AI and IoT-Based Intelligent Automation in Robotics

Scrivener Publishing
100 Cummings Center, Suite 541J
Beverly, MA 01915-6106

Publishers at Scrivener
Martin Scrivener (martin@scrivenerpublishing.com)
Phillip Carmical (pcarmical@scrivenerpublishing.com)

AI and IoT-Based Intelligent Automation in Robotics

Edited by
Ashutosh Kumar Dubey,
Abhishek Kumar, S. Rakesh Kumar,
N. Gayathri, Prasenjit Das

Scrivener
Publishing

WILEY

This edition first published 2021 by John Wiley & Sons, Inc., 111 River Street, Hoboken, NJ 07030, USA and Scrivener Publishing LLC, 100 Cummings Center, Suite 541J, Beverly, MA 01915, USA
© 2021 Scrivener Publishing LLC
For more information about Scrivener publications please visit www.scrivenerpublishing.com.

Wiley Global Headquarters
111 River Street, Hoboken, NJ 07030, USA

For details of our global editorial offices, customer services, and more information about Wiley products visit us at www.wiley.com.

Limit of Liability/Disclaimer of Warranty
While the publisher and authors have used their best efforts in preparing this work, they make no representations or warranties with respect to the accuracy or completeness of the contents of this work and specifically disclaim all warranties, including without limitation any implied warranties of merchantability or fitness for a particular purpose. No warranty may be created or extended by sales representatives, written sales materials, or promotional statements for this work. The fact that an organization, website, or product is referred to in this work as a citation and/or potential source of further information does not mean that the publisher and authors endorse the information or services the organization, website, or product may provide or recommendations it may make. This work is sold with the understanding that the publisher is not engaged in rendering professional services. The advice and strategies contained herein may not be suitable for your situation. You should consult with a specialist where appropriate. Neither the publisher nor authors shall be liable for any loss of profit or any other commercial damages, including but not limited to special, incidental, consequential, or other damages. Further, readers should be aware that websites listed in this work may have changed or disappeared between when this work was written and when it is read.

Library of Congress Cataloging-in-Publication Data

ISBN 978-1-119-71120-9

Cover image: Pixabay.Com
Cover design by Russell Richardson

Set in size of 11pt and Minion Pro by Manila Typesetting Company, Makati, Philippines

Printed in the USA

10 9 8 7 6 5 4 3 2 1

Contents

11 Real-Time Mild and Moderate COVID-19 Human Body Temperature Detection Using Artificial Intelligence   189
K. Logu, T. Devi, N. Deepa, S. Rakesh Kumar and N. Gayathri

12 Drones in Smart Cities   205
Manju Payal, Pooja Dixit and Vishal Dutt

Preface

It is widely believed that the current technologies are not the only factors that limits the building of an efficient human-machine intelligent processing engine. The emotions and the cognitive abilities are also playing an important role in understanding the various aspects through various intelligent technologies.

Artificial Intelligence (AI) is one of the trending technologies in the recent era. The emergence of the robotics and application of AI in it brings out a significant change in the domain. Various algorithms that emerge in AI and the computational efficiency of the systems has made it possible to address a number of applications through robotics. The Internet of Things (IoT) is the important domain that plays a major role in robotics. With the aid of IoT and AI, robotics an exponential development in providing solutions to complex technical problems have been explored.

This book aims at providing an overview of robotics and the application of AI and IoT in robotics. It contains the deep exploration of AI and IoT based intelligent automation in robotics. The various algorithms and frameworks for robotics based on AI and IoT have been presented analyzed and discussed. This book also provides insights on application of robotics in education, healthcare, defense and many other fields with the utilization of IoT and AI. It also includes the idea of smart cities using robotics.

This book contains twenty-four chapters. Chapter 1 reports the introduction about the robotics. Chapter 2 explores the techniques of robotics for automation using AI and IoT. Chapter 3 descriptively investigates the role of the defense in the same technological aspects. Chapter 4 examines the role of AI and IoT based intelligent automation of robotics in case of healthcare. Chapter 5 explores the skill transfer to robots based on semantically represented the activities of humans. Chapter 6 illustrates the healthcare robots enabled with IoT and artificial intelligence for old aged patients. Chapter 7 explores the robotics, AI and IoT in defense system. Chapter 8 describes the techniques of robotics for automation using AI and IoT. Chapter 9 discusses an artificial intelligence based smart task responder that is android robot for human instruction using LSTM technique. Chapter 10 explores the robotics, AI and IoT in medical and healthcare. Chapter 11 scrutinizes real time mild and moderate Covid'19 human body temperature detection using AI. Chapter 12 shows the role of drones in smart cities. Chapter 13 presents UAV's in terms of agriculture prospective. Chapter 14 discussed the semi-automated parking system by using DSDV and RFID. Chapter 15 reviews on the various technologies involved in vehicle to vehicle communication. Chapter 16 explores about the smart wheelchair. Chapter 17 explores defaulters list using facial recognition. Chapter 18 introduces visitor/intruder monitoring system using machine learning. Chapter 19 provides a comparison of machine learning algorithms for air pollution monitoring system. Chapter 20 discusses a novel approach towards audio watermarking using FFT and Cordic Q-R decomposition. Chapter 21 explores the performance of DC biased optical orthogonal frequency division multiplexing in visible light communication. Chapter 22 illustrates the microcontroller based variable rate syringe pump for microfluidic application. Chapter 23 illustrates the analysis of emotion in speech signal processing and rejection of noise. Chapter 24 discusses regarding securing cloud data by using blend cryptography with AWS services.

Overall, this book is designed for exploring global technological information about the AI and IoT based intelligent automation in robotics. Armed with specific usage practices, applicability, framework and challenges readers can make informed choices about the adoption of AI and IoT based intelligent automation. It may be helpful in the development of efficient framework and models in the adoption of these techniques in different domains.

It is a great pleasure for us to acknowledge the contributions and assistance of many individuals. We would like to thank all the authors who submitted chapters for their contributions and fruitful discussion that made this book a great success. We hope the readers find value and future insights into the contributions made by the authors. This book also opens up further avenues and opportunities for the future research. We are very thankful to the team of Scrivener publishing specially to Martin Scrivener for providing the meticulous service for timely publication of this book.

We would like to express our deep sense of gratitude for the encouragement and support offered by our Institutions/Universities and colleagues. Last but not least, we gratefully acknowledge the support, encouragement and patience of our families.

Ashutosh Kumar Dubey
Abhishek Kumar
S. Rakesh Kumar
N. Gayathri
Prasenjit Das
February 2021

Introduction to Robotics

Srinivas Kumar Palvadi[1], Pooja Dixit[2] and Vishal Dutt[3]*

[1]Department of Computer Science Engineering,
University of Madras, Chennai, Tamil Nadu, India
[2]Sophia Girls' College (Autonomous), Ajmer, Rajasthan, India
[3]Department of Computer Science, Aryabhatta College,
Ajmer, Rajasthan, India

Abstract

These days, automation plays a major role in all sectors of society and the technology of robotic automation is very much in demand along with other significantly trending concepts such as the Internet of Things (IoT), Machine Learning (ML), Artificial Intelligence (AI) and Cloud Computing. Many people are showing interest in purchasing things which have process automation; for example, do not increase speed once they reach a certain point and automatically turn off the water tank when it is about to overfill. Robotics is also the technology where when an instruction is given to the device it acts accordingly based on the user instruction. When we want the robot to perform based on the user instruction, we first have to train the device or robot with the instructions for the particular task we want to do. For example, if we give a data set to the robot for creation of coffee and we give an instruction to the robot to "Prepare Tea," the robot doesn't respond to the request because the request doesn't match the available datasets in the robot. In this chapter, I will focus on a basic introduction to robots, their architecture and the equipment needed for designing robots.

Keywords: Machine learning, IoT, AI, energy, drones, nano tubes, energy, actuation

1.1 Introduction

"Robotics" or "robots" is a very popular term which we are increasingly hearing day by day. The word "robotics" was derived from the word "robot,"

Corresponding author: vishaldutt53@gmail.com

Ashutosh Kumar Dubey, Abhishek Kumar, S. Rakesh Kumar, N. Gayathri, Prasenjit Das (eds.) *AI and IoT-Based Intelligent Automation in Robotics*, (1–14) © 2021 Scrivener Publishing LLC

which comes from the Slavic word "robota," meaning slave/servant. Robots were introduced to society by George C. Devol, who generally referred to them as artificial people. Generally, robots consist of different components such as sensors, controlling devices, manipulators, power supply as well as software to perform the defined action. A combination of these characteristics forms the robot. For preparing the perfect robot we have to proceed with designing, building, programming as well as testing the robot using a combination of physics, mathematics, computational techniques, mechanical engineering, electrical engineering and structural engineering. In some of the particular scenarios the concepts of biology, chemistry and medicine are also involved based on the requirements. Generally, robot technology is used [1] in environments where a human cannot perform the action.

Many people treat robots as machines but in many of the real-time applications robots replace the person and also act as a person, such as the androids in the movies *Star Wars*, *Terminator* and *Star Trek: The Next Generation*. The robots capture human faces and activities and perform tasks as a person does. Even though developers are implementing many advancements in robots and using them in many applications, they are not able to develop enough common sense in them because robots perform the task based on the user's instructions but can't predict future actions by doing tasks in a dynamic manner. So, regarding this topic, many of the researchers are working in this domain under the research domain named "humanoid robots."

Most of the robots which were created till now are very dangerous, boring, onerous and just plain nasty. We can find these types of robots in the medical, automobile, manufacturing, and industrial industries among others, as well as the space industry. Robots, such as the Mars rover Sojourner and the upcoming Mars Exploration rover or the underwater robotic vehicle Caribou, were designed and sent to places where humans cannot go, such as volcanoes, mars, etc., for the purpose of helping to conduct research in those particular places. On the other hand, other types of robots were designed for the purpose of entertaining small children and others. A few of them are Techno, Polly and AIBO ERS-220, which often arrive at the stores around Christmas time.

Robots are very efficient, fun and easy to design. In his book *Being Digital*, Nicholas Negroponte relates an excellent story that took place about eight years ago at the time of the televised premier of the Media Lab's LEGO/Logo work at the Hennigan School. When the robot was first introduced to the children in school, they didn't show interest in adopting it. However, in a third attempt, the children talked, played and had fun with the robot. The children asked the robot questions and the robot started giving responses to the children. The children in the class felt very excited and had fun with the robot.

Finally, what exactly does robot mean?

Many authors gave definitions based on their understanding. There is really no standard definition of robotics. When designing the robot, every designer needs to have the following properties and features, if not it is not considered a robot [2].

The robot should have following characteristics:

- Sensing
  First, robots have to recognize the surroundings and respond according to them. The robots will not behave in all the environments. We have to imbue robots with sensitivity to light (eyes), touch, pressure (like hands), chemicals (nose), sound (ears) and taste (tongue) among others. By combining all these we will get the correct working robot for the environment.
- Movement
  The robot should be capable of identifying surroundings/ environment in order to perform actions such as moving its body all around the surroundings.
- Energy
  Robots should be capable of identifying the power in their battery and should charge by themselves.
- Intelligence
  Robots need to become smarter than humans. Those who make robots smart are called programmers. Robots should require a minimum amount of knowledge to understand and perform the task that the user instructed.

So, the definition of the term robot encompasses a sensor, controlling device, physical device, manipulator, and a programming testing device, with mechanical engineering, electrical engineering, mathematics, and a small portion of chemistry also being involved.

1.2   History and Evolution of Robots

Table 1.1 shows the origins of robotics along with detailed information of when the robots came into existence, the developer's name, etc. Presently, there are various types of robots which are used for various environments

Table 1.1 History of the earliest robots.

Date	Significance	Robot name	Inventor
3rd century BC and earlier	First humanoid automata based on an earlier description		Yan Shi
1st century AD and earlier	Descriptions of more than 100 machines and automata which include a fire engine, a wind organ, a coin-operated machine, and a steam-powered engine		Ctesibius, Philo of Byzantium, Heron of Alexandria, and others
c. 420 BC	Robot designed like a bird, which will fly	Flying Pigeon	Archytas of Tarentum
1206	First humanoid robot with automata mechanism	Robot band, hand-washing automaton [11], automated moving peacocks [12]	Al-Jazari
1495	Humanoid robot	Mechanical Knight	Leonardo da Vinci
1738	Mechanical duck which can eat, flap its wings, and excrete	Digesting Duck	Jacques de Vaucanson
1898	First radio-controlled device	Teleautomaton	Nikola Tesla
1921	First fictional autom-atons called robots	Rossum's Universal Robots	Karel Čapek
1930s	Humanoid robot exhibited at the 1939 and 1940 New York World's Fair	Elektro	Westinghouse Electric Corporation
1946	First general-purpose digital computer	Whirlwind	Multiple people

(Continued)

Table 1.1 History of the earliest robots. (*Continued*)

Date	Significance	Robot name	Inventor
1948	Simple robots exhibiting biological behaviors	Elsie and Elmer	William Grey Walter
1956	First commercial robot from the Unimation company	Unimate	George Devol
1961	First installed industrial robot	Unimate	George Devol
1967 to 1972	First full-scale humanoid intelligent robot	WABOT-1	Waseda University
1973	First industrial robot with six electromechanically driven axes	Famulus	KUKA Robot Group
1974	First microcomputer controlled electric industrial robot, IRB 6 from ASEA, which was already patented in 1972.	IRB 6	ABB Robotics
1975	Programmable universal manipulation arm, a Unimation product	PUMA	Victor Scheinman
1978	First object-level robot programming language, which allows robots to handle variations in object position, shape, and sensor noise	Freddy I and II, RAPT robot programming language	Patricia Ambler and Robin Popplestone
1983	First multitasking, parallel programming language used for a robot control	ADRIEL I	Stevo Bozinovski and Mihail Sestakov

for various users. Moreover, the robots were classified into mechanical construction, electrical components and computer programming mechanism.

The mechanical part of the robot is designed for mechanical purposes such as designing the particular shape and processing of the particular task. With the mechanical components it also follows the physics friction mechanism for processing of the task.

The robots have the electrical power capable of handling the mechanical products because the electricity is capable of handling the machine [3]. Even though there are petrol-based robots, they still require electrical energy in order to function, just as a car works with a battery.

1.3   Applications

Because the lives of people were becoming busier, robots were designed to help meet the needs of their users. Initially we assigned the task or multiple tasks as per the instructions of humans and the robots performed the task if the particular task was programmed and vice versa. Later on, the robots were designed in such a way that specific robots or customized robots were designed for specific tasks. The main theme in designing customized robots was to make them work more efficiently. Generally, the robots were designed in an assembly manner for making them more adaptive as well as making the tasks speedier. Such types of robots were categorized as "assembly robots." Now robots were also used in the automobile industry for procedures such as welding, tightening, etc., and the robots were the products called "integrated units" because they were designed in such a way that they were integrated with different fields like mechanical and electrical engineering and computers. For example, robots that performed welding tasks were called "welding robots." Any type of robot had the capability of performing various types of tasks [4]. Some robots were exclusively designed for making the heavy load changes and such type of robots were treated as "heavy duty robots." Finally, "humanoid robots" were designed for addressing all the emergencies that a human does.

The robots described above are just some of the various robots and their applications in specific fields. Some of the various types of robots and various places where they are being used include:

- Military robots
- Industrial robots
- Collaborative robots

- Construction robots
- Agricultural robots
- Medical robots
- Robots for kitchen automation
- Spot robot for combat
- Robots for cleaning up contaminated areas
- such as toxic sites or nuclear facilities
- Domestic robots
- Nanorobots
- Swarm robots
- Autonomous drones
- Robots for sports field line marking

1.4   Components Needed for a Robot

Electricity, mechanical power and programming are the main things needed to successfully design a robot. First, when designing the robot, the planning and outlook of how it should be viewed after implementation are the main things to keep in mind [5]. Below are the requirements for designing a full-fledged robot:

1) Power Source

   For the power source the main thing which we use is batteries. The power taken from electricity will convert to the thermal energy stored in the batteries. All robots need a battery in order to work. The robot will work up to a certain number of hours when it is fully charged. The batteries, such as silicon batteries and acid batteries, are used because batteries, such as silver-cadmium batteries, are too expensive. While designing the required battery for a particular robot, initially we only have to think about the power consumption of the robot based on its working capacity. If the robot work capacity is less and if we give more power the electricity inside the robot may short circuit and total loss or damage to the robot may ensue. We also have to consider the weight of the robot while designing because if the robot is heavier it will consume more power when performing the user requests [6]. If the robot is heavier there are many disadvantages such as not cost-effective, difficult to manage the tasks, higher power consumption, inefficient, etc. Apart from electric power there are a few other alternatives which are beneficial, such as

- Pneumatic power
- Solar power
- Hydraulic power
- Flywheel energy storage
- Anaerobic digestion
- Nuclear power

2) Actuation

In human terminology, the actuator is like muscles for the robot. Here the overall thing depends on the momentum of the device. Most of the devices work in an electrical and mechanical manner. These robots help in controlling, managing and monitoring the works. After designing the particular robot for a particular manner in the customized way, many of the alterations were performed on the robot and many of the software updates and alterations were made either in terms of hardware or software or battery or capacity, etc., based on the load and capacity of the robot.

3) Electric Motors

A large number of robots use electrical and mechanical power for performing tasks. The robots use mechanical power as well as electrical power for performing tasks. The robots use DC motors and AC motors for industrial purposes for performing the heavy loaded type of tasks. There will be motors which perform the heavy loaded as well as light loaded tasks. Here, when performing the heavy loaded and light loaded tasks the capacity of battery as well as the usage of the battery varies from time to time.

4) Linear Actuators

There are various types of actuators which have faster speed as well as direction. Here, when the speed changes the direction also changes and vice versa. There are various types of robots which have more pneumatic and hydraulic actuators. There is an actuator called a "linear actuator" which has a motor as well as a lead screw. Another type of actuator which is powered by hand is the rack and pinion actuator commonly found in cars.

5) Series Elastic Actuator

This part is designed in a flexible and elastic manner and works in a more robust manner in controlling things like energy efficiency, robust force control and shock absorption. The generated results, weakens the overall interaction with humans if the measurement is high.

6) Air Muscles

Air muscles were also treated as pneumatic muscles or air muscles. These will extend up to the range of 40%. The air muscles are used to provide privacy in applications. This mechanism is used in the application of robots.

7) Muscle Wire

This technique is also called shape memory alloy mechanism. For this method a procedure of exactly 5 percent electricity was needed for the development of the small type of mini robot applications.

8) Electroactive Polymers

These are the materials used because they consume more electricity. They are used in the muscles and hands when making the robot because using electroactive polymers activates the hands and legs shaking moments and also help in the waking, swimming, floating and running of the robots.

9) Piezo Motors

Piezo motors are widely used alternatives to DC motors. This working principle is also very different. It depends on the rotator motion. There are different operations such as one which uses a vibration mechanism and another which uses an oscillation mechanism of the elements. The main advantage of using a piezo mechanism is that it makes the motor more efficient.

10) Nanotubes

Nanotubes are used in the robots during the design process in order to conduct experiments on how the electricity flows and the level of elasticity in the body of robot.

11) Sensing

The main theme in developing sensing is that it helps to measure the environment and also says how to react based on the situations from moment to moment. The reaction of the robot to what action has happened is very important. The response of the robot changes as per the environment.

12) Touch

Here, sensing mainly depends on the software we are using. Recently, for touch sensing the tactile sensors used vary widely. The sensor is a mechanism which has a rigid body and all the touch properties from top to bottom for the robot. The sensor was designed in such a way to have a rigid cone surface with all the objects. This mechanism helps in forming the grip of the robots in a very strong manner for the purpose of handling objects.

13) Vision

The computer vision of the robots is very important. The vision helps in the extraction of the images and if needed the data which is captured by the robot will be stored in the server for recollecting what tasks are done by the robot from the start to the end of the day, which can help the user for cross-checking purposes if needed [7]. The vision of the robot may take many forms; it takes images or it records video based upon the settings made by the user. The vision mechanism is based purely on the computer sensor and electromagnetic radiation and the light rays generated are visual light or infrared light.

14) Manipulation

Minute manipulations are done on robots from time to time like replacing hands and legs for better moment; in other words, it is an endless effort.

15) Mechanical Grippers

Grippers play a major role in designing the robot for some important things like vision, sensing and responding in a particular manner. Mechanical grippers help a robot catch any object with its hands using the grippers to catch things without dropping them. Like hands, grippers also play a major role in handling objects using friction [8]. There is another type of gripper known as a "vacuum gripper," which is simple to add in a block to the robot. Vacuum grippers are very active in nature and are mainly used in windscreens.

These above components are needed for building an efficient robot.

1.5   Robot Interaction and Navigation

Navigation is very important to how the robot works and plays a major role in different tasks, such as locating the robot, its position, its condition, etc. There are a few advanced robots, such as ASIMO, which will automatically charge themselves based on their position.

1.5.1   Humanoid Robot

Humanoid robots are the majority of those used in homes and restaurants for task automation. Once the timetable of when the tasks should be done is set, the tasks are assigned to the robot and it will automatically perform the task as part of its daily routine per the schedule [14]. Not until the user makes any alteration to the existing timetable will the robot change its task. While making the schedule or adding the new task for the robot to perform on a daily basis, first we have to train the robot by giving instructions like the step-by-step procedure for performing the task, which is called an "algorithm." The algorithm given to the robot it treated as the training set. First, while implementing the task the task should be tested by the user to confirm whether all the steps are working correctly [9]. This is the basic thing that the robot performs. There are some types of robots that have advanced features or characteristics such as speech recognition, robotic voice, gesture, facial expression, artificial emotions, personality and social intelligence.

1.5.2   Control

The mechanical structure of a robot must be controlled to perform errands. The control of a robot includes three distinct stages: perception, processing, and action (mechanical standards). Sensors give data about the earth or the robot itself (for example, the situation of its joints or its end effector). This data is then prepared to be stored or transmitted to ascertain the proper signals to the actuators (engines) which move the mechanical device.

The handling stage can run intricately. At a responsive level, it might decipher crude sensor data legitimately into actuator orders. A combinations of sensors may initially be utilized to gauge boundaries of intrigue (for example, the situation of the robot's gripper) from boisterous sensor information. A prompt undertaking (for example, moving the gripper a specific way) is deduced from these evaluations. Procedures from the control hypothesis convert the assignment into orders that drive the actuators [10].

At longer time scales or with progressively modern undertakings, the robot may need to assemble and dissuade a "subjective" model. Subjective models attempt to speak to the robot, the world, and how they collaborate. For example, acknowledgment and PC vision can be utilized to follow objects; mapping strategies can be utilized to assemble maps of the world; lastly, movement arranging and other man-made consciousness procedures might be utilized to make sense of the proper behavior. For instance, an organizer may make sense of how to accomplish an undertaking without hitting deterrents, falling over, and so forth [11].

1.5.3   Autonomy Levels

This mechanism has a lot of various levels of algorithms, which are classified below along with the steps followed for performing the task.

- Direct interaction with the help of telephone or teleported devices.
- Specifying the particular position to the robot and where it should move or giving step-by-step instructions from beginning to end until it reaches its destination.
- An autonomous robot performs some tasks beyond user specified ones because some robots are capable of performing tasks and alerting the user when the robot is in trouble, etc. [12].
- There are a few types of robots which are operated by the user's instruction via telephone.
- There are a few robots which perform specific moves based on the instructions given upon starting.
- There are a few robots which only perform the tasks specified by one person. Whichever task is specified first by the instructor is identified by the robot as the task specified, which is stored in its memory and performed as the stored task. Such types of robots are called "task level autonomous."
- There are a few robots which do whatever task it is instructed to do by the user; such types of robots are called "fully autonomous" [13].

1.6   Conclusion

Robotics is a technology spreading throughout all industries because of its many advantages, including its ability to reduce man power, save money by reducing man power, complete tasks very effectively and quickly, prevent human mistakes, be more easily maintained, quickly respond in a more responsive manner; along with many other applications in fields where the robot performs, such as in multinational corporations (MNCs). Because of the automation process used for unit testing, integration testing, system testing and acceptance testing in MNCs being performed only by robots, many people are losing their jobs. Moreover, there are many applications where the robot performs or plays a major role in various areas, a few of which are industry, business, research, dynamics, kinematics, bionics, biometrics, quantum computing, education, training, career training, certification, summer robotics camp, robotics competition, employment, software industry, software projects testing, occupation safety and health implications and many more. Future development of robots or the robotic field is vast, and in a decade there is a chance that people will be replaced with robots for all tasks in every sector. This is because of the many advantages of robots which have already been adopted in a few sectors, with many more sectors ready to adopt the process. On one hand, this will lead to many good changes, but on the other hand many small jobs will be lost and unemployment will increase, etc.

References

1. Qin, T., Li, P., Shen, S., VINS-Mono: A Robust and Versatile Monocular Visual-Inertial State Estimator. *IEEE Trans. Rob.*, 34, 4, 1004–1020, Aug. 2018.

2. Pequito, S., Khorrami, F., Krishnamurthy, P., Pappas, G.J., Analysis and Design of Actuation–Sensing–Communication Interconnection Structures Toward Secured/Resilient LTI Closed-Loop Systems. *IEEE Trans. Control Network Syst.*, 6, 2, 667–678, June 2019.

3. Chang, X. and Yang, G., New Results on Output Feedback H_{∞} Control for Linear Discrete-Time Systems. *IEEE Trans. Autom. Control*, 59, 5, 1355–1359, May 2014.

4. Li, Z., Zhang, T., Ma, C., Li, H., Li, X., Robust Passivity Control for 2-D Uncertain Markovian Jump Linear Discrete-Time Systems. *IEEE Access*, 5, 12176–12184, 2017.

5. Yang, C., Ge, S.S., Xiang, C., Chai, T., Lee, T.H., Output Feedback NN Control for Two Classes of Discrete-Time Systems with Unknown Control Directions in a Unified Approach. *IEEE Trans. Neural Networks*, 19, 11, 1873–1886, Nov. 2008.

6. Münz, U., Pfister, M., Wolfrum, P., Sensor and Actuator Placement for Linear Systems Based on Optimization. *IEEE Trans. Autom. Control*, 59, 11, 2984–2989, Nov. 2014.

7. Sui, S., Tong, S., Chen, C.L.P., Finite-Time Filter Decentralized Control for Nonstrict-Feedback Nonlinear Large-Scale Systems. *IEEE Trans. Fuzzy Syst.*, 26, 6, 3289–3300, Dec. 2018.

8. Rakovic, S.V. and Baric, M., Parameterized Robust Control Invariant Sets for Linear Systems: Theoretical Advances and Computational Remarks. *IEEE Trans. Autom. Control*, 55, 7, 1599–1614, July 2010.

9. Li, Y., Sun, K., Tong, S., Adaptive Fuzzy Robust Fault-Tolerant Optimal Control for Nonlinear Large-Scale Systems. *IEEE Trans. Fuzzy Syst.*, 26, 5, 2899–2914, Oct. 2018.

10. Zhang, H. and Feng, G., Stability Analysis and H_{∞} Controller Design of Discrete-Time Fuzzy Large-Scale Systems Based on Piecewise Lyapunov Functions. *IEEE Trans. Syst. Man Cybern. Part B (Cybernetics)*, 38, 5, 1390–1401, Oct. 2008.

11. Bakule, L., Rodellar, J., Rossell, J.M., Robust Overlapping Guaranteed Cost Control of Uncertain State-Delay Discrete-Time Systems. *IEEE Trans. Autom. Control*, 51, 12, 1943–1950, Dec. 2006.

12. Liu, Y. and Tong, S., Adaptive NN Tracking Control of Uncertain Nonlinear Discrete-Time Systems with Nonaffine Dead-Zone Input. *IEEE Trans. Cybern.*, 45, 3, 497–505, March 2015.

13. Li, D. and Li, D., Adaptive Control via Neural Output Feedback for a Class of Nonlinear Discrete-Time Systems in a Nested Interconnected Form. *IEEE Trans. Cybern.*, 48, 9, 2633–2642, Sept. 2018.

14. Alzenad, M., El-Keyi, A., Yanikomeroglu, H., 3D placement of an unmanned aerial vehicle base station for maximum coverage of users with different QoS requirements. *IEEE Wirel. Commun. Lett.*, 7, 38–41, 2018.

2

Techniques in Robotics for Automation Using AI and IoT

Sandeep Kr. Sharma, N. Gayathri*, S. Rakesh Kumar
and Rajiv Kumar Modanval

*School of Computing Science and Engineering, Galgotias University,
Uttar Pradesh, India*

Abstract

Gone are the days when people use manual methods to perform every task; now the world has evolved and we have advanced technologies like artificial intelligence (AI) and the internet of things (IoT) that have changed our world outlook. With the rapid advancement in technology, we are gifted with lots of modern technologies that are being integrated into our day-to-day lives, making it much easier.

In this chapter, we will discuss various techniques used for automation, like AI and the IoT, which form the basis for robotics. There's a technique called robotic process automation (RPA) which is very popular nowadays, which can be used to automate any computational process. One software that is used to practice and build the RPA system is UiPath Studio, which comes in handy for all sorts of scripts and contains many tools that can be used to make automated bots. Apart from that, we will be discussing and proposing some other such techniques and studying the requirements for AI and IoT in the automation of robots.

Defining the roles and algorithms in integration with machine learning (ML), we will also be looking at some case studies and various other applications for automation in different scenarios. With the increase in the popularity of AI, the day is not very far off when we will have a replacement for humans—not only a replacement, but also a more advanced form of humans. Today, robots are so smart that they are capable of mimicking human behavior and are so efficient that it will take a normal human about 100 to 1000 times more time to complete the task. In this way, they are making our lives so easy and comfortable.

Corresponding author: n.gayathri@galgotiasuniversity.edu.in

Ashutosh Kumar Dubey, Abhishek Kumar, S. Rakesh Kumar, N. Gayathri, Prasenjit Das (eds.) AI and IoT-Based Intelligent Automation in Robotics, (15–34) © 2021 Scrivener Publishing LLC

Keywords: Artificial intelligence (AI), internet of things (IoT), robotics, automation, robots, machine learning

2.1   Introduction

Technically the word automation refers to the running of some action or process that mimics human behavior without or very little involvement of humans. Earlier this was not very popular and things were mostly processed via humans but with the advancement of technology and computation power we now have access to the most advanced robots and automation [1] tools with which one can perform any task easily and rapidly. If we look at the broader aspects of automation it mainly finds application in industries and manufacturing sectors which were the provenience for the automation and the automated machines used for various jobs like painting, manufacturing parts, storage, monitoring, etc. Still, almost all industries are utilizing these automated robots in their day-to-day processes.

The Industrial Revolution [2] played a big role in making automation so popular that it is considered foolish not utilize the automation procedure, as not using automation will lead to a waste of time and money as "time is money."

2.2   Brief History of Robotics

Robotics has always been a fascinating topic for research and innovation which has its origin in ancient times, but the modern notion began to be established with the inception of the Industrial Revolution. The term "robot," which in Czech means slave, was first coined in a play about the men working on the assembly lines of factories [3]. Also, the term "robotics" [4] was neologized by the American science fiction writer Isaac Asimov in his story "Runaround" in the year 1942. Who knew the robots dreamed of in fiction would become one of the revolutionary technologies in the near future [5]?

The first robot was invented in the year 1950 by George C. Devol [3], who patented a reprogrammable manipulator termed "Unimate." He tried selling it to industry but failed. A few years later, in 1960 Joseph Engelberger, an engineer and businessman, procured the patent from Devol and modified it to make an industrial robot and established a company called Unimation to produce and sell the robots. His works and endeavors gave him the honorary title of "Father of Robotics" [6] in industry. So, it is uncanny that the robots that we have today were idealized from science fiction and now are revolutionizing technology.

2.3   Some General Terms

- Artificial Intelligence: Refers to making machines capable of mimicking human behavior and intelligence in a way to act and think like humans. And it is called artificial because the intelligence has been given to machines by means of some programming which is dissimilar to the natural intelligence exhibited by humans. The term "artificial intelligence" (AI) was first coined in 1856 by John McCarthy. AI is one of the disruptive technologies with powerful features and can be used in a wide variety of applications; for example, AI can be used to play games, monitor the health of patients and used as a traffic controller system. In the education sector it can act as an independent and effective tutor; apart from that it can be used to predict diseases and weather, etc. The list is countless [7] as it finds endless possibilities of applications due to its advanced characteristics and tools.

  The Venn diagram of AI in Figure 2.1 below shows that it is the superset of machine learning (ML) and deep learning (DL).

- Machine Learning: Describes the learning behavior of machines by means of data fed to it. Based upon learning the machine makes predictions based on statistical inference and finding a pattern in data by using some advanced mathematical models [8]. It is the branch of artificial intelligence

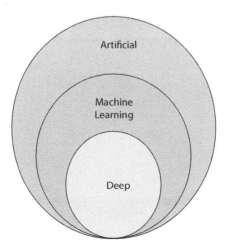

Figure 2.1 Venn diagram of AI, ML and DL.

that works in its backend and defines various algorithmic procedures to be followed to make the machine intelligent so as to make accurate predictions [9]. Based on the learning behavior and the type of data, it is divided into four types:

– Supervised learning
– Unsupervised learning
– Semi-supervised learning
– Reinforcement learning

- Agent: Refers to something that perceives the environment through sensors and performs action via actuators based on some predefined rules for which the agent is trained. Just like in humans, there are five sense (i.e., sight, sound, smell, taste, and touch), and based on the information of our senses we perform actions through our limbs, etc. A simple diagrammatic representation of an agent is shown in Figure 2.2 below.

  The agents act as a backbone for AI techniques that govern how they are working and what sorts of applications they are dealing with. Based on utility there are different types of agents [10]:

  – Simple reflex agent
  – Model-based agent
  – Goal-based agent
  – Utility-based agent

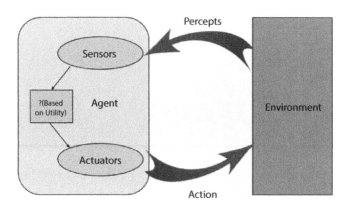

Figure 2.2 Representation of an agent.

- Internet of Things: Refers to the interconnection of the things that we use in our daily lives with the internet. The basic idea of the IoT [11] is to connect all the devices through the internet via short-range wireless devices, such as Zigbee, Bluetooth, RFID, and various sorts of sensors and devices [12], by which they can communicate with each other and share the sensor data among the peer devices in order to facilitate the end-user/client via cloud services. It is one of the most demanding technologies in any industry and from 2019 to 2025 it is expected to grow by 33.81% [13]. The basic architecture of the IoT is shown in Figure 2.3 below.

- Robots: Programmable machines capable of performing complex tasks in intense and rigorous environments. They are designed as in Figure 2.4 to automate any human tasks with the controllers built-in or outside based on the requirements. Robots are now being used in many places [14] to perform dangerous or repetitive tasks to safeguard humans, and are being used especially in industry in painting jobs, warehouses, assembly lines, etc. So, basically, they are automating the environment in order to reduce human efforts. And now robots have become an essential commodity of many sectors; for example, they find application in healthcare [15], education, research and development, and are used in architecture, as waiters in restaurants, and almost

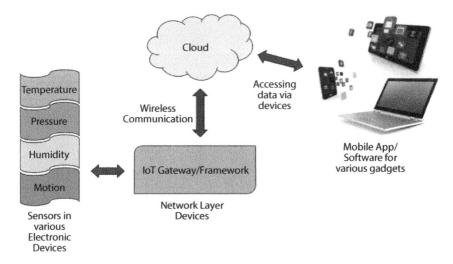

Figure 2.3 Architecture of the Internet of Things.

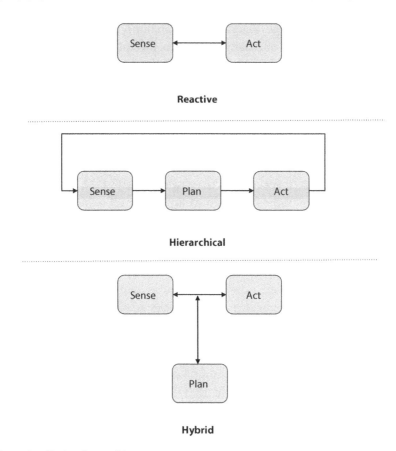

Figure 2.4 Basic robot architecture.

all the sectors of our economy. With the increase in research and innovation, more and more intelligent systems are being prepared that are forming the foundation of modern society and helping in reshaping the future.

2.4   Requirements of AI and IoT for Robotic Automation

Robotic automation is one of the most challenging and lengthy tasks without the use of any proper tools and techniques and today that requirement is fulfilled by one of the most advanced techniques available to us, so-called Artificial Intelligence and the Internet of Things, with the help of which we are able to design more complex and more powerful robots. For instance, if we look at the very first form of computer and the computers now available to us, i.e., powerful computers in our pockets, we can see a huge difference. In the same way, the technologies are transforming our lives and giving birth to more advanced forms of machinery that we had once only thought possible.

So, while AI and IoT are required because they are bundled with full-fledged tools and techniques, which are enough to make a powerful robot using traditional programming, it will take months writing the same code-base in comparison to the codes that are written using these technologies. Basically, AI and IoT are efficient and effective enough to work in developing any robotic system.

2.5   Role of AI and IoT in Robotics

Artificial intelligence (AI) and Internet of Things (IoT) are the technologies of today and they are becoming more and more advanced day by day. These technologies are in very high demand in the industry as all the innovations taking place are based on them. AI comprises mathematical and statistical models that govern the working of algorithms that are used to develop intelligent systems and the IoT consists of various tools and techniques to effectively manage the sensors and their intercommunications via the use of various protocols and devices. Due to the high capabilities of these technologies, they are highly adopted in industries, healthcare, businesses, and various sectors of the economy [16].

Both of these technologies, when used together, can be much more beneficial as IoT is better at collecting data and AI is a great tool to process huge amounts of data. As IoT uses other technologies like big data or AI for data processing, this implies that AI works on the backend of IoT and plays a major role in working on any system or framework comprising the two [17]. The perfect example can be our voice user interface devices such as Alexa or Google Home. They were trained with some data and that data has been processed via AI whose engine gives output on the basis of data.

Similarly, in robotics, which is a complex system consisting of various types of sensors, various electrical and mechanical devices work together to perform an assigned task. In robotics for the case of recognizing and classifying tasks, it uses computer vision in which the thousands of raw images of objects are fed into machines, and once trained it can classify and recognize objects. In this case, the camera will capture the images from the surrounding (which falls in the IoT domain) and gives it to the ML engine for processing, and once processed the output is shown via actuators or via any output devices.

Some of the major roles of AI and IoT in robotics are:

- To program various aspects like learning, understanding, thinking, and inferring based on rules into the robot so as to perform accordingly.
- To implement various supervised, unsupervised, semi-supervised, or reinforcement learning algorithms into the robots based on the utility of robots either in industry, business, or for commercial purposes.
- To establish various connections between different parts of the robot-like camera connection, wireless modules like Zigbee or Bluetooth, connections between microcontrollers to actuators, etc.
- To set up a trained classifier or model so that it can be used by the robot.
- To install sensors and actuators so as to sense the environment and perform accordingly.
- To create an inference engine for performing inference on the basis of a percept sequence or percept history.
- In some cases, to enable speech synthesis so as to talk or control via voice, i.e., voice user interface (VUI) [17].
- To establish connections via the cloud so that it can be remotely configured or controlled.

The performance of a robot is governed by its memory or percept sequence and, while training, the model finds some sort of patterns in data that form the basis for learning. While creating a robot there are various aspects that need to be taken care of and the aim is to develop a cognitive architecture in which integration of reasoning, planning, reacting, creating, learning from the past, etc. [18] exists. Inspired by human biology, we try to mimic every biological behavior artificially in robots, like neural networks being built to mimic the behavior of our brain into machines, and various joints being artificially created which were inspired by the human body.

Apart from that, artificial organs are being created to help needy people. Although mimicking the human brain is such a typical task, various companies/researchers are working day and night to build a replacement for the human brain. One such project is SpiNNaker, a machine built at the University of Manchester [19] that is a supercomputer capable of very quickly mimicking a human brain which not only thinks but can create the models of neurons in our brains, and is capable of simulating it in real-time far faster than any other computer in the world [20].

In any IoT-enabled devices [24] which are equipped with sensors (temperature, humidity, pressure, vibration, speed, etc.), percepts are formed of the environment and that information is transferred over the cloud via wireless devices through routers. That data is then input into our android phones or any user interface devices, where the data is then compared with the existing database based on how it performs some actions via actuators, whether it is an alarm, buzzer or fan, to inform the system administrator or user. Then, with the use of AI, the system now acts to resolve the problem on the basis of the percept sequence about the situation stored in the cloud database [16].

2.6 Diagrammatic Representations of Some Robotic Systems

- Industrial Robot
  The admin of the robotic arm is controlled via a controller embedded with a wireless chip so as to control the arm remotely. The central system enables the admin to manage the settings and set up various modes at which the arm needs to run. The system is connected with the robotic arm that collects data from the system via some protocols like file transfer protocol (FTP) that gives instructions on what task is to be done and how. A representation of the process is shown in Figure 2.5.
- Healthcare Robot
  The various steps to perform robotic surgery are shown in the flow diagram in Figure 2.6 below. The benefits of robotic surgery is that it can precisely perform the surgery without any extra cuts and cannot make mistakes like human doctors can, as continuous monitoring is done during surgery to check if everything is going well.

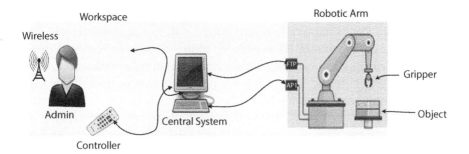

Figure 2.5 Workings of an industrial robot.

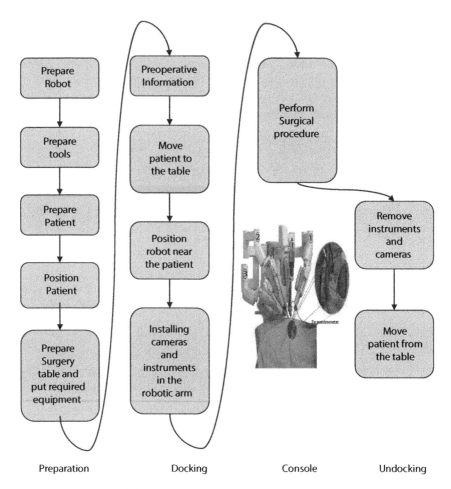

Figure 2.6 Workingsof a healthcare robot.

- Agricultural Robot
  Agricultural robots can be very helpful to farmers as they really work very hard to cultivate the crops and don't think about seasonal weather—from the harsh sun of summers to the chilly winters. By using agricultural robots, farmers can perform all sorts of work on their land remotely—while just sitting at home. Figure 2.7 is a representation of how these robots works.

The robotic machinery is connected wirelessly via the cloud, which is connected to the farmer's home or phone. A farmer can use a phone or

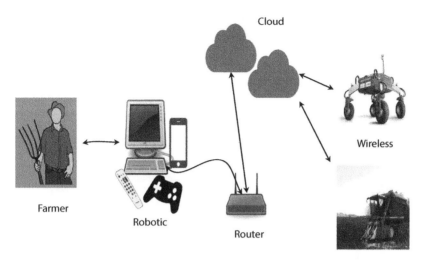

Figure 2.7 Workings of agricultural robots.

controller system to control the robotic machinery to carry out actions in the field.

2.7   Algorithms Used in Robotics

Artificial intelligence works based on some algorithms and those algorithms are studied under machine learning (ML). These algorithms are used based on the requirement of the type of task to be carried out and the final goal to be achieved. ML algorithms are categorized into the four basic types depicted in Figure 2.8 below.

The algorithms that fall under each category have been derived on the basis of mathematical and statistical inferences and work as per some mathematical model—everything can be depicted in terms of mathematical models and those models form the basis of machine learning algorithms that are to be used in robotics. In some industrial robots, the motion planning of robotic arms is done via algorithms such as the Bayesian filter. The Bayes' rule has some fascinating roles in robotics that is hidden under a single equation:

$$Bel(x_t) = \eta P(z_t \mid x_t) \int P(x_t \mid u_t, x_{t-1}) Bel(x_{t-1}) dx_{t-1}$$

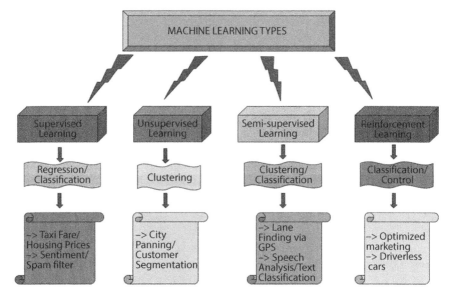

Figure 2.8 Types of machine learning algorithms.

The above expression can be understood as:

- Expression before the integral can be understood as: make a guess and improve it by reading the sensor data.
- Expression within integral or after integral can be understood as: draw what we already know and try to guess to make it better.

The above algorithm can be used to derive some other algorithms like:

1. Algorithms for linear and non-linear systems:
   Linear:
   – Linear Kalman filter
   Non-linear:
   – Extended Kalman filter
   – Unscented Kalman filter
2. Improved version of Kalman filter: Information filter
3. Particle filter: Used in the Monte Carlo method
4. Histogram filter: For making multidimensional items and histograms

For more algorithms used in robotics please refer to [21, 22].

2.8   Application of Robotics

The growth in technology brings more innovation on a daily basis due to the fact that continuous research and experimentation are going on in every field, and robotics has such a vast application and scope that almost every field is utilizing it in their day-to-day lives to perform intensive tasks where humans fail to perform. Some of the robotics applications include:

1) Industrial Applications
   Beginning with the Industrial Revolution, there has been continuous incremental progress in the uses of robots for manufacturing purposes, and automation has become a key aspect in the industry as robotic arms are capable of performing various tasks such as welding, cutting, bending, moving, painting, etc. Therefore, they are intensively utilized to perform various operations in industry.
   Some of the most common robots that are used in industry are:

   - Articulated robots
   - Scararobots
   - Delta robots
   - Cartesian coordinate robots
   - Cylindrical coordinate robots
   - Spherical coordinate robots

   For more details refer to [23].

2) Healthcare Service Applications
   Healthcare is the most prominent and sophisticated industry that requires the greatest attention as it counts as a basic entity for any nation. So, it becomes important to open the doors of innovation for this sector also. Although it is under development, some experiments are going on to use robots to replace nurses to perform some of their common tasks such as providing timely medicine to patients, changing their clothes, dressing their wounds, lifting patients up, etc.
   Some of the medical robots changing the healthcare industry are:

   - DaVinci is a system capable of performing surgical operations with tiny incisions and utmost precision.

- EndoscopyBot is a camera embedded in the robot which enters the body through a natural opening and searches for the damaged parts or any foreign material stuck somewhere in the body and traces the disease caused by them.
- Orthoses (Exoskeletons) are useful for patients with walking abnormalities due to surgery to help them walk and also provoke the weak muscles and make them heal faster.
- Targeted Therapy Microrobots are of microscopic size and help in therapy for specific targets in the body.
- Some other robots include Disinfectant Bots, Clinical Training Bots, Companion Bots, Telepresence Robot Surrogates, Robotic Nurses, Robotic-Assisted Biopsy, etc. [25].

3) Outer Space Applications

Robots are now widely used in outer space exploration. They are sent as unmanned vehicles to space to explore new planets, stars, and other celestial bodies. The most famous robot was the Mars Rover by NASA which was sent to explore the planet Mars. Spirit and Opportunity were two other robots sent to Mars, whose robotic arms were used to investigate soil and rocks on the Red Planet. Other robots, such as the Phoenix Mars Lander and Curiosity Rover, were also sent for further exploration.

4) Military Applications

Defense is the key element for running a nation and therefore any nation invests much more in their defense system. So, robots can play a major role in making defense systems [26] more effective and secure. Lots of research is going on to make advanced robotic systems for the army and defense. One such pioneering robot developed was the Predator drone with unmanned aerial vehicles that can take photographs with greater accuracy and can launch missiles accurately to the target without any pilot.

Some key points of why robots can be used in military applications are:

- They can't get tired
- They don't know what fear is
- They can open their eyes day and night
- They don't hide
- They don't talk while on duty
- They can perform their duty in any weather

- They don't have health risks

The above points are enough to describe why robots can be beneficial for military purposes.

5) Other Applications
   Other applications include:

- Smart home systems that intelligently monitor home security, manage energy usage, maintain proper temperature, clean houses, and provide proper lighting and airconditioning based on requirements
- Smart traffic system
- In making real-life games
- Robotic police/cops
- Driving assistant, etc.

Figure 2.9 below depicts various applications of robots in our day-to-day lives.

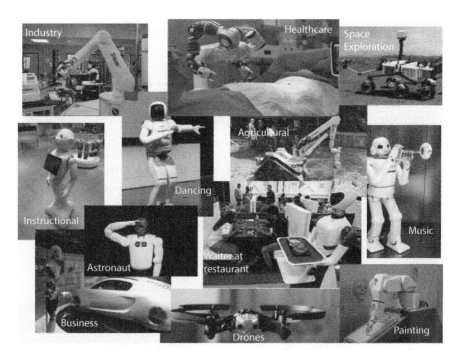

Figure 2.9 Applications of Robotics.

2.9   Case Studies

2.9.1   Sophia

Sophia, a robot that became the world's first robot citizen [28], is also the first robot that can express feelings. It is a humanoid robot that is the brainchild of the American company Hanson Robotics and was developed in Hong Kong by the head creator David Hanson. The main quality of Sophia is that it understands and learns from human behavior by interacting with people. It looks just like humans, with a face which was designed to look similar to Audrey Hepburn, a British actress. It is her amazing qualities that led the Saudi government to honor her with the first robot citizen of the country at the Future Investment Summit held in Riyadh on October 25, 2017 [29]. Sophia has an attractive female face and her eyes are the camera that can recognize the person and say hello to them by their name [30]. Sophia can make about 62 facial expressions and also has a sense of humor. She keeps on learning and is getting better every day. The gap between humans and robots is decreasing day by day. Sophia is a state-of-the-art humanoid that has changed the robotic world and the day is not far off when there will be no difference between the thoughts of machines and humans.

2.9.2   ASIMO

Honda's ASIMO is a four feet tall humanoid robot that can work as a perfect companion in our homes. It was developed by scientists at Honda technologies. The design of its body is human-like, and it can talk and can recognize and interact with people. It can play with children by tossing a coin and also can serve cold drinks by opening the bottle with his own hands. It has a great working capability and can be used in stores for customer service. ASIMO can also run like humans with a speed of 3.5 mph.

However, it is not yet available for the proposed purpose and Honda [27] is continuously working to perform some advanced upgrades to make it more human-like.

2.9.3   Cheetah Robot

The Cheetah robot created at MIT [31] was the first robot capable of doing a backflip. It is a lightweight and springy robot that can perform a range of motions such as walking right-side up or upside down. Apart from that, it can walk two times faster than a normal human being on uneven terrain.

The robot has four legs, with each leg consisting of three low-cost motors that can be easily replaced, and gives a wide range of motion with low inertia and high torque design. It can recover from an unexpected force. Also, its balancing capability is far better than other robots and can easily and instantly balance itself. So, one can say that it is the only state-of-the-art balancing and backflipping robot present till now [32].

2.9.4 IBM Watson

IBM Watson is the smart question-answering system that can answer any question that has been asked in natural language. It was named after Thomas J. Watson, IBM's founder and first CEO. Initially, It was built for serving the purpose of QA(question answering) and it uses machine learning and cognitive thinking to perform the QA, but recently the capabilities of Watson have been increased [33]. Now, it's not only a QA system but also has the capability to talk, hear, see, learn, interpret, and perform as a recommendation system.

2.10 Conclusion

In this chapter, we have discussed various robotics techniques that are used for automation via two of the most in-demand and trending tech systems of the industry—AI and the IoT. Based on their capabilities they are used for automation in a wide range of robotic applications, including healthcare, manufacturing, defense, space exploration, restaurants, agriculture, houses, etc. Looking at the requirements we have defined the roles of various robots and diagrammatically described each role. Apart from that, we have also discussed some of the algorithms that are used in robotics and how they can be used to derive other algorithms based on requirements. Defining the application we have discussed various case studies of some of the most popular and astonishing accomplishments of various institutions or companies with a description of their inventions and the innovative changes they have brought to our modern world which have helped in making it a better place to live.

References

1. Trevathan, V.L. (Ed.), A Guide to the Automation Body of Knowledge, in: *Research Triangle Park*, 2nd ed., International Society of Automation, NC, USA.

2. Jenkins, R. *Science and Technology in the Industrial Revolution*, By A. E. Musson and Eric Robinson. Toronto, University of Toronto Press, 1969. pp. viii 534. Business History Review, 45, 3, 397–399, 1971.

3. https://cs.stanford.edu/people/eroberts/courses/soco/projects/1998-99/robotics/history.html

4. Kurfess, T. R. (Ed.), Robotics and automation handbook, CRC press. Page 3-4, 2018.

5. Robots then and now Archived 2010-12-20 at the Wayback Machine. BBC, http://news.bbc.co.uk/cbbcnews/hi/find_out/guides/tech/robots/newsid_3914000/3914569.stm.

6. https://www.robotics.org/joseph-engelberger/about.cfm

7. Russell, S. J., Edwards, D. D., RUSSELL, S. J. A., Norvig, P., Canny, J., Malik, J. M., *Artificial intelligence: a modern approach*. Prentice Hall, United Kingdom, 1995.

8. Sarle, W. S., *Neural Networks and statistical models*, SAS Institute Inc., Cary, NC, USA, p. 1, 1994.

9. Alpaydin, E., *Introduction to Machine Learning*, The MIT Press, London.

10. https://www.educba.com/agents-in-artificial-intelligence/

11. Miraz, Dr, Ali, M., Excell, P., Picking, R., A review on Internet of Things (IoT), in: *Internet of Everything (IoE) and Internet of Nano Things (IoNT)*, pp. 219–224, 2015.

12. Feki, M.A., Kawsar, F., Boussard, M., Trappeniers, L., The Internet of Things: The Next Technological Revolution. *Computer,* 46, 2, 24–25, Feb. 2013.

13. https://www.prnewswire.com/in/news-releases/global-internet-of-things-iot-market-size-was-valued-at-usd-164-billion-in-2018-and-is-expected-to-grow-at-a-cagr-of-38-62-by-2025-valuates-reports-842976853.html

14. Akins, C., 5 jobs being replaced by robots, in: *Excelle. Monster,* https://web.archive.org/web/20130424145057/http://excelle.monster.com/benefits/articles/4983-5-jobs-being-replaced-by-robots?page=1.

15. Robotic future of patient care, in: *E-Health Insider,* 2007-08-16, https://web.archive.org/web/20071121041811/http://www.e-health-insider.com/comment_and_analysis/250/robotic_future_of_patient_care.

16. Spyros, G.T., Synergy of IoT and AI in Modern Society: The Robotics and Automation Case. *Robot Autom. Eng. J.,* 3, 5, 555621, 2018.

17. Cohen, M. H., Cohen, M. H., Giangola, J. P., Balogh, J., Voice user interface design. Addison-Wesley Professional, page 5-6, 2004.

18. Bogue, R., The role of artificial intelligence in robotics. *Ind. Robot,* 41, 2, 119–123, 2014. https://doi.org/10.1108/IR-01-2014-0300.

19. https://www.humanbrainproject.eu/en/follow-hbp/news/breakthrough-in-construction-of-computers-for-mimicking-human-brain/

20. https://www.scientificamerican.com/article/a-new-supercomputer-is-the-worlds-fastest-brain-mimicking-machine/

21. Fedak, V., Durovsky, F., Uveges, R., Kyslan, K., Lacko, M., Implementation of Robot Control Algorithms by Real-Time Control System. *Int. J. Eng. Res. Afr.*, 18, 112–119, 2015.
22. Thrun, S., Probabilistic Algorithms in Robotics, in: *AI Magazine,* vol. 21, no. 4, 2000.
23. http://www.robotiksistem.com/robotics_applications.html
24. Vermesan, O., Bröring, A., Tragos, E., Serrano, M., Bacciu, D., Chessa, S., Gallicchio, C., Micheli, A., Dragone, M., Saffiotti, A., Simoens, P., Cavallo, F., Bahr, R., Internet of Robotic Things – Converging Sensing/Actuating, Hyperconnectivity, in: *Artificial Intelligence and IoT Platforms,* 2017, 10.13052/rp-9788793609105.
25. https://interestingengineering.com/15-medical-robots-that-are-changing-the-world
26. http://www.indiandefencereview.com/military-applications-of-artificial-intelligence/
27. Kim, M. and Kang, K.C., Formal Construction and Verification of Home Service Robots: A Case Study, in: *Automated Technology for Verification and Analysis. ATVA 2005. Lecture Notes in Computer Science,* vol. 3707, D.A. Peled and Y.K. Tsay (Eds.), Springer, Berlin, Heidelberg, 2005.
28. Parviainen, J., and Coeckelbergh, M., The political choreography of the Sophia robot: beyond robot rights and citizenship to political performances for the social robotics market. *AI & Society*, 1–10, 2020.
29. https://www.forbes.com/sites/zarastone/2017/11/07/everything-you-need-to-know-about-sophia-the-worlds-first-robot-citizen/#2880b5d946fa
30. Peterson, B., I met Sophia, the world's first robot citizen, and the way she said goodbye nearly broke my heart. Enterprise, in: *Digital version,* 2017, Retrieved of http://uk.businessinsider.com/sophia-the-words-first-robot-citizen-nearly-broke-my-heart-2017-10.
31. http://news.mit.edu/2019/mit-mini-cheetah-first-four-legged-robot-to-backflip-0304
32. Four-legged Robot, 'Cheetah,' Sets New Speed Record, in: *Reuters,* 2012-03-06, Archived from the original on 2013-10-22.
33. Upbin, B., IBM Opens Up Its Watson Cognitive Computer For Developers Everywhere, in: *Forbes,* November 14, 2013, https://www.forbes.com/sites/bruceupbin/2013/11/14/ibm-opens-up-watson-as-a-web-service/.

3

Robotics, AI and IoT in the Defense Sector

Rajiv Kumar Modanval, S. Rakesh Kumar*, N. Gayathri
and Sandeep Kr. Sharma

*School of Computing Science and Engineering, Galgotias University,
Uttar Pradesh, India*

Abstract

As the world grows and advances, so too does technology. Rapid tech advancements have paved lots of pathways that have given us various types of applications for robotic processes. In this chapter, some of the most common robots used for the defense sector will be described; also proposed are some robots for creating helping hands for our armies along with more modernized and effective robots that further advance our defense systems via some of the most trending technologies like IoT and AI. The defense sector is one of the most crucial elements of any country in which they invest the most. According to data, India invests around $40 billion on its army and defense systems. But nowadays, with the availability of such modern and advanced technologies, the overall expenditure can be minimized. Robots can perform far better than humans as they can provide untired service to the nation with little investment and less maintenance. Robots are useful in doing repetitive task like walking at a border to secure it. Artificial intelligence is used to make robots capable of understanding the situation and react according to it. The internet of things plays a big role in connecting the robots so they can share data with each other and perform their task sefficiently. Robots also ensure zero life loss and high security at a very low cost.

Keywords: Artificial intelligence (AI), internet of things (IoT), robotics, automation, robots, machine learning

Corresponding author: s.rakeshkumar@galgotiasuniversity.edu.in

Ashutosh Kumar Dubey, Abhishek Kumar, S. Rakesh Kumar, N. Gayathri, Prasenjit Das (eds.) AI and IoT-Based Intelligent Automation in Robotics, (35–52) © 2021 Scrivener Publishing LLC

3.1   Introduction

According to Sun Tzu, a Chinese general, military strategist, writer and philosopher who lived in the Eastern Zhou period of ancient China, "The supreme art of war is to subdue the enemy without fighting."

Robotics is a rapidly growing field of technology with potentially significant applications in the defense sector which can play a significant role in warfare. Nowadays, the United States of America using drones to target enemies in countries like Afghanistan and Pakistan is the best example of the use of robotics in warfare [10]. The United States Department of Defense and countries like China, Russia, and India are developing robots for a wide range of military operations. Artificial intelligence gives robots the ability to make a decision on what to do, how to react, etc. The IoT ensures better connectivity between robots to perform tasks effectively. The combination of AI, IoT and robotics helps to make robots or automatic weapons which can destroy the enemy within a second without losing a single life from our side. To understand the role of AI in robotics first we have to understand the difference between an autonomous system and an automated system. Automated systems are based on computer reasoning that uses clear if–then rules, which are rule-based and return a fixed output for each input. An autonomous system will not return a fixed output for each input, it collects the data through sensors, analyzes the situation, and then takes the decision on action. Its action can vary from situation by situation. All autonomous systems that interact with the world will construct a database which stores arange of behaviors and continuously maintains it.

3.2   How Robotics Plays an Important Role in the Defense Sector

Humans are always searching for new kinds of weapons for warfare. They have always made weapons based on the current technology, availability of resources, etc. Humans made their first weapon, called a spear, in 400,000 BC in a part of Germany between 40,000 to 25,000 BC and they developed a flexible dot in Northern Africa which can kill a deer in a 40-meter range. Arrows and bows were developed in 20000 BC, with some believing they were developed much earlier, pointing to a 60000 BC old stone that may or may not have an arrowhead.

By 1000 BC, swords were entwined with Celtic folklore and custom in Britain, mirroring their significance in the public arena. The first rocket, known as "fire arrow," was developed in China between 800 to 1300 AD [13]. As the technology grew, humans invented many weapons like guns, tanks, missiles, nuclear bombs, and hydrogen bombs. Robotics is being used to eliminate human interaction in warfare, with many countries currently working on this and some countries also working on innovating new weapons [17].

Figure 3.1 shows the journey of weapons, from spears to nuclear bombs. The journey of exploring new ways of developing new weapons is currently continuing in the United State of America with the use of drones to target terrorist bases in foreign countries like Iran and Pakistan. Their use got a tremendous response, successfully killing terrorists without losing a single life [11]. Robotics can be the best replacement for armed forces in warfare, which eliminates the risk of losing human life. Many countries like the USA, China, Russia, and India are developing robots for warfare. This is a new type of warfare based on technology and utilization of available resources.

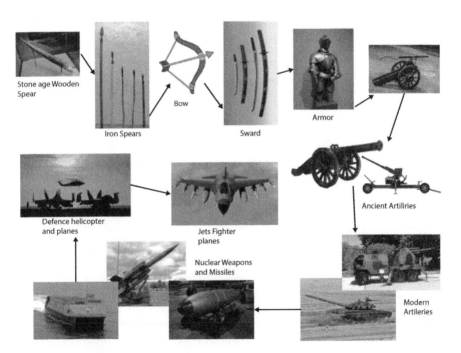

Figure 3.1 The journey of weapons in warfare.

3.3   Review of the World's Current Robotics Capabilities in the Defense Sector

China and the United State have emerged as leaders in the field of artificial intelligence and they are trying to do the same for the field of Robotics. The world's current capabilities in the field of robotics are reviewed below.

3.3.1   China

The Chinese government is investing billions of dollars to promote the development in the field of artificial intelligence. Chinese companies are also investing billions of dollars for startups in Silicon Valley and in the development of AI in local areas. It is expected that by 2020 China's progress in the application and technology of robotics will be at an advanced level in the world, while it's artificial intelligence industry will make a significant impact on its economic growth rate. In July 2017, China announced that it is expected to be a world leader in the field of artificial intelligence by 2030 with an industry potentially worth 150 billion dollars [15]. By now, China hopes to have achieved vital progress in next generation AI technologies, together with massive knowledge, swarm intelligence, hybrid increased intelligence, and autonomous intelligent systems. At that time, the worth

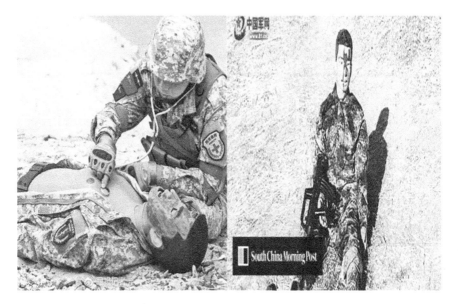

Figure 3.2 "Warrior," the first Chinese patient robot.

of China's core AI trade is targeted to exceed a hundred and fifty billion RMB (over \$22 billion) in value, with AI-related fields valued at one trillion RMB (nearly \$148 billion). At the same time, China is advancing in gathering high-quality talent and establishing initial frameworks for laws, ethics, and policy.

Dr. Cameran Ashraf, an assistant professor at Central European University who researches the geopolitics of internet censorship and cyber-war, said in *The Defense Post* that "China is very likely to remain highly competitive in the AI space by 2030, and barring substantial geopolitical instability will be a global leader in AI and cyber warfare" [15].

As reported in the *PLA Daily*, the Chinese army has created a lifelike golem mannequin, complete with a pulse and beating heart, to assist in training its medics to treat tract wounds. The medical robot named "Warrior" shown in Figure 3.2 is even ready to provide medics feedback on how well they're treating the injuries and is provided with over thirty sensors to assist in simulating over three hundred tract injuries [32].

3.3.2   United State of America

The United States government is providing billions of dollars to get ready for the following stage of warfare that it believes is going to be defined by advances in AI. Ideas like drone motherships releasing little baby drones from the air and the sea, infantrymen and women sporting exoskeletons and wearable electronics loaded up with combat apps, and lone mission commanders directing swarms of remote-controlled vessels to carryout operations are areas that are already being tested at MIT's Computer Science and AI Laboratory [18]. On May 3, 2016, the US Administration announced that it will establish a new National Science and Technology Council (NSTC) Subcommittee on Artificial Intelligence and Machine Learning responsible for helping coordinate Federal activity on AI. This Subcommittee directed the Subcommittee on Networking and Information Technology Research and Development (NITRD) to create a National Artificial Intelligence Research and Development Strategic Plan. A NITRD Task Force on Artificial Intelligence was then formed which outlined the Federal strategic priorities for AI research and development, with explicit attention on areas of national security that industry is unlikely to handle [18].

The Defense Advanced Research Project Agency (DARPA) of the U.S. Department of Defense has been one of the largest sources of funding for AI research and development workover the last few decades, including funding for the virtual machine reality (VMR) system which aids

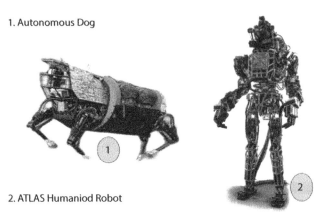

Figure 3.3 Armed robots being developed for U.S. armed forces.

intelligence analysts in searching, filtering, and exploring visual media through advanced computer vision and reasoning techniques.

Figure 3.3 shows the humanoid robot Atlas and an autonomous dog. DARPA is strenuously working to complete these projects for its armed forces.

3.3.3   Russia

The United States and China are busy competing with each other to become the leader in the field of artificial intelligence. The Russian government also understands the importance of robotics in warfare. Nobody would call Russia's administration and budgetary organization especially deft, nor its protection industry especially developed. Without a doubt, Russia trails the Western economies in such key areas as correspondence hardware, microelectronics, innovative control frameworks, and other key advances. However, in specific areas of the field of unmanned military frameworks, Russia might be creeping in front of its opposition in planning and testing a wide assortment of frameworks and conceptualizing their future use.

Before the eventual fate of war is acknowledged in combat zones, it is formed in labs and practice ranges. As Russia's Ministry of Defense iterates design around the Marker unmanned ground vehicle, the Ministry of Defense is learning the opening plays of future robot fights. In the first half of 2020, Russia is expected to test robot swarms guided by armed humans in exercises to learn exactly how the nation should prepare for robot

Figure 3.4 Some advanced Russian military robots.

warfare in the future [16]. The Russian Ministry of Defense is bringing two robot tank designs in-house, following advancements from industry in developing these forms [17]. The Ministry of Defense has asked those involved in different military-mechanical endeavors to provide recommendations which will be surveyed ahead of schedule one year from now by the military's Combined Arms Academy. The Russian state news agency has written that the initiative is intended to address "the virtual absence of a unified concept for the use of military robotics by the Russian armed forces" [18]. Figure 3.4 shows some advanced autonomous military robots.

3.3.4 India

Artificial intelligence (AI), also known as the Industrial Revolution 4.0, has been making great strides in scientific and technological development across varying fields. It is capable of making noteworthy changes in the manner in which activities of civilians and military operations are conducted [22]. Countries across the world are busy making their armed forces more efficient using emerging technologies like AI, IoT, and robotics. Russia, China, and the United States are competing with each other to become the leader in this technology, with India also wanting to join this race [24]. India is planning to secure its border against autonomous armed robots from two major neighboring countries, China and Pakistan, using a smart surveillance alert system. The Indian Ministry of Defence has directed the Defence Research and Development Organisation to develop armed robots and other military equipment like autonomous tanks, unmanned aerial vehicles (UAVs), etc.

In August 2017, the Indian Army stated that it intends to utilize several indigenously assembled robots to fight against terrorists in Jammu and Kashmir. Purportedly these robots can convey ammo at the planned areas in the event of perilous and crisis circumstances has just endorsed a military proposition to enlist 544 robots for this reason. These robots are lightweight and consist of reconnaissance cameras and transmission frameworks with a scope of 200 meters [25, 36].

The Defence Research and Development Organisation (DRDO) was established in 1958, and ever since it has been working to make the Indian Army powerful in terms of technology. The DRDO has more than 1800+ industry partnerships and has collaborated with these companies to make equipment, systems, products and technologies for the army, some of which are [25]:

- Daksh – Remotely Operated Vehicle (ROV)
- NETRA – Unmanned Aerial Vehicle (UAV)
- Confined Space Remotely Operated Vehicle (CSROV)

Figure 3.5 Indian military robots.

- Surveillance Remotely Operated Vehicle (SROV) (on the verge of induction)
- Unexploded Ordnance Handling Robot (UXOR)

Figure 3.5 shows a few autonomous robots developed by India's Defence Research and Development Organisation. The DRDO is responsible for research and development of weapons based on new technology in India and has more than 1800+ industrial partners for development and research of new weapons [25].

3.4   Application Areas of Robotics in Warfare

Robotics has a broad area of application in warfare because there are many dangerous tasks which should be performed by robots instead of humans like diffusing IEDs and bombs. In warfare there are several tasks to perform for which there are many types of specially designed robots. Armed forces can use robots to search out enemies in any kind of situation and destroy them. Robots can be a surveillance system, an autonomous tank, an aerial drone or an armed soldier. Some of the application areas of robotics are presented below.

3.4.1   Autonomous Drones

Drones or unmanned aerial vehicles (UAVs) are used all over the world by armies. They are armed with GPS, an infrared camera, and lasers, which makes them more dangerous. Unmanned aerial vehicles are IoT enabled. They are all connected with each using IoT techniques. The internet of things (IoT) provides a platform to connect devices so they can communicate with each other, transfer data using the cloud for better user experience or to perform military operations very efficiently [34]. As per a report by Goldman Sachs, global militaries will have spent $70 billion on UAV innovationsby 2020 [27].

The U.S. Defense Advanced Research Projects Agency (DARPA) is as of now taking a shot at semi-autonomous Demon UAVs that can be launched and recovered by a mothership [33]. Additionally, in the United Statespocket-sized observation bots are being tried. In the meantime, Germany and France have lately reported on designing and building another military aircraft named the "Eurodrone," which is set for take-off in 2040. Utilizing drones for military purposes might make sure that errands progress successfully and in a cost-efficient manner, in addition to

Figure 3.6 Autonomous drones in action.

sparing lives [35]. Drones can be sent in circumstances where keeping an eye on flight is considered excessively hazardous or troublesome, go about as a day in and day out eye in the sky, and convey arms with more note worthy exactness [27].

Figure 3.6 shows autonomous drones in action. They can play an important role in any type of warfare. Using these drones, militaries can destroy enemies without entering their borders. They are especially useful for anti-terror military operations, and the United States have used these drones against terrorists in countries like Iraq and Afghanistan and have gotten amazing results.

3.4.2 Autonomous Tanks and Vehicles

Unmanned aerial vehicles (UAVs) are used for security in the skies in a similar manner as autonomous tanks and vehicles are used for security on ground. They help reduce the risk of losing human life in warfare. Tanks can be autonomous or semi-autonomous and are equipped with surveillance systems, sensors, cameras, and weapons. UAVs are connected with each other through the internet of things (IoT) and communicate with each other on IoT platforms using the cloud. The IoT is an emerging technology like artificial intelligence (AI), the cloud and big data.

Russia, close to the United States, is one of the nations driving advances in unmanned ground vehicle (UGV) innovation. Lately, JSC 766 UPTK, a producer of military equipment, sent their Uran-6 UGVs to Syria to incapacitate bombs and mines and investigate unknown territories. They're

Figure 3.7 Autonomous tanks.

also building a 10-ton battle UGV with a 30mm gun and 7.62mm automatic rifle to be used against tank rockets, just as the T-14, a semi-self-governing tank. UGVs are getting basic to ground missions, going about as eyes, ears and even battle troopers. By sending robots in first, people are kept securely out of risk. Their abilities likewise empower better non-military personnel security, even in the outcome of battle, as they can defuse remaining bombs and mines [27].

Figure 3.7 shows the autonomous tanksin action. Autonomous tanks and vehicles can play an important role on the battle ground. Future wars will be the same as now, but human soldiers will be replaced by humanoid robots, tanks will be replaced by autonomous tanks, and ships and submarines will be replaced by autonomous ships and submarines.

3.4.3   Autonomous Ships and Submarines

Submarines are the hidden players of any warfare, which have the capability to change the result of warfare. Submarines have capabilities to surprise enemies. Since they operate under the water, it is very difficult to trace them. One drawback with submarines is that they need crew members to operate them. Autonomous submarines will solve this problem, and this type of submarine is currently under development.

The Defense Advanced Research Projects Agency (DARPA) developed the Sea Hunter in 2018, having a length of 40 meters, speed of 27 knots. The Sea Hunter operates up to three months at a time without a crew or anyone controlling it remotely. As of late, the U.S. Office of Naval Research showed an armada of self-ruling pontoons imparting and swarming an objective altogether. Their possible future use? Shielding harbors from assault [19]. Asia and Europe are additionally dealing with different unmanned boat ventures. In the UK, the Royal Navy as of late took was responsible for an autonomous minesweeper framework that can clear ocean mines.

Autonomous ships and submarines that utilize on-board PC frameworks, GPS, sonar, laser, infrared and different sensors, are improving reconnaissance and warranting a substantial amount of investments to fund. For Sea Hunter, the operational quotes run from US$15,000 to US$20,000 every day. Contrast that with an everyday cost of around US$700,000 to operatea destroyer [23].

As per DARPA, these submarines could transform United State naval operations and can lead the way to a new type of naval warfare. These autonomous ships and submarines are capable of changing the result of any warfare, without losing a single life. Figure 3.8 shows autonomous submarines and ships that are in the testing phase of development.

Figure 3.8 Autonomous submarines and ships currently under development.

3.4.4   Humanoid Robot Soldiers

In the twentieth century, approximately 108 million people were killed due to warfare, and it is estimated that approximately 150 million to 1 billion people have been killed in wars throughout all of human history [28]. Humanoid robot soldiers will help to reduce these kinds of deaths in the future. Humanoid robots are modeled like humans. Since they are designed for specific tasks, the functional abilities of these robots are different from each other. We all have seen humanoid robots in movies in which they are fighting to achieve some specific goal. Humanoid robot soldiers are a type of humanoid robot designed to model armed soldiers to participate in warfare.

The world is busy developing humanoid robot soldiers which can replace armed forces. Some countries have developed really good humanoid robots which they keep upgrading [27]. FEDOR, a humanoid robot developed by Russia, can shoot at targets using both hands. FEDOR, which is short for Final Experimental Demonstration Object Research, is also known as Skybot F-850 [16]. There are many humanoid robot soldiers in development. The United States is developing an advanced humanoid robot which can replace the soldiers in the armed forces.

Humanoid robots will be part of future wars, and a country having the latest technologies for armed robots will most probably defeat its opponent. China and the United States are busy competing with each other to become the leader in AI technology. China wants to become the leader of this emerging technology, with 2030 being the deadline to achieve this goal. It is investing billions of dollars to promote home invention and many start-ups in the Silicon Valley [18]. Currently, many humanoid robot soldiers are under development. Some of the military robots of the future are [31]:

- Atlas
- Avatar III
- Corrosion Resistant Aerial Covert Unmanned Nautical System (CRACUNS)
- TALON
- Black Knight
- Guardium

Currently some humanoid robot soldiers have been developed and many are in the testing phase of development. Russia has developed Fedor, the United States is developing Atlas, and so on. Figure 3.9 shows some humanoid armed soldiers who will replace human armed soldiers in the future.

Figure 3.9 Some examples of humanoid armed robots.

3.4.5   Armed Soldier Exoskeletons

What is an armed soldier exoskeleton? Is it a robot or a human? It's neither a robot nor a human, it's a combination of both. Most probably everyone has seen the movie *Iron Man* in which there was an Iron Man suit; it is the same as that. The United States Special Operations Command, with the cooperation of the Defense Advanced Research Projects Agency (DARPA) and Harvard, is presently inventing a Tactical Assault Light Operator Suit (TALOS), which is a battery-powered exoskeleton intended to be worn by fighters to enhance strength, endurance and ergonomics [28].

Notwithstanding a strong exoskeleton that bolsters the administrator, the suit includes physiological and organic sensors, actuators that fill in as the muscles to control the suit, processors and PCs, a cap with advanced presentation and different correspondence frameworks.

TALOS and other exoskeletons being created in nations such as Europe, China, and Russia, will help support soldiers when walking long distances or carry heavy loads, including casualties. Additionally, they can possibly offer ballistic and bomb protection in an assault [27].

By conserving human energy and reducing injuries, soldiers will be able to keep moving longer, reducing the amount of down time, which is a huge military advantage. Regardless of some lingering issues, the work on the main model is expected to be finished by the end of 2018. The connection between robots and the military is experiencing some dramatic changes. Rightly or wrongly, this forward-moving innovation is changing how countries handle defense, from observing enemy activity and completing missions to who we send into battle.

Be that as it may, while robots utilized in military positions can help decrease costs, empower efficiencies and spare lives when on our side, when in the hands of the foe, or whenever given an excess of self-rule, they could introduce new dangers which could be deadlier. Therefore, new ethical protocols need to be developed to decrease the dangers.

Armed soldier exoskeletons, which are a combination of humans and robots, are shown in Figure 3.10 [21].

Figure 3.10 Armed soldier exoskeletons.

3.5   Conclusion

A complete long-range vision of the vital job that AI has in the military is the basis of the innovative work being done in AI development. The vision must cover different key aspects of AI, taking into consideration the role AI plays in autonomous weapons and digital barriers, and figuring out precise arrangements for every one of them. It isn't necessary that these approaches be in accordance with either broad universal supposition or strategy shifts in different nations on these issues, as long as they sufficiently serve national interests. The advancement of such an exhaustive vision will enable the Indian government to enhance the assignment of its significant research capacities towards the improvement of explicit AI abilities that would most profit the nation.

3.6   Future Work

The days are gone when armed soldiers will fight during warfare. Future wars will be fought based on technology, and countries who strike with advanced warfare technology will probably win the war. The world is preparing for future warfare. Currently, in the United States, DARPA is investing billions of dollars in research and development of robots for warfare. China is trying to become the leader in this technology by 2030; to achieve this goal they are investing billions of dollars to promote in-house innovation and Silicon Valley startups.

As of now, many robots have been developed and many are still under development. Some of the names of upcoming robots are [31]:

- Ripsaw MS1 (autonomous tank)
- DRDO Daksh (support UGV)
- Goalkeeper CIWS (autonomous ship defense system)
- Atlas (search and rescue bipedal UGV)
- Black Knight (UGV tank)
- Protector USV (unmanned patrol boat)

References

1. http://www.academia.edu/download/59339185/2017-01-26-artificial-intelligence-future-warfare-cummings-final20190521-119589-196oqd3.pdf
2. https://search.informit.com.au/fullText;res=IELAPA;dn=200609450

3. https://books.google.com/books?hl=en&lr=&id=xU0MDziPSpMC&oi=fnd&pg=PP2&dq=robotics+in+warfare&ots=HP94esGseU&sig=hsiBAmRQR_Px-R41yk5pdsIOIZ4
4. Robotics at War: Survival: Vol 57, No 5
5. https://heinonline.org/hol-cgi-bin/get_pdf.cgi?handle=hein.journals/jlinfos21&section=23
6. https://www.seas.upenn.edu/~modlab/publications/dsto.pdf
7. https://search.proquest.com/openview/d8bc29fac458c2e6cb2437074ff84cfa/1?pq-origsite=gscholar&cbl=18750&diss=y
8. https://usiofindia.org/publication/usi-journal/robotics-in-warfare/
9. https://ieeexplore.ieee.org/abstract/document/4799405
10. https://www.sciencedirect.com/science/article/pii/S0262407909602372
11. https://www.sciencedirect.com/science/article/pii/S0926580518309932
12. https://www.sciencedirect.com/science/article/pii/B9780123739858001987
13. https://www.newscientist.com/article/dn17423-timeline-weapons-technology/
14. https://www.orfonline.org/research/a-i-in-the-chinese-military-current-initiatives-and-the-implications-for-india-61253/
15. https://www.thedefensepost.com/2018/01/02/china-artificial-intelligence-drones/
16. https://www.c4isrnet.com/unmanned/2019/12/13/russia-will-test-swarms-for-anti-robot-combat-in-2020/
17. https://www.c4isrnet.com/unmanned/robotics/2020/01/11/russian-army-will-develop-of-storm-robot-tank-and-ally/
18. http://www.indiandefencereview.com/military-applications-of-artificial-intelligence/
19. https://www.defenseone.com/ideas/2019/11/russias-military-writing-armed-robot-playbook/161549/
20. https://cdn.defenseone.com/media/img/upload/2018/07/19/shutterstock_610303184/defense-large.jpg
21. https://cdni.rbth.com/rbthmedia/images/web/in-rbth/images/2015-01/top/Top_robots.png
22. https://www.orfonline.org/expert-speak/artificial-intelligence-military-operations-where-does-india-stand-54030/
23. https://timesofindia.indiatimes.com/india/india-moves-to-develop-ai-based-military-systems/articleshow/64250232.cms
24. https://analyticsindiamag.com/us-chinas-military-future-robots-india-competing/
25. https://drdo.gov.in/headquarter-directorates/area-of-work/industry-interface-technology-management
26. https://drdo.gov.in/robotics
27. https://www.distrelec.de/current/en/robotics/how-robots-are-changing-the-defence-sector/

28. https://www.nytimes.com/2003/07/06/books/chapters/what-every-person-should-know-about-war.html
29. https://www.space.com/russia-launching-humanoid-robot-into-space.html
30. https://www.thehindu.com/sci-tech/science/russia-sends-its-first-humanoid-robot-fedor-into-space/article29220831.ece
31. https://interestingengineering.com/a-brief-history-of-military-robots-including-autonomous-system
32. https://www.thestar.com.my/tech/tech-news/2019/06/11/chinese-military-develops-its-first-robot-patient-as-it-seeks-to-prepare-medics-for-battlefield-role.
33. Alzubi, J.A., Manikandan, R., Alzubi, O.A., Gayathri, N., Patan, R., A Survey of Specific IoT Applications. *Int. J. Emerging Technol.*, 10, 1, 47–53, 2019.
34. Muthuramalingam, S., Bharathi, A., Gayathri, N., Sathiyaraj, R., Balamurugan, B., IoT Based Intelligent Transportation System (IoT-ITS) for Global Perspective: A Case Study, in: *Internet of Things and Big Data Analytics for Smart Generation*, pp. 279–300, Springer, Cham, 2019.
35. Kumar, S.R. and Gayathri, N., Trust based data transmission mechanism in MANET using sOLSR, in: *Annual Convention of the Computer Society of India*, pp. 169–180, Springer, Singapore, 2016, December.
36. Kumar, S.R., Gayathri, N., Balamurugan, B., Enhancing network lifetime through power-aware routing in MANET. *Int. J. Internet Technol. Secured Trans.*, 9, 1-2, 96–111, 2019.

Robotics, AI and IoT in Medical and Healthcare Applications

Pooja Dixit[1]*, Manju Payal[2]†, Nidhi Goyal[3]‡ and Vishal Dutt[4]§

[1]Sophia Girls' College (Autonomous), Ajmer, India
[2]Academic Hub, Ajmer, India
[3]GD Memorial College, Jodhpur, India
[4]Aryabhatta College, Ajmer, India

Abstract

Today, the vital role of robotics, AI and IOT technologies have recast healthcare. Healthcare apps enabled by these technologies help manage the health of consumers, thus ensuring their health. The main focus of this chapter is to study the applications for the techniques that make the healthcare system more affordable, provide better outcomes and also access patients' records in order to provide better solutions. Thus, when these technologies merge, there is a chance that they will be capable of better operational efficiency for tracking and monitoring patients, with automation making more optimistic solutions possible.

Keywords: Artificial intelligence, robotics, IoT, internet of medical robotics things (IoMRT)

4.1 Introduction

4.1.1 Basics of AI

Artificial intelligence (AI) is a computer system able to perform tasks that usually require human intelligence like reasoning, training, remodeling,

---

*Corresponding author: poojadixit565@gmail.com
†Corresponding author: manjupayal771@gmail.com
‡Corresponding author: ng56665@gmail.com
§Corresponding author: vishaldutt53@gmail.com

Ashutosh Kumar Dubey, Abhishek Kumar, S. Rakesh Kumar, N. Gayathri, Prasenjit Das (eds.) AI and IoT-Based Intelligent Automation in Robotics, (53–74) © 2021 Scrivener Publishing LLC

understanding, and interplay. Nowadays, AI has many applications. It performs certain tasks or solves predefined problems based on principles and tools, which can include math, logic, and biology. Existing computer-based intelligence innovations significant feature is that they are logically ready to legitimate of various unorganized data; for example, natural language content and pictures [1]. AI and machine learning have become the most successful techniques for the fundamental approach used by many applications in recent years. Machine learning permits a system to turn up new patterns and acquire its own rules for existing data and new circumstances. AI is potentially used in personal health and social care services planning and resource allocation; for example, UK's Harrow Council uses the IBM Watson Care Manager to provide services for less money. After first meeting with individuals to discuss their needs, the care provider enters their requirements within the care budget. The care provider also creates and individual care plan which professes to give individuals more control and flexibility over what care and health services they receive. In this process AI is used to improve the patient's experience.

In Liverpool, Alder Hey Children's Hospital used IBM Watson to help create UK's first "cognitive hospital" to make the interrelationship with the patient easier with the introduction of an app. This app is mainly used to reduce patients' anxiety before a visit, accessing required information, and providing clinicians with knowledge to help provide the correct surgery [2].

4.1.1.1　AI in Healthcare

Artificial intelligence can make it possible to accurately inspect and recognize sample compounds faster in dataset. For appropriate studies, AI is used to search the scientific literature and synthesize various types of data like drug discoveries.

For scientific research, the Institute of Cancer Research's canSAR database homogenizes generic clinical data collected during ongoing patient care along with necessary information, which helps to create a predication for new aims of cancer drugs. Recently, an AI "robot scientist" named Eve has emerged for making drug discovery faster, effective and very profitable. AI is important in healthcare and relevant in medical research. AI also finds better-matching patients for clinical trials [3]. Figure 4.1 illustrates that in 2014 and 2021, there has been a rapid growth in the artificial intelligence market for healthcare applications in the world.

Since AI techniques assuredly support the prognosis of disease they are being used in UK hospitals. AI is commonly used to research publications,

Figure 4.1 Artificial intelligence market for healthcare applications in the world for the years 2014 and 2021. (Frost & Sullivan Report, Transforming Healthcare Through Artificial Intelligence Systems, 2016).

clinical data and professional guidelines, and can also guide advice about medical treatment. In clinical care, AI may include:

- Medical Scheme: Scanned medical information is methodically assembled to make it easily accessible to instruct the AI system. AI helps reduce the cost as well as time involved in examining scans for better targeted treatment with more assurance. It allows more scans and provides favorable outcomes by ascertaining what the situation is in skin and breast cancer, pneumonia, and other diseases [4].
- Echocardiography: In Oxford, at John Radcliffe Hospital the Ultromics framework uses AI to study echocardiograms, which are utilized to design models of pulses and confirm coronary thrombosis.
- Televise Neurological Conditions: AI techniques are being developed to examine verbal expression patterns which anticipate psychotic insane scenes and recognize side effects of neurological conditions like Parkinson's disease.
- Operation: AI acquires mechanical autonomy instruments like robotics, which are utilized in analyses to convey how to perform some specific functions in keyhole surgery, like suturing and wound closure [5].

4.1.1.2   Current Trends of AI in Healthcare

Parts of healthcare are quickly being reshaped following current universal AI trends in healthcare. AI is being introduced in some hospitals to examine critical diseases, such as cancer, and helps detect conditions at an early stage with more accuracy. For example, the U.S. startup Enclitic has developed deep learning AI-based medical imaging software to detect tumors. Its design algorithm helps to discover human lung tumors using a CT scan.

Some trends of AI in healthcare are:

- AI as a tool for data mining medical records: IBM's Watson Health can analyze large volumes of patient healthcare data to aid healthcare organizations by using cognitive technology to offer a prognosis [6].
- AI-based health chatbots as health assistant and personal trainer: Chatbots are sometimes used in healthcare to schedule doctor's appointments, furnish medical reminders, and for conditions-based symptom recognition. Babylon MD Health is a familiar AI-enabled health support application which is used by doctors, patients, and health professional for the above functions.
- Use of AI in healthcare companies: AI-powered robots are being externalized for use in robotic surgical systems. Many healthcare companies are using machine learning (ML) applications such as Google DeepMind, IBM Watson, etc., and the new AI-enabled robots developed for healthcare result of undamaged, more accuracy and recovers speedily.
- Drug discovery: AI technologies use apps like Helix for drug discovery. AI apps endowed with machine learning are capable of responding to verbal questions and requests, and also permit more efficient research, expand effectiveness, upgrade lab security, stay up-to-date on significant research topics, and oversee stock.
- Automation of drug design and compound selection: Peptone uses AI with Keras and TensorFlow integration to predict protein characteristics which would enable certified researchers to reduce complexity in protein design.
- Machine learning models for healthcare: GNS Healthcare converts a biomedical and healthcare data stream into a computer model in clinical trials. This customized model helps doctors identify a patient's response and deliver medicine and treatment that match the patient's needs [7].

4.1.1.3   Limits of AI in Healthcare

Artificial intelligence (AI) is dependent on computer-based information, inconsistencies, accessibility, the nature of the data stored, and the capacity. Additionally, significant computing processing power is essential for inspecting large and complicated datasets, keeping computerized records, and marking the information. There are questions concerning how many patients and masters approve of cutting-edge sharing of individuals health information. People have characteristics that an AI framework presumably will not have; for instance, sympathy. Most times, medical training includes complex choices and limitations that AI at present cannot suggest; for instance, contextual data and the ability to examine expressive gestures [8].

4.1.2   Basics of Robotics

In 1921, the Czech writer Karel Čapek introduced a "robot" in his play *R.U.R. (Rossuum's Universal Robots)*. In Czech, "robot" derives from the word "robota," which means "essential work." The term robot is defined by the Robot Institute of America as "a reprogrammable, multifunctional manipulator designed to move material, parts, tools, or specialized devices through various programmed motions for the performance of a variety of tasks." In the 1940s, based on Isaac Asimov's Robot series of books, there are essentially three fundamental laws of robots:

1) A robot may not injure a human or, through inaction, allow a human being to come to harm.
2) A robot must obey the orders given it by human beings except where such orders would conflict with the First Law.
3) A robot must protect its own existence as long as such protection does not conflict with the First or Second Laws.

A main application or serious after the innovation of robots for work like people, and it was created bit by bit and including highlights this shows it can more accomplish than it was created. Today until uses of mechanical autonomy in numerous territories to be grown yet there are still new extension are accessible around there. A basic meaning robot is: "whichever machine is modified to accomplish work." In any case, essential machine computerization is currently so common that this exemplary definition is being progressively supplanted with an expression that better suits it, which is "a machine with knowledge." This field of mechanical autonomy includes telemanipulation and numerical control frameworks [9].

4.1.2.1   Robotics for Healthcare

Mechanical technology for medicine and healthcare is seen as the zone of systems prepared to perform mechatronic exercises (power or development efforts) which depend on data preparation which accept through sensor innovation, with the expect help the working of obstructed individuals,

Medical intercessions, care and restoration of patients and besides to help individuals in shirking programs

The definition of what makes a robot continues to change. In any case, there is general agreement regarding the fundamental qualities that robots must have, three of which are captured within the parameters of healthcare technology, as illustrated in Figure 4.2:

- Sensors: Robots utilize detecting innovation to secure data about their condition.
- Knowledge: Robots process data caught through sensor innovation and produce outputs for dynamic decision-making, coordination, and control.
- Movement: Robots follow the directions that are pre-programmed, or created in real-time on sensor input, to perform conscious, controlled, and frequently repeated mechatronic activity.

Robotics for medical healthcare and healthcare enterprises are deployed to coordinate responsibility utilizing the field of automation and electronics, similar to power or development estimation or domain, sensing element framework technology, etc. The functions carried out by robots include considerations for patients, restorations, artificial prosthetics, necessary healthcare mediations, e-health, and observations [10].

Robotic systems can increase the value of healthcare in four ways that are illustrate in Figure 4.3:

- Less labor costs: This can be accomplished by simply giving explicit human exercises to robots by robotizing logistic exercises within expert care.
- Growing freedom and social support for vulnerable individuals: Both social and economic benefits can assist in an

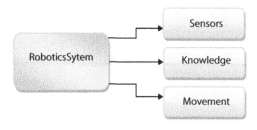

Figure 4.2 Robotics system.

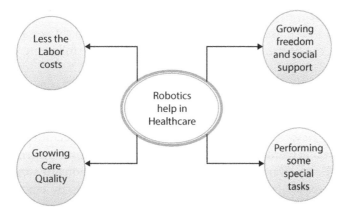

Figure 4.3 Robotics in healthcare.

individual's increased sense of freedom and support in the daily routines of life. An example of this is simply the capacity to take care of oneself.

- Growing quality of care given by robotic systems: Robots are able to answer accurately and can repeat activities which humans cannot perform. An example of this are automated bone cutters for hip surgery.
- Performing tasks that cannot be done by humans: Robots are able to perform tasks which are impossible for surgeons to do because of limitations based on size or accuracy. An example of this are the microcapsules used for taking internal body tissue samples [11].

4.1.3   Basics of IoT

The primary purpose of the internet of things (IoT) is to connect smart devices with the internet in a straightforward way. This allows data to be exchanged between all devices and for users data to be stored in an increasingly secure way. In healthcare, the IoT is capable of accessing numerous medical applications; for example, observing health remotely, scheduling, monitoring chronic health conditions, and elderly care services. The IoT has the potential to significantly change medical services and how hospitals, health centers, and other medical care facilities accumulate data by combining significant practical, scientific, and trading patterns of motility in the form of computerized data that medical practitioners can use to deliver patient care. As previously mentioned, physical devices are connected with the network; for example, implanted sensing elements, actuators, and other types of devices that gather and transfer real-time data through the network system [12]. This information accumulated from different networking devices can be use by healthcare institutions for the following purposes:

- AI helps improve patient care by enhancing and supporting various services that maintain and modify a healthcare organization based on data.
- AI elevates procedure by developing new facilities and arrangements that expand productivity and lower expenses.
- AI empowers healthcare institution associations to suggest increasingly customized care and experiences by continuously studying the needs and inclinations of patients.
- AI creates a network of more intelligent healthcare systems by proactively observing the foundation and robotizing the arrangement and the board of the IT framework [13].

4.1.3.1   IoT Scenarios in Healthcare

The internet of things provides answers to healthcare by constructing associations that it is more astute and increasingly effective at to perform tasks. The IoT can possibly reclassify how individuals, technology and devices interface and associate with one another in healthcare situations, advancing better options, diminished expenses, and improved results.

Examples of IoT-driven healthcare include:

- Connecting medical devices, such as MRI and CT scanners, can produce a huge amount of data which can be used through a connected network with computing infrastructure, generating explication, visualization and analysis.
- Wearable healthcare devices can be used by health providers for remote patient monitoring, which provides more secure and increasingly powerful social healthcare for real-time checking of a patient's vital signs, post-surgery recuperation, and observation of patients in medical clinics remotely. By using the wearable sensors, specialists are able to track patients remotely and progressively follow their well-being status [14].
- Electronic ID-enabled security doors and video surveillance cameras enhance security and prevent threats and unauthorized entries and departures in healthcare facilities.
- Bluetooth low energy (BLE) tags are used to screen healthcare devices, cure doses and supplies.

- Communicate effectively with clinical personnel by providing proactive updates on solutions for health-monitoring equipment to decrease unexpected repairs of necessary devices, frameworks, and medical tools.

4.1.3.2   Requirements of Security

Security is essential for IoT-based healthcare services systems. Therefore, to achieve safe administrations, it is necessary to focus on the following additional security prerequisites:

- Privacy: Guarantees the unavailability of medical facts for unapproved clients.
- Integrity: Maintains all information trustworthiness during the transmission of information between devices.
- Authentication: Authentication is checked between peers with which it is communicating.
- Availability: Information is accessible on the IoT to all health and social services management (which can be either vicinity or global/cloud management) only to sanctioned assemblies to help prevent denial-of-service attacks. Figure 4.4 shows the various app symbols that are used in mobile healthcare system by clicking on these app's, patients can

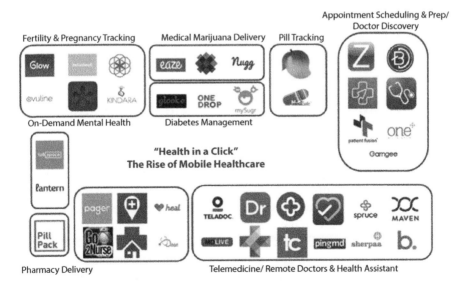

Figure 4.4 Some of the apps symbolic of the rise of mobile healthcare.

track their requirements and follow the guidelines provided by these mobile app's.

- Data Freshness: This involves the newness of information, which is a key element of each IoT healthcare network delivery. Sometimes changing estimations is a necessity to guarantee that each message is new.
- Non-Repudiation: This is the assurance that someone cannot deny the validity of something sent previously.
- Authorization: This guarantees that only approved nodes are open for network services or resources.
- Flexibility: Some interconnected devices are undermined; even when that happens a security scheme should indeed guarantee the network/device/information from any attack.
- Fault Tolerance: A security plan should keep on operating properly to provide security even if a fault exists (e.g., a software glitch, a device compromise, or a device failure).
- Self-Healing: In an IoT healthcare network a medical device may crash or can run out of energy. At that point, the devices remaining or working together should provide a basic degree of security.
- Secure Booting: There is a verification mechanism for ensuring that code launched by firmware is trusted software, which is confirmed by the user's cryptographically created digital signature.
- Interoperability: This is when various systems collaborate to offer the ideal support at the perfect time.
- Privacy: It is a compulsory issue because sensitive and crucial data are exchanged across the network [15].

4.2   AI, Robotics and IoT: A Logical Combination

4.2.1   Artificial Intelligence and IoT in Healthcare

The IoT and AI work together. The IoT deals with enormous amounts of information which must be comprehended and managed. Accordingly, AI algorithms are capable of learning from data, which is genuinely significant for clients or potential clients, and can enhance the efficiency of the IoT. Since the IoT is still in its infancy, the ability to connect gazillions of brilliant gadgets is flawed. For example, characteristics such as the exactness and speed of IoT information transmission are yet to be improved. In addition, a man-made consciousness framework not only emulates

1	2	3	4	5
Medical staff, patients, and inventory tracking	Chronic disease management	Drug management	Emergency room wait time reduction	Remote health control

Figure 4.5 Uses for AI-enabled IoT.

the way humans perform tasks, it also gains from what it designs itself [16]. When AI and IoT are combined in healthcare, it is probable that they will improve operational effectiveness in this field. Gathering, observing (examining), controlling, streamlining (preparing), and mechanization (displaying, foreseeing) are the key advances that accommodate the savvy and proficient utilization of AI calculations in IoT devices.

This technology helps to decrease the workload of managerial and clinical staff, helps to increase the work process, gives clinical officials the option to invest extra time with patients, and undoubtedly will make it easier for healthcare services to adopt an increasingly patient-centric strategy.

The ways in which AI-enabled IoT are used in medicinal services are shown in Figure 4.5 and listed below:

- Keep track of medical personnel, patients, and inventory
- Manage chronic diseases
- Manage drugs
- Decrease emergency room waiting time
- Provide remote control of health

4.2.2 AI and Robotics

The use of AI is becoming more advanced at doing whatever people want in a proficient and rapid manner at less cost. The role that AI with IOT plays in human life is huge, and it has progressively become a piece of our medical care eco-framework.

The eight different areas of healthcare which are being changed by AI-enabled technology are described below and depicted in Figure 4.6.

- Keeping Well: Probably one of the greatest advantages of AI is that it assists in making sure that people remain safe and healthy so they do not need to consult with a specialist or at least not as routinely. Application of AI and the internet of medical things (IoMT) originally used to lower cost of care is presently being used to help people.

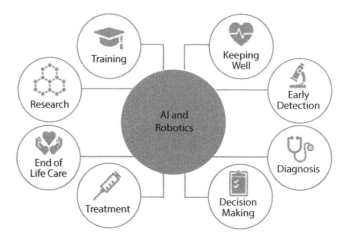

Figure 4.6 Areas of healthcare being enhanced by AI and robotics.

Technology applications promote healthy living and help people take charge of their health. It puts consumers in a position to monitor their own well-being and prosperity. Another AI technology relevant in healthcare is claims and payment administration, in which regular models and patterns of the individuals being cared for are used by administration specialists to gain insight into their lives in order to provide better analysis of underwriting factors to estimate how likely a potential policyholder is to become ill.

- Early Detection: AI techniques are already being utilized to recognize diseases such as cancer to help identify malignant growths more exactly and at early stages. As indicated by the American Cancer Society, a high proportion of mammograms yield incorrect results, and screening mammograms do not find about 1 in 5 breast cancers. The utilization of AI is empowering auditing and interpretation of mammograms 30 times quicker with 99% exactness, decreasing the requirement for unnecessary biopsies.
- Diagnosis: IBM Watson Health is assisting human services spread the AI revolution by unlocking enormous amounts of rich data and prognostics. Watson is able to store a vast amount of information and can review clinical information from each clinical journal and related investigations on treatments and responses from around the world faster than any human can.

Another example is Google's DeepMind, which is working in association with clinicians, scientists and patients to address the cause of disease and real-world healthcare issues. This technology incorporates machine learning and systems neuroscience to construct strong and effective neural network learning algorithms that mimic the human brain.

- Decision-Making: To improve decision-making a large amount of suitable healthcare information needs to be prepared, including possible healthcare choices. Ongoing evaluation can be used to endorse clinical supervision and events and also organize regulatory administrative tasks.

  Utilizing design acknowledgment to recognize patients at risk for working up a constrain—and visualize that separate cause of behavior, circumjacent, genomic, or various reasons—is a different domain where AI is starting to catch on in medical services [17].

- Treatment: Checking the fitness of medical care records can assist healthcare workers in recognizing consistently sick individuals who may be at risk for an unfavorable event. AI can assist clinicians in adopting a comprehensive strategy for disease, executives to better facilitate care plans, and help patients to more earnestly run and follow drawn out treatment programs.

- End-of-Life Care: We are living longer than in previous years, and it is likely that when we arrive at the final years of life we will die at a slower rate, resulting in an increase of conditions like dementia, cardiovascular disease and osteoporosis. It is also a period of life which is frequently afflicted by feelings of loneliness.

- Robotics: The final stage of life can be transformed by the great inherent capabilities of robotics, which help people stay self-sufficient longer, diminishing the need for medical care and assisted living facilities. AI-integrated robots are designed in humanoid form to move impressively and carry on a "discussion" and different public interactions with humans to continue keeping personalities sharp.

- Research: The process of getting drugs for patients from a research lab is a progressively costly enormous task. According to the California Biomedical Research Association, it takes approximately 12 years for a drug from a research laboratory to reach needy patients. Just five of every 5,000 drugs that enter preclinical testing progress to human testing, and only one of these five are accepted for human use.

Drug research and disclosure is probably the most used AI application for clinical healthcare. By managing the newest advancements in AI to smooth out the drug disclosures or prescriptions, repurposing structures there is the chances to deduction both a chance to publicize for recently developed medications and their costs.

- Training: Different types of knowledge in AI are used to prepare realistic models in a way that a straightforward computer-based algorithm cannot. The arrival of naturalistic vocal expression and the capability of AI to immediately describe an enormous sequence of events in a database implies that the reaction to questions, conclusions, and advice from a student can challenge what a human cannot. Furthermore, the training programs can cognize from past responses from the student. In other words, the challenges can consistently change and adapt in accordance with student needs. In addition, preparation should be possible anywhere with AI intensity embedded on a cell phone [18].

4.2.2.1   Limitation of Robotics in Medical Healthcare

Regardless of the upsides of AI and robotics, some noteworthy disadvantages have to be given serious consideration. For instance, the 78-year-old father of Catherine Quintana was taken to Kaiser Permanente Medical Center in Fremont, California, because he was unable to breathe due to chronic lung disease. Catherine was stunned when a robot machine was rolled into his room and a doctor told him by video call that he would likely die within days and that treatment was no longer an option.

Despite the facts of this story being extraordinary, this model focuses on one of the principal impediments of mechanization in human services. Indeed, even with top of the line robotic innovations, robots are incapable of acting like humans. Specifically, they can't have human feelings and deal with complex inquiries. This restricts the role of robots in social situations [19].

4.2.3   IoT with Robotics

Robotics technology is one of the most exceptional rising technologies in the field of healthcare. This technology incorporates electronic sensors to control mechanical frameworks, which improves the presentation and adaptability of frameworks enormously. Innovations in robotics are utilized to develop arms, that was not precise and unfit to send the specific sensory feedback, accurate development, and positioning.

At present, robotization is used in huge areas of healthcare that especially affect the conditions of patients or decisions about their care. Mechanical autonomy, which is part of innovation in healthcare, is the focal point of the medical services carried out in ICUs, general use rooms, and medical procedure rooms. It is beneficial for diminishing dangers to patients and specialists; and is also used in labs to gather samples followed by transportation of tests whenever required, examining, and protecting them for long-term storage [20].

The significant advantages of the IoT-driven social healthcare units are:

- Decreased expenses of clinical treatment
- Improved treatment results
- Improved disease management
- Reduced number of errors
- Enhanced patient experience
- Enhanced administration of medications

The social healthcare services supported by robotics have become unpredictable, difficult for sharing data, information communication and appropriation of the sensors' information. The internet of medical robotics things (IoMRT) approaches consist of robots as "things" and develop new connections with new correspondence; for example, Li-Fi innovation and data-driven innovation on the web.

4.2.3.1   Overview of IoMRT

Robotics technology innovation has made enormous changes in various dimensions of human culture. The advanced clinical robots have been extensively conveyed and utilized in a wide range of administrations, from seat to bedside checking of patients to perform, nonstop, basic or potentially unsafe errands such as nursing, research center testing, prognostics, and patient care, as shown in Figure 4.7. These prearranged robots are especially compelling at their accomplishments in a couple of composed therapeutic clinical applications in light of their high precision, exactness, constancy, and speed. Robotization developments have been combined with existing framework progression to extend the scope of practical assessment of these robots when conveyed in unstructured conditions [21].

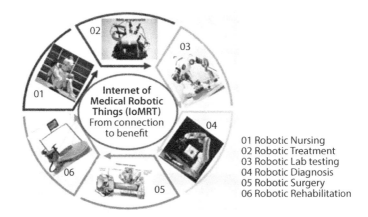

01 Robotic Nursing
02 Robotic Treatment
03 Robotic Lab testing
04 Robotic Diagnosis
05 Robotic Surgery
06 Robotic Rehabilitation

Figure 4.7 Uses for the IoMRT.

Figure 4.8 illustrates the architecture of IoMRT that is divide into four layers: Abstract and service layer, Transport layer, Network layer, Sensors and Actuator layer. Each layers has its own responsibility which can accumulate patient healthcare information.

The IoMRT does a significant and noticeable job under clinical conditions to enhance the viability, speed, and accuracy of the clinical gadgets

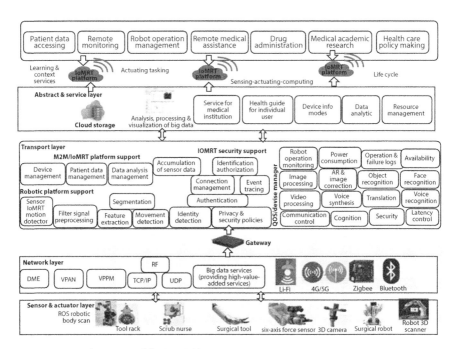

Figure 4.8 Architecture of the IoMRT.

being used. The IoMRT is able to gather the patient health data by using the sensors and gadgets associated with the web-based well-being checking frameworks through online systems. The IoMRT works by associating and transmitting data from clinical gadgets outfitted with Wi-Fi or Li-Fi machine-to-machine (M-to-M). The information received from the IoMRT gadgets is stored in the cloud server database, which is connected with cloud stages and then examined.

The IoMRT is a sustained procedure of checking and offering types of assistance based on the status of a patient's health by strongly suggesting a course of action and using a complex level of detection that keeps an eye on what is happening and what is likely to occur. The IoMRT is especially involved in clinical and diagnostic health issues and restorative care. It might incorporate various services like nursing, laboratory examinations, sample testing, recovery, and clinical findings. Robotic innovation combined with the IoT permits a physician or specialist to utilize smart gadgets to control the activity of a robot and execute distinct work in real time.

A robotics service has developed the ability of doctors or specialists to observe and operate on patients in nontraditional clinical frameworks in a more efficient manner. The IoMRT uses modern strategies to accumulate patient healthcare information, such as from patients in their homes, and transmit the information to health services providers to study in order to propose therapies for illnesses and execute the programs using robots [22].

4.2.3.2   Challenges of IoT Deployment

The IoT handles an extraordinary amount of information, introducing execution, operational and circuit board difficulties in the infrastructure of a network operating system, along with expanded security dangers for all end-users. For solving these problems, health services associations need to adjust conventional system plans to provide new degrees of system knowledge, computerization and protection. Hospitals, clinics, health centers and care offices require an economical foundation that meets security and protection needs while taking care of an ever-increasing amount of data, and is likewise easy to oversee and handle. The framework must:

- Provide a basic, mechanized on-boarding procedure for IoT devices. Enormous IoT frameworks can include a huge number of devices or sensors, and physically supplying and dealing with these them is unpredictable and error-prone. Computerized on-boarding empowers the system framework to powerfully perceive gadgets and allot them to the suitable secured system.

- Supply the right system assets for the IoT framework to manage appropriately and productively. Numerous gadgets in the IoT framework convey crucial data that demands a particular degree of QoS. For instance, some clinical frameworks, such as 3D and color imaging, need data transmission protection on an elite system network to guarantee administration conveyance and unwavering quality.
- Prevent cyberattacks and information deprivation. Since many arranged gadgets could prompt a sufficient number of potential attack vectors, security is basic for relieving the dangers of cybercrime. Security is important at numerous phases, including regulation of the IoT systems themselves [23].

4.3   Essence of AI, IoT, and Robotics in Healthcare

Human services is a broad and manifestly important field. Therefore, robotics, AI and IoT are used together in numerous areas of human services. They all combine with each other and play a major role in medical healthcare services. The fundamental advantage of IoT is a patient's comfort and speedy extraction of all their crucial information to prevent critical situations (an opportunity to check vital signs at home versus finding an opportunity to go to a specialist). Connected devices are proving to be extremely critical for an effective healthcare quality assurance process. Some basic reasons for using healthcare-associated medical devices are:

- Monitor patient health records in real-time.
- Quick response time.
- Less congestion in emergency rooms/clinics to free up space for the critically ill.
- Healthcare services can be accessed that benefit more people every day.

As per the Mayo Clinic, robotic procedures "permit specialists to perform numerous kinds of composite strategies with more accuracy, adaptability and control than is conceivable with ordinary systems." The minimally invasive type of robot-assisted medical procedure is a key advantage.

The combined use of robotics, the IoT and AI does not end with finding new treatments, but is also involved in the clinical trials of drugs. The IoT and AI are combined to help find patient records electronically, medical applications, and both office and medical services resources in emergency clinics. AI with IOT are used together in the context of interoperability and data interchange between all healthcare centers to give the user or operator a clear concise view of what is happening within the facility in real-time. Because healthcare services have some administrative maintenance backlog issues, AI and the IoT are also being utilized to improve clinical work processes for clinical staff so they can invest more time with patients. These are only a couple of instances of robotics with IoT and AI being used in medical services, yet they are only a portion of the many applications today, which is precisely the point we need to make. For instance, real-time health systems (RTHS) use robotics in healthcare, use smart beds in clinics, remote medical services, etc., and the combined utilization of AI and the IoT to advance changes in social insurance will continue to develop.

4.4   Future Applications of Robotics, AI, and IoT

In the coming years, AI systems will become more advanced and have the ability to perform more tasks in an extensive range. If this technique is used, then some people have suggested that it be required to be "ethical" and capable of making ethical decisions. This is the subject of much philosophical discussion, bringing up issues about whether and how moral qualities or standards can always be coded or learnt by a machine. With every passing year, the uses for robotics frameworks in medical services keep on growing. Industry specialists predict a significant shift in how medical services are conveyed throughout the following decades. For instance, robots are completely ready to expand access to clinical administrations in rural or underserved zones. In a telehealth model, robots may gather regular clinical data such as a patient's blood pressure, pulse, breathing rate, and early symptoms of disease. A remote master would then be able to utilize the clinical data to make an analysis and offer a treatment plan.

Robots may also be sent to rehabilitation settings to help with exercise-based therapy programs for patients with spinal cord injuries or neurological diseases. Incorporating mechanical autonomy with computer-generated reality can assist patients with improving portability, equalization, quality, and coordination.

Human-sized mechanical technology frameworks are not by any means the only ways that robots may upend medication regimens. Microbots or nanobots are tiny mechanical devices created to deliver medications to explicit sites. Right now, chemotherapy and other medical interventions cannot be explicitly targeted to one area of the body. Therefore, scientists are creating microbots and nanobots using biodegradable materials that can deliver drugs without being attacked by the human immune system [24].

4.5 Conclusion

In the upcoming era, there will be more modern and less expensive innovations in the areas of healthcare and medicine that will be completely dependent on robotics, AI and the IOT. Frameworks based on AI, the IOT and robotics will be able to work easily under various conditions and in difficult situations. In addition, AI is more than comfortable working in unpredictable environments. Presently, AI and the IOT are revolutionizing the healthcare profession, with AI being built into the system. Robotics and IoT-enabled wearable and intelligent machines—from Bluetooth-enabled hearing aids to robotic caretakers and from smartphones to robots—are greatly adding to the advancement of medical healthcare services.

References

1. Habeeb, A., Introduction to Artificial Intelligence, Research gate, https://www.researchgate.net/publication/325581483, September 2017.
2. Nuffield Council on Biothics 2018 artificial intelligence in healthcare and research. *Bioethics Briefing Note*, 2018. http://nuffieldbioethics.org/wp-content/uploads/Artificial-Intelligence-AI-in-healthcare-and-research.pdf. Accessed 06 Jan 2019. Nuffield Council on Bioethics, Bedford, London.
3. Patel, A., Singh, N.M., Kazi, F., Vitality of Robotics in Healthcare Industry: An Internet of Things (IoT) Perspective, 91-109, 2017. https://link.springer.com/chapter/10.1007/978-3-319-49736-5_5
4. https://www.roboticsbusinessreview.com/health-medical/healthcare-robotics-current-market-trends-and-future-opportunities/
5. https://vilmate.com/blog/why-use-ai-enabled-iot-in-healthcare/
6. The Internet of Things in Healthcare Build a secure foundation to leverage IoT solutions and optimize the care pathway, in: *solution brief IOT in Healthcare*, Alcatel-Lucent Enterprise. https://www.spacewalkers.com/wp-content/uploads/2018/10/IoT-for-Healthcare-Solution-Brief-1.pdf.
7. Camaz, P., Nogueira, V., An overview of IoT and healthcare. in: S. Abreu. V.B. Nogueira (Eds.). Actas das 6as lomadas de Infonnatica de Universidade de Evora. Eccola de Ciencias e Tecnologia da Universidade de Evora. Evora, 2016 Retrieved inmi Intp://hdllandlemet/10174/19998.
8. https://www.pwc.com/gx/en/industries/healt
9. https://www.techsupportofmn.com/what-role-do-robots-play-in-healthcare
10. Guntur, S. R., Gorrepati, R. R., & Dirisala, V. R., Robotics in healthcare: An intemet of medical robotic things (IoMRT) perspective. *Machine Learning in Bio-Signal Analysis and Diagnostic Imaging*, pp. 293–318. Academic Press, 2019.

11. https://www.einfochips.com/blog/the-future-of-healthcare-iot-telemedicine-robots-artificial-intelligence/
12. https://www.i-scoop.eu/internet-of-things-guide/iot-and-ai/
13. Baker, S., Xiang, W., Atkinson, I.M., Internet of Things for Smart Healthcare: Technologies, Challenges, and Opportunities, *IEEE*, 26521 - 26544, 17496914, November 2017.
14. Gerard T. Capraro "Artificial Intelligence (AI), Big Data, and Healthcare" ChemRx Seminar, 52238608, 2017-11-02.
15. https://plato.stanford.edu/entries/ethics-ai/
16. https://iot.eetimes.com/the-internet-of-robotic-things-how-iot-and-robotics-tech-are-evolving-together/
17. Raveendranathan, K.C., Future directions: IoT, robotics and AI based applications, 15 November 2019, IOP, 2020, 15-1 to 15-24.
18. NarasimaVenkatesh, A., Reimagining the Future of Healthcare Industry through Internet of Medical Things (IoMT), Artificial Intelligence (AI), Machine Learning (ML), Big Data, Mobile Apps and Advanced Sensors. *Int. J. Eng. Adv. Technol. (IJEAT)*, 9, 1, 3014–3019.
19. Butter, M., Rensma, A., van Boxsel, J., Kalisingh, S., Schoone, M., Leis, M., Gelderblom, G.J., Cremers, G., de Wilt, M., Kortekaas, W., Thielmann, A., Cuhls, K., Sachinopoulou, A., Korhonen, I., Robotics for Healthcare Final Report, October 3rd, European Commission, DG Information Society, Verson no 19, 2008.
20. Nagasubramanian, G., Sakthivel, R.K., Patan, R., Gandomi, A.H., Sankayya, M., Balusamy, B., Securing e-health records using keyless signature infrastructure blockchain technology in the cloud. *Neural Comput. Appl.*, 3, 1–9, 2018.
21. Kumar, S.R., Gayathri, N., Muthurumalingam, S., Balamurugan, B., Ramesh, C., Nallakaruppan, M.K., Medical big data mining and processing in e-Ilealthcare. *In Internet of Things in Biomedical Engineering*, pp. 323–339, Academic Press. San Diego. CA, 2019.
22. Dhingra, P., Gayathri, N., Kumar, S.R., Singanamalla, V., Ramesh, C., Balamurugan, B., Internet of Things-based pharmaceutics data analysis. *In Emerge: Kr of Phan: Jamaica? industry Gruwth with Industrial lert Appruat Academic Press*. Elsevier. San Diego. CA, pp. 85– I 31, 2020.
23. Nagasubramanian, G., Sankayya, M., Al-Turjman, F., Tsaramirsis, G., Parkinson Data Analysis and Prediction System Using Multi-Variant Stacked Auto Encoder. *IEEE Access,* 2020-07-06.

5

Towards Analyzing Skill Transfer to Robots Based on Semantically Represented Activities of Humans

Devi.T[1]*, N. Deepa[1], S. Rakesh Kumar[2], R. Ganesan[3] and N. Gayathri[2]

[1]Saveetha School of Engineering, Saveetha Institute of Medical and Technical Sciences, Chennai, India
[2]School of Computing Science and Engineering, Galgotias University, Uttar Pradesh, India
[3]SCSE, Vellore Institute of Technology, Chennai, India

Abstract

Human robots follow the instructions given by users and work based on their activities. The proposed framework works by depicting how the user's movements are received by robots and how their performance gets increased in an effective manner. Representing the user activities semantically is the most important feature in the proposed work. This makes the robot understand which activity has to be presented based on the instructions provided. User activities as well as attributes help in framing the rules which can be represented semantically to make robots perform better. Real-time working of the system shows how the user activities can be changed dynamically and how the response of robots varies accordingly. The goal of the user is attained by varying inputs dynamically to make the robots show the varying functions online. The experimental results show how well the system works and also showcase the effective behavior even in the case of inputs being changed dynamically.

Keywords: Human activities, robot, semantic rules, transfer of skills

Corresponding author: devi.janu@gmail.com

Ashutosh Kumar Dubey, Abhishek Kumar, S. Rakesh Kumar, N. Gayathri, Prasenjit Das (eds.) AI and IoT-Based Intelligent Automation in Robotics, (75–86) © 2021 Scrivener Publishing LLC

5.1   Introduction

Robots are involved in many types of work such as assisting in house cleaning, restaurant services and so on [1]. When it comes to human-computer interaction, the work related to the field has always been less [2]. Human actions as well as attributes associated with their objectives play a significant part in the interaction between human and computer. In order to achieve such interaction, features such as knowing what the minds of humans are very important [3]. Activities of humans can be observed and their skills can be transferred to robots in order to increase the system capabilities. Representing the user activities in a semantic way helps these system capabilities which drive the robots to understand the behavior of humans [4]. Humanoid robots need to identify the behavior of the user, thereby reacting to the instructions by showing them either in their movements or by using actions [5]. Facial expressions of humans, their gestures as well as voice can be shared in order to make the robot interact in a similar way by observance [6].

Observation of activities of humans by robots enables them to learn more about them [7]. In this way the robots are able to achieve the objectives of the human by paving the way to an effective communication path and better interaction between both the human as well as computer [8–10]. For example, the behavior of humans can be observed, and the robots are made to learn and perform according to the requirements at the time [11].

The procedure involves certain steps, including retrieving [12] the significant features of tasks, data processing to help in achieving the user goal, and finally showing relevant movement to depict the objective attained as shown in Figure 5.1. In order to attain the objective of the user, an observation module is necessary to determine which features of tasks are significant [13]. One of the important characteristics to be noted is to retrieve the input data from several sources, including the movement of users as well as environmental factors that help to get useful data of the system [14].

The goal of a user needs to be translated as the objective of the system to be attained. For this, behavior of the user can be represented semantically [15]. After this comes the final stage where the robot identifies which characteristic feature of the user is to be represented as motion or action [16]. Such mapping stands as a significant problem as it is the robot which makes decisions regarding whether to use the users' method or to do the task on its own [17]. The relationships between objects can be understood by the robots by knowledge representation based on ontology [18].

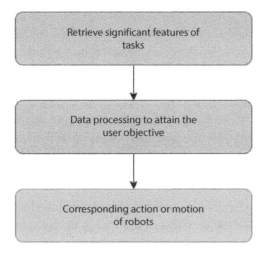

Figure 5.1 Steps in attaining the objective.

Such representations make the system more useful compared to all other systems in the literature.

Our contributions to the chapter include:

- By observing the activities of users, the proposed system will be imitating all of them.
- Rules are designed semantically to make the system help the robot understand user activities.
- Improvisation in the representation of rules semantically also improves the performance of robots accordingly.

This chapter is organized as follows: Section 5.2 presents the related work, Section 5.3 is an overview of the system, Section 5.4 presents the results and Section 5.5 concludes the chapter.

5.2 Related Work

Understanding the activities of the user in an automatic manner has attracted many researchers to focus on the research problem of how robots perform the activities of the user [19–22]. Several fields in computer science have been utilized to identify robot movements based on user activities [23]. Activities of users were identified and those activities were further classified into different sections depending on the complexity of the problem [24]. Partitioning of activities of humans along with detecting the features associated with the motion of users are the important aspects to be addressed by the system [25]. Translation methods still stand as an obstacle for such systems, thereby reducing the performance of the systems on the whole [26].

In the case of movement of robots, the main issue is to detect what kind of user activity is to be focused on. Several existing systems do not allow dynamic movement of robots and also do not allow them to depict changes online [27, 28]. Static input behavior observed in several humanoid robots is one of the issues which needs the real attention in the field of robot research.

Translation can be done in an effective way to allow the robots to behave efficiently for the dynamic changes in input with the help of representing data semantically [29]. Rules framed semantically also help the users identify the gap in the existing systems, thereby enhancing the version of the rules proposed to overcome all the pitfalls faced by the existing ones [30].

5.3   Overview of Proposed System

Our proposed system (Fig. 5.2) has three components, namely, examining the actions of users along with their attributes, representing user behavior in a hierarchical manner, and finally the corresponding movement by the robot. The proposed architecture is shown in Figure 5.2.

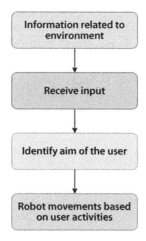

Figure 5.2 Proposed system steps.

The recordings from the video and many more sources are retrieved and used as input for the first component in the proposed system. Several attributes examined from the recordings are first sent through the process of pre-processing where the visual attributes are analyzed. Based on such inputs, categorization is done as P_r - progress, DP_r - don't progress, as well as UD - usage of devices, which actually are the movements of users along with their attributes.

The video recordings serve as input for the next component of the system that helps in achieving the user objectives. It acts as a significant component of the entire system as it helps to define rules semantically in order to achieve the user actions. The main part here is to check whether the actions of humans can be attained by the given input to the system. But all the existing systems fail in such situations. These existing works mainly focus on static works of users to be used as input whereas the proposed work allows attributes to be included even in the testing phase also, which stands as a major advantage of the system. Predefined instructions are present which reduces the difficulty of computing the instructions semantically every time.

The final component makes the robot react to the user activities, which is attained by executing the pre-planned method of the robot to react to the inputs from the second component. Finally, the objective of the user is attained and the robot reacts in a way expected by the user.

5.3.1   Visual Data Retrieval

User activities can be represented as robot movements by taking the visual data as input from many various sources. Many methods are available to extract the input information as the data is always online. Most of the existing work focuses on processing of offline data only.

The first component of our proposed system works on extracting data online from the actions of the users using a hierarchical method of representing the user movement. This component works in two phases where the first phase is to determine the data related to the user to be used and the second phase is to allocate the extracted information to categorization. Categorization is done as P_r - progress, DP_r - don't progress, as well as UD - usage of devices, which actually are the movements of users along with their attributes.

The main reason for using a hierarchical approach is the advantage of an increase in accuracy in the case of input data, thereby reducing the time it takes to train the data as well. Several existing systems work by execution of their algorithm offline. The main advantage of our proposed work over the other systems is identification of features of humans online itself. For this feature, the system makes use of an algorithm to identify images as well as for tracking an image.

The main use of the algorithm is to find the movement of hands by the positions of hands mentioned. The proposed system not only identifies a single object and performs the motion, it also identifies multiple objects simultaneously and produces motion accordingly.

5.3.2   Data Processing to Attain User Objective

One of the important phases in the proposed system is processing of data to obtain the objective of the user. Movement of user hands (U_{mov}) along with attributes of the entity (Eattr) are taken as input for the current phase. Activities of users, such as playing, running, and eating, are inferred in order to produce the output. Upon failure of the inference, the usage of parental class (Par_{cls}) comes into the picture. The incorporation of Par_{cls} is an important enhancement in our proposed system which makes it different from the other existing systems.

a) Extraction of Entity Depicted Semantically
   Representing the entities semantically stands as the next step. The proposed method first recognized the relationship between U_{mov} as well as E_{attr}, which helps in understanding the movements of the user promptly. In order to define such movements of users, categorization is made to identify them including the inputs from Phase 1. For this purpose, decision trees are utilized to classify in a better way. Absence of uniqueness in the user action semantics makes the incorporation of the decision tree slow. When the classification is done, the focus is on user activities and how they can be converted to robot movement. Here, the two-step process includes primary and secondary steps as shown in Figure 5.3 and Figure 5.4 where the former includes movements such as come, go and so on and the latter include movements such as cook, wash and so on.

Figure 5.3 Steps in extraction of information.

Progress	Don't progress	Idle

Figure 5.4 Mapping user activities with movement of robots.

b) Recognizing Primary Steps
The tree can be shorter than those which are longer to produce better results. This allows the entities to be represented in a proper manner. how the frames can be represented in an effective manner.

The algorithm makes use of following conventions such as set of data (D_s), set of cases (C_{as}) and Core concept (C_{con}). The input is obtained from the set of data (D_s).

Algorithm 1: Understanding Activities of User

Input: Set of data (D_s), set of cases (C_{as}), core concept (C_{con})

If the data = Tr_p (training phase) then

Construct DT (Ca_s, C_{con}) (decision tree)

return DT

or else

Find Core concept (C_{con})

end for

return C_{con}

end if

The algorithm clearly depicts how the decision tree is constructed as well as helps in understanding the activities of the user.

c) Recognizing Secondary Steps
The properties of entities need to be increased in order to represent the activities of the user such as cook, wash and so on. The activities used may be the same, but the tool used to represent them differs. The main reason for the secondary step is to incorporate the decision tree in an effective way. The movement activities have P_r - progress and DP_r - don't progress as entities for the action and also help in movement of robots. The example can be viewed as,

{Progress, noodles, spoon}, eat}
{Don't progress, oil, pan}, Pour}

5.3.3   Knowledge Base

The interaction between users and robots occurs in an effective way which helps robots make decisions in the proper way. Representing semantically can be incorporated by using the data engine, which is mainly used to represent the real-world activities of the user as well as identify what has to be done next from the inference derived.

Acquiring knowledge is one of the significant abilities of humans which helps their reasoning skills. This helps to predict the activities performed by humans. The main reason for this is that this system merges knowledge which is commonly known along with real-world insights to identify aspects that are hidden.

The rules related to interpretation skills have to be defined in a proper manner to identify the relationship with the real world. Many doubts arise regarding the interpretation about their origin, their guarantee and also issues related to their generalization. Such queries need to be identified and solutions to those queries help us in improving the knowledge about the environment and our reasoning skills.

Web ontology language (OWL) is mainly used in representing knowledge because of its significance in modeling of data. An example representative of OWL is shown in Figure 5.5 below which gives a clear picture of representation of a subclass.

a) Ontology Expansion

Defining rules to represent human activities is significant for the robots to represent their actions properly. The attributes associated with the objects need to be understood in a better way to know more about the instances that are newly created. These newly produced samples serve as a main part of the ontology expansion. This can be done by adding

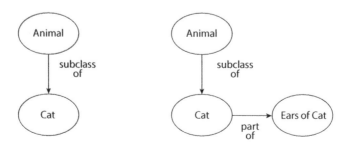

Figure 5.5 Representation of subclass.

activities performed by humans on a daily basis and representing them in order to make the algorithm work well.

Our knowledge engine works in an effective way in which human activities like go, come, as well as work, were all embedded in the knowledge engine in a manual way in the existing systems. But our proposed system works in a different manner where such activities are not entered manually. The main reason behind this automatic nature is the optimization of methods.

The interpretations used here stand as the main feature in ontology. Here, the activities used as samples included progress, don't progress, and be idle. This is an important step to be noted in making the robot understand the human activities. The relationship between the reasoning process with the outside environment plays a significant role in the knowledge engine. This action is achieved by the sensors in the robot that were clearly understood by labeling the records in the database.

Attributes as well as objects need to be represented semantically; for this a map represented in a semantic manner is used as a relationship between attributes and objects as well, which plays an important role here.

5.3.4   Robot Attaining User Goal

The robot and user have to interact in such a manner that the system identifies similarities in the behavior of both activities. The major advantage of the system is the real-time behavior of the system as the input can be changed dynamically to suit the real-time working of the system.

5.4   Results and Discussion

The proposed system works effectively as the rules are represented semantically, thereby identifying the relationship between entities and attributes, and robots are made to respond in real time. The user activities are first observed, and based on those observations, semantic representations are performed. After which rules are framed semantically, as the robots are able to deliver the goal of the user. The performance of the robot compares with that of the human as well, and it can be said that the robot performs well in the case of an increase in number of activities.

The performance of the system as shown in Figure 5.6 mainly depends on the response time of the robot to several activities performed by the users. It depends on the main understanding level of the robot. In comparison with the existing system, the proposed one outperforms due to its dynamic nature.

As shown in Figure 5.7, the proposed system works in an effective way when compared with the existing system when the number of activities to be performed by the robot increases as well as when the time it takes to perform them also decreases.

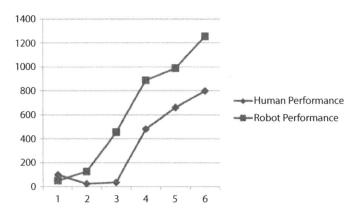

Figure 5.6 Performance comparison chart.

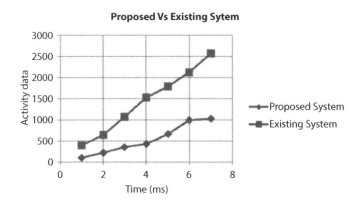

Figure 5.7 Comparison of proposed system with existing system.

5.5   Conclusion

Robots face the challenging problem of recognizing user activities. The proposed system stands as an effective system to enhance the interaction between users as well as the robots. The system mainly focuses on extraction of user activities along with the attributes associated with them. The above-mentioned activities along with the attributes act as input for the system and the output stands as the chosen user activity which the robot performs online. Based on the activities observed from the users, rules were framed semantically that help the system provide better accuracy and better performance of the system in various environments.

Skill transfer to robots from the activities of the user was also performed in the system to make the robot perform activities in a reduced amount of time. The main advantage of the system is in calculating the relationship between entities and their associated activities. Dynamic updating of knowledge based on eradicating manual updating has also been added as another advantage to the system. The rules represented semantically therefore increase the overall performance of the system.

References

1. LeCun, Y., Bengio, Y., Hinton, G., Deep learning. *Nature*, 521, 7553, 436–444, 2015.
2. Ali, L., Rahman, A., Khan, A., Zhou, M., Javeed, A., Khan, J.A., An automated diagnostic system for heart disease prediction based on χ^2 statistical model and optimally configured deep neural network. *IEEE Access*, 7, 34938–34945, 2019.
3. Lei, Z., Sun, Y., Nanehkaran, Y.A., Yang, S., Islam, M.S., Lei, H., Zhang, D., A novel data-driven robust framework based on machine learning and knowledge graph for disease classification. *Future Gener. Comput. Syst.*, 102, 534–548, 2020.
4. Hao, Y., Usama, M., Yang, J., Hossain, M.S., Ghoneim, A., Recurrent convolutional neural network based multimodal disease risk prediction. *Future Gener. Comput. Syst.*, 92, 76–83, 2019.
5. Wang, T., Qiu, R.G., Yu, M., Zhang, R., Directed disease networks to facilitate multiple-disease risk assessment modeling. *Decis. Support Syst.*, 129, 113171, 2020.
6. Geras, K.J., Wolfson, S., Shen, Y., Wu, N., Kim, S., Kim, E., Cho, K., High-resolution breast cancer screening with multi-view deep convolutional neural networks. *Computer Vision and Pattern Recognition*, arXiv preprint arXiv:1703.07047, 3, 1-9, 2017.

7. Li, Z., Wang, C., Han, M., Xue, Y., Wei, W., Li, L., Fei-Fei, L., Thoracic disease identification and localization with limited supervision, in: *Proceeding of the Conference on Computer Vision and Pattern Recognition*, pp. 8290–8299, 2018.

8. Shadmi, R., Mazo, V., Bregman-Amitai, O., Elnekave, E., Fully convolutional deep-learning based system for coronary calcium score prediction from non-contrast chest CT, in: *Proceedings of the 15th International Symposium on Biomedical Imaging (ISBI)*, pp. 24–28, 2018.

9. De Fauw, J., Ledsam, J.R., Romera-Paredes, B., Nikolov, S., Tomasev, N., Blackwell, S. *et al.*, Clinically applicable deep learning for diagnosis and referral in retinal disease. *Nat. Med.*, 24, 9, 1342–1350, 2018.

10. Khosravi, P., Kazemi, E., Zhan, Q., Malmsten, J.E., Toschi, M., Zisimopoulos, P. *et al.*, Deep learning enables robust assessment and selection of human blastocysts after *in vitro* fertilization. *NPJ Digital Med.*, 2, 1, 1–9, 2019.

11. Zhou, X., Menche, J., Barabási, A.-L., Sharma, A., Human Symptoms–disease network. *Nat. Commun.*, 5, 1, 1–10, 2014.

12. Bronstein, M.M., Bruna, J., LeCun, Y., Szlam, A., Vandergheynst, P., Geometric deep learning: Going beyond euclidean data. *IEEE Signal Process. Mag.*, 34, 4, 18–42, 2017.

13. Scarselli, F., Gori, M., Tsoi, A.C., Hagenbuchner, M., Monfardini, G., The graph neural network model. *IEEE Trans. Neural Networks*, 20, 1, 61–80, 2008.

14. Kipf, T.N. and Welling, M., Semi-supervised classification with graph convolutional networks, *Machine Learning*, arXiv preprint arXiv:1609.02907, 4, 1-14, 2016.

15. Pedregosa, F., Varoquaux, G., Gramfort, A., Michel, V., Thirion, B., Grisel, O., Duchesnay, E., Scikit-learn: Machine Learning in Python. *J. Mach. Learn. Res.*, 12, 2825–2830, 2011.

6

Healthcare Robots Enabled with IoT and Artificial Intelligence for Elderly Patients

S. Porkodi[1]* and D. Kesavaraja[2]

[1]*Dr. Sivanthi Aditanar College of Engineering, Tiruchendur, Tamil Nadu, India*
[2]*Associate Professor, Dr. Sivanthi Aditanar College of Engineering, Tiruchendur, Tamil Nadu, India*

Abstract

As the demand for doctors is increasing day by day, a need has arisen to provide personalized healthcare for elderly patients and those with chronic conditions in addition to taking necessary actions during emergency situations. So, healthcare in the digital era is experimenting with adopting robotics to provide personal healthcare to patients in need. In this chapter, the needs of elderly patients are identified and solutions are provided with a personalized robot. Emergency situations can also be predicted more quickly with the vital information provided by IoT devices and necessary action can be suggested using artificial intelligence. IoT-based wearable devices are used to obtain necessary health data from patients. These data are processed and decision-making is carried out by AI, whereas the required action is taken by the designed robot. Humanoid robots can be designed for providing healthcare and physical assistance to elderly patients and those with chronic conditions. Animal-like robots can also be designed that act like pets as a solution for those with psychosocial issues. The major goal is to review robots to develop a robot in the future that can prevent interventions, perform multiple functions, provide motivational interaction style, provide better educational data, and alert an ambulance in case of an emergency.

Keywords: Internet of things (IoT), robotics, healthcare, artificial intelligence (AI)

*Corresponding author: ishwaryaporkodi6296@gmail.com

Ashutosh Kumar Dubey, Abhishek Kumar, S. Rakesh Kumar, N. Gayathri, Prasenjit Das (eds.) AI and IoT-Based Intelligent Automation in Robotics, (87–108) © 2021 Scrivener Publishing LLC

6.1   Introduction

6.1.1   Past, Present, and Future

The technologies of the current world enable a new digital world and different way of living. Only recently have researchers started studying how these technologies can help in the field of medicine and healthcare. The advanced technology in the medical field not only reduces cost but also improves the efficiency of the treatment and creates a better recovery of patients without as many difficulties. Around 2007, electronic health record (EHR) systems were developed to maintain healthcare records. EHR systems mainly reduce paperwork, maintain the history of patients' records, and store more information that can be accessed for providing better treatment.

In today's world, telemedicine and mHealth are being used. Telemedicine can be a video consultation between a patient and a doctor. The vital signs and symptoms of the patients can be monitored using IoT sensors and devices using computer or mobile apps. The healthcare or the prescription can be conveyed to the patient directly or sent to a nearby pharmacy at the time of emergency. Mobile health, also known as mHealth, is mainly designed to provide all the mobile applications that are relevant to healthcare, including healthcare provider tools, patient education, wearable sensors, decision support, electronic health records (EHRs), healthcare data management, disease registries and much more. As of 2016, there were more than 250,000 mHealth applications available for supporting healthcare providers and patients [1]. Adaption of blockchain is also in an early stage of use in the healthcare industry. Blockchain is capable of solving problems concerning transparency, unity, cohesiveness and security in the electronic health record system.

The future technologies in the healthcare industry will be robotics with artificial intelligence. Vital signs can be taken by robotic nurses, and robots can also be built to assist in surgeries and administration tasks and to take care of the elderly. These innovations could lead to the development of personalized healthcare treatment with greater accuracy [2].

6.1.2   Internet of Things

Sensors and devices are capable of acquiring data, processing it or sending the data over the internet. In healthcare, any patient data that is collected by the sensors or wearable devices is sent to the healthcare provider in real time to monitor the health of the patient [3]. The IoT connected devices also provide support in monitoring elderly patients, those with chronic diseases, and also in self-monitoring. It is highly used in telemedicine and telehealth services. The data collected by the IoT devices could be sent to robots, where the robots can process the data and take the necessary action according to the condition of the patient [31]. One example of an IoT device is a wireless glucometer that monitors the glucose level of a patient regularly, and when the glucose level falls, the patient is notified via a mobile device to inject insulin. The benefits of the IoT are real-time remote health monitoring, a faster response time, prevention of unwanted hospitalization, and lower costs [30].

6.1.3   Artificial Intelligence

In healthcare, artificial intelligence is used to analyze the complex medical and healthcare data to arrive at appropriate solutions only with algorithms and without any human interactions. The data collected are processed and the necessary output is generated for the patients. Machine learning algorithms are used to make the system learn from the given data and situations with which correct decisions can be made when a new situation occurs or predict the problem before it occurs. The relationship between the treatment program and the outcome for the patient are analyzed. The AI algorithm and programs are designed and developed for development of a treatment program, diagnosis process, real-time patient monitoring, personalized medicines and drug development [4]. The benefits of using AI include improved patient satisfaction, fulfillment of workforce needs, optimization of staff, lower overall cost, increased utilization of healthcare facilities, and reduction in unplanned hospitalizations [5].

6.1.4   Using Robotics to Enhance Healthcare Services

Robots have been developed in every industry for minimizing work done by people and to provide efficient treatment of patients, thereby having a huge impact in all areas of the healthcare field. Robots also make the healthcare and medical processes safer and minimize overall cost. The robots are even capable of performing surgeries within very small places inside the human body with more accuracy [6, 7]. Also, a robot is capable of acting as a nurse to monitor the health and vital signs of patients and report immediately when an emergency situation arises [8]. Furthermore, robots can act as a cart that can carry supplies and medicines throughout the hospital. Even if an outbreak of a new contagious disease arises, like coronavirus, a personalized robot can be used for monitoring and analyzing patients' individually, thereby preventing a doctor or nurse from getting infected with the disease. Even though the robots are costlier, here there is a huge chance for robots to replace health workers and change healthcare in a few years.

6.2   Existing Robots in Healthcare

A healthcare robot is mainly used to monitor health, assist complex task that are difficult for patients due to their health issues and much more. Healthcare is required to address problems in physical, emotional, mental and psychosocial areas. These robots can perform multiple tasks and can act as rehabilitation robots and also as social robots. The rehabilitation robots are mainly developed to assist physical tasks of the patient; they either perform a complex task or the task is made easier for patient. The social robots are companions that interact with patients in a friendlier manner, which can make information much easier to understand. There are two categories of social robots: service robots and companion robots. The service type can help patients perform tasks in order to make patients live independently by providing assistance in mobility, health monitoring, safety, and completing or assisting in household tasks. The patients can interact with the social robots, where the robot determines how to assist them using the information collected and inputted from them. The companion robot only communicates or interacts with patients for improving the patient's quality of life and it does not do any other assistance work or complex task. Some robots are designed to provide assistance like service type robots and also communicate like companion robots. The robots are discussed based on how they will assist or provide solutions for the problems faced by older people.

6.3   Challenges in Implementation and Providing Potential Solutions

The main challenge in designing and implementing a new technology, such as robots in the field of healthcare, is acceptance. There are several challenges in the acceptance of healthcare robots and theoretical models determining how useful, trustworthy, enjoyable, and easily accessible they are can predict their intended use. Other challenges of the technology are its complexity, low self-efficacy, problem solving, and trust issues with technology itself. These issues can be solved by identifying the fears and resolving them with the help of accessible technologies and the case studies have shown that the use of healthcare robots has been implemented successfully.

The acceptance and usage of robotic solutions by the elderly is as important as the roles of the robot considered by the developer while developing a healthcare robot. The robots should be smart for people who are dubious of the use of robots due to the bigger leap between technologies. Also, a robot with expressive features is deemed to be more desirable and accessible. Older people should also be included while developing the robot in order to make it easily accessible to them. If any needs or concerns of the elderly are not met in the design phase, then it is advisable to research more while taking the elderly patient using the healthcare robot into consideration. If the healthcare robot is found useful for older people, then it can be rated as acceptable. Research is conducted among the elderly before designing a robot and the information gained is based on what tasks a healthcare robot has to do for them. This can be used to increase the usability of a healthcare robot to its maximum. In a survey, the elderly suggested that a robot can be useful if it reduces falls, cleans, makes calls, gives medication alerts, monitors locations and controls appliances. Many of the given tasks lead to maintaining a dignified and independent life. Residential care creates an image in the minds of the elderly that their independence is lost, which in turn leads them to think that they are not capable of taking care of themselves and so their lives are under the control of someone else and they have very little privacy.

Elderly people agree with using a robot in their homes but they worry about privacy issues and how a robot will act in a home environment [9]. Many elderly people prefer a robot that won't frequently move about in their home but only do the assigned tasks. Robots are always praised for being capable of offering better communication among healthcare professionals and patients and they give support to healthcare providers. Moreover, the way in which a robot communicates is accepted as a helpful feature in accepting a robot. Research surveys show that the interactions between a robot and a person determines whether further engagements with robots are possible or not [10]. The research results prove that robots with more social intelligence are better received [11, 13, 57]. Therefore, the research is focusing on aesthetic design and robotic functions for different problems and programming. Identifying the needs of the elderly are very important to successfully build a healthcare robot. The problems faced by older people are identified and possible technical solutions along with their applicability in robots in healthcare field are reviewed to find the

Table 6.1 Existing robots and their physical appearance and functionalities in various countries.

Name of robot	Physical appearance	Functionalities	Country
Pearl	Humanoid with facial expression Height: 1 meter	Daily activity reminder, health monitor, home guide, appointment reminder, operates refrigerator, and telepresence system	USA
Care-O-bot	Humanoid with static face Height: 1.5 meters	Health monitoring, watering plants, cleaning, heating food, navigation aid, patient safety, controls security, home environment control, carries and fetches things, sets the table, medication reminder, and telepresence system.	Germany
AILISA	Machine without a face Height: 1 meter	Monitors falls, monitors physiological parameters, and mobility aid	France
Hector	Machine with static face and touch screen interface Height: 1.5 meter	Medication reminder, daily routine recorder, reviews daily agenda, helps prevent falls, cognitive training, home environment control, and helps assess emergency situations	Europe

(*Continued*)

Table 6.1 Existing robots and their physical appearance and functionalities in various countries. (*Continued*)

Name of robot	Physical appearance	Functionalities	Country
MOVAID	Machine without face Height: 2 meters	Delivers food, heats food, cleans kitchen table, and changes bed linen	Italy
HRIB	Machine without face Height: 1 meter	Bathes patient while sitting inside the robot	Japan
RI-MAN	Humanoid with static face Height: 1.5 meters	Carries or lifts people and works on small problems	Japan
Guido	Machine without face Height: 1 meter	Navigation and walking aid	Ireland
Cafero	Machine without face Height: 1 meter	Vital signs monitoring and recording, cognitive training, telepresence system, schedules activities, entertainment and reminiscence	New Zealand
Ifbot	Humanoid with static face Height: 0.3 meter	Health monitoring, cognitive training, and entertainment	Japan
IRobiQ	Humanoid with static face Height: 0.3 meter	Vital signs monitoring, cognitive training, telepresence communication, medication reminder, and entertainment	Korea

(*Continued*)

Table 6.1 Existing robots and their physical appearance and functionalities in various countries. (*Continued*)

Name of robot	Physical appearance	Functionalities	Country
Hopis	Fluffy dog with static face Height: 0.3 meter	Measures temperature, blood sugar level and blood pressure	Japan
Teddy	Bear robot with facial expression Height: 0.4 meter	Health monitoring, medication reminder, daily routine recorder, and conversation	Japan
Wakamaru	Humanoid with facial expression Height: 1 meter	Face recognition, schedule management, medication reminder, conversation, reports unusual situations, and security	Japan
Robear	Bear robot with facial expression Height: 0.4 meter	Health monitoring, medication reminder, telepresence system, conversation, and entertainment	Japan
PARO	Fluffy seal with facial expression Height: 0.25 meter	Companion	Japan
ICAT	Hard cat with facial expression Height: 0.38 meter	Companion	The Netherlands

(*Continued*)

Table 6.1 Existing robots and their physical appearance and functionalities in various countries. (*Continued*)

Name of robot	Physical appearance	Functionalities	Country
NeCoRo	Fluffy cat with facial expression Height: 0.25 meter	Companion	Japan
Wandakun	Fluffy koala with facial expression Height: 0.3 meter	Companion and entertainment	Japan
AIBO	Hard dog with facial expression Height: 0.25 meter	Companion and entertainment	Japan
Tama	Fluffy cat with facial expression Height: 0.25 meter	Health monitoring, appointment reminder, companion and entertainment	Japan
Sophia	Humanoid with facial expression Height: 1.83 meter (6 feet)	Chatbot	Hong Kong

gap in current technology and develop it to increase the acceptance rate. Robots along with their physical appearance and functionalities in developed countries of the world are shown in Table 6.1. The issues faced by the elderly, solutions to those issues and robotic functions to solve those issues are shown in Table 6.2.

Table 6.2 Robot functions that solve issues faced by the elderly.

Issues faced by the elderly	Current solutions	Robots that can solve issues
Medications and health management	Memory device [13], personal digital assistant (PDA), medicine dosage regimes [14]	Hector [15], Care-O-bot [16], Teddy [17], Wakamaru [18], IRobiQ [19]
Mobility for the physically disabled	Walking stick, wheelchair, mobility scooters, and transportation services	Guido [20] and robotic wheelchairs [21]
Health monitoring and illness management	Telemonitoring [22], Teleconferencing [23], internet websites [24]	Hector [15], Care-O-bot [16], Teddy [17], Wakamaru [18], IRobiQ [19], Hopis [25], Ifbot [25], Pearl [26]
Housework	Housekeeping services	Pearl [26], MOVAID (cleaning kitchen, changing bed) [27] and Roomba (vacuum cleaner) [21]
Bathing	Non-slip bath mats, home care services, walk-in shower installation	HRIB (robotic bathtub) [28]
Fall prevention	Fall monitoring, physical therapy [29]	Hector [28], AILISA (fall monitor) [30]
Toileting	Home care services; mechanical toilet seats	No robot available

(*Continued*)

Table 6.2 Robot functions that solve issues faced by the elderly. (*Continued*)

Issues faced by the elderly	Current solutions	Robots that can solve issues
Safety monitoring	Smart homes, Medic alert bracelets	Care-O-bot [16], Wakamaru [18], Hector [15], AILISA [30]
Sensory decline	eyeglasses, hearing aids, audiobooks, contact lenses	No robot available
Companionship needs	Friends and family visit, pets	Wakamaru [18], Paro [31], Icat [32], NeCoRo [33], Wandakun [34], AIBO [35], Tama [34]
Prevention of cognitive decline	Video conference [36], cognitive training with computer [37], group activities [38, 39]	Cafero [40], Ifbot [25], Hector [15], IRobiQ [19]
Communication	Telephone, video calling, social activities	Care-O-bot [16], Cafero [40], Pearl [26], Ifbot [25], Hector [15], IRobiQ [19], Robear [23]
Healthcare service details	Websites on internet	No robot available
Easily understood illness details	Websites on internet	No robot available

6.4   Robotic Solutions for Problems Facing the Elderly in Society

6.4.1   Solutions for Physical and Functional Challenges

The main focus of robotic technology is to assist the elderly in performing their day-to-day tasks, ensuring that they will stay safe while at home. Some of the robotic products are robotic vacuum cleaners [21], kettles and spoons [25], lawn mowers, laundry sorters, and food heating equipment. Robotics is currently focused on mobility assistance like exoskeletons, artificial limbs, and smart wheelchairs [20]. Also, robots are developed to carry or lift people, and for those who walk using a cane, robotic walkers are being developed; for example, a personal mobility aid was developed by Dublin researchers which can be operated like smart walker [42]. For the visually impaired, a prototype of a robotic walker named Guido was developed in 2004, which can help the elderly navigate by providing information about surroundings and nearby objects.

Some of the robots which are currently under development are Pearl [26], Care-O-bot [16], and AILISA [30]. Pearl is capable of monitoring health, has telecommunication capabilities and reminds patients about their appointments. Care-O-bot has the ability to monitor health, control home security, use the microwave, fetch objects, and communicate with family members and healthcare providers. AILISA monitors the falls [43] and physiological symptoms of the patient.

Robots are even developed to carry out the daily activities of elderly patients such as bathing. One such robot which helps the elderly bathe is the Harmony in Roll-lo Bathing (HIRB) robotic machine [28], in which a person sits in a chair that rolls backward into a chamber that encloses the body, leaving the shoulders and head outside the chamber. Then the robot is set to release soap and water into the chamber to bathe the person. This robot is being tested in Japan and the feedback received is positive. These types of robots are said to protect the dignity and privacy of the users, and are also easier to operate and take less time to use. Bathing is one of the difficult tasks performed by the elderly, so these robots can be very useful. They can also replace the shower, thereby minimizing the risk of slipping in the bathroom.

6.4.2   Solutions for Cognitive Challenges

Robots are developed with built-in software that helps stimulate the brain with cognitive training exercises. The robot Cafero monitors health, offers telecommunications services, and also provides cognitive training [40]. A trial of this robot was carried out in dementia units and nursing homes [44]. Robots are designed especially for dementia patients which provide games for cognitive stimulation, music therapy, and reminiscence therapy [54]. These patients are kept stimulated and engaged so that their disruptive behavior can be minimized, thereby reducing caregiver stress and improving the quality of life of patients. Robots like Ifbot [25] and IRobiQ [55] are built to provide cognitive games and many other services. The experts suggest these robots with built-in software for dementia patients. Thus, these robots can encourage cognitive brain training exercises and can also measure and check their physical health.

6.5   Healthcare Management

6.5.1   Internet of Things for Data Acquisition

Various IoT devices or sensors are attached to patients in the form of wearable or biometric bracelets to regularly monitor vital signs [27]. The IoT devices include sensors to measure heart rate, body temperature, blood pressure, blood oxygen saturation, glucose, electrical signals in your heart, volume of air inspired and expired by the lungs, brain waves, motion, etc. [28]. A representation of some of the sensors used to collect health data are shown in Figure 6.1 below.

Cognitive behavior data on the patient, such as social activity, physical activity, stress, diet, etc., are also collected. These data, which are monitored and analyzed by the robot, consist of different software such as navigation, user localization, environmental monitoring, calendar, speech, and database. Robot navigation is based on the map stored in the database. User localization is designed to locate the patient in need of robot support. The home environment is monitored by various sensors such as humidity, light, water leak, temperature, etc. This can alert the user to critical situations. Natural-language user interface, which is used to interact with patients, consists of vocal synthesis and speech reorganization tools. A calendar is integrated to manage medications and doctor appoints. The database is basically used to store all the information collected from the patient and also knowledge about what to do in emergency situations. Maps for localization are also stored in the database [29]. The modules in the healthcare management system are shown in Figure 6.2 below.

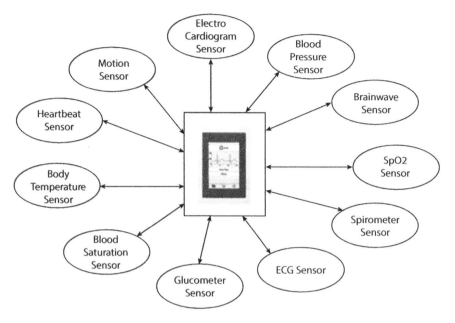

Figure 6.1 Sensors that are used to collect patient's health data.

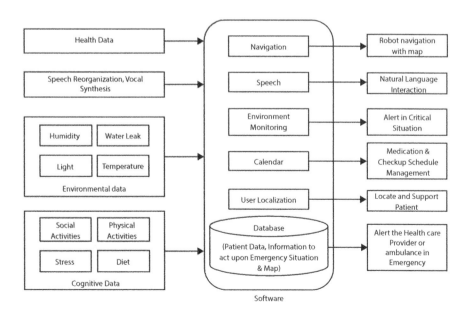

Figure 6.2 Flowchart of modules in the healthcare management system.

Healthcare Monitoring Algorithm:

Inputs:

Sensor 1 = Heartbeat Sensor;

Sensor 2 = Body Temperature Sensor;

Sensor 3 = Blood Saturation Sensor;

Sensor 4 = Glucometer Sensor;

Sensor 5 = ECG Sensor;

Sensor 6 = Spirometer Sensor;

Sensor 7 = SpO2 Sensor;

Sensor 8 = Brain Wave Sensor;

Sensor 9 = Blood Pressure Sensor;

Sensor 10 = Electrocardiogram Sensor;

Sensor 11 = Motion Sensor;

Begin

Collect User Data and Store in Database;

Function Patient Health Monitor (Sensor 1, Sensor 2, Sensor 3, Sensor 4, Sensor 5, Sensor 6, Sensor 7, Sensor 8, Sensor 9, Sensor 10, Sensor 11);

Send Data to Healthcare Provider;

Call Ambulance if Anything Found to be Unusual;

End

Home Environment Control Algorithm:

Inputs:

Sensor 1 = Humidity Sensor;

Sensor 2 = Temperature Sensor;

Sensor 3 = Light Sensor;

Sensor 4 = Water Leak Sensor;

Begin

Collect Environmental Data and Store in Database;

Function Home Environment Control (Sensor 1, Sensor 2, Sensor 3, Sensor 4);

Send Data to User's Mobile Phone;

Alert User if Anything Found to be Unusual;

End

Medication Management Algorithm:

Inputs:

Prescription;

Calendar;

Begin

Get Tablet Name and Dosage Allotment from Prescription;

Allot Concern Tablets According to Its Dosage Allotment in the Calendar;

Function Medication_Management (Prescription, Calender);

Alert User When It Is Time to Take the Medicine;

End

6.5.2   Robotics for Healthcare Assistance and Medication Management

In healthcare robots, one of the common features is health monitoring. Robots can measure vital signs with various sensors and the data can be sent to doctors for consultation. The robots can also be built with telecommunication facilities that can allow consultation with a doctor through a video call. The robots have the capability to combine all the existing technologies within them, making the interface simple and easy. Some of the existing robots are Pearl [26], Hector [15], and Cafero [40], which perform health monitoring and also other services, whereas robots like Hopis [25] are only developed for monitoring vital signs such as blood pressure, body temperature, and blood sugar level. But the Hopis robot is no longer being produced, as its sales were poor and its usage was low. Actually, the problem with this robot is that its physical appearance looks like a fluffy animal which perform serious tasks. The designer gave the robot such an appearance only to make it more approachable and likable, but it seems that elderly people do not like to interact or communicate with a toy. Another robot called Ifbot [25] that can provide health monitoring, entertainment and cognitive training is also currently not in production due to its toy-like appearance. Testing of the Ifbot robot found that elderly people slowly started liking the robot initially but got bored within five weeks [41]. Small-sized robots so far only have positive and good reactions among the elderly. These types of robots, such as Teddy [23], Wakamaru [53], and Robobear [45], are currently in the research and exploratory phase. The smaller robots can perform health monitoring, give medication reminders and can also be a companion [56]. If anything unusual occurs in the elderly, Wakamaru sends an emergency signal to the doctor so that necessary steps can be taken. Robobear has telepresence capabilities and can play games to help avoid boredom.

6.5.3   Robotics for Psychological Issues

In the future, healthcare robots under development should not only consider the healthcare and functional needs of the elderly, but also provide information and support to the whole community, as robotics may become one of the most important aspects in the development of the smart digital world. Robots that consist of telecommunication facilities can not only contact doctors and healthcare providers, but also family and friends.

Robots are being developed as social companions to minimize the loneliness of the patient or user. Robots, such as Paro, AIBO, etc., are developed mainly to provide companionship for the elderly and act as pets which interact with patients and also take care of them. Studies done on the fluffy animal-like robots Paro (seal robot) [31] and AIBO (dog robot) [35] only had positive results; and interaction with the robots reduced the depression and loneliness of the elderly [29, 46–48]. Paro has been commercially available on the market since 2005, with the number of robots sold estimated to be 1000, around 65% of which were for individual use [49]. A survey was conducted by Shibata *et al.* [50] to find the reason for the purchase of these kinds of robots. The survey concluded that patients who can't have pets buy these robots; additionally, the robots won't get sick like pets, instead the robots take care of patients and are cute and huggable. Also, some participants stated that they prefer a robot over a real pet since they worry about being sad if the pet dies or who will take care of the pet after they died. Research was also carried out with elderly owners of AIBO robots on whether patients became attached to pet robots and the psychological benefits of owning them [51, 52]. The survey concluded that the interaction with these robots is easy and more suitable for home use, and also that only a minimum amount of learning is needed to operate them.

6.6   Conclusion and Future Directions

This chapter reviewed what is needed by a community for ensuring that the elderly can continue to live independently in their homes with the help of robots. These needs continue to be addressed with the continuing development of robotics in the field of healthcare. This chapter showed how the elderly need help to perform their daily tasks and physical activities. Falls and injuries become of greater concern as people age, and also when they live on their own. As people age they grow forgetful and may require formal care. The elderly also experience lots of health problems and cognitive issues, thus monitoring their physical and mental health and managing their medical issues become much important as they need support to live independently. Even if the elderly have the ability to manage the challenges related to aging, they may end up feeling depressed, isolated, and lonely. Also, the demand for doctors is increasing nowadays mainly due to contagious diseases like coronavirus, so the need has arisen to provide personalized healthcare for elderly patients and those with chronic conditions and take the necessary actions during an emergency situation. So, IoT wearable devices are used to obtain necessary health data from the patients. These data are processed and decision-making is carried out by artificial intelligence, whereas the required action is performed by the robot designed for the purpose. The robots are being developed to prevent interventions, perform multiple functions, provide motivational interactions, contain a greater amount of educational data, and alert an ambulance in case of any emergency.

References

1. Astell, A.J., Ellis, M.P., Bernardi, L., Alm, N., Dye, R., Gowans, G., Campbell, J., Using a touch screen computer to support relationships between people with dementia and caregivers. *Interact. Comput.*, 22, 267–275, 2010.

2. Banks, M.R., Willoughby, L.M., Banks, W.A., Animal-assisted therapy and loneliness in nursing homes: Use of robotic versus living dogs. *JAMDA*, 9, 173–177, 2008.

3. Banning, M., A review of interventions used to improve adherence to medication in older people. *Int. J. Nurs. Stud.*, 46, 1505–1515, 2009.

4. Barlow, J., Singh, D., Bayer, S., Curry, R., A systematic review of the benefits of home telecare for frail elderly people and those with long-term conditions. *J. Telemed. Telecare*, 13, 172–179, 2007.

5. Baun, M. and Johnson, R., Human-animal interaction and successful aging, in: *Handbook on animal-assisted therapy*, 3rd edition, A. Fine (Ed.), pp. 283–299, Academic Press, San Diego, 2010.

6. Belew, B., *Japan's Ifbot understands language and emotional tone, gets rejected*, Rising Sun of Nihon, Japan, 2007.

7. Broadbent, E., Jayawardena, C., Kerse, N., Stafford, R.Q., Mac Donald, A., Human-robot interaction research to improve quality of life in elder care: An approach and issues, in: *Proceedings of the 25th Conference on Artificial*

Intelligence. Workshop on Human-Robot Interaction in Elder Care, San Francisco, CA, pp. 13–19, 2011.

8. Brooke, J., Japan seeks robotic help in caring for the aged. *Caring*, 23, 7, 56–59, 2004.

9. Buckwater, K.C., Davis, L.L., Wakefield, B.J., Kienzle, M.G., Murray, M.A., Telehealth for elders and their care givers in rural communities. *Fam. Community Health*, 25, 31–40, 2002.

10. Davenport, R.D., Robotics, in: *Smart technology for aging, disability, and independence*, W.C. Mann (Ed.), pp. 83–126, Wiley, Hoboken, 2005.

11. Dario, P., Guglielmelli, E., Laschi, C., Teti, G., MOVAID: A personal robot in everyday life of disabled and elderly people. *Technol. Disabil.*, 10, 77–93, 1999.

12. De Ruyter, B., Saini, P., Markopoulos, P., Van Breemen, A.J.N., Assessing the effects of building social intelligence in a robotic interface for the home. *Interact. Comput.*, 17, 522–541, 2005.

13. Desai, A., *The Future of Healthcare: IoT, Telemedicine, Robots & Artificial Intelligence*, Einfochips, https://www.einfochips.com/blog/the-future-of-healthcare-iot-telemedicine-robots-artificial-intelligence/, San Jose, 2016.

14. Duggan, A., Robo-pet: a human's best friend? - https://www.iol.co.za/mercury/world/robo-pet-a-humans-best-friend-212637, 2004.

15. Durán-Vega, L.A., Santana-Mancilla, P.C., Buenrostro-Mariscal, R., Contreras-Castillo, J., Anido-Rifón, L.E., García-Ruiz, M.A., Montesinos-López, O.A., Estrada-González, F., An IoT System for Remote Health Monitoring in Elderly Adults Through a Wearable Device and Mobile Application. *Geriatrics (Basel, Switzerland)*, 4, 2, 34, 2019.

16. Foulk, E., *Lonely robots ignored by elderly luddites*, The New Zealand Herald, https://www.nzherald.co.nz/technology/news/article.cfm?c_id=5&objectid=10465061, New Zealand, 2007.

17. Friedman, B., Kahn, P.H., Hagman, J., Hardware Companions? What Online AIBO Discussion Forums Reveal about the Human Robotic Relationship, in: *Proceedings of the SIGCHI conference on Human factors in computing systems*, Lauderdale, Florida. CHI '03, pp. 273–280, 2003.

18. Gillespie, L.D., Robertson, M.C., Gillespie, W.J., Lamb, S.E., Gates, S., Cumming, R.G., Rowe, B.H., Interventions for preventing falls in older people living in the community (Review). *Cochrane Database Syst. Rev.*, 2012, 9, CD007146, https://pubmed.ncbi.nlm.nih.gov/22972103, Accessed December 2020.

19. Giuliani, M.V., Scopelliti, M., Fornara, F., Elderly people at home: technological help in everyday activities, in: *Proceedings of the 2005 IEEE International Workshop on Robots and Human Interaction Communication*, Nashville, TN, pp. 365–370, 2005.

20. Graf, B., Hans, M., Schraft, R.D., Care-O-bot II—development of a next generation robotic home assistant. *Auton. Robots*, 16, 193–205, 2004.

21. Grandia, L., Healthcare Information Systems: A Look at the Past, Present, and Future - https://www.healthcatalyst.com/insights/healthcare-information-systems-past-present-future, 2014.

22. Heerink, M., Ben, K., Evers, V., Wielinga, B., The influence of social presence on acceptance of a companion robot by older people. *Journal of Physical Agents*, 2, 2, 33–40, 2008.

23. Heerink, M., Krose, B., Evers, V., Wielinga, B., The influence of a robot's social abilities on acceptance by elderly users, in: *Proceedings of the 15th IEEE international symposium on robot and human interactive communication RO-MAN06*, Hatfield,UK, pp. 521–526, 2006.

24. Hicks, J., *Hector: robotic assistance for the elderly*, Forbes, https://www.forbes.com/sites/jenniferhicks/2012/08/13/hector-robotic-assistance-for-the-elderly/#15acc18b2443, Paris, 2012.

25. Jesswalrack, The Past, Present, and Future of Technology in Healthcare. Brightscout - https://www.brightscout.com/the-past-present-and-future-of-technology-in-healthcare/, 2018.

26. Kahn, P.H., Friedman, B., Hagman, J., I care about him as a pal: conceptions of robotic pets in online AIBO discussion forums, in: *Proceedings of the CHI '02 extended abstracts on Human factors in computing systems*, New York, NY, pp. 632–633, 2002.

27. Nagasubramanian, G., Sakthivel, R.K., Patan, R., Gandomi, A.H., Sankayya, M., Balusamy, B., Securing e-health records using keyless signature infrastructure blockchain technology in the cloud. *Neural Comput. Appl.*, 3, 2020, 1–9, 2018.

28. Kumar, S.R., Gayathri, N., Muthuramalingam, S., Balamurugan, B., Ramesh, C., Nallakaruppan, M.K., Medical Big Data Mining and Processing in e-Healthcare, in: *Internet of Things in Biomedical Engineering*, pp. 323–339, Academic Press, Bethesda, Maryland, 2019.

29. Dhingra, P., Gayathri, N., Kumar, S.R., Singanamalla, V., Ramesh, C., Balamurugan, B., Internet of Things–based pharmaceutics data analysis, in: *Emergence of Pharmaceutical Industry Growth with Industrial IoT Approach*, pp. 85–131, Academic Press, United States, 2020.

30. Alzubi, J.A., Manikandan, R., Alzubi, O.A., Gayathri N. and Patan, R., A Survey of Specific IoT Applications. *Int. J. Emerg. Technol.*, 10, 1, 47–53, 2019.

31. Sharma, S.K., Modanval, R.K., Gayathri, N., Kumar, S.R., Ramesh, C., Impact of Application of Big Data on Cryptocurrency, in: *Cryptocurrencies and Blockchain Technology Applications*, pp. 181–195, 2020.

32. Lytle, J.M., *Robot care bears for the elderly*, News BBC, http://news.bbc.co.uk/2/hi/science/nature/1829021.stm, Japan, 2002.

33. Matthews, K., *The Growing Emergence of Robots in Healthcare: Key Opportunities & Benefits*, Hit Consultant, https://hitconsultant.net/2019/12/05/the-growing-emergence-of-robots-in-healthcare-key-opportunities-benefits/#.Xml-cKgzbIU, Atlanta, Georgia, 2019.

34. Marius, E., *6 Ways AI and Robotics Are Improving Healthcare*, Robotics Business Review, https://www.roboticsbusinessreview.com/health-medical/6-ways-ai-and-robotics-are-improving-healthcare/, United States, 2019.

35. Noury, N., AILISA: Experimental platforms to evaluate remote care and assistive technologies in gerontology, in: *Proceedings of 7th International Workshop on enterprise networking and computing in healthcare industry HEALTHCOM 2005*, Busan, Korea, pp. 67–72, 2005.

36. Onishi, K., Wakamaru, the robot for your home. *J. Jpn. Soc. Mech. Eng.*, 109, 448–449, 2006.

37. Owen-Hill, A., *5 Ways Robotics Are Used in Medicine and Healthcare*, Robotiq, https://blog.robotiq.com/5-ways-cobots-are-used-in-medicine-and-healthcare, Canada, 2019.

38. Pollack, M.E., Engberg, S., Matthews, J.T., Thrun, S., Brown, L., Colbry, D., Orosz, C., Peintner, B., Ramakrishnan, S., McCarthy, C.E., Montemerlo, M., Pineau, J., Roy, N., Dunbar-Jacob, J., Pearl: A mobile robotic assistant for the elderly. AAAI Technical Report WS-0202, AAAI Workshop on Automation as Eldercare, https://www.semanticscholar.org/paper/Pearl%3A-A-Mobile-Robotic-Assistant-for-the-Elderly-Pollack-Brown/1bc1535414684083ecef59 7f704bb069a6b6f38f., Aug., 2002.

39. Poon, P., Hui, E., Dai, D., Kwok, T., Woo, J., Cognitive intervention for community-dwelling older persons with memory problems: Telemedicine versus face-to-face treatment. *Int. J. Geriatr Psychiatry*, 20, 285–286, 2005.

40. Robert, N., How Artificial Intelligence is Changing Nursing. Nursing Management: September 2019. *Nurs. Manag.*, 50, 9, 30–39, 2019.

41. Rentschler, A.J., Cooper, R.A., Blasch, B., Boninger, M.L., Intelligent walkers for the elderly: Performance and safety testing of VA-PAMAID robotic walker. *J. Rehabil. Res. Dev.*, 40, 423–431, 2003.

42. Robinson, H., Mac Donald, B., Kerse, N., Broadbent, E., A randomized controlled trial. The psychosocial effects of a companion robot. *JAMDA*, 14, 9, 661–667, 2013.

43. Robinson, H., Mac Donald, B.A., Kerse, N., Broadbent, E., Suitability of healthcare robots for a dementia unit and suggested improvements. *JAMDA*, 14, 34–40, 2013.

44. Shibata, T., Kawaguchi, Y., Wada, K., Investigation on people living with Paro at home, in: *Proceedings of the 18th IEEE International Symposium on Robot and Human Interactive Communication*, Toyama, Japan, pp. 1131–1136, 2009.

45. Shibata, T. and Tanie, K., Physical and affective interaction between human and mental commit robot, in: *Proceedings of the IEEE International Conference on Robotics and Automation*, Seoul, Korea, pp. 2572–2577, 2001.

46. Siek, K.A., Rogers, Y., Connelly, K.H., Human-computer Interaction-INTERACT 2005, in: *Fat finger worries: How older and younger users physically interact with PDAs*, M.F. Costabile and F. Paterno (Eds.), pp. 267–280, Springer, Berlin Heidelberg, 2005.

47. Taggart, W., Turkle, S., Kidd, C.D., An interactive robot in a nursing home: preliminary remarks, in: *Proceedings of Toward Social Mechanisms of Android Science*, Stresa, Italy, pp. 56–61, 2005.

48. Wada, K., Shibata, T., Kawaguchi, Y., Long-term robot therapy in a health service facility for the aged: A case study for 5 years, in: *Proceedings of the IEEE International Conference on Rehabilitation Robotics*, Kyoto, Japan, pp. 930–933, 2009.

49. Wada, K., Shibata, T., Saito, T., Tanie, K., Effects of Three months robot assisted activity to depression of elderly people who stay at a health service facility for the aged, in: *Proceedings of the SCIE 2004 Annual Conference*, Sapporo, Japan, pp. 2709–2714, 2004.

50. Willis, S.L., Tennstedt, S.L., Marsiske, M., Ball, K., Elias, J., Koepke, K.M., Morris, J.N., Rebok, G.W., Unverzagt, F.W., Stoddard, A.M., Wright, A., Long-term effects of cognitive training on everyday functional outcomes in older adults. *JAMA*, 296, 2805–2814, 2006.

51. Wilson, R.S., Mendes de Leon, C.F., Barnes, L.L., Schneider, J.A., Bienias, J.L., Evans, D.A., Bennett, D.A., Participation in cognitively stimulating activities and risk of incident Alzheimer disease. *JAMA*, 287, 742–748, 2002.

52. Yi-Lin, S., Other devices and high technology solutions, in: *Smart technology for aging, disability, and independence*, W.C. Mann (Ed.), pp. 49–82, Wiley, Hoboken, 2005.

53. Kato, S., Ohshiro, S., Itoh, H., Kimura, K., Development of a communication robot Ifbot, in: *Proceedings of IEEE International Conference of Robot Autom*, vol. 1, pp. 697–702, 2004.

54. Lauriks, S., Reinersmann, A., Van der Roest, H.G., Meiland, F.J.M., Davies, R.J., Moelaert, F., Mulvenna, M.D., Nugent, C.D., Droes, R.M., Review of ICT-based services for identified unmet needs in people with dementia. *Ageing Res. Rev.*, 6, 223–246, 2007.

55. Lee, D., Yamazaki, T., Helal, S., Robotic companions for smart space interactions. *Pervasive Comput.*, 8, 78–84, 2009.

56. Libin, A.V. and Cohen-Mansfield, J., Therapeutic robocat for nursing home residents with dementia: Preliminary inquiry. *Am. J. Alzheimer's Dis. Other Demen.*, 19, 111–116, 2004.

57. Looije, R., Cnossen, F., Neerincx, M.A., *Incorporating guidelines for health assistance into a socially intelligent robot*, pp. 515–520, University of Hertfordshire, Hatfield, UK, 2006.

7

Robotics, AI, and the IoT in Defense Systems

Manju Payal[1]*, **Pooja Dixit[2], T.V.M. Sairam[3] and Nidhi Goyal[4]**

[1]Academic Hub, Ajmer, India
[2]Sophia Girls' College, Ajmer, Rajasthan, India
[3]Andhra Loyola Institute of Engineering and Technology, Vijayawada, India
[4]GD Memorial College, Jodhpur, India

Abstract

Robotics, AI, and the IOT is an expeditiously growing field of technology with the potential to considerable impact defense systems. As such, the U.S. Department of Defense (DOD) and some defense organizations in other nations are focusing on developing various applications for a range of military functions. Research is ongoing in areas such as intelligence collection, analysis, logistics and transportation, cyber operations, target recognition, command and control, and autonomous and semiautonomous vehicles. AI is used to make intelligent machines that perform intellectual tasks based on experiences. Military autonomous robots are increasingly being designed for military applications with sensors, which can be deployed in all domains and allow acquiring full situational awareness and monitoring in diverse conflict-affected areas or battle zones. A combination of these technologies have the perceptual knowledge to manage and process information and the ability to build a machine that emulates human behavior.

Keywords: Internet of things, robotics, artificial intelligence, computer vision, machine intelligence, defense systems, militaries, unmanned aerial vehicles

Corresponding author: manjupayal771@gmail.com

Ashutosh Kumar Dubey, Abhishek Kumar, S. Rakesh Kumar, N. Gayathri, Prasenjit Das (eds.) AI and IoT-Based Intelligent Automation in Robotics, (109–128) © 2021 Scrivener Publishing LLC

7.1   AI in Defense

7.1.1   AI Terminology and Background

Artificial intelligence (AI) does not have one accepted definition which is accepted in almost all academic studies. AI consists of several approaches for research in the field, which is the reason why it does not have one accepted definition. Here, AI refers to artificial intelligence. Similarly, the FY2019 NDAA directed the SecDef to submit a definition of AI. This directs the SecDef according to Section 238. Here, NDAA refers to the National Defense Authorization Act and SecDef refers to the Secretary of Defense. According to the directive, this definition was to be provided by August 13, 2019 to the FY2019 NDAA. Figure 7.1 shows the relationship of related AI definitions. However, as of now there is no proper definition of AI provided by the official U.S. government. There are some definitions available that were provided by the FY2019 NDAA to address Section 2019 are given below:

1) Any artificial system that performs tasks under varying and unpredictable circumstances without significant human oversight, or that can learn from experience and improve performance when exposed to data sets.
2) An artificial system developed in computer software, physical hardware, or other context that solves tasks requiring

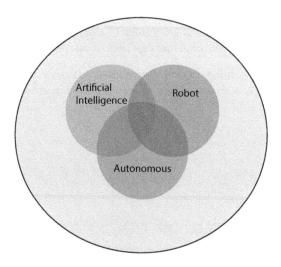

Figure 7.1 Relationship of related AI definitions [3].

human-like perception, cognition, planning, learning, communication, or physical action.

3) An artificial system designed to think or act like a human, including cognitive architectures and neural networks.

4) A set of techniques, including machine learning, that is designed to approximate a cognitive task.

5) An artificial system designed to act rationally, including an intelligent software agent or embodied robot that achieves goals using perception, planning, reasoning, learning, communicating, decision making, and acting.

There are some definitions available that contain many of the descriptions above which are shown in Table 7.1. These definitions are summarized and explained in the table [3].

7.1.2 Systematic Sensing Applications

Some of the available systematic sensing applications of AI are:

- The first application is related to mining. Drone bots are extensively used in mines that can use feature maps to identify and analyze mines, deactivate them, or remove them.
- The second application is related to the enemy segmentation and detection. AI is also used for identifying enemy tanks under several conditions.

Table 7.1 Taxonomy of historical AI definitions.

AI Concepts	
System That Thinks Like Humans "The automation of activities that we associate with human thinking, activities such as decision making, problem solving, and learning." **Bellman, 1978**	**System that Thinks Rationally** "The study of the computations that makes it possible to perceive, reason, and act" **Winston, 1992**
System That Thinks Like Humans "The art of creating machines that perform functions that require intelligence when performed by people." **Kurzweil, 1990**	**System that Thinks Rationally** "The branch of computer science that is concerned with the automation of intelligent behavior." **Luger and Stubblefield, 1993**

- The third application is related to virtual reality (VR) circumstances. Warfare simulation in the context of VR circumstances can be used to train soldiers for more realistic combat situations.
- The fourth application is related to compact helmets with visors. Battle helmets with visors are used to examine the environment of war zones or give enhanced vision.
- The fifth application is related to the missiles fired. It is used in the analysis of the status of missiles fired for satellite defense grid systems to shoot down the right missile [1].

7.1.3   Overview of AI in Defense Systems

The use of AI in defense systems is a rapidly growing field of technology. This technology has captured the attention of policymakers, industrial investors, international competitors, and defense intellectuals, as confirmed by several novel initiatives. On July 20, 2017, the Chinese government released a plan identifying its scheme to start taking the lead in artificial intelligence by 2030. About two months after the fact, Vladimir Putin squarely positioned Russia in the technological arms race for AI innovations, stating "Whoever becomes the leader in this sphere will be the ruler of the world," Accordingly, the U.S. National Defense Scheme announced in January 2018 distinguished AI as one of the fundamental innovations that will assure the U.S. will have the capability to battle and win the wars of the future [2]. The United States military is as of now incorporating AI frameworks in battle through a program called Project Maven, which utilizes AI methods to fight against radicals concentrated in Syria and Iraq. The use of AI methods brought up a few issues that Congress tended to in hearings that took place in 2017 and 2018: What kind of military AI applications are conceivable, and what restrictions, assuming any, ought to be forced? What particular points of interest and vulnerabilities accompany utilizing AI for resistance? By what means will AI change fighting and what impact will it have on the military parity with U.S. competitors? Congress has access to various budgetary, oversight, and authorization tools that it might use to respond to these inquiries and shape the future advancement of AI innovation.

Some of the AI uses available to militaries and defense systems are:

- Surveillance
- Cybersecurity
- Autonomous vehicles
- Logistics

- Autonomous weapons and weapons targeting
- Homeland security

Interested readers might be interested in studying our report on AI used mainly by U.S. defense contractual workers; however, here we will focus mainly on the use of AI for independent weapons and related topics (https://emerj.com/ai-sector-overviews/artificial-intelligence-at-the-top-5-us-defense-contractors/).

- Autonomous Weapons and Weapons Targeting
  Framework targets are decided based on their precision and how quickly they can bolt onto an objective. As countermeasures for this style of focusing are commonly developed, electronic focusing frameworks should be enhanced so they are less vulnerable to those countermeasures. It follows that machine intelligence (MI) and computer vision (CV) would be the next applications for this innovative round of cat and mouse

  Now self-sufficient weapon stages are utilizing CV to recognize and follow goals. An independent weapon fundamentally becomes self-sufficient when the framework can recognize and track goals in the area it has been sent to monitor.

  The AI behind the targeting must be prepared on precisely what key objective is worth concentrating its capability on and cautioning the administrator how to handle the platform. This might be an adversary airplane flying into challenged airspace at an extraordinary rate of speed, a rocket fired at a town, or a defensively covered staff carrier driving up a mined street.

  At present, there are no self-governing weapon stages that are intended to shoot its arms without the express endorsement of an observing administrator. One vital advantage that autonomous weapons mainly have in their operational framework is that they can select and engage targets without further intervention by a human operator. Self-sufficient weapons permit the ever-cautious "eyes" of CV to be fixed on the skies above to forestall shock rocket assaults by focusing on and downing enemy rockets seen all around before they can explode in a populated region. Significant seconds to react might be lost if a human administrator is occupied or snoozes off while posted.

  Artificial intelligence can be utilized as a weapon in cybersphere. The behavioral learning for adaptive electronic warfare (BLADE) program is a framework proposed to impair and assault remote correspondence systems utilizing artificial intelligence. The BLADE program, which is a framework developed by Lockheed Martin in a $29 million agreement with the Defense Advanced Research Projects Agency (DARPA), has entered the late stage of testing. We installed this innovation at work in RAPIDFire, a self-propelled anti-aircraft gun system developed by Thales, in our article on the AI ventures at the AI programming at the top European protection workers.

- Surveillance
  Militaries around the world obtain colossal amounts of visual reconnaissance information daily from several assets such as PCs, telephone cameras, video observations, planted cameras, satellite film, and unmanned aerial vehicles (UAVs). Surveillance not only gathers information, but also mines it for vital data, and this is where AI and machine vision could be useful.

  MI programming can possibly figure out enormous amounts of information for bits of useful knowledge quicker than expert human examiners. The US Department of Defense and other national associations presently use CV and AI programming for reconnaissance activities. For instance, as depicted in our report on machine vision (https://emerj.com/ai-sector-overviews/military-applications-of-machine-vision-current-innovations/).

- Predictability
  Artificial intelligence methods frequently produce unpredictable and strange outcomes. In March 2016, the AI organization DeepMind developed a game-playing algorithm called AlphaGo, which vanquished Lee Sedol, the best Go player on the planet, four games to one. After the match, Sedol remarked that AlphaGo made astonishing and inventive moves, and other vanquished master Go players also expressed opinions along the lines that AlphaGo enabled them to amass insights into how to play the game. The ability of AI to deliver comparatively unpredictable outcomes in a military setting may give it a favorable edge in battle, especially if those outcomes shock the enemy.

  AI-based recognition algorithms outperformed human performance in 2010, most recently achieving an error rate of 2.5% as opposed to the average human error rate of 5%; however, some commonly cited experiments with these systems demonstrate their capacity for failure [3].

7.2   Overview of IoT in Defense Systems

The IoT is a dispersed computing framework for collecting and transmitting information. It empowers heterogeneous devices to share data and organize choices by incorporating transducers that gather information on physical and environmental situations. These gadgets transmit information over a wired or remote correspondence system to servers and PCs that store and process data utilizing programming applications and investigation. The information gathered from the investigation can be utilized for error identification, control, prediction, checking, and improvement of procedures and frameworks. IoT advances can possibly increase strategic proficiency, viability, security and produce huge cost savings in the long run. These advancements can assist the military and specialists on call in adapting to a cutting-edge world in which foes are put in increasingly refined and complex rural situations (sensitive urban areas) while funding is decreasing.

Guard and public safety (PS) associations assume a basic societal job of guaranteeing national security and reacting to crisis occasions and catastrophic events. Rather than PS associations, a few groups utilize public protection and disaster relief (PPDR) radiocommunnications [4], characterized in ITU-R Resolution 646 (WRC-12) as a mix of two key methods to react to crisis situations:

- PP Radiocommunication: Here, PP stands for public protection. These radio exchanges are utilized by offices and associations liable for managing the upkeep of lawfulness, security of property and life, and crisis circumstances.
- DR Radiocommunication: Here, DR stands for disaster relief. These interchanges are utilized by agencies and organizations dealing with a serious disruption in the functioning of society, posing a significant, widespread threat to human life, health, property or the environment, whether caused by accident, nature or human activity, and whether suddenly or as a result of complex, long-term processes [1].

Now, the challenge of crisis managment is to minimize the effect and injury to resources and individuals. This work calls for a collection of capabilities already definite through TCCA [5], ETSI [6] and European TETRA [4] normalization bodies and American APCO Project-25 [7]. It is including supply chain management and assests, secure communication and access to wider scope of data. The military and specialists on call ought to have the option to exchange data in an ideal way to organize aid projects and create awareness of a situation. FY 2016 SAFECOM Guidance provides current information on emergency communications policies. The ability to communicate should exist especially under trying conditions where foundations are regularly abandoned or annihilated. disasters, catastrophic events or different crises are normally spontaneous events, alarming civilian populations and influencing existing assets. In the case of cataclysmic events, a wide range of PS associations, such as military associations, volunteer groups, non-governmental organizations and other neighborhood and national associations, might be included. Simultaneously, communication frameworks and assets of businesses should likewise be utilized to alert and speak with civilians. Moreover, explicit security requirements concerning communications and data can also worsen while there is a lack of interoperability. Sharing different sorts of information is required so as to set up and maintain a common operational picture (COP) among organizations and among field and headquarters staff [9].

7.2.1 Role of IoT in Defense

The arrangement of IoT-related technologies for defense and Public Security is based on applications for C4ISR fire control frameworks. Here, C4ISR stands for command, control, communications, computers, intelligence, surveillance and reconnaissance. This is driven by an overwhelming view that sensors primarily serve as instruments to collect and share information, and make a progressively viable Command and Control (C2) of advantages. IoT advancements have likewise been received in certain applications for coordination and preparation; however, their arrangement is constrained and ineffectively incorporated within different frameworks. In addition, IoT functionalities are valuable for setting up innovative situational awareness in the region of activities. Leaders settle on choices that are dependent on constant investigation created by incorporating information from unmanned sensors and reports from the field. These administrators profit from a wide range of data provided by sensors and cameras mounted on the ground, and by unmanned vehicles or warriors. These devices analyze the mission scene and feed information to a forward operating base. A portion of the information might be transferred to a command center where it is coordinated with information from different sources [9].

The IOT can change every aspect of a business, from coordination to creation to appropriation. Also, the IoT can reform defense systems. Defense forces in India currently tackle a ton of IT frameworks and applications. Vital, strategic, operational and calculation applications currently utilize a great deal of IT-empowered arrangements. Network-centric warfare and situational awareness sensor systems are currently using innovations like the IoT. Selection of AI and machine learning (ML), which overlap the IoT system, are currently being attempted. Moreover, they have particularly unique structures and designs compared to their non-military personnel partners.

7.2.2   Ministry of Defense Initiatives

Intent on developing a biological system which encourages advancements, the Ministry of Defence (MoD) in India has instituted the Defence Innovation Fund (DIF), Defence Innovation Organization (DIO) and Innovation for Defence Excellence (iDEX). Notwithstanding these, the Defence Research & Development Organisation (DRDO) of India has also established the Technology Development Fund. The Army Design Bureau has distributed four volumes of Compendium of Problem Definition Statements, which documents numerous problems which can be addressed by the IoT. This will open doors for pioneers in industry and academia to team up with defense organizations to find creative arrangements.

The IoT technology could likewise help improve the quality of defense production, particularly those of critical ammo, thereby significantly reducing the danger of ammo mishaps. Ammo, along with the environmental condition around it, can be tracked with blockchain-based IoT devices in its journey from factory to depots to units to ranges until the time they are fired, thereby improving the confidence of the firer in the ammo. Another area which will benefit enormously is in improving the mission reliability of the equipment and weapon system being used by the Indian Defence Forces. An IoT/AI-based system can anticipate impending defects in the framework and can recommend the correct action to forestall the failure of the system [10]. A surveillance system grid augmented with IoT sensors can enhance the intelligence gathering capability and improve situational awareness during combat missions.

There are numerous such areas where defense forces can profit from the IoT. Concepts like Internet of Battlefield Things (IoBT) and Internet of Military Things (IoMT) are being imagined today, with the IoT being adapted to the anomalies and difficulties of a battlefield.

7.2.3   IoT Defense Policy Challenges

Most current national-level digital defense strategies are centered around identifying attacks against military and government frameworks and financial resources characterized as "basic foundation" (e.g., national defense forces, broadcast communications, and aviation authority frameworks). These frameworks and resources are checked, and approaches for recognizing cyberattacks are entrenched. Nevertheless, recognizing the many types of attacks against IoT targets presents various problems concerning approaches to safeguard systems. There are three types of problems: specialized, authority related, and incentive related.

A specialized test for identifying coordinated attacks against the IoT from devices used to dispatch distributed denial-of-service (DDoS) attacks are hard to recognize and can be in place weeks or months before the attacks are really launched. A commonly used software application programmed to lead DDoS attacks is a "bot" (e.g., the Mirai bot used in the Dyn cyberattack). The "bot" programming can be secretly present on any unsecure web framework (switches, webcams, DVD players, or any framework inside the IoT) and activated on order. A huge number of DDoS attacks occur when huge quantities of bot-tainted frameworks (a "botnet") are activated and coordinated against explicit targeted frameworks on the IoT.

In light of the fact that the attackers can harbor malicious intentions over an extended period of time, and do so without activating cautions or alerts, DDoS testing is the technique used against this type of attack. The manufactured challenges ahead are difficult when associated with authority. The majority of the huge number of frameworks associated with the IoT are owned and operated by private people or associations. Except in certain special cases, which are presented below, governments are for the most part not allowed to conduct covert observations of these private frameworks, regardless of whether or not it is practical to do so. Exclusive frameworks, such as building computerization, production line controls, and private communications hardware, are present to prevent administration attacks, yet most governments are not positioned to recognize attacks against them. Nor do the proprietors of private frameworks have any motivation to report attacks to government specialists. Regardless of whether an attack is in progress, a framework proprietor (for instance, the administrator of a business building) is probably going to attempt to relieve the impacts without quickly informing national specialists and gambling on exposing the framework. This motivating force related test further confounds the government's approach for ideal recognition of attacks against the IoT. Current government approaches underscore the difficulty of distinguishing attacks against the IoT at each stage of the decision-making cycle.

7.3   Robotics in Defense

Defense robotics are proficient in assisting robots that are sent by the military into battle situations. They are regularly planned to improve a fighter's current abilities while keeping them out of harm's way, as much as can be reasonably expected. Defense robots contribute to military superiority by giving soldiers an advantage at the ground level. Militaries as a whole gain a technical advantage by using defense robots.

Defense robots saw a moderate gain in 2018, growing by 4% to around 12,500 installed units, as per the International Federation of Robotics World Robotics 2018 Service Robots report. In 2017, defense robots represented roughly 11% of all service robots, at an approximate value of $902 million, and will continue to become an entrenched technology as an ever-increasing number of units are sold.

Defense robots come in numerous shapes and sizes, yet most serve the same basic functions of protecting and enabling troops in battle. The military has a long history with robotic exoskeletons for defense applications, which enhance the endurance and agility of soldiers.

At different times, these have come in the form of:

- Lower body-powered exoskeletons
- Energy scavenging exoskeletons
- Full body exoskeletons
- Stationary military exoskeleton
- Stationary military exoskeletons

Field robots, another type of professional serve robot, are also extensively used in defense applications. These defense robots have many functions, including:

- Carrying heavy equipment
- Rescuing wounded soldiers in combat zones
- Operating in dangerous situations to keep soldiers at a safer distance

Some field robots in defense applications are beginning to be outfitted with weapons for offensive capabilities. Defense robots are beginning to become a common part of military campaigns, assisting with maintaining the safety of troops and providing a tactical advantage in almost any combat situation. As the military keeps on testing and succeeding with various types of defense robots, the market is expected to see strong growth.

The Indian Army has submitted a request for 200 Daksh remotely operated vehicles (ROVs) to defuse explosives (Figure 7.2). Furthermore, the Defence Acquisition Council (DAC) has endorsed approximately 544 robots for the Indian Army from indigenous source. The robots will be utilized for reconnaissance and can convey appropriate ammo [11].

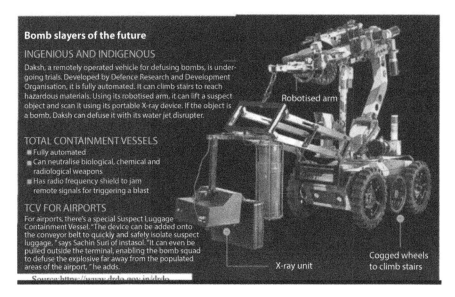

Bomb slayers of the future

INGENIOUS AND INDIGENOUS

Daksh, a remotely operated vehicle for defusing bombs, is undergoing trials. Developed by Defence Research and Development Organisation, it is fully automated. It can climb stairs to reach hazardous materials. Using its robotised arm, it can lift a suspect object and scan it using its portable X-ray device. If the object is a bomb, Daksh can defuse it with its water jet disrupter.

TOTAL CONTAINMENT VESSELS
■ Fully automated
■ Can neutralise biological, chemical and radiological weapons
■ Has radio frequency shield to jam remote signals for triggering a blast

TCV FOR AIRPORTS
For airports, there's a special Suspect Luggage Containment Vessel. "The device can be added onto the conveyor belt to quickly and safely isolate suspect luggage," says Sachin Suri of instasol. "It can even be pulled outside the terminal, enabling the bomb squad to defuse the explosive far away from the populated areas of the airport," he adds.

Source: https://www.drdo.gov.in/drdo

Robotised arm

X-ray unit

Cogged wheels to climb stairs

Figure 7.2   Daksh remotely operated vehicles.

7.3.1   Technical Challenges of Defense Robots

1) Discriminating Between Targets
   In some situations it is extremely difficult to design a robot that can differentiate between a soldier and a civilian in order to apply the principles required by the Rules of Engagement (ROE) and Law of War (LOW), especially as agitators act like regular people. Moreover, robots would also need to differentiate between enemy soldiers that are alive and those who have died or surrendered, which is an overwhelming task. Even though differentiation between targets is also an extremely difficult, error-prone task for human soldiers, we should be sure about how precise this differentiation should be. So, should we hold robots to a better standard when we still can't seem to accomplish this ourselves, at any rate in the near future?

2) First-Generation Problems
   We recently referenced that it is naïve to think that another mishap with military robots will not occur again. Likewise, as with some other advances, errors or bugs will unavoidably exist. This problem can be adjusted in the innovations of up-coming years. With internet innovations, for example,

original missteps are not too difficult and can be fixed with programming patches or updates. Nevertheless, with military mechanical technology, the stakes are a lot higher, since human lives might be lost because of programming or different errors. Nonetheless, with the testing currently occurring on robots, it is still frustrating if not difficult to guarantee that any given robot is error free, given that (a) testing situations might be significantly unique in relation to increasingly unpredictable, unstructured, and dynamic front line conditions in which we can't foresee every conceivable possibility; and (b) the central processing unit (CPU) utilized to control the robot's "brain" may consists of a large number of lines of code.

Beta testing of a program (testing before the official item is dispatched, regardless of whether identified with mechanical technology, business applications, and so forth) is conducted today; yet real clients routinely find new errors in programming long after the official item is dispatched. It is just impractical to run a mind-boggling bit of programming through every conceivable use in a testing stage; surprises may occur during its real use. Likewise, it is not reasonable to expect that testing of robots will remove all imperfections; the robots may carry on in surprising and unintended manners during genuine field use. Once more, a lot is on the line with sending robots into combat situations, since any error could be lethal. This makes the original issue of continuous security and dependability a particularly delicate matter.

3) Robots Running Amok

As portrayed in sci-fi books and films, some envision the likelihood that robots may break free from their human programming as a result of their own learning, or making different robots without such requirements (self-recreating and self-revising), or breaking down, or programming mistake, or even deliberate hacking. In these situations, since robots can be programmed to be tough and even attack, they would be amazingly hard to overcome—which is the purpose of utilizing robots as power multipliers. Some of these situations are more probable than others; we would not see the ability of robots to completely make different robots or to profoundly increase their insight and depart from any established ethical conduct for a long time. Nevertheless, different situations, such as hacking, appear to be near-term prospects, particularly if robots are not given solid self-defense capabilities (see below).

That robots may start to run amok is an up-dated version of the concern that foes may utilize our own creations against us; however, it likewise has another component in that past weapon frameworks, despite everything, need a human controller, which gives robots a state of helplessness, which is the "delicate underbelly" of the framework. Self-ruling robots would be intended to work without human control. What measures can be taken to keep robots from being captured and figured out or reconstructed to attack our own control? In the event that we structure an "off button" that can consequently stop a robot, this may introduce a key defenselessness that can be abused by the foe.

4) Unauthorized Overrides

The concern about overrides, especially in relation to atomic weapons, is that a rogue official might assume responsibility for these awful weapons and release them without approval or, in any case, abrogate their programming to submit some unlawful activity. This is a constant concern with any new disruptive innovation and is a multi-faceted test: It is a human issue (to create moral, able officials), an authoritative issue (to give procedural protections), and specialized issue (to give fundamental protections). So, there isn't anything as of yet which gives the impression that there is anything special about this concern, which ought to frustrate the turn of events or arrangement of cutting-edge mechanical autonomy, to the degree that it should affect the improvement of different innovations. Yet, in any case, this concern should be considered in the planning and organization stages.

5) Competing Ethical Frameworks

If we try to fabricate a moral structure for robot activities, it isn't clear which moral hypothesis should be used as our model. In this section, we have asserted that a half-and-half method identified with ethics as the hypothesis that appears to prompt the least intuitive outcomes; however, any modern hypothesis is by all accounts ineffective against irregularities and contending mandates (particularly if a three-or four-rule framework as basic as Asimov's can't work consummately).

This concern is identified with the primary specialized test portrayed here, that it is too hard to even think about embedding these rules of conduct or programming into a machine. Yet, we should review what we consider to be crucial; our underlying objective should not be to make a very moral robot—particularly one that demonstrates more moral behavior than people—and, unfortunately, this might be a low bar to clear.

6) Coordinated Attacks

Generally, it is smarter to have more information than less when making a decision, especially one as profound as a military strike choice. Sometimes robots are intended to effectively connect with different robots and frameworks; yet this may confuse matters for robots built just as administrators. We may need to set up levels of leadership inside robots when they work as a group, just to guarantee coordination of their activities. The hazard here is that as the multifaceted nature of any framework expands, the more open doors exist for errors to be present, and any errors made by military robots might be lethal.

7.4   AI, Robotics, and IoT in Defense: A Logical Mix in Context

7.4.1   Combination of Robotics and IoT in Defense

Robotics and AI till now have been utilized primarily for business matters, not for defense automation in India. However, there is gigantic potential in this field; for example, the Indian government recently established the Task Force on Artificial Intelligence to transform the economy of India [12].

Robotization of defense is currently big business, and military robots and AI applications guarantee to act as "power multipliers" and spare lives. Nevertheless, the ghost of another arms race and mutually assured destruction still remains. Automotive manufacturers are still the main clients of mechanical robots, but the military is also interested in AI-enabled robotic land vehicles. This is probably going to happen in the not so distant future. According to Goldman Sachs, by 2025, worldwide spending on defense automation is expected to reach $16.5 billion, more than three times the $5.1 billion spent on military robotics in 2010.

In 2010, India's military divulged its ambitious "military robot doctrine," which calls for having robots lead half of all military operations within 10 years. At that point, the Indian military had 16 top-secret programs for defense automation. In 2013, the Defence Research and Development Organisation (DRDO), India's equivalent to the U.S. Defense Advanced Research Projects Agency (DARPA), was reportedly creating robot soldiers with a "very high level of intelligence." India needs to send robot soldiers into various areas, such as the Line of Control between it and Pakistan. In accordance with this goal, the country wants an "advanced robotic soldier" watching and securing its borders by 2023. Also, Israel Aerospace Industries (IAI) developed the Harop unmanned aerial vehicle (UAV) to follow the radio frequencies of enemy planes and crash into them; hence, the moniker "suicide drones." Furthermore, Harop is furnished with an "autonomous platform" that is seen as a "precursor" to fully autonomous weapons.

In March, the Indian Internet of Things (IoT) company CRON Systems said it will work with Israel's Automotive Robotic Security on border security. The multimillion-dollar deal will combine ARI's AGVs and CRON's intrusion-detection systems [13].

7.4.2   Combination of Robotics and AI in Defense

The advancement in defense technology and the geo-political environments requires more defense spending every year because of the necessity for weapons and arms. Therefore, the recent trend to replace conventional equipment by smart robots and intelligent machines that learn by observation and experimentation to enhance operational effectiveness, are a cost-effective alternative. Artificial intelligence can provide many options for military applications for strategic, operational and tactical level planning, some of which are shown in Figure 7.3.

There is an increasing preference for the unmanned ground systems (UGS), unmanned aerial vehicles (UAV), guided bomb and missile systems, longer ranges and accuracy of smart ammunition, and so on which are beginning to be manufactured. The Indian Army is increasingly utilizing indigenously sourced remotely operated vehicle (ROV) Daksh robots for bomb disposal, unmanned autonomous vehicles (Netra UAV, Rustom, Searcher, etc.) for surveillance, and other miniature robotic machines [11].

In the next level of robotics with AI, unmanned systems could rule the future war systems. AI reasoning and robotics will have the following applications:

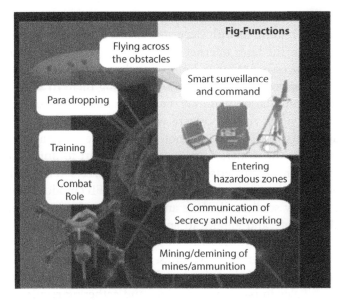

Figure 7.3 Applications of Artificial Intelligence For Militaries.

- The first application relates to image interpretation. It is used for target classification and identification.
- The second application relates to expert systems. These systems are used for maintenance and diagnosis of sophisticated weapon systems such as missiles and radars.
- The third application relates to robotic equipment. This equipment can be used for precision targeting support and carriage of ammunition and accuracy.
- The fourth application relates to camera equipment. Applications such as camera-equipped and shock-resistant platforms provide fire power remotely.
- The fifth application relates to the systems. This is used to maintain and diagnosis sophisticated weapon systems.
- The sixth application relates to missile targeting. Missile target range and trajectory analysis is used to assess kill zones, launch time and simulation to assist with qualifying trajectory analysis in different situations.
- The seventh application relates to the enhanced use of robots. Robots are increasingly being used for extraction of personnel, improvised explosive devices, firing of guns and other types of applications [12].

The robot is an electromechanical machine or device that is constrained by a computer program or with electronic circuit to perform an assortment of physical tasks. The term internet of things (IoT) refers to an established network and processing capacity connecting devices, sensors and items not ordinarily considered to be computers, permitting them to share and collect data with minimal human intervention. In this framework, the robot utilizes a night vision remote camera which can stream and record environmental factors of the robot. Remote surveillance cameras are battery-powered, making the cameras genuinely remote start to finish. The robot has a shoot sensor, which alerts soldiers, as with buzzers in metal detectors, senses when the robot is attacked with bullets. A RFID module is utilized to recognize friendly soldiers. RFID is an abbreviation for "radio-recurrence recognizable proof" and alludes to an innovation whereby computerized information encoded in RFID labels or keen marks are caught by a pursuer by means of radio waves. Laser weapons, which have had even and vertical development, are provided to shoot at the enemy. A pick and spot arm is affixed which helps in picking land mines and gathering required items in dangerous zone where people can't enter [14].

The goals of using IOT with robotics are:

- The first goal is to control the area under attack.
- The second goal is to secure the lives of people during rescue operations.
- The third goal is to recognize harmful and hazardous materials.
- The fourth goal is to reduce unauthorized access to defense areas.
- The fifth goal is to assemble a framework which can conceivably do all the things referenced above with high unwavering quality and ease.

7.5   Conclusion

Emerging technologies like AI, IOT and robotics potentially have considerable ramifications for national security. As such, the U.S. Department of Defense (DOD) and other nations are merging various AI applications with robotics and IOT for diverse military functions. Research is underway in the fields of intelligence collection and analysis, logistics, cyber operations, information operations, command and control, and in diverse semiautonomous and autonomous vehicles.

The vision must cover the different military facets of AI, robotics and the IOT that include autonomous weapons and cyber defense to formulate distinctive policies for each of them. The development of such a comprehensive vision will help defense organizations optimize the allocation of their considerable research capabilities towards the development of specific AI, IOT and robotics capabilities that would most benefit countries [8].

References

1. Deepak Kumar Gupta, *Military Applications of Artificial Intelligence*, http://www.indiandefencereview.com/author/deepakkumargupta/IDR Blog Date: 22 Mar, 2018.
2. Marcus Roth, *Artificial Intelligence in the Military - An Overview of Capabilities*, February 22, 2019 https://emerj.com/ai-sector-overviews/artificial-intelligence-in-the-military-an-overview-of-capabilities/by Emerj the AI Research and advisory Company.
3. Congressional Research Service, *Artificial Intelligence and National Security*, https://fas.org/sgp/crs/natsec/R45178.pdf Nov, 2019, CRC report prepared for Members and Committees of Congress.
4. Fraga-Lamas, Fernández-Caramés, Suárez-Albela, Castedo, González-López, A Review on Internet of Things for Defense and Public Safety, 16, 10, Oct, 2016.
5. TETRA Association, Public Safety Mobile Broadband and Spectrum Needs, 16395-94, Analysis Mason; Technical Report, Analysis Mason Limited, London, UK, 2010.
6. TETRA Critical Communications Association (TCCA), The Strategic Case for Mission Critical Mobile Broadband: A Review of the Future Needs of the Users of Critical Communications; Technical Report, TCCA, Newcastle Upon Tyne, UK, 2013.
7. European Telecommunications Standards Institute (ETSI), Emergency Communications (EMTEL); Requirements for Communications from Authorities/Organizations to Individuals, Groups or the General Public During Emergencies; Technical Report ETSI TS 102 182-V1.4.1, ETSI, Sophia Antipolis, France, 2010.
8. Telecommunications Industry Association (TIA), APCO Project 25 Statement of Requirements (P25 SoR); Technical Report, TIA, Arlington, MA, USA, 2013.
9. Fraga-Lamas, P., Fernández-Caramés, T.M., Suárez-Albela, M., Castedo, L., González-López, M., A Review on Internet of Things for Defense and Public Safety, October 2016.
10. Kalghatgi, A.T., Former Director (R&D), Bharat Electronics Ltd Track chair, Defence, IoT India Congress 2019, http://iotindiacongress.

com/internet-of-things-possibilities-for-the-indian-defence-forces/#:~: text=IoT%20or%20IoBT%20can%20be,case%20of%20a%20military%20 conflict.

11. Service Robots Pioneering Technology for the Challenges of Today's Marketplace, https://www.robotics.org/service-robots/defense-robots#:~:text= Defense%20Robots%20Keep%20Soldiers%20Safe,the%20military%20 in%20combat%20scenarios.&text=Defense%20robots%20contribute%20 to%20military,advantage%20at%20the%20ground%20level.

12. Defence ProAc Biz News Indian Defence Production and Acquisition, 2020 https://defproac.com/?p=6000#:~:text=Robotics%20and%20Artificial%20 intelligence%20in%20defence%20can%20be%20a,sector%20for%20 the%20private%20players.&text='NeuroNet'%20is%20an%20artificial%20 neural,the%20underwater%20systems%20of%20tomorrow.

13. Prakash, A., *Defense Automation Leads to New Capabilities, Worries*, May 29, 2017.

14. Hemkumar, Mahima, Rachana, R.S.I., Rangaswamy, Multifunctional War Field Robot using IOT. *IJCSMC*, 8, 11, 104–107, November 2019.

8

Techniques of Robotics for Automation Using AI and the IoT

Kapil Chauhan[1]* and Vishal Dutt[2]

[1]*Aryabhatta College of Engineering and Research Centre, Ajmer, India*
[2]*Department of Computer Science, Aryabhatta College, Ajmer, India*

Abstract

This chapter discusses a strategy for creating and improving the mechanical autonomy field by means of artificial intelligence (AI) and the web of things. Today, we can say that AI brings autonomous autonomy to the world. Practically all businesses use robots for some of their work. They use co-usable robots to frame unmistakable sort of works. In addition, the significance of information, on the grounds that it is found in primates and other phenomenal animals for instance, it will in general be arrived at bowed fuse an interleaved set of cutoff points, including creative mind, energetic data, and care.

This chapter proposes another thought which handles the issues for supporting control and checking practices at association goals and current robotizations, where sharp things can screen periphery events, impel sensor data got from a collection of sources, use off the cuff, close by, and scattered "machine information" to settle on a choice reasonable course of exercises, and a short time later act to manage or disperse static or dynamic position careful mechanical things inside the physical world through a uniform route by offering how to utilizing them as Internet of Robotics things.

Keywords: Internet of things, internet of robotic things, agent, reasoning

**Corresponding author*: kapilajmer86@gmail.com

Ashutosh Kumar Dubey, Abhishek Kumar, S. Rakesh Kumar, N. Gayathri, Prasenjit Das (eds.) AI and IoT-Based Intelligent Automation in Robotics, (129–148) © 2021 Scrivener Publishing LLC

8.1   Introduction

An automation framework as illustrated in Figure 8.1 may mean everything from a basic, single controller to fully complete robotized frameworks; single controllers and robots, frameworks of at least two robots, and flexible manufacturing and flexible assembly systems with administration robots are the run-of-the-mill models. Indeed, even explicit automated applications, such as miniaturized robots, medical procedure robots, space and underwater robots, strolling and divider-climbing robots, and so on may be considered. Design (as well as arranging) implies just a few stages in the life cycle of a robot or mechanical framework. The primary stages of the actual life cycle are: prerequisite determination, investigation, structure, execution, testing, activity, support, exiting, and reuse of the framework or its parts. Every one of these stages consists of a few distinct parts which may contrast on account of various items/frameworks. For example, configuration might be part of the theoretical structure, fundamental plan, itemized plan, and so on. Recreation, which is not referenced independently, is usually significant in the structure and also in the activity stage. Moreover, the reproduction of different advances might be valuable as well.

The mechanical framework has generated huge changes in different areas of human culture. Mechanical robot manipulators have been broadly deployed and utilized in a wide range of ventures to perform dull,

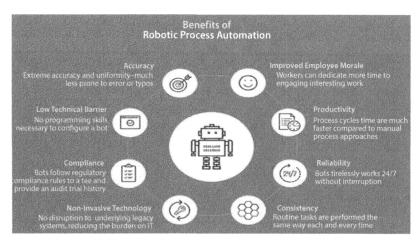

Figure 8.1 Robotic process automation (RPA). [https://www.google.com/search?
q=robotic+process+automation&safe=active&sxsrf=ALeKk00dA3YCBv-R5PjBbf2OVaLi
XCl7Sw:1608279600090&source=lnms&tbm=isch&sa=X&ved=2ahUKEwjI1YyyjNftAhX
zwTgGHV1DBDEQ_AUoAnoECAEQBA#imgrc=gNXxr4Yp-6UN9M]

monotonous, basic, as well as hazardous tasks such as item gathering, vehicle components, and box bundling [1].

The suppression have animated the investigators to consider new types of profitable mechanical structures, i.e., "Cloud Robotics." Cloud mechanical self-sufficiency may be depicted as a structure that relies upon the "Cloud computing" establishment to get an enormous amount of administrative power and data to help its action. This infers that not all identification, computation, and memory is joined into a single free structure as it was in the case of resolved mechanical innovation. Cloud robot structures constantly shut down some of your capacity by taking care of low-passivity when the framework found it difficult or faulty to reach the correct responses, i.e., decomposed. One example of Cloud robotics is Google's self-driving car program that creates accurate road maps by extracting data from satellites and street views and held in Cloud to support exact limitation.

8.2   Internet of Robotic Things Concept

Computerized reasoning, mechanical technology, AI, and a multitude of innovations will continue to improve applications of the internet of things. Mechanical autonomy frameworks generally give the programmable measurement to machines intended to perform serious and tedious work, just as a rich arrangement of innovations to bode well their condition and follow up on it, while computerized reasoning and AI permit/enable these machines work dynamically. These logical orders open the way to self-sufficient programmable frameworks advancements, joining mechanical autonomy and AI for planning automated frameworks that are self-sufficient [2]. AI is a piece of a propelled condition of knowledge utilizing factual example acknowledgment, parametric/non-parametric calculations, neural systems, recommender frameworks, swarm advances and so forth to perform autonomous tasks. Likewise, the modern IoT is a group of things, where edge devices and processing systems communicate with their surroundings to produce information to improve forms. It is around there where self-governing capacities and Internet of Things can practically allot IoRT (internet of robotic things) innovation. The utilization of correspondence focused robots utilizing remote correspondence and availability with sensors and other system assets has been developing and uniting patterns in mechanical technology. An associated or "organized robot" is a mechanical gadget associated with an interchange system.

The robots thusly can convey, fix, and maintain the sensor system to expand its life span and utility. Diverse testing in the two subclasses of organized robots is being used to develop a scientific base that partners correspondence for controlling and enabling new capacities. A robot is a closed system with high cutoff points and where refreshes in handiness and movement requires authority and normally long upkeep periods [3].

The concept of the internet of robotic things (IoRT) goes beyond arranged and shared/cloud autonomy and incorporates heterogeneous smart gadgets into a disseminated design of stages working both in the cloud and at its edge. Along with the IoT, the IoRT provides numerous advancements and a combination of automated "gadgets" to increase mechanical abilities, which when accumulated enhance the IoT's usefulness and increase its novel applications. This in turn opens the way for business ventures in new areas as well as in pretty much every division where automated help and IoT innovations and applications can be envisioned (home, city, structures, foundations, health, and so forth) [4].

8.3   Definitions of Commonly Used Terms

- Artificial Intelligence (AI): This is intelligence demonstrated by machines, unlike the natural intelligence displayed by humans and animals. The term was coined in 1956 by John McCarthy at Massachusetts Institute of Technology. Man-made mental aptitude consolidates games playing, programming PCs to play, for instance, chess and checkers. AI systems program PCs to make decisions, in fact, assignments (for example, some AI systems help experts diagnose illnesses based on symptoms). AI is also used in natural language processing to understand basic human language; in neural networks that endeavor to recognize underlying relationships in a set of data through a process that mimics the way the human brain operates; and in mechanical innovations (programming PCs to see and hear and react to other material upgrades) [5].
- Agent: An agent is anything that can perceive its environment through sensors and acts upon that environment through effectors. A human agent has sensory organs such as eyes, ears, nose, tongue and skin parallel to the sensors, and other organs such as hands, legs, mouth, and other body parts for effectors. A motorized star replaces cameras and infrared range sensors, leading to separation of connects engines [6].

- Robots: Articulation "robot" for the first time is present; Consider a robot "weapon" for welding. Try to imagine a robot that looks like a human Articulation can begin at the starting line "Robot" [7].
- Internet of Things: The next wave of processing will occur outside the domain of the conventional work. At present, the meaning of "Internet of Things" is complex, as it changes based on the unique situation and from the perspective of the individual being impacted by it [8].

8.4   Procedures Used in Making a Robot

8.4.1   Analyzing Tasks

Dissecting the experience of analyzing tasks can be an exceptionally confusing procedure. Therefore, the tasks which need to be actualized by a robot need to be highlighted by writing them down or listing them in a table so as to determine without much difficulty the number of tasks that need to be actualized by the robot. This is the actual method generally used to make parts of different types of robots in the world.

8.4.2   Designing Robots

After analysis of the user needs, the second step in designing a robot is to use these needs to determine which sensors are utilized to make a customized robot. General programming concepts are used in designing the robot [9] as illustrated in Figure 8.2. Therefore, programming sensors and different parts used in the computer, such as microchips and other chip sets, are also used. For instance, to make a robot that can perform tasks, sensors need to be included in the robot to program components to perform the task agreed upon.

8.4.3   Computerized Reasoning

Using AI concepts, it is expected to build robots that can learn tasks on their own. Along these lines, programming fake ideas for each independently is important, which includes the concept of computerized arguments in each assignment are discovered in this process. These man-made thoughts of consciousness can be legitimately explored by undertakings and different from the general idea of making robots [10].

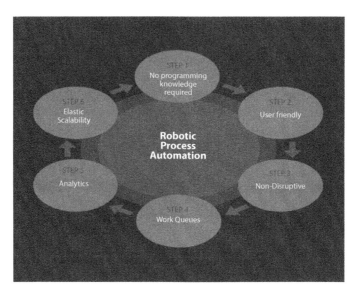

Figure 8.2 Cycle of robotics process automation. Hand drawn.

8.4.4   Combining Ideas to Make a Robot

Computer-aided reasoning and general ideas about each assignment are difficult to combine when making a robot that can be taught to think and act like a human. In this procedure, sensors are considered to proficiently execute man-made reasoning.

8.4.5   Making a Robot

Utilizing all the above procedures, the robot is made. All equipment parts are combined in the robot and the tasks are programmed into the sensors and the different parts.

8.4.6   Designing Interfaces with Different Frameworks or Robots

Robots can be designed to interface with other frameworks or robots using Bluetooth or some other remote gadgets. We can utilize these remote gadgets connected to PCs or other devices on the network in a versatile manner. In this way, the robot can be reached by PCs or other comparative gadgets [11].

8.5   IoRT Technologies

The meaning of the Internet of Things utilized in the Internet of Robotic Things (IoRT) is that it is a unique worldwide network with self-designing capacities dependent on standard and interoperable correspondence conventions where physical and virtual "things" have characteristics, physical qualities, and virtual characteristics that utilize shrewd interfaces, and are flawlessly incorporated into the data arrange as illustrated in Figure 8.3. The "things" are heterogeneous, have various degrees of unpredictability, detecting/impelling, correspondence, handling, insight, and portability and are coordinated in various stages. The "automated" things are a class of intricate, keen, self-ruling "things" that consolidate strategies from mechanical technology and from man-made reasoning and are incorporated into

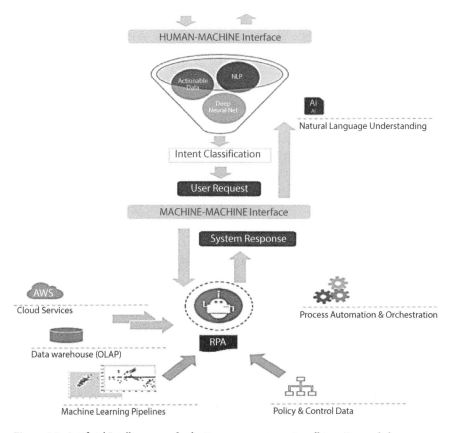

Figure 8.3 Artificial Intelligence and robotics process automation. [https://towardsdata science.com/artificial-intelligence-and-robotic-process-automation-284daecf3e55].

edge processing and cloud internet-of-things-based stages. Robotics consolidates the highlights of a powerful worldwide system framework with self-designing capacities with the independent, self-learning conduct of associated mechanical things making an arrangement of frameworks that utilize self-learning and movement arranging and movement control to provide benefits and give answers for explicit errands. In this unique situation, Internet of Things engineering coordinates the independent framework design based on six primary qualities [12]:

1. Detecting is a standard quality of the robotic structures and the key feature that enables the correspondence of "things" with other internet of things devices and people, in which most of the events occur in a device to human manner through articulation "recognizing," thus attracts people little earth belongs to his Internet of things Approach or approach to the organization.

2. Impelling is dependent on a comprehensive way of thinking and is the quality that drives "things" to act physically and also conduct effective exercises to prevent a fragment or breaking point from striking in the Internet of Things vertical markets it is not yet accessible in the Internet of Things market. Filtering requirements to ensure a reliable, and guaranteed about an unexpected turn of events and actions. It is open for multi-vendor Internet of things activity applications [13]. Must stop active Novel game-plans as a possible outcome of research "Praised as Service" as another point connecting with ease of use for viewing the Internet of things obligation to confirm and control end customer certification Internet of Things gadgets.

3. Control is filtered through social events and activities where cutoff points and associations are depicted by a "circle." The interfaces must be portrayed to offer access to perceive data correspondingly as to offer access to required control structures and the far-reaching security contemplations of the planning must be reflected in the interface definitions to empower the required sequencing parts [14]. The control circle can be mapped out for each viable plan for anything, from applications to associations in the cloud to structures and contraptions in the systems framework, on the off chance that the last one is conceivable. By then it isn't hard to recognize that the Internet of Things can be

dematerialized and tended to by methods for autonomic measures gadgets.

4. Designing based on the game plan is a proposed capability It motivates the internal parts for the working organization ask and make sure quality levels contribute weather for life cycle held in Internet Application of things. Must be the cause of coordination open assets, adjust to the demands of collaboration with data management and information parts, and their foundations are uneven Illustration [15]. Thinking, thinking about strategy for planning a robotic work process relies on the motor to dispatch the basic incentive base is based on every aid demand would like to think, affiliation technique the way the data is portrayed and customer friendly circumstances to enable the process of association definition.

5. Recognition means that we can say that interdisciplinary strategy where the installation of sensor data in mechanical progress more visible information, robots expect robot-human installation participation using human correspondence planning, programming system, federation-based, cloud-based and information evaluation structures, multi-chairman frameworks, machine sensor frameworks and now and again man argued [16]. Jealousy becomes a robot in excitement the environmentally sensitive(s) subsequently empowered Ae. Constantly expressing movement for singular people.

8.6   Sensors and Actuators

Two basic advances in the Internet of Things have focused one attempts to decide which are depicted around and are alleged sensor gadgets and actuators are reliably honest for execution. Robotics is the Internet of Things, especially structures with both features. Interfaces (for example, for identification or response) and for offering This functionality for the Internet of Things robot by strategies for related parts. Unusual sensors such as the Internet of Things and actuators force everyone through the Internet of Robotics construction material.

Mechanical things gain the possible for contrasted and difficult identifying and incitation from the long show of apply self-rule. From the recognizing side, mechanical science and advancement gives methodologies and use both fundamental and refined sensors, including inertial sensors, going sensors, 3D sensors, too continuously ordinary sensors like cameras, collectors and force sensors. Convenient robots or various robots can accumulate sensor data from different stance or conceivably at various events, and strategies exist to join these data in a coherent picture of the earth and of its progression in time. From the initiation side, the ability to alter the state of being is apparently the most phenomenal piece of mechanical things. Actuation can take a wide extent of structures, from to movement of clear contraptions like a modified gateway to the transportation of product and people and to the control of articles.

8.7   Component Selection and Designing Parts

The segment determination of mechanical technology and assembling frameworks is one of the assignments which requires the use of a master knowledge-based (KB) framework, as every single essential piece of information, prerequisites, potential outcomes and results are easily characterized as illustrated in Figure 8.4. As information, for the most part the assignments to be carried out ought to be characterized as procedure or activity plans. The potential outcomes are characterized by methods for certain information bases containing every single accessible asset, and by methods for KBs to characterize all imperatives, connections, and explicit

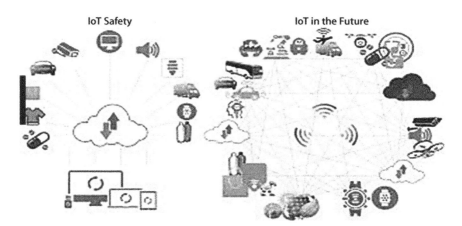

Figure 8.4 Internet of robotic things – converging sensing/actuating, hypoconnectivity, AI and IoT platforms. [https://www.google.com/search?q=Internet+of+robotic+things+%E2%80%93+converging+sensing/actuating,+hypoconnectivity,+AI+and+IoT+platforms.&safe=active&hl=en&sxsrf=ALeKk02kxn6e3ryDxE0-i6JxUJLl27AYpQ:1608279799793&source=lnms&tbm=isch&sa=X&ved=2ahUKEwj5z6mRjdftAhX5wjgGHYTwCh0Q_AUoAXoECAQQAw&biw=1366&bih=600#imgrc=uI9GA_QbDdAGRM].

essentials. The KBs contain all material improvement standards, as well as rules and realities (now and then given in outlines). Indeed, even doubtful and incomplete information can be overseen without issues. The fundamental assignment of the KB framework is therefore match making between the objectives to be accomplished and the methods accessible, contemplating all prerequisites and requirements, and some streamlining rules. This segment choice is called arrangement, or structure in a few cases; this configuration also contains format arranging when the physical space of the workshop is geared toward the accessible space and the chosen segments. On the off chance that another arrangement of segments is chosen for a given errand, or changes of a current framework are important, or distinctive advancement rules are utilized, a re-design or update happens [17].

First the determination of robots, instruments, grippers, and so forth occurs, then format arranging, the reenactment, and afterward final arranging happens. Determination of coming together depends on the essential Functions, characterized as underdeveloped development. First the subassemblies, at that point the congregations are structured. Initial a lot of particular is made to fill in as practical detail for robot configuration dependent on the examination of the mechanical necessities of a particular arrangement of robot-related errands, at that point the best fit robots are chosen from the arrangement of accessible robots. The robot details contain around 25 extraordinary, significant parameters such as force necessities, control, precision, power, torque, gripper, combination prospects, cost, and so forth. A scientific programming technique and a standard-based master framework is introduced to locate the best arrangement of mechanical advances that are required by the arrangement of thoughts about errands (stage one). For the second stage the satisfactory arrangement of robots is chosen and afterward the existing list is organized with both of the above techniques. At long last the combination of the scientific apparatuses (whole number programming) and rule-based master frameworks is recommended. In Gear maintenance the most parts are used for transportation, robots or moving robots, as autonomous guided vehicles (AGVs), or essentially trucks, and so on. Dragone, M. *et al.* (1993) manage modern truck choice, as model. Their study examines how to develop an information base and afterward how to utilize it for determination. The subsequent robot determination incorporates kinematics, tomahawks, drives, programming, speed, and so forth.

The contribution of the framework was to depict the necessary design (process plans). This was mapped by methods for suitable guidelines to specialized and value parameters. Similar parameters were utilized for the determination of the subsequent framework, which implied that depending on the improvement measures set forth in the projects the best-fit instruments and gear were chosen as an underlying arrangement of machines, robots, and so forth to be utilized. At that point an arrangement (design), and planning framework checked the chosen set of components, and a few refinements were made, all in reenactment mode. In the case of any issues arising, a reconfiguration calculation began to discover better arrangements. A similar rearrangement was utilized because of changes, increments, breakdowns, and so on, and if the design prerequisites changed [18].

8.7.1   Robot and Controller Structure

In this section, AI-enabled parts of the robot, controller and robot framework configuration will be examined. It is interesting how adequately such calculations can be utilized to settle specific structural undertakings. The multipopulation-based genetic algorithm (MPGA) is an exceptionally effective enhancement method for nonlinear issues. It is equal in use to the genetic algorithm (GA), which is a sort of versatile search technique that is greatly used in the controller configuration to best fit the errands highlighted. The optimality depends on the utilization of an aptitude measure; here it is the relative manipulability. This is a regular task-based design (TBD). The quantity of capacity developments is equivalent to the quantity of errands being focused on. A dynamic plan structure is added to the framework. For the most part, the streamlining capacity is an aggregate of a targeted work and a few limitations, which builds the multifaceted nature of the TBD exponentially with the expansion of the quantity of errands being focused on, because of the immense inquiry space and nonlinearity. In the event that a different enhancement process is requested for all errands being focused on, and these are connected by interfacing limitations, the intricacy is practically consistent. There is no need for coherence in the subordinates, so any wellness capacity can be applied. The structure limitations are reachability, heuristics, joint cut-off, and joint edge change between two adjoining task focuses, all of which are task explicit. A theoretical model of an autonomous operator has been introduced. It coordinates receptive and subjective conduct. For such incorporation the following characteristics ought to be cultivated: reactivity, ideal conduct, and symbolic information portrayal. Information portrayal, arranging, planning and execution in addition to the procedure of assessment is included. The assessment module continually regulates nature and the specialist's activities to guarantee the operator's reactivity.

8.8   Process Automation

Organizations are sufficiently aware of the fact that increasing business efficiency and worker productivity is of paramount importance to flourish in a highly-competitive environment. Any process can be automated as long as a clear operating procedure is accessible.

There were times when programming content for semi-automatically doing ordinary daily tasks such as network provisioning, system administration, and so on were highly sought for expanding operational efficiency. Despite the fact that a human was required for managing those tasks, the advantages of a software approach quickly became clear and began to gain prominence in the industry. With the development in system design, the trend mainly shifted towards service oriented architecture (SOA), with systems becoming larger and more complex. Different methods of integrating with external or internal services began to emerge, increasing the demand for "orchestration" and "automation" for flawless execution [19].

Utilizing low-level knowledge of application engineering in addition to access to various instruments and application interfaces, software modules are used to draft a strategy for tasks, so those tasks can be activated on-demand or in a predefined manner as a software routine without human intervention.

8.8.1   Benefits of Process Automation

Organizations are starting to realize that increasing business efficiency and worker profitability is of paramount importance to flourish in a highly competitive world.

Automation through programming is of utmost importance in order for corporations to remain competitive and accomplish operational excellence by meeting or outperforming service level agreements (SLAs). By using the power of robotics programming, engineering companies have opened up new roads for process designing in the IT industry. Mechanisms for data management that are presently being created consider robotic process automation (RPA) tools to be a suitable option that is more obtainable than any other time in recent memory.

8.8.2   Incorporating AI in Process Automation

For the accomplishment of the work, identify it clearly and understand the mechanics behind a fruitful acceptance of RPA proximity to an air driven process. RPA framework, where AI is considered the center stage, requires a central understanding of both innovations exist collectively. Configuration of the two points must be clearly delineated before going into usage phase.

Taking an all encompassing viewpoint, recorded information for model preparing is unavoidable. Moreover, different perspectives, for example, entertainers, trigger focuses, sub-framework limits, area information, interfacing API/snares, guidelines, just as corner situations where human mediation might be required, special case taking care of, and so on are for the most part going to be significant.

8.9   Robots and Robotic Automation

In order to perform different tasks in our homes or workplaces, robots come in all shapes and sizes, from mechanical arms on a shop floor to welcome robots in retail locations, coffee shops, or lodgings.

Robots are also showing up in frameworks of related and persistently adroit devices. For example, a self-driving related vehicle is a robot: yet it consolidates different smaller robots or sharp interface sensors and actuators. All of these devices, smaller robots, and smart sensors need to be arranged in order to work together to accomplish the goals of the more noteworthy complete robot: the related vehicle [20].

8.10   Architecture of the Internet of Robotic Things

Over the years, the Internet of Things has progressed in various planning standards and Internet of Things organized and created mechanizing the exceptionally distinct Internet of Things scene storage facilities and courses of action that are not interconnected with other Internet of Things steps and applications. Beat the irregularity of vertical-orchestrated shutdown system to defeat the vagina of structures and application domains and proceed to open applications and steps that help in various applications, new ideas are needed to improve open internet planning passing in topology and joining new parts makes things orderly. Identify, and initiate the necessary for planning framework organization and interface headway.

This fuses from beginning to end security in circled, heterogeneous, dynamic Internet of Things circumstances by using composed fragments for ID, confirmation, data affirmation and evasion against computerized attacks at the device and structure levels, and can help ensure an anticipated method to manage Internet of Things standardization structures.

The internet of things open stages can access correlation, structure improvement and access by empowering the creative, physical and spectrum related assets expected to help IoRT applications and associations. Internet of Robotics Things game plans are rising and will scale and become progressively confounding as different heterogeneous self-administering shrewd devices will be added to the edge and this requires Internet of Things stages and applications that are open, flexible, extensible, prosperity and secure.

8.10.1   Concepts of Open Architecture Platforms

The heterogeneous internet of things devices transmit information to different devices, portals and cloud-based IoT platforms where the information is examined and exchanged among applications through frameworks that make choices, come up with examples, direct forms and create new services.

In this, dynamic heterogeneous condition the open stages structural ideas assume a basic job as there are associations among astute gadgets over the stages and application spaces.

8.11   Basic Abilities

8.11.1   Discernment Capacity

The sensor and information investigation innovations from the Internet of Things unmistakably can give robots a more extensive skyline contrasted with nearby, on-board detecting as far as space, time and kind of data. Then again, putting sensors on board versatile robots permits situating them in an adaptable and dynamic manner and empowers refined dynamic detecting methodologies. A key test of recognition in an internet of robotic things (IoRT) domain is that the ecological perceptions of the IoRT substances are spatially and transiently distributed. Some methods must be set up to permit robots to investigate this circulated information. A key part of the robot's recognition capacity is getting information on their own area, which incorporates the capacity to fabricate or refresh models of the environment. Despite extraordinary advancement in this area, self-restriction may at present be difficult in swarmed or potentially Global Positioning System-denied indoor situations, particularly if high dependability is requested. Straightforward internet of things-based frameworks;

for example, a radio recurrence recognizable proof (RFID) improved floor has been utilized to give solid area data to local robots. Other methodologies use range-based procedures on signals radiated off-board [21].

8.11.2   Motion Capacity

The capacity to move is one of the crucial included estimations of automated frameworks. While mechanical structure is the key factor in deciding the inborn viability of robot portability, IoT availability can help versatile robots by helping them to control programmed entryways and lifts; for instance, in assistive robotics and in calculated applications. Internet of Things stage administrations and M2M and systems administration conventions can encourage appropriated robot control designs in large-scale applications; for example, last-mile delivery, exactness agribusiness, and observational ecology. Such an interface is appropriate for robots to act as a versatile sensor that distributes perceptions and makes them accessible to any intriguing IoT administrations [22]. In application situations, such as search and salvage, where correspondence framework might be missing or damaged, versatile robots may need to set up specially appointed systems and utilize each other as sending hubs to look after correspondence.

8.11.3   Manipulation Capacity

In the reception of RFID, the difference within signal quality received wires were used for all or any more precise positioning.

More significant level capacities of decisional self-governance or decisional self-rule alludes to the capacity of the framework to make a decision based on the simplest game plan to satisfy the errand or mission. This is often generally not considered in IoT middleware; applications simply call for an activation API of so-called smart codes that hide the inner complexity. Roboticists frequently depend upon AI arranging techniques hooked into prescient nature of the model and the potential activities. The characteristics of the plans basically relies upon the characteristics of those models and of the gauge of the underlying state. In this regard, the improved situational mindfulness overseen by an IoT domain can prompt better plans. Human mindful assignment planners use information on the expectations of people deduced through an IoT domain to supply designs that regard imperatives on human association. The IoT also increases the extent of decisional self-rule by making more on-screen features and activities accessible; for instance, controllable lifts and doors. However, IoT gadgets may progressively open up or become unavailable [23]. A solution for this is to try to arrange theoretical administrations which are mapped into genuine gadgets at runtime.

8.12   More Elevated Level Capacities

8.12.1   Decisional Self-Sufficiency

Decisional independence implies the limit of the system to settle on a choice for the most straightforward course of action to fulfill its endeavours and missions. This is frequently commonly not considered in IoT middleware: applications essentially call an incitation API of alleged smart things that spread within multifaceted nature of robotics. Roboticists as often as possible rely on AI orchestrating methods embedded in judicious models of the world and of the potential exercises. the character of the plans essentially depends upon the characteristics of those models and of the measure of the basic state [24]. Human mindful assignment planners use data on the points of the individuals induced through an IoT circumstance to create flexible structures that respect the needs of human interaction. The IoT also increases the degree of decisional independence by making more on-screen features and exercises open; for example, controllable lifts and entryways. Even though, IoT contraptions may continuously open up or become inaccessible, which challenges conventional multi-administrator masterminding moves. An answer for this is to attempt to orchestrate similar dynamic organizations which are mapped into genuine gadgets at runtime.

8.12.2   Interaction Capacity

This is the capacity of a robot to communicate genuinely, psychologically and socially either with clients, administrators or different frameworks around it. While M2M protocols can be straightforwardly embraced in mechanical programming, here we focus on how IoT innovations can encourage human–robot associations at useful (instructing and programming) and social levels only as a method for telecollaboration. Useful unavoidable IoT sensors can make the practical methods for human–robot communication increasingly stronger. Regular language directions are an attractive method to educate robots, particularly for non-master clients, yet they are frequently obscured or contain verifiable assumptions. The IoT can provide data on the position and condition of articles to disambiguate these guidelines. Signals are another instinctive method to order robots; for example, by highlighting objects. Acknowledgment of pointing motions from sensors on board the robot just works inside a restricted field of view [25].

8.12.3   Cognitive Capacity

By thinking about and inducing information for a fact, subjective robots can comprehend the connection between themselves and the earth and among objects, and to evaluate the conceivable effect of their activities. In the previous areas there were some aspects of comprehension at the speaking point, for instance, multi-modular recognition, consultation and social insight. Here, we focus on the subjective states of thinking and learning in an IoRT multi-entertainer setting [26]. This necessity is generally conspicuous in the areas of strategic and cutting-edge design, where a quick response to disturbances is required, along with adaptable adjustment to fluctuating creation destinations.

8.13   Conclusion

This chapter has proposed an IoT-based mechanical technology design concept, known as the Internet of Robotic Things, which is making headway in the current cloud organized robots. The Web of Robotic Things permits robots or mechanical frameworks to associate, share, and scatter the disseminated calculation assets, business exercises, setting data, and ecological information with each other, and to get novel information and particular aptitudes not learned by themselves, all under a hood of advanced engineering structure. Presently, robots are especially required for quick assembling. Utilizing this technique, we can make robots effectively and productively. Obviously, as of today the utilization of computational, multi-operator and AI strategies and apparatuses to structure and work automated frameworks has some extremely positive outcomes around the world. However, the greater part of these outcomes are known and applied by the scholarly network, as industry needs more time to be persuaded to implement the most up-to-date procedures. There is a pattern of becoming increasingly more multidisciplinary, combining instrument design and information with PC procedure devices and information as well as with mental outcomes too. That is why the future will demand additional testing, but also what makes it a fascinating field of study.

References

1. Craig, A.B., *Understanding Augmented Reality – Concepts and Applications*, Morgan Kaufmann, U.S, pp. 1-37, 9780240824086, 2013, https://doi.org/10.1016/B978-0-240-82408-6.00001-1.

2. Gluhak, A. and Vermesan, O., Report on Internet of Things platform activities, H2020 Work Programme 2014-2015, ICT-30-2015: Internet of Things and Platforms for Connected Smart Objects, pp-102-13. Retrieved from http://www.internet-of-thingsresearch. eu/pdf/D03 01 WP03, 2016.
3. Riazuelo, L., RoboEarth semantic mapping: A cloud enabled knowledge-based approach. *IEEE Trans. Autom. Sci. Eng.*, 432–443, Apr. 2015, Vol: 12(2).
4. Shim, B.-K., Kang, K.-W., S.-B., Automation and Systems, in: *Bitcoin: Beyond money*, Deloitte University Press, DUPress.com, online at https://dupress.deloitte.com/content/dam/dup-us-en/articles/bitcoinfact-fiction-future/DUP 847 BitcoinFactFictionFuture.pdf. (n.d.), 2012, Birmingham, AL.
5. Bacciu, D. and Barsocchi, P., An experimental characterization of reservoir computing in ambient assisted living applications. *Neural Comput. Appl.*, 24, 6, 1451–1464, 2014.
6. Ferrer, E.C., *The blockchain: A new framework for robotic swarm systems*, Cornell University Library, August 2016, Springer, Cham.
7. Friess, O.V., *Building the Hyperconnected Society – Internet of Things Research and Innovation Value Chains, Ecosystems and Markets*, 2015, River Publisher, Denmark.
8. Friess, O.V., *Digitising the Industry Internet of Things Connecting the Physical, Digital and Virtual Worlds*, 2016, River Publisher, Denmark.
9. Hu, G. and W.P., Cloud robotics: Architecture, challenges and applications. *IEEE Netw.*, 26, 3, 21–28, May/Jun. 2012.
10. Sukhatme, G.S. and a. M., Embedding Robots Into the Internet. *Commun. ACM*, 67–73, May 2000.
11. A. Florea, & C. Buiu (2017). An Overview of Swarm Robotics. IGI Global. http://doi:10.4018/978-1-5225-2280-5.ch001.
12. IEEE Society of Robotics and Automation's Technical Committee on Networked Robots. (n.d.). Retrieved from www.ieee-ras.org/technical-committees/117-technical-committees/networked-robots/146-networked-robots. www.ieee-ras.org/technicalcommittees/117-technical-committees/networked-robots/146-networkedrobots.
13. Wan, J. and Tang, S., Cloud robotics: Current status and open issues. *IEEE Access*, 4, 2797–2807, 2016.
14. Jaeger, M.L., Reservoir computing approaches to recurrent neural network training. *Comput. Sci. Rev.*, 3, 3, 127–149, 2009.
15. Medagliani, Paolo & Leguay, Jeremie & Duda, A. & Rousseau, Franck & Duquennoy, Simon & Raza, Shahid & Ferrari, Gianluigi & Gonizzi, Pietro & Cirani, Simone & Veltri, L. & Montón, Màrius & Domingo Prieto, Marc & Dohler, M. & Villajosana, I. & Dupont, O. (2014). Internet of Things Applications - From Research and Innovation to Market Deployment.
16. Parker, L. and a., Building multirobot coalitions through automated task solution synthesis. *Proc. IEEE*, 94, 7, 1289–1305, 2006.

17. Di Rocco, M. and e. a., A planner for ambient assisted living: From highlevel reasoning to low-level robot execution and back. *AAAI Spring Symposium Series*, 2014.
18. Dragone, M. and Amato, G., (n.d.). A Cognitive Robotic Ecology App.
19. Gianni, M. and Ferri, F., Augmented Reality Environment for Mobile Robots, 2013, Conference Towards Autonomous Robotic Systems, Springer, Berlin, Heidelberg, 470-483.
20. Lukoševičius, M. and Jaeger, H., Reservoir Computing Trends. *KI – Künstliche Intelligenz*, 26, 4, 365–371, 2012.
21. Financial Times, Silver Economy Series, November 2014, The Silver Economy: Japan embraces future of robot care, Tokyo, 2014.
22. Vermesan, O. and Bahr, R., Internet of Things Business Models Framework, Retrieved from http://www. internet-of-things-research.eu/pdf/D02 01 WP02 H2020 UNIFY-Internet of Things Final.pdf, 2016, H2020 Work Programme 2014-2015 ICT-30-2015: Internet of Things and Platforms for Connected Smart Object, pp.: 1-57.
23. Schladofsky W. *et al.* (2017) Business Models for Interoperable IoT Ecosystems. In: Podnar Žarko I., Broering A., Soursos S., Serrano M. (eds) Interoperability and Open-Source Solutions for the Internet of Things. InterOSS-IoT 2016. Lecture Notes in Computer Science, vol 10218. Springer, Cham. https://doi.org/10.1007/978-3-319-56877-5_6
24. Lundh, R., Karlsson, L., Saffiotti, A., Internet of Things. Dynamic selfconfiguration of an ecology of robots, in: *2007 IEEE/RSJ International Conference on Intelligent Robots and Systems*, pp. 3403–3409, 2007, IROS.
25. Dragone, M. and Saunders, J., On the Integration of Adaptive and Interactive Robotic Smart Spaces. *Paladyn*, 6, 1, (2012), 2015. Strategic Intelligence Monitor on Personal Health Systems, Phase 2 – Impact Assessment Final Report. In http://ftp.jrc.es/EURdoc/JRC7 1183.pdf.
26. Organisation for Economic Cooperation and Development (OECD), *The wellbeing of nations: The role of human and social capital, online: The wellbeing of nations: the role of human and social capital*, 2017, OECD, Paris.

9

An Artificial Intelligence-Based Smart Task Responder: Android Robot for Human Instruction Using LSTM Technique

T. Devi[1*], N. Deepa[1], SP. Chokkalingam[1], N. Gayathri[2]
and S. Rakesh Kumar[2]

Saveetha School of Engineering, Saveetha Institute of Medical and Technical Sciences, Chennai, India
School of Computing Science and Engineering, Galgotias University, Uttar Pradesh, India

Abstract

Robots have become a central part in the day-to-day activities of humans. Communication between the two still remains a challenging task and processing methods should be developed to map out the problems. Human and robot communication can be enabled by incorporating natural language processing (NLP) techniques from the artificial intelligence field. The proposed system enables the movement of robots based on instructions as well as constraints from humans. The system works in three phases: (i) text transformation using NLP, (ii) categorization of instruction, and (iii) post processing of data. Long short-term memory (LSTM) is used for categorization of input instructions given by the user. The experimental results show how single instruction accuracy plays an effective role in movement of robots.

Keywords: Constraints, instructions, movement, natural language processing

Corresponding author: devi.janu@gmail.com

Ashutosh Kumar Dubey, Abhishek Kumar, S. Rakesh Kumar, N. Gayathri, Prasenjit Das (eds.) AI and IoT-Based Intelligent Automation in Robotics, (149–164) © 2021 Scrivener Publishing LLC

9.1   Introduction

The interaction between human beings and robots has become very significant due to the coexistence of robots with humans. Considering the safety of humans, robots help them in achieving success rates in several sectors such as factories or housework and so on. The interaction between human and robot increases as we communicate and give several instructions to robots in order to make them work in an effective manner (Figure 9.1).

In today's technological world, Google search and language translation are frequently used by everyone in day-to-day life. Due to the increasing use of AI-based platforms, the interaction between humans and robots has also evolved. Robots are activated in many ways, especially when NLP handles the AI in critical aspects such as natural language understanding and generation of various languages into the machine understandable language many of us frequently use in our virtual assistants such as Siri owned by Apple, Amazon's version of Alexa, Cortana developed by Microsoft, etc. Even though there are many examples like this which are based on AI-enabled platforms, Google Assistant, Netflix and Amazon Prime are some of the most frequently used voice-activated services in telecommunications. These services customize our use based on multiple steps by giving direct voice commands with our own language by applying NLP.

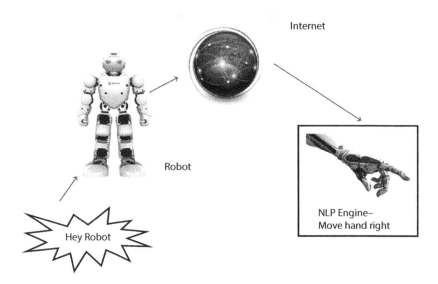

Figure 9.1 Robot movement based on human instructions.

For human communication, AI-enabled chatbots deliver speed and accuracy, which has transformed the field of today's online markets that apply NLP. Since AI enables many types of processes for human interaction, such as data search, voice control, etc., we mainly concentrate on "voice search," which uses NLP to improve search engine optimization (SEO), online marketing, etc. Not only is NLP used in search engine optimization, but also AI-enabled virtual assistants or chatbots. NLP has its own complex process such as voice recognition, separate voice clipping, words to voice conversion, feature extraction, audio samples and so on. When voice process technology has many drawbacks based on the conversion recorded to text and audio is recognized as input the steps are analyzed based on the voice input which has been considered here. Several systems follow the following steps to carry out the process (Figure 9.2).

The objective of this chapter includes:

1. Making movement of robots easy by human instructions and parameters.
2. Increased accuracy in instruction and movement precision.

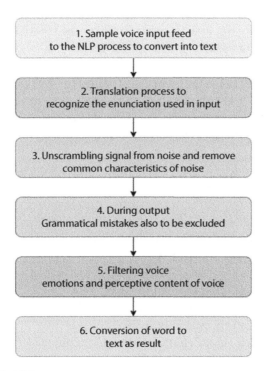

Figure 9.2 Sample NLP process.

The chapter is organized as follows: Section 9.2 reviews the literature on the topic; Section 9.3 discusses the proposed system; Section 9.4 presents the results and discusses them; and Section 9.5 concludes the chapter.

9.2   Literature Review

Translation of language of humans as instructions to machines is a challenging task. Each and every word from the human can be translated, yet there are difficulties in understanding the context of the entire document. A few systems [1–3] utilized hardware to identify the commands and make the robot interact. These systems [4, 5] suffered from several limitations such as every word being translated as well as the static state of the set of commands.

Several systems focused on recognizing the audio from the humans [6–8]. The system focused on implementing limited commands, thereby also increasing the time to respond. At the same time, the system suffers from the same limitation [9, 10] of every word being translated as well as limited constraint passing while communicating due to the format of words. Later systems [11, 12] were designed to focus on the constraints to be passed but were not able to concentrate on the translation process that hinders NLP being used.

The system proposed [13] takes the entire document as input and also provides efficient results compared to traditional systems that translated every word. First the message [14, 15] taken as input is encoded to the vector and from that the original message is later decoded. So, our system incorporates NLP methods to help robots to respond [16, 17].

9.3   Proposed System

The proposed system receives instructions from humans and translates them to make the robots move. As illustrated in Figure 9.3, there are three basic steps to the process, namely:

- Step 1: Text Transformation Using NLP
  Takes document as input and gives instruction list as output.
- Step 2: Categorization of Instructions
  LSTM helps in categorizing the instructions.
- Step 3: Post-Processing of Data
  All the instructions are listed for movement of robot.

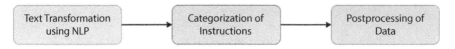

Figure 9.3 Steps in proposed system.

- Step 1: Text Transformation Using NLP
  The input text from humans needs to be converted to instructions understood by robots. Transforming text to extract information using NLP involves the steps given below, which are also illustrated in Figure 9.4.

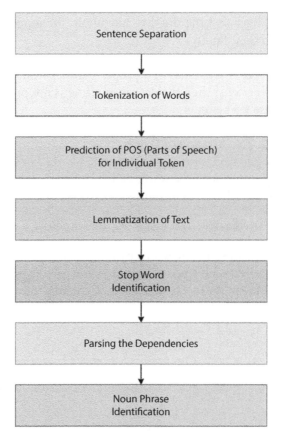

Figure 9.4 Text transformation using NLP.

Consider the text given below:

"The calm tiger jumps over the lazy dog. The dog is also happy to see his long-time missing friend and it plays with him. The tiger and the dog live happily in the jungle forever with their family."

- Step 1.1: Sentence Separation
  Sentence separation stands as the first step in the proposed system which gets the sample input data (single sentence or a paragraph of lines) and breaks it down into single sentences separately. From the example, separation of sentences gives the following single sentences.

  1. The calm tiger jumps over the lazy dog.
  2. The dog is also happy to see his long-time missing friend and it plays with him.
  3. The tiger and the dog live happily in the jungle forever with their family.

  The text is separated in a proper manner using NLP methods and also works when the data formatting is not proper, as shown in Figure 9.5 below.

- Step 1.2: Tokenization of Words
  After separating into single sentences, we need to split these sentences into separate words called "tokens," and the above process is called "tokenization."

  The calm tiger jumps over the lazy dog.

  Tokenization splits the words by finding the spaces between them and also full stop is also noted as a token separately as it adds meaning to the sentences. Generally, punctuations

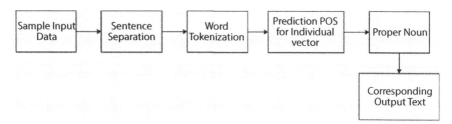

Figure 9.5 Sentence separation sample text.

are taken into account while tokenizing the sentences as they play an important role in providing meaning to the sentences. The result of the above sentence after tokenizing is as follows:

"The", "calm", "tiger", "jumps", "over", "the", "lazy", "dog", "."

- Step 1.3: Prediction of POS (Parts of Speech) for Individual Token
  By examining each token, the POS of an individual token can be predicted as to whether a noun or a verb or an adjective is used. We will be able to find out the predicted meaning of the sentence by identifying the part of every word in the given sentence. When each word is fed into the classification model it will be tagged with the POS of each word and the behavior is replicated. The POS can be guessed for sentences that are similar as well as the words that were found before.
  Consider the following example:

  The calm tiger jumps over the lazy dog.

  - tiger, dog - noun
  - calm, lazy - adjectives
  - jumped - verb

  From the above example it is clear that the nouns identified are "tiger" and "dog" which depicts clearly that the text is telling us about a "tiger."

- Step 1.4: Lemmatization of Text
  In the case of sentences, identification of a word's lemma is an important step. A look-up table is constructed according to POS (parts of speech) along with the rules associated with the words (Figure 9.6). From the example, the following result appears after lemmatization.

  Original Text:
  The dog is also happy to see his long-time missing friend and it plays with him.

  Lemmatized Text:

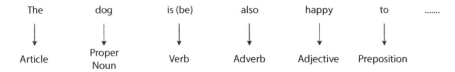

Figure 9.6 Lemmatized sample text.

- Step 1.5: Stop Word Identification
  Every word in the sentence plays an important role which appears frequently, such as a few verbs as well as adjectives. The reason behind this is because of the introduction of noise by such words. So, they are noted as gray in the example text shown in Figure 9.7.

- Step 1.6: Parsing the Dependencies
  The relationship between words in a sentence is identified in the step called parsing the dependencies. The main aim is to assign an individual node as a parent to every word in the sentence. The root of the tree is chosen to be the verb and a parse tree is constructed (see Figure 9.8). This also helps us to relate every word in the sentence with another word to help us understand in a better way.

Figure 9.7 Stop word recognition of sample text.

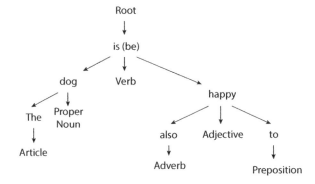

Figure 9.8 Parsing dependencies in sample text.

Figure 9.9 Recognition of noun phrases in sample text.

Non-instructional Word	Instruction	Constraints
"Hey"	"Move", "down"	"25 cm"

Figure 9.10 Input data given to robots.

- Step 1.7: Noun Phrase Identification
  The noun phrases can be grouped together, as shown in the example grouping in Figure 9.9. The main reason for grouping is to simplify the sentence.

  With the above steps, we were able to extract some information from the given document.

  The above steps are for sample text when given as input for robots. Our system mainly focuses on movement of robots and also associated constraints with the movements. Consider the text, "Hey android robot possibly will you move ahead 25 cm then bend down". The data taken as input consist of instructions like "move" and "down" and constraints like "25 cm". The robot takes the input and shows changes in its movement, which is considered as output. The input given to the robot is shown in Figure 9.10. The instructions as well as constraints can be added dynamically to the proposed system for better functioning.

  Input dataset is trained and performed using LSTM to make the robots work in the desired manner according to human instructions.

9.4   Results and Discussion

When the proposed system is implemented it works in the following way:

- Step 1: Text Transformation Using NLP
  The input text given by user is taken as
  "Hey android robot possibly will you move ahead 25 cm then bend down" --------- Input 1

will produce following output:
["possibly will you move ahead 25 cm", "bend down"]

- Step 2: Categorization of Instructions
  Here we give the above instruction to the robot as input and apply LSTM, as illustrated in Figure 9.11.

  We used LSTM here to overcome the drawback of a deep learning techniques named Recurrent neural network (RNN) where most of the words fetched from the sentence are inappropriate, so we introduce LSTM (long-short term memory) which has a "forget" layer that is used to take the input only if it is appropriate or else ignore the word to be forgotten. There are three layers or conditions to be followed in LSTM when there is a massive amount of information to be processed in a dataset. The three states of LSTM are depicted in Figure 9.12.

  LSTM used an activation sigmoid (σ) function According to [1], when LSTM is trained, the model can be used to make a logical decision "yes" or "no" to move to the next state if not deciding to forget the state of input which was used before. Sigmoid gives two values; yes defines '0' and no defines '1'. According to the current state the value has to be multiplied and the output of the already visited state will be determined by how much of each value has to be elapsed, since sigmoid is a non-linear activation function used with tan h function as illustrated in [1].

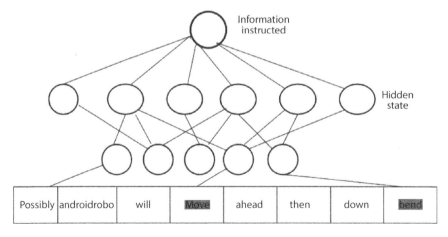

Figure 9.11 LSTM processing information in instructions given to robots (Sentence).

Figure 9.12 States of LSTM.

When a series of input data with expressions that use the remaining gates as update gates and output gates. Whenever there is a process update, the gate takes the count of state value. Deep learning tanh activation function defined as tanh is used to make the value to fall between "yes" or "no" state where the hidden layers which have communicated between input and output layer states increased their cell count according to the communication between each layer. Once the state is updated, a hyper tangent function will evolve to make the procedure based on the input given to get the appropriate results. After the output state, a track no. (T_r) is created as its identity, which is the number of gates according to the stream of input (here we need approx. 5–550 gates). The data are trained according to tanh and sigmoid function which is gathered as input and hidden layer is processed via tensor flow process where the Tr. Number will be converted here after the input is processed. Now, class will be identified according to the process:

Ex: command "move" is categorize as class 1 and "Bend" as class 2
Now
input: ["move ahead 25 cm", "bend down"]
output: [1, 2]
For example, the expression "move ahead 25 cm" and the expression "move behind 25 cm" have 2 factors, which are "ahead/behind" and "cm/km".
Results as

Table 9.1 Instruction and categorization of instruction accuracy for user input.

Input of raw text	25	23	21	15	11	7	5
Message classification precision (%)	80.7	81.5	90.1	88.9	91.1	80.1	92.3
Gates required	550	550	550	550	550	550	500
After process precision (%)	84.7	84.7	78.9	76.4	82.8	95.7	74.7

Table 9.2 Instruction and categorization of instruction accuracy for gates.

Input of raw text	10	10	10	10	10	10	10
Message classification precision (%)	80.7	81.5	90.1	88.9	91.1	80.1	92.3
Gates required	2700	2000	1500	700	250	25	10
After process precision (%)	76.7	74.7	68.9	66.4	72.8	85.7	64.7

Table 9.3 Single instruction insertion precision.

Words as instruction	Track no. (Tr.)	Verified Tr	No. of corrected constraints	No. of track	Precision (%)
Move	25	25	25	25	100
Ahead	17	17	17	17	17
Possibly	11	11	11	11	99
behind	7	7	7	7	56.6
bend	5	5	5	5	100
left	3	3	3	3	33.7
End	1	1	1	1	64.5

input: ["move ahead 25 cm", "bend down" and [1, 2]
output: [[1, 15], [1, 100]] C.

- Step 3: Post-Processing of Data
  This process receives the track id (T_r) and message classification id and deciphers robot actions based on the activities

Table 9.4 One expression translation.

Raw text input with one expression	Conversion
"hey android robot ahead"	set out incessantly ("ahead");
"hey android robot move ahead"	set out_incessantly ("move ahead");
"hey android robot amplify tempo to 8 m/s"	set_amplify_m(5);
"hey hey android robot amplify tempo to increase to 6 km/hr"	set_tempo_km(6);
"hey android robot tempo 8 cm/s"	set_tempo_cm(8);

the movements have been monitored. Table 9.1 depicts the instructions and categorization of data accuracy for user input; Table 9.2 indicates how instruction and categorization of instructions works for gates; Table 9.3 depicts how the proposed system works when a single instruction is inserted; and Table 9.4 indicates how translation occurs if one expression is used as input.

The Table 9.3 defines the single instruction insertion precision where there are various words given as instructions and to identify the instruction track number is provided. Once the assigned track number is verified the number of constraints which are in corrected form from the given words are measured along with the precision value. Based on the precision highest value the choice of words have been noticed.

9.5 Conclusion

The proposed system presented in this chapter takes three steps to make the robot move in the desired manner. An LSTM approach makes the system stand out from other existing systems and also makes the robot respond immediately. The instructions given by humans are preprocessed and categorized and finally post-processing enables robots to respond in an appropriate manner. The dynamic nature of the proposed system allows it to include instructions and constraints at any time, which is advantageous to how the system works; therefore, the corresponding robot movement also varies. Our future work will be extended by incorporating a cost function to help the system work in an optimized fashion.

References

1. Abadi, M., Barham, P., Chen, J., Chen, Z., Davis, A., Dean, J., Devin, M., Ghemawat, S., Irving, G., Isard, M. *et al.*, Tensorflow: A system for large-scale machine learning, in: *OSDI*, vol. 16, pp. 265–283, 2016.
2. Chai, J. and Li, A., Deep Learning in Natural Language Processing: A State-of-the-Art Survey, in: *IEEE Xplore*, 06 January 2020, Beijing Normal University, Hong Kong Baptist University United International College, Division of Business and Management, Zhuhai, China.
3. Chandhana Surabhi, M., Natural language processing future. *2013 International Conference on Optical Imaging Sensor and Security (ICOSS)*, 06 January 2020, IEEE EXplore.
4. Yao, L. and Guan, Y., An Improved LSTM Structure for Natural Language Processing. *IEEE Xplore*, Qingdao No.2 Middle School, Qingdao, China, 15 April 2019, April 2019.
5. Nigam.V., Natural Language Processing: From Basics to using RNN and LSTM, in: *A detailed introduction to all the concepts prevalent in the world of Natural Language Processing,"Towards data science"*, May 17, 2019.
6. Chiu, J.P. and Nichols, E., Named entity recognition with bidirectional LSTM-CNNs, *Transactions of the Association for Computational Linguistics*, arXiv preprint arXiv: 1511.08308, 4,2016, 357–370, 2015.
7. Ling, Y., Hasan, S.A., Farri, O., Chen, Z., van Ommering, R., Yee, C., Dimitrova, N., A Domain Knowledge-Enhanced LSTM-CRF Model for Disease Named Entity Recognition. *AMIA Jt Summits Transl. Sci. Proc.*, 2019, 761–770, 2019.
8. Cho, K., van Merrienboer, B., Gulcehre, C., Bougares, F., Schwenk, H., Bengio, Y., Learning phrase representations using RNN encoder-decoder for statistical machine translation, in: *Conference on Empirical Methods in Natural Language Processing (EMNLP 2014)*, 2014.
9. Rambabu, D., Naga Raju, R., Venkatesh, B., Speech Recognition of Industrial Robot. *Int. J. Comput. Math. Ideas*, 3, 2, 92–98, 2011.
10. Norbeto Pires, J., Robot-by-voice: Experiments on commanding an industrial robot using the human voice. *Ind. Rob.: An International Journal*, 32, 6, 505–511, 2005.
11. Fezari, M. and Bousbia Salah, M., A voice command system for autonomous robots guidance. *International Workshop on Advanced Motion Control, AMC*, 2006, pp. 261–265, 2001, 10.1109/AMC.2006.1631668.
12. Wu, Y., Schuster, M., Chen, Z., Le, Q.V., Norouzi, M., Macherey, W., Krikun, M., Cao, Y., Gao, Q., Macherey, K., Klingner, J., Shah, A., Johnson, M., Liu, X., Kaiser, L., Gouws, S., Kato, Y., Kudo, T., Kazawa, H., Dean, J., Google's Neural Machine Translation System: Bridging the Gap between Human and Machine Translation, arXiv:1609.08144, 2, 1–23, 2016.
13. Sutskever, I., Vinyals, O., Le, Q.V., Sequence to sequence learning with neural networks. *Process. Adv. Neural Inf. Process. Syst.*, 2, 3104–3112, 2014.

14. Scheutz, M., Cantrell, R., Schermerhorn, P., Toward Humanlike Task-Based Dialogue Processing for Human Robot Interaction. *AI Mag.*, Winter 32, 4, 77–84, 2011.
15. Levesque, H.J., The Winograd Schema Challenge. Department of Computer Science. University of Toronto, Canada, 2011.
16. She, L., Cheng, Y., Chai, J.Y., Jia, Y., Yang, S., Xi, N., Teaching Robots New Actions through Natural Language Instructions. *The 23rd IEEE International Symposium on Robot and Human Interactive Communication*, Edinburgh, Scotland, August 25–29, 2014.
17. Sutherland, A., Bensch, S., Hellström, T., Inferring Robot Actions from Verbal Commands Using Shallow Semantic Parsing. *International Conference on Artificial Intelligence, ICAI'15*, Department of Computing Science, Umeå University, Umeå, Sweden.

10

AI, IoT and Robotics in the Medical and Healthcare Field

V. Kavidha[1], N. Gayathri[2]* and S. Rakesh Kumar[2]†

*[1]Department of Computer Science and Engineering, National Engineering College,
Kovilpatti, Tamil Nadu, India
[2]School of Computing Science and Engineering, Galgotias University,
Greater Noida, India*

Abstract

AI-enabled robotics-based coaching systems have demonstrated results in complex treatment areas such as joint replacement, behavioral health, and spinal surgery. AI technology shows adequate promise in advancing treatment and provable outcomes across a range of conditions. Data-driven strategic partnerships and joint ventures are expected to continue their prominence, with industry leaders redefining their methods to improve business and partnerships to maintain an aggressive advantage in an outcome-driven new health economy [1]. IoT devices are also managing the sudden sprint to user-centric environments for increasing application in self-monitoring, rather than health services being offered in hospitals and offices alone. This goes hand in hand with the perception of telehealthcare with devices ranging from wearables to communication devices and wireless monitoring services. The main benefit of robotics, AI and IoT for patients is expediency and quick access to vital information and avoiding emergency situations such as the time-saving monitoring of vital signs at home versus finding the time to go to a doctor.

Keywords: Artificial intelligence, robotics, internet of things, patients, machine learning

*Corresponding author: n.gayathri@galgotiasuniversity.edu.in
†Corresponding author: rakesherme@gmail.com

Ashutosh Kumar Dubey, Abhishek Kumar, S. Rakesh Kumar, N. Gayathri, Prasenjit Das (eds.) AI and IoT-Based Intelligent Automation in Robotics, (165–188) © 2021 Scrivener Publishing LLC

10.1   Introduction

Robotics, Artificial Intelligence (AI), and the Internet of Things (IoT) will infiltrate the healthcare system. Machines will not only assist, but in many circumstances, will substitute for humans as caregivers, medical service providers, diagnosticians and expert decision makers. In so doing, they will generate a number of novel issues for Canadian health law and policy. The appropriate application of existing law, the need for new laws and the formation of wise policy choices require our early attention in order to ensure beneficial uses of robotics, AI, and the IoT [2, 3].

Robots are already automating various physical tasks traditionally carried out by healthcare professionals, such as lifting, suturing, delivering goods, administering medications, monitoring vital signs, tracking patients, and assisting with mobility. Kinova, a Montreal-based robotics company, has developed robotic arms that increase the mobility and independence of wheelchair users. The Smart Tissue Autonomous Robot (STAR) is already outperforming human surgeons at suturing incisions. Transcending the physical, AI is achieving measurable success in carrying out various intellectual tasks in the fields of psychotherapy, medical diagnostics and decision-making elements of healthcare that historically were within the exclusive domain of human clinical experts. For example, IBM Watson, a cognitive supercomputer designed to glean meaningful information from countless sources of structured and unstructured medical information, is able to diagnose lung cancer with a success rate of 90%, significantly outperforming human doctors' 50% success rate. After scouring more than 20 million journal articles, an impossible task for human experts, Watson was recently praised for correctly diagnosing a rare form of leukemia in a patient whose doctors had misdiagnosed her. Health benefits are not limited to sophisticated supercomputers. Robotics, AI and the IoT were used in designing PARO, a small social robot in the form of a baby seal that responds to human touch and noises, which was shown to improve the well-being and social interaction of elderly patients who were exposed to it.

These early successes prefigure the anticipated impact that robotics, AI and the IoT will have in the coming decades on the healthcare system, its many industries, professionals and caregivers, as well as the patients and family members who use them. At the same time, various features of robotics, AI and IoT will create emerging challenges for healthcare, requiring careful reflection on the appropriate bounds of delegating human tasks and decision-making to machines. In addition to their potentially huge impact on labor markets, robotics, AI, and the IoT will force us to rethink several traditional legal and moral concepts, including liability, responsibility, and redress [4, 5]. Thus, as we march down the road to automation, it is worth taking stock of the various robots, AI and IoT technologies currently deployed and under development in the health sector. Doing so will help us identify, anticipate, and better understand some of the social, legal, and policy challenges that these technologies are generating.

10.2   A Survey of Robots and AI Used in the Health Sector

This section provides a survey of various categories of robotics, AI and IoT used in the healthcare setting. Although the level of uptake and impact of the technologies described below remains uncertain, this snapshot will help foreshadow the social, legal and regulatory issues.

10.2.1   Surgical Robots

Surgical robots are perhaps the most well-known robots in use in the medical sector. Robotic surgery is proliferating in medical centers eager to position themselves as leaders in cutting edge treatment. At the same time, questions remain about the effectiveness and overall cost benefit of robot-assisted surgery. Trading proximity for precision, the surgeon uses computer-assisted vision, joystick-like controls and advanced 3D imaging technology to guide the da Vinci's robotic arms through small incisions in the patient's body. The system's control algorithms enhance the surgeon's expert abilities by filtering out hand tremors and allowing for more complicated and precise movements than would be possible by human hands alone. While these control algorithms are the catalyst to better than human surgical capability, they simultaneously mediate the doctor's relationship with her/his own expertise, as a kind of third party whose operations are beyond the surgeon's control. For example, the integrity of a surgery could be undermined by a bug in the algorithm or "biases" in the software that presume certain machine responses are appropriate when they are not. Telesurgery could also be hacked. The technological challenge is to find ways to allow the machine to correct for human imperfection while, at the same time, allowing the human operator to maintain control in the case of a machine malfunction. This is a more general aim of robotics, AI and IoT, with humans and machines working symbiotically to achieve results that neither could achieve alone [6].

Figure 10.1 depicts a surgical robot with the da Vinci arm and similar teleoperated surgical systems, the surgeon is meant to dictate the

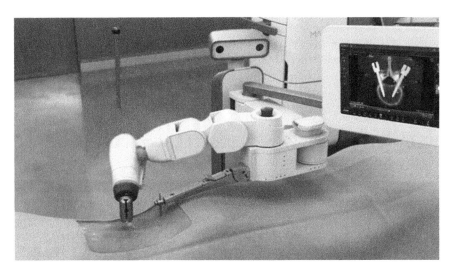

Figure 10.1 Surgical robot.

procedure and its outcome. The robot merely assists the surgeon in carrying out her/his task. More recent innovations however have generated robots that are meant to perform autonomously and the robots carry out procedures from start to finish without human intervention. Significant research and development on autonomous surgery is underway. For less complicated procedures like laser eye surgery, knee replacements and hair transplants, automated surgeries of these sorts are now possible. Already much progress has been made in autonomous soft tissue surgery. The STAR robot described in the introduction can stitch a pig's small intestines using its own computer vision, tools and AI to carry out the procedure without human help. It is already performing with greater precision than human surgeons. As autonomous robotic surgery continues to advance and success rates continue to increase, there will be increasing pressure on surgeons to relinquish control to the machines [7, 8].

10.2.2   Exoskeletons

The robotics, AI and IoT ideal described above is no more evident than in the recent development of wearable robotic systems used to rehabilitate, restore and enhance human mobility. Lower body robotic exoskeletons like the Ekso are being used for gait rehabilitation of stroke and spinal cord injury patients. The magical interplay between the Ekso's AI/algorithms and its robotic hardware allows physically disabled patients to move without human help, increasing independence, accelerating strength development and reducing the physical toll on human rehabilitation therapists. This fascinating merger of humans and machines is not limited to the therapy setting. People with mobility disorders are now using exoskeletons quite successfully as alternatives to wheelchairs. The ReWalk Personal and the Indego Personal have met the safety standards required by the FDA for all day use at home and in the community. As these machines are more broadly adopted like canes, crutches and electric wheelchairs, robotics, AI and IoT will become further normalized [9, 10].

As in many robotic technologies under development, it is possible to tweak exoskeletons, like the one in Figure 10.2, initially designed to restore human function in a therapeutic context in ways that ultimately augment human function beyond typical human performance capabilities. Consequently, physically assistive wearable robots are also being created for able-bodied users to enhance their strength and mobility. In the healthcare setting, medical applications such as Cyberdine's HAL have been developed to enable smaller framed healthcare workers to safely and easily lift and move patients without strain. Although such applications have very practical benefits, it is important to realize that the commercial development of non-therapeutic exoskeletons creates the possibility of a shift away from traditional restorative medicine in favor of an enhancement-based approach, the aim of which is to make those who can afford it better than well. Although this vision smacks of Dr. Tony Stark's "Iron Man," it in fact raises serious policy considerations associated with resource allocation in the healthcare system.

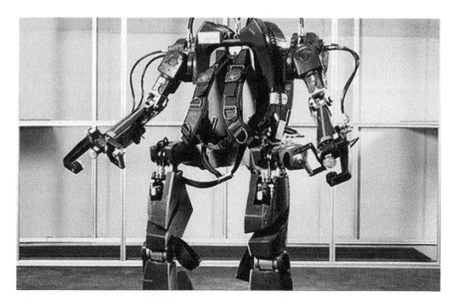

Figure 10.2 Robotics exoskeletons.

10.2.3   Prosthetics

Prosthetics raise similar concerns. The possibility of prosthetics as enhancements emerged at least a decade ago when Oscar Pistorius, a Paralympic cum Olympic athlete, was subject to scrutiny by the International Association of Athletics Federations. At issue was whether "the fastest man on no legs" was "too able" when running on his Össur bionic legs. Although Pistorius (an elite athlete endorsed by Nike to the tune of US 2 million dollars per year) could easily afford several pairs, the same is not true of the broader community of amputees, many of whom might also prefer performance enhancing rather than merely therapeutic prosthetics. The healthcare system will continue to feel pressure as more people demand enhancement quality hip and knee replacements and the like [11, 12].

There have been significant technological advances in prosthetics in past decades. For amputees, smart robotic prosthetics, like the DEKA Arm System, that can be controlled through MG signals sensed in the amputee's own muscles, are now being developed. Similar systems are being developed for prosthetic hands, as shown in Figure 10.3. These systems will use implanted electrodes to measure prosthesis control signals from muscles and motor nerves and will provide sensory feedback to the amputee via electrodes implanted in sensory nerves. This will allow for a more "natural" human control of the prosthetics and better integration with the body.

Currently, most smart prosthetics use Bluetooth and other device-based connectivity rather than wireless networks to support these interactions. Soon, however, cloud computing and the so-called IoT will drive robotic

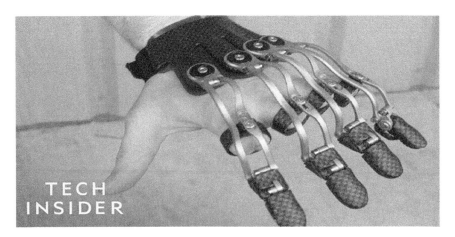

Figure 10.3 An example of robotic prosthetics.

devices of this sort. Much in the same way that the internet currently uses various software protocols to link communications devices, our expanding networks will increasingly permit the connection of bodies and other physical objects. These objects will be embedded with electronics, software, sensors, processors and actuators, allowing novel forms of cybernetic interactions between biological and non-biological entities. Many of today's exoskeletons and prosthetics are already internet enabled and this tendency towards greater connectivity is sure to increase. This will of course raise a series of issues relating to privacy and information security. Devices with wireless capabilities are prone to being hacked, and protocols and standards will be required to minimize the possibility of such interference. As discussed below, former Vice President Dick Cheney realized this need in 2007 when he became worried that his heart implant would be subject to a denial of service attack. The application of data protection and privacy laws will also have to be refined in response to the enormous amounts of health data transmitted between such devices, our bodies, device makers and healthcare providers. These issues are not novel, but the sheer magnitude of data and the serious consequences of breaches will require careful attention [13, 14].

10.2.4   Artificial Organs

Like other implantable technologies, artificial organs like those depicted in Figure 10.4 give rise to hacking, information-security and failure concerns. They also raise novel issues for health law and policy by virtue of their location inside the human body. With artificial organs, patients' bodies are now being driven by life-sustaining software that resides inside of them but is entirely beyond their control. The software is most often proprietary, meaning that some company owns it (usually treating its source code as a trade secret). The patient's use of the device is strictly regulated by the terms of an end user license agreement (EULA). As a result, manufacturers are able to adopt the controversial business models used for mass marketing consumer goods known as planned obsolescence and vendor lock-in (think Apple's iPhones and iPads). By regularly requiring software updates, or by developing new hardware that is not forward/backward compatible, EULAs permit the possibility of serious injustice.

Will a patient's damaged bionic knee be replaced if her/his lifestyle did not comport with the User Manual? Will the warranty for a cochlear implant be void if the CI is plugged into peripheral devices made by competitors? While courts have yet to make any such pronouncements, existing Terms of Service agreements provide clear answers to these questions (respectively;

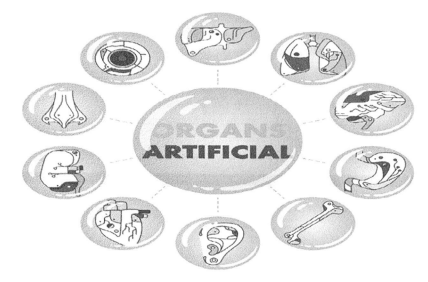

Figure 10.4 Examples of artificial organs.

"no" and "yes"). These one sided, take it or leave it contracts are becoming the rule, and device manufacturers the rule makers. Consumer protection legislation will not provide an easy fix for this. Law reform in the health sector is necessary to protect patients who are dependent on these devices and yet do not own or control the software that drives them.

10.2.5 Pharmacy and Hospital Automation Robots

Robots are also driving changes in hospitals and pharmacies. In an effort to cut costs, hospitals are taking cues from the manufacturing sector and using robots to increase efficiency. Autonomous delivery robots are being used for intra hospital deliveries of medicine, meals, linens and equipment, freeing up time for nurses and support staff to take on other tasks. Delivery bots like TUG, RoboCourier and HOSPI, are programmed to intelligently navigate hospital corridors and avoid obstacles [15].

Figure 10.5 shows that robots are also encroaching on the traditional role of pharmacists as large robotic systems like ScriptPro, ROBOT-Rx and RIVA are able to autonomously compound and dispense drugs. These machines can increase the number of prescriptions that can be completed in a day and reduce human error in those tasks. Scientists and engineers are working on automating other complex and specialized medical procedures like embryo vitrification, a highly technical and cumbersome operation in

Figure 10.5 Outpatient pharmacy automation.

the processing of embryos that are then frozen for subsequent IVF pro-cedures. Robots are also being designed to replace healthcare workers performing needle-based procedures [21–23]. The Veebot system is being developed to fully automate venipuncture procedures used to draw blood from patients and could help reduce many needlestick injuries common among healthcare workers. Another emerging class of robots in this cate-gory is disinfection robot devices that can eliminate human error during the disinfection process (e.g., surgical and other reusable medical equip-ment) and thus reduce infections. While the introduction of robots into hospitals and other care facilities may result in greater overall efficiency, it also generates new risks. Robots have the capacity to do physical harm. They might one day also have the capacity to eliminate entire categories of the healthcare workforce [16].

10.2.6   Social Robots

Many robots used in healthcare will have social attributes, interacting with patients to provide companionship, therapy and an extended ability to mon-itor vital signs and other health-related functions. As robots become better able to mimic human facial gestures, voices, expressions, language and emo-tions, people will increasingly develop social bonds with them. This in turn will establish the kind of trust necessary for the delegation of certain tasks and decision-making previously carried out by human caregivers and doc-tors. Robots are already being designed to optimize interaction with demen-tia and autism patients, providing the optimal level of social engagement to facilitate learning, companionship and in some cases increasing the capacity for independence among those patient populations [17].

Another strategy for imbuing robots with sociality involves telepresence. Telepresence robots are semi-autonomous robots that can be remotely operated but can also carry out some operations on their own (Figure 10.6). The purpose of these robots is to give a sense of presence both to the teleoperator and those co-located with the robot. These robots use telecommunications to monitor health and provide support services to outpatients and others in need of care, without tethering them to an institution. The physical embodiment of these robots usually includes a body made of plastic and metal and a "face" (usually a screen that projects the face of the distant operator). The Giraff, a European made telepresence robot targeted at elderly populations, uses a variety of smart home sensors to measure patients' blood pressure changes and detect when they fall down. It also has a Skype-like interface to connect the patient with caregivers and relatives.

Social robots do not need all of these bells and whistles. Some of the most effective social robots to date are much simpler machines. Perhaps the most well known of these is PARO, a socially assistive companion robot that resembles a baby seal. PARO is, in essence, an animated "sniffle" that uses tactile, light, auditory, temperature and posture sensors to perceive people and react to its environment. PARO allows the documented benefits of animal therapy to be administered to patients by reducing stress, promoting relaxation and stimulating interaction between patients and caregivers [18–20].

Figure 10.6 Educational robots.

10.2.7   Big Data Analytics

Today's medical information technologies are generating truly staggering quantities of unstructured data, ushering in an era of information overload. From Fitbits and medical imaging to electronic patient records and peer-reviewed scientific studies, it has become impossible for health care professionals to analyze all of the relevant data in a way that gleans useful, actionable information. Neuroimaging alone was estimated to have generated 10 petabytes of data in 2017, (the equivalent of 3.3 billion pictures on an iPhone). The amount of data generated globally tends to double every 12 to 14 months. Even with the aid of conventional computing techniques, this information overload presents an intractable problem. Thankfully, sophisticated AIs such as IBM Watson are finally starting to make a serious dent in the big data problem [24].

As we have seen, Watson already outperforms human diagnosticians. Like other big data analytics AIs, Watson is essentially a sophisticated computer program. However, its design differs from conventional computing approaches in a way that raises unique legal and ethical challenges since it uses machine learning to excel at its diagnostic tasks. Watson is programmed to "ingest" vast quantities of unstructured medical data and related medical literature, and "learns" how to perform a diagnosis under the directed tutelage of human expert diagnosticians who train it using question-answer pairs and reinforcement learning. Once the human experts declare that Watson has reached a certain level of proficiency at the task, it is deemed expert enough to go into production. Just like human experts, Watson undergoes periodic "training updates," reading the latest curated sets of information, and answering more questions under supervision designed to test its new knowledge. Compared to conventional computer programs, Watson is less like a tool, and more like a medical student always learning new medical information and occasionally making discoveries that would astonish an attending supervisor.

In addition to its growing success as a diagnostician, Watson is also being trained to help people navigate complex health institutions, identifying personalized treatments by analyzing patient and genomics data, and improving cancer treatment recommendations. Watson's early successes are only the beginning. Google has plans to enter the world of healthcare AI with its own DeepMind technology. As previously stated, the need for big data analytics are changing the role of human experts in the world who will need to grapple with the complexities of working alongside their emerging AI counterparts.

10.3   Sociotechnical Considerations

In addition to those issues previously discussed, robotics, AI and IoT raise or amplify a number of traditional medical ethics issues, including disagreements about treatment decisions, access to healthcare for vulnerable populations, medical error, informed consent and substitute decision-making. Though these issues are important and worthy of mention, this section focuses instead on three particular sociotechnical considerations that arise alongside an increased interaction between humans, robotics, AI and IoT in the healthcare setting: (i) Sociotechnical Influence; (ii) Social Valence; (iii) The Paradox of Evidence-Based Reasoning.

10.3.1   Sociotechnical Influence

It is well known that technology can have a significant influence on the people who use it. It can introduce new modes of thought and action, while simultaneously eliminating others. Robotics, AI and IoT can potentially influence traditional modes of medical practice by shifting the manner in which healthcare practitioners understand evidence, engage in scientific reasoning, and execute decision-making processes and protocols, as IBM Watson demonstrated when it discovered the right leukemia diagnosis in a case that had stumped doctors for months. Also, they may well become agents of change, capable of suggesting novel interpretations or approaches previously unconsidered. As some scholars have described it, the implementation of health technology is a process of mutual transformation in which the organization and the system transform each other. Since this can lead to good or bad outcomes, it will be important to better understand these transformative processes in order to inform and implement the most beneficial modes of robotics, AI and IoT policy.

Consider for example a very different technological transformation that led to a tragic outcome with a system called the Therac-25. After use of this popular radiation therapy machine was well established, a malfunction of the machine's radiation sensors resulted in massive radiation overdoses in six patients. The operators trusted the "all is normal" messages that the machine delivered even after observing clinical symptoms to the contrary. The trust that operators had developed for the Therac-25 caused them to disregard contradictory evidence. This example illustrates the need for designers, health professionals, practitioners and policy makers to reflect critically on the mediating influence that technologies are capable of exerting when determining how best to integrate them into well-established healthcare practices. Among other things, there is a need to be careful not to put too much trust in robotics, AI and IoT to unduly project onto these machines superior intelligence, reliability or objectivity.

Even if robotics, AI and IoT one day outperform human clinicians and healthcare practitioners in tasks and decision-making, it will still be important to develop checks and balances that ensure more than just beneficial outcomes. We must avoid the risk that robotics, AI and IoT be treated like oracles of previous times that humans unquestioningly relied upon to their detriment. In related contexts, such as autonomous vehicles or autonomous weapons, laws and policies under consideration would require meaningful human control of those systems by keeping humans in the decision loop. Canadian health law and policy will eventually need to confront similar considerations for healthcare workers and their patients.

10.3.2   Social Valence

One novel form of sociotechnical influence is that robots and machines tend to have social valence. The popular image of robots, after all, is not one of prosthetics, artificial organs or hospital automation, it's of mechanical people. True to the popular imagination, social robots are often designed to promote anthropomorphism, the psychological tendency to treat inanimate objects as though they have human qualities thus blurring the line between human and instrument. Anthropomorphic design increases our tendency to blur that line. Some human robot interaction experts believe that this suggests a new ontological category of beings. Robots are not persons but neither are they merely toasters. Our tendency to think of robots as possessing some form of agency is gaining currency. Anthropomorphic design appears to be useful in psychology research, where pediatric patients are often willing to trust psychotherapy robots to a greater degree than human adults, suggesting that robots might be better at providing therapeutic interventions with certain patient populations.

Although anthropomorphic design is already providing obvious therapeutic benefits with robots like PARO, it is important from a policy perspective to continue to ask the question: "When is it appropriate to substitute machines for human caregivers?" Although robots may provide vital and effective support, they are not a panacea to the problems generated by an aging population. Likewise, it is important to appreciate how easily anthropomorphic design can be used to influence perceptions of trust and the underlying trustworthiness of technologies, opening the door to manipulation by those who develop or employ the robot. As the sociality of these machines becomes more sophisticated, Canadian health law and policy will need to pay attention to the risk of manipulation through the use of social and companion robots especially when they are interacting with vulnerable populations.

Of course, machines need not be anthropomorphic to generate social valence. Consider the seemingly simple implantable cardioverter defibrillator (ICD) used to shock a potentially deadly cardiac arrhythmia into a normal heartbeat. After receiving painful and unexpected shocks from this small implanted device, some recipients report fears that their device might decide to shock them again, while others see their ICDs as their protectors. Researchers describe this perceived agency as stemming from the ICD recipients' perception that the device has them in a state of persistent surveillance. Like the prison guards in Foucault's famous panopticon, the ICD is perceived to exert a constant though unverifiable power over its host, the consequences of which come unexpectedly and swiftly whenever the recipient's heart steps out of line. Other researchers have gone even further, making a strong case for understanding the ICD as a moral proxy, an entity that makes a number of deeply moral decisions on the patient's behalf by virtue of its design. In an increasing number of cases, there are good reasons for understanding the robot as having its own ontology. For example, it may one day make more sense for judges assessing liability to treat an AI as an expert rather than merely as a tool used by experts. But we can also slip into careless thinking about the ontological nature of robotics, AI and IoT, thereby come to entrust them with tasks and decision-making though they are in fact unreliable or unsafe. We saw this in the case of the Therac-25.

10.3.3   The Paradox of Evidence-Based Reasoning

Evidence-based reasoning will be a key practice in ensuring that robotics, AI and IoT are functioning safely and appropriately and will also be an important safeguard in our critical reflections about the more general sociotechnical influence that robotics, AI and IoT have on the healthcare system. Perhaps the central role that evidence-based reasoning will play, however, is to assist with policy determinations about whether, or under what circumstances, it is appropriate and permissible to delegate human tasks or decision-making to robotics, AI and IoT in the first place. Figure 10.7 shows how the question of whether to substitute machines for humans in any given instance requires an evidence-based perspective: if there is good evidence to suggest that a particular action produces the most favorable outcome, then that action is the most justifiable one. Similarly, if the evidence demonstrates that a robot is better at producing beneficial outcomes and is equally cost effective, then it becomes more difficult to reject

Figure 10.7 The six As of evidence-based practice.

the idea that the use of the robot evidence-based reasoning provides a normative pull.

Although the requirement of evidence seems straightforward and obvious, it becomes much more complicated with robotics, AI and IoT. As we described above in discussing Big Data Analytics, IBM Watson and other AIs employ machine learning. This means that these AIs have the ability to do things that they were not explicitly programmed to do. This novel form of agency allows AIs to change and adapt their operations when exposed to new data, transcending their own programming. Consequently, the developers of such programs will not always be able to predict, foresee, or immediately comprehend what the AI will do in the future. As long as the AI is functioning well and its evidentiary track record is successful, this is of little concern. Problems will arise, however, when things go wrong. This is because general responsibility, accountability and liability standards require explanations when harm results.

Thus, even in situations where the robotics, AI and IoT has a vastly superior performance record compared to a human expert and there is good reason to delegate the task or decision-making to the machine, there is now a new problem when it comes to assigning responsibility or liability when things go wrong. Unlike our more traditional product liability regimes where the product can be characterized as defective owing to the manufacturer's negligence, which in turn can be understood to have caused the harm in the case of machine learning (and possibly other AI techniques), there is no equivalent defect. This is because the AI was not explicitly programmed to perform in any one particular way. Developers of Machines will in many cases be unable to provide a traditional causal explanation of the AI's behavior based on their programming inputs. The complexity of the massive informational inputs combined with the machine's ever-shifting learned behaviors break the traditional causal links between the programmers' inputs and the system's behavior. It would likely be equally or more difficult to demand an account from the healthcare administrators and professionals who adopted the AI.

Here we are confronted with a paradox: the normative pull leading to a decision to delegate to the robotics, AI and IoT, namely, evidence-based reasoning generates a system in which we now have no straightforward evidentiary rationale for explaining the outcome generated by the AI. This will create significant problems in the assessment of liability. Ironically, medical malpractice law may escalate this paradoxical result. In areas where AIs outperform human healthcare providers without mishap, the looming threat of negligence law will pressure hospitals and other healthcare providers to adopt these technologies, generating an AI monoculture where exclusive AI decision-making undermines the further attainment of human medical knowledge. This could become a very serious problem and is but one of the many legal considerations that robots and AI will require.

10.4   Legal Considerations

10.4.1   Liability for Robotics, AI and IoT

It is extremely likely that delivering care using robotics, AI and IoT will in some instances cause harm. Establishing liability in such cases will present novel legal issues. For example, in the case of the AI medical diagnostics discussed above, negligence claims against the AI will require determination of who (or what) counts as a medical expert, and decisions about how to deal with robot evidence in situations where it is unlikely that a human expert understands how or why the robot did what it did. For now, as discussed in the two subsections that follow, accountability will likely be an issue only for doctors and hospitals using AI, robotics and IoT, rather than for the AI, Robotics and IoT themselves. As noted above, this is because traditional product liability law is likely inapplicable in the case of robotics, AI and IoT, which are designed to be autonomous or have emergent characteristics.

Liability for medical malpractice is grounded in negligence law. A successful claim requires that the defendant be found to owe a duty of care to the plaintiff. Could a robot owe a duty of care to a patient? Or could its manufacturers or developers? As explained above, the development of a trust relationship is the underlying strategy in the emerging field of social robotics. Indeed, it is the functional glue in human–robot interaction. It is therefore possible to imagine that one day proof of a sufficient relationship between human and machine could lead to a duty of care being ascribed to the robot, its manufacturer or the software developer.

Even if we reach a point where we treat robots as though they owe duties of care, the standard of care aspect of the negligence claim would give rise to strange and difficult questions about whether robotics, AI and IoT are even capable of apprehending and following standards of care requirements that usually apply only to members of an interpretive community. Such considerations lead us back to some of the foundational questions briefly mentioned above: Is a robotics, AI and IoT to be understood as an instrument, a person or some intermediate form of agency? Along these lines, one might also ask: Could robotics, AI and IoT owe duties or be expected to adhere to standards of care as are other inanimate entities like hospitals? Conversely, are robots capable of being rights-bearing entities, or are there ever pragmatic reasons for treating them as such? As anthropomorphic lines continue to blur the distinction between robot and person, these may one day become actual legal and policy issues in the healthcare context. For now, such considerations are speculative and fanciful. They are interesting but also distracting. The remainder of this section focuses instead on more mundane but crucial legal considerations that need to be resolved in the short term.

10.4.2   Liability for Physicians Using Robotics, AI and IoT

Medical negligence claims against a doctor can be of two very different sorts. The first sort is the more typical case where it is alleged that the physician was negligent in delivering care. The second involves cases where the physician failed to obtain the patient's informed consent to the proposed medical treatment or intervention. The lawsuits against doctors using the da Vinci robot mentioned previously, provide a clear example of the first sort of lawsuit. But robots and Us can also be implicated in cases where the physician failed to obtain the patient's informed consent. In such cases, the general duty of care that physicians owe to patients includes a duty to disclose to the patient all material information relating to the proposed treatment. In the context of untested or experimental therapies, a higher level of disclosure is required than for established therapeutic treatments. An important policy consideration, therefore, is whether the use of robotics, AI and IoT, in cases where their operations are autonomous or their outcomes are emergent, should be understood as experimental. If so, their use would attract the more onerous standard of disclosure. In such instances, physicians would, for example, be required to disclose not only that they are consulting robot diagnosticians but also to fully inform patients of the robot's diagnosis and recommended course of treatment. This would include disclosure of options the physician may have chosen not to pursue. Similar considerations would arise with autonomous robots used to carry out surgical or other care-related procedures. Cases where there is a discrepancy in approach or outcome between the doctor and robot could undermine trust between physicians and patients regarding the best course of treatment.

As suggested above, another important question that will arise relates to the standard of care applicable when physicians use robotics, AI and IoT in the course of treatment. The current approach is tempered when it comes to assessing whether an emerging technology is part of the required standard of care or not. AI and healthcare robots certainly have not yet found their way into common use and, as such, a physician who chooses to use them now will risk challenges in establishing the reasonableness of such decisions: Thus, a certain level of caution is required in the initial decision of whether to use robotics, AI and IoT, though this may be less significant in hard medical cases, where even the best diagnostician or surgeon is up against significant uncertainty or unlikelihood of success.

The luxury of nearly a century of hindsight provides an established line of evidence-based reasons to the contrary. For starters, x-rays have clearly become a technology of common usage. By current standards, it is practically inconceivable for a physician not to consult an x-ray or some other form of imaging in her/his diagnosis of a broken bone. Only time will tell whether it will be equally inconceivable to imagine a medical diagnosis or a surgical procedure to be made by a human alone without the help of a robot or IT AI history may very well repeat itself: like the x-ray machine, the appropriate use of robotics, AI and IoT may need to be litigated in court many times before similar human biases and prejudices give way to seeing it as a standard component of treatment.

10.4.3   Liability for Institutions Using Robotics, AI and IoT

One way of imposing institutional liability is through the device of vicarious liability, holding hospitals or other care facilities liable for the actions of their employees. The question of whether a robot could ever be considered by law to be an employee will reinvigorate a number of the foundational questions discussed previously and would have tremendous implications in the fields of labor and economics that go beyond the scope of this chapter. That said, one could easily imagine the development of targeted legislation that stipulates strict or vicarious liability for the robotics, AI and IoT when used in certain ways by hospitals or other care facilities. One could imagine, for example, holding hospitals liable for sending a patient home with a faulty exoskeleton that causes injury, or as a result of an autonomous robotic procedure run amok.

Whether to carve out such liability regimes is in fact part of a broader set of legal and policy considerations concerning the appropriate scope of liability for hospitals and other care facilities. The traditional view, which still holds much currency today, is that hospitals remain primarily responsible for providing a location and support staff for physicians to practice. However, fundamental changes to our healthcare system mean that the hospital is no longer merely a place where a doctor treats patients but a sophisticated facility designed to provide a plethora of services from a wide variety of health professionals. Indeed, the provision of care services in the coming decades is more likely to be distributed among a wide array of care locations, including the home. As care robots begin to populate these other spaces, will it still be reasonable to maintain the claim that a care facility is a mere location where competent human personnel provide treatment? When a patient receives tele or virtual care, should they not expect safe and reliable medical treatment, irrespective of whether it is delivered by fleshy or mechanical hands? Courts seem to have already recognized this in principle: The provision of a wide range of medical services is thus an integral and essential part of the operation of a modern, general hospital. This is so regardless of the way in which the hospital has structured its relationship with the professional personnel who provide those services. It is medical care that is sought by the patient; and it is proper medical care that should be provided. The primary responsibility for the provision of this medical care is, in my opinion, that of the hospital, and the hospital cannot delegate that responsibility to others so as to relieve itself of liability. It would therefore seem wrongheaded if a hospital or other institution could escape liability in such situations simply by delegating the medical task to a robot rather than a human.

10.5 Regulating Robotics, AI and IoT as Medical Devices

The final legal consideration in this chapter focuses on the regulation of robotics, AI and IoT as medical devices. This approach to regulating medical devices is pre-market, seeking to ensure that their interactions with people and their bodies are proven safe and effective before such devices are allowed to go to market. The Food and Drugs Act and Food and Drug Regulations govern most medical technologies employed in Canadian healthcare. The Food and Drugs Act defines a "device" as: an instrument, apparatus, contrivance or other similar article, or an in vitro reagent, including a component, part or accessory of any of them. for use in (a) diagnosing, treating, mitigating or preventing a disease, disorder or abnormal physical state, or any of their symptoms, in human beings or animals, (b) restoring, modifying or correcting the body structure of human beings or animals or the functioning of any part of the bodies of human beings or animals, (c) diagnosing pregnancy in human beings or animals, (d) caring for human beings or animals during pregnancy or at or after the birth of the offspring, including caring for the offspring, or (e) preventing conception in human beings or animals.

From this definition one immediately sees that the current regime may not cover many of the medical enhancement devices discussed, which are not therapeutic in nature. Likewise, while the current regime works for traditional hardware-based medical devices driven by pre-programed software, it is not well suited for devices whose operations are autonomous or emergent by virtue of machine learning and other AI techniques. Such devices by their very nature will make it impossible to comport with a section of the regulations, which specifically states that: if a medical device consists of or contains software, the software shall be designed to perform as intended by the manufacturer and the performance of the software shall be validated. As we have seen, it is possible with complex AI that software performance is not always capable of validation in the traditional sense. Either these laws will require reform, or else many beneficial health innovations in the years to come will not be allowed to go to market. The larger point is that this regime is not meant to protect beyond basic safety and efficacy in the narrowest sense. For example, the regulations are not sufficiently flexible to ensure the safety and efficacy of robotics, AI and IoT that learn and adapt as they go. Furthermore, the current regime does not address any of the ethical or sociotechnical concerns enumerated above. This is in part because the regime is premised on the idea that medical devices are purely mechanical.

As we have seen, the introduction of emergent characteristics and social valence will move us far beyond this realm. We are slowly accepting the idea that we are not Newtonian, stand alone and unique agents; rather we are informational organisms, mutually connected and embedded in an informational environment, which we share with other informational agents, both natural and artificial, that also process information logically and autonomously. We shall see that such agents are not intelligent like us, but that they easily outsmart us, and do so in a growing number of tasks. We stand on the precipice of a society that increasingly interacts with machines, many of which will be more akin to agents than mere mechanical devices. If so, our laws need to reflect this stunning new reality. Treating machines imbued with artificial intelligence merely as tools reduces them to something quite other than what they are; it strips them of a legitimate descriptive richness in order to fit them into comfortable metaphors which suggest established categories of liability even though those categories may no longer be fitting. By doing so we sacrifice accuracy for tradition, precision for metaphor. Although this makes regulation appear more straightforward, it actually undermines the safety and efficacy that such laws were initially designed to achieve.

10.6 Conclusion

The rise of robots and AI in healthcare is part of a larger effort to leverage technology in order to meet increasing demand and provide more accessible and efficient healthcare services. As we have seen, our current social, legal and policy frameworks are insufficient to deal with a number of issues that will arise. Canadian health law and policy can either support the development of beneficial robots and AI or impede it. Moving forward, decisions about the uptake, permissible use and regulation of robots and AI in the healthcare setting will require some careful juggling of multiple balls in the air but only two hands to guide them. There will always be the risk of under- and over-regulation, either of which could impact human flourishing. It is therefore crucial to develop clear social, legal and policy frameworks that minimize risks, so that hospitals and the broader public might enjoy a range of benefits that could only be delivered by a co-robotic healthcare system.

References

1. Alston, P., Lethal robotic technologies: The implications for human rights and international humanitarian law. *J. Inform. Sci.*, 21, 35, 2011.
2. Broadbent, E., Stafford, R., MacDonald, B., Acceptance of healthcare robots for the older population: Review and future directions. *Int. J. Soc. Robot.*, 1, 319–330, 2009.

3. Smarr, C.A., Prakash, A., Beer, J.M., Mitzner, T.L., Kemp, C.C., Rogers, W.A., Older adults' preferences for and acceptance of robot assistance for every-day living tasks, in: *Proceedings of the Human Factors and Ergonomics Society Annual Meeting*, pp. 153–157, 2012.
4. O'Reilly, R.C. and Munakata, Y., *Computational explorations in cognitive neuroscience: Understanding the mind by simulating the brain*, MIT press, Cambridge, 2000.
5. Yang, G.Z., *Robotics and AI Driving the UK's Industrial Strategy*, UK, Ingenia, 2017.
6. Andreu Perez, J., Poon, C.C., Merrifield, R.D., Wong, S.T., Yang, G.Z., Big data for health. *IEEE J. Biomed. Health Inf.*, 19, 1193–1208, 2015.
7. Ravi, D., Wong, C., Deligianni, F., Berthelot, M., Andreu Perez, J., Lo, B. *et al.*, Deep Learning for Health Informatics. *IEEE J. Biomed. Health Inf.*, 4–21, 21, 2017.
8. Chen, Z., Jia, X., Riedel, A., Zhang, M., A bio-inspired swimming robot. *Robotics and Automation (ICRA), 2014 IEEE International Conference on*, pp. 2564–2564, 2014.
9. Ohmura, Y. and Kuniyoshi, Y., Humanoid robot which can lift a 30kg box by whole body contact and tactile feedback, in: *Intelligent Robots and Systems, 2007. IROS 2007. IEEE/RSJ International Conference on*, pp. 1136–1141, 2007.
10. Kappassov, Z., Corrales, J.A., Perdereau, V., Tactile sensing in dexterous robot hands Review. *Rob. Auton. Syst.*, 74, 195–220, 2015.
11. Arisumi, H., Miossec, S., Chardonnet, J.R., Yokoi, K., Dynamic lifting by whole body motion of humanoid robots, in: *Intelligent Robots and Systems, 2008. IROS 2008. IEEE/RSJ International Conference on*, pp. 668–675, 2008.
12. Asada, M., Towards artificial empathy. *Int. J. Soc. Robot.*, 7, 19–33, 2015.
13. Zhang, L., Jiang, M., Farid, D., Hossain, M.A., Intelligent facial emotion rec-ognition and semantic-based topic detection for a humanoid robot. *Expert Syst. Appl.*, 40, 5160–5168, 2013.
14. Mavridis, N., A review of verbal and non-verbal human robot interactive communication. *Rob. Auton. Syst.*, 63, 22–35, 2015.
15. Kruse, T., Pandey, A.K., Alami, R., Kirsch, A., Humanaware robot naviga-tion: A survey. *Rob. Auton. Syst.*, 61, 1726–1743, 2013.
16. Mochizuki, K., Nishide, S., Okuno, H.G., Ogata, T., Developmental human-robot imitation learning of drawing with a neuro dynamical sys-tem, *in: Systems, Man, and Cybernetics (SMC), 2013 IEEE International Conference*, pp. 2336–2341, 2013.
17. Oudeyer, P.Y., Socially guided intrinsic motivation for robot learning of motor skills. *Auton. Robots*, 36, 273–294, 2014.
18. Chan, M.T., Gorbet, R., Beesley, P., Kulic, D., CuriosityBased Learning Algorithm for Distributed Interactive Sculptural Systems, in: *Intelligent Robots and Systems (IROS), 2015 IEEE/RSJ International Conference on*, pp. 3435–3441, 2015.

19. Virgillito, M.E., Rise of the robots: Technology and the threat of a jobless future. *Labor Hist.*, 58, 240–242, 2017.
20. Colombo, M., Why build a virtual brain? Large scale neural simulations as jump start for cognitive computing. *J. Exp. Theor. Artif. Intell.*, 29, 361–370, 2017.
21. Nagasubramanian, G., Sakthivel, R.K., Patan, R., Gandomi, A.H., Sankayya, M., Balusamy, B., Securing e-health records using keyless signature infrastructure blockchain technology in the cloud. *Neural Comput. Appl.*, 1–9, 2018.
22. Kumar, S.R., Gayathri, N., Muthuramalingam, S., Balamurugan, B., Ramesh, C., Nallakaruppan, M.K., Medical Big Data Mining and Processing in e-Healthcare, in: *Internet of Things in Biomedical Engineering*, Elsevier Academic Press, US, pp. 323–339, 2019.
23. Dhingra, P., Gayathri, N., Kumar, S.R., Singanamalla, V., Ramesh, C., Balamurugan, B., Internet of Things–based pharmaceutics data analysis, in: *Emergence of Pharmaceutical Industry Growth with Industrial IoT Approach*, pp. 85–131, Elsevier, Academic Press, US, 2020.
24. Alzubi, J.A., Manikandan, R., Alzubi, O.A., Gayathri N. and Patan, R., A Survey of Specific IoT Applications. *Int. J. Emerg. Technol.*, 10, 1, 47–53, 2019.

11

Real-Time Mild and Moderate COVID-19 Human Body Temperature Detection Using Artificial Intelligence

K. Logu[1]*, T. Devi[1], N. Deepa[1], S. Rakesh Kumar[2] and N. Gayathri[2]

[1]*Saveetha School of Engineering, Saveetha Institute of Medical and Technical Sciences, Chennai, India*
[2]*School of Computer Science and Engineering, Galgotias University, Uttar Pradesh, India*

Abstract

Day by day, COVID-19 cases are increasing all over the world. Without a proper vaccine to control the disease, the only solution so far is social distancing and identifying the disease at an early stage. In more than 80% of confirmed cases there are only mild symptoms, like fever; therefore, we have to check the body temperature of people in public places like shopping malls, hotels, airports, schools and universities, etc. In this chapter we propose contactless temperature (CT) measurement utilizing thermal (TS), RGB, and 3D sensors. We also propose a fever location camera (FLC) which gives high-quality estimates from up to 2 or 3 meters away. Using cutting-edge technology, the fever location framework (FLF) estimates the internal heat level of individuals in groups of three or four by checking and filtering their face temperatures. If a high temperature is identified, the framework sounds an alarm or cautioning message, which has propelled face recognition technology. The framework, which is based on the investigation of face temperature, guarantees high-quality estimations. Using facial recognition (FR) likewise limits false readings; for example, an individual carrying a hot beverage. Using a devoted programming stage, a signal can be set to inform us of unusual temperatures. It can precisely recognize the facial temperature (FT) of numerous

*Corresponding author: klogu786@gmail.com

Ashutosh Kumar Dubey, Abhishek Kumar, S. Rakesh Kumar, N. Gayathri, Prasenjit Das (eds.) AI and IoT-Based Intelligent Automation in Robotics, (189–204) © 2021 Scrivener Publishing LLC

individuals quickly, with an exactness of ≤ 0.3 °C. Temperature recognition range can be set with the ideal location of up to 3 meters in the framework highlighted by a bi-directional double-channel (infrared light + visible light) camera utilizing a heated sensor and low level interference signals.

Keywords: Contactless temperature (CT), thermal sensor (TS), RGB, fever location camera (FLC), fever location framework (FLF), facial temperature (FT), facial recognition (FR)

11.1   Introduction

The World Health Organization (WHO) has called COVID-19, previously known as "2019 novel coronavirus," a pandemic. A supported effort is needed to stop the further spread of the disease. A pandemic is defined as "an epidemic occurring over a very wide area, crossing international boundaries, and usually affecting a large number of people." In the spring of 2009, a novel influenza A (H1N1) virus emerged. On 31 December 2019, the World Health Organization was formally notified about an outbreak of pneumonia spreading from Wuhan, the capital of Hubei province in China. In January 2020, a decline in new cases of the disease, called the 2019 novel coronavirus, and tests from cases and evaluation of the disease's fundamental characteristics showed what had taken place behind the scenes. This epic disease was named Coronavirus Disease 2019 (COVID-19) by WHO in February 2020 [1]. The SARS-CoV-2 virus is the cause of COVID-19.

Artificial intelligence (AI) is increasingly being used to build suitable machines to perform tasks that normally require human intelligence. Automated reasoning is an interdisciplinary science with various perspectives, and sorts of progress in AI and essential learning are uncovering an improvement in setting in practically every division of technology. Man-made adroit cutoff (AI) is a rapidly moving new unforeseen development, made possible by the Internet, that may in a short time impact our standards a little at a time. Artificial intelligence mimics the human brain, which can learn, reason, plan, see, or structure fundamental language. These attributes of AI have huge budgetary possibilities, while also introducing unique money-related challenges. As an AI-enabled Internet is being developed, the Internet Society sees that understanding the odds and loads related with AI is essential to designing an internet that people can trust. As AI is used essentially capably as a sensational piece of the time in things and relationships, there are some fundamental issues concerning customers' trust in the internet. Two or three issues must be taken into account when applying artificial intelligence, including its money-related impacts; issues of trustworthiness, propensity, and commitment; new uses for data, security, ethical issues; and how AI reinforces the development of new ecosystems. In the near future, there are express challenges facing the ever-changing field of AI which must be addressed, including enhancement of interpretability for better verification and trustworthiness; data quality and desirable design; recommendations relating to growth and security; assessments concerning obligations; and possible dangerous repercussions for social interactions and budget planning.

The age of artificial intelligence (AI) has arrived, and is transforming the way we live. Improvements made possible through the internet combined with AI have improved our standard of living. These advances, which are central to improving standard of living and ethical issues, apply AI for various cutting-edge applications. Industry's interest in AI is rapidly growing, and governments are attempting to fathom what the improvement could mean for their environments [2]. The social implications of "big data" and the improvement of the Internet of Things (IoT) has created the perfect area for new AI applications and relationships. Artificial intelligence is beginning to be used in applications such as human diagnostics, treatment support, transportation, open security, service robots, and service sector will continue to be applied in more fields, and will continue to be applied in more fields in the coming years. Next to the internet, AI changes the ways we experience the world and can be another engine to address money-related unexpected turn of events.

11.2 Contactless Temperature

Every object releases electromagnetic radiation, and the range and intensity of this radiation generally fluctuates with temperature. The zenith of heat radiation is usually around close to infrared frequencies. For bodies close to room temperature, the peak radiation is around 10 μm. As the temperature of the body goes up, the peak also decreases and the intensity of the transmitted radiation gets shorter. Precisely when an object's temperature reaches about 800 °C, it begins to glow red. By and by, the peak of the heat radiation expands and moves into the prominent frequencies. Perceiving the transmitted radiation of an object explains contactless temperature estimation [3]. An achieving energy saving and human-centered intelligent control. Therefore, many researchers have been studying thermal comfort measurements for indoor environments in recent decades. Many methods were generated, including the questionnaire survey method, environmental measurement method and contact measuring method of human body physiological parameters. In recent years, the semi-contact measuring method and contactless measuring method for human body physiological parameters were also generated. For example an infrared sensor was fixed on the frame of eyeglasses in order to measure skin temperature

Contact and non-contact temperature estimations is major to paying extraordinary psyche to flourishing, security and quality issues in a wide level of affiliations [4]. The use of thermometers to evaluate temperature has been around for a long time and it is the second normally an exceptional bit of the time outlined physical absolute after time. Various fields, including standard, mechanical, clinical, design, quality control, and maintenance, unequivocally depend upon cautious temperature estimations. They provide a huge amount of information such as the condition of a machine, screens that monitor weather temperature and pattern, and help single out icing conditions for flight planning and agribusiness. Positive temperature checks ensure that systems are working dependably and flawlessly, thereby improving quality, increasing security, allowing greater leeway in making decisions and reducing time. Temperature measurement falls into two categories: contact and non-contact. In contact thermometers, contact sensors measure their own temperature. Contact thermometers measure temperature using the heat transfer phenomenon known as "conduction." They require physical contact with the measured object to bring the sensor body to the object's temperature [5]. While in non-contact thermometers, measurements are taken by an infrared sensor which is used to review the temperature of an object by looking at the level of infrared light released.

11.2.1　Bolometers (IR-Based)

The distinguishing feature of a bolometer is its resistance temperature detectors (RTDs), which are sensors used to measure the temperature of material with high heat absorptivity. The Bolometer based on a high-finesse silicon its coated silicon wafer was then broken into small fragments can be surveyed in a manner similar to some other RTDs. The distinctive section is organized to face the object to be surveyed and radiative heat is exchanged between the distinguishing fragment and the object, which impacts the part's temperature [6]. The heat concordance arrived at by the sparkle relies on its emissivity, its Bolometers based on structural data obtained from a sparkle model limit and the heat conductivity between the sensor and its casing. High emissivity, low heat capacity and low heat conductivity of the barrier help to create the affectability and a reduction of the reaction time of the sensor. Bolometers are reliably sensitive to IR frequencies from 14 down to 8 micrometers, normally relating to 250 K to 400 K. They are generally utilized in ear clinical thermometers.

11.2.2 Thermopile Radiation Sensors (IR-Based)

A thermopile radiation sensor (Figure 11.1) is similar to a bolometer in that the temperature change of an absorptive surface is surveyed. However, in a thermopile sensor the absorptive surface includes a thin film on which the "hot" assemblies of a thermopile are found. The thermopile is composed of several thermocouples connected usually in series with hot and cold junctions, which is built on a massive base. By virtue of its low heat limit, the temperature of the layer is sensitive to radiative heat Cooling is s commonly experienced on cloudless nights.

The temperature separation between the film and the sensor base creates a quantifiable voltage over the thermopile by strategies for the thermoelectric impact. A substitute sensor on the base measures its superior temperature.

11.2.3 Fiber-Optic Pyrometers

Fiber-optic pyrometers or "disappearing filament" pyrometers (Figure 11.2) are devices which incorporate optical fiber which is heated by an

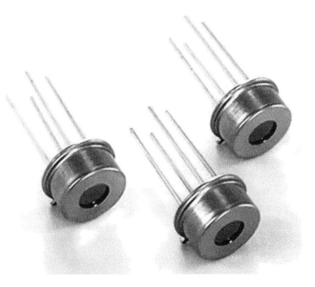

Figure 11.1 Thermopile radiation sensors.

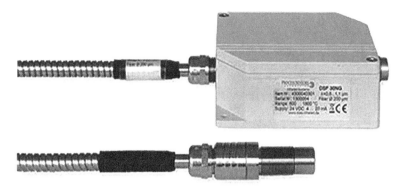

Figure 11.2 Optical fiber pyrometers.

electrical current. Right when the object to be assessed is seen through the optics, the heated and glowing fiber is found in the frontal region. The client changes the current through the fiber until its brilliance "vanishes" away from plain sight. By the fibre is close to the measuring unit corresponds to the fiber optic switch.

In a manner of speaking, the fiber radiates in the same near infrared range (Full body sense of touch or sensation) as the seen object, so the temperatures of the two objects must be indistinguishable [7]. The relationship between fiber current and temperature is known from calibration. An issue with this estimation technique is that the purposeful thing may have a dull emissivity. A pyrometer regularly utilizes two repeated wavelength channels. By then the degree of the wonder of the two frequencies can be utilized to choose the temperature of the object.

11.2.4   RGB Photocell

Color sensor products include both RGB (red, green, blue) sensors (Figure 11.3) and high-accuracy photocell light sensors for precise color measurement, determination, and discrimination. When reflection of light occurs, depending on the surface characteristics of the object the light will either be reflected, transmitted, or absorbed. For example, green paper can absorb both red and blue in varying amounts while reflecting the greenish bit of the range, making it radiate an impression of being greenish to the observer.

Surveying the colors of objects is done in basically two indisputable ways. The most straightforward way is to use a covering to change the light source and a sensor that surveys the strength of the light. Most mechanical masking sensors contain a white light maker and three separate masters.

Figure 11.3 RGB sensor with IR filter.

As expected, there are three blueprints of masking source or concealing channel with top sensitivities at frequencies that we see as red (580 nm), green (540 nm) and blue (450 nm). All hues can be provoked by their parts.

11.2.5   3D Sensor

The cutting-edge 3D sensors (Figure 11.4) associated with the ShapeDrive course of action offer a high one of a kind range concerning the object's concealment and wonder [8]. The sensors pass on trustworthy results for both metallic and glossy surfaces. ShapeDrive sensors perceive even the smallest component features due to their extremely high resolution, as well as large measuring volumes; for example, the entire content of Euro boxes and Euro pallets can be quickly scanned. Simultaneous measurement of signal strength makes it possible to deliver high-contrast grey tone images, which can be used for the detection of data matrix codes and barcodes or contamination on objects with no additional hardware. The 3D sensors are

Figure 11.4 A 3D sensor.

non-contact metrology instruments that can evaluate with high precision anytime. They come in a wide range of standard models with differently sized fields of view (FOV) and working partition.

The 3D sensors adventure a couple of models onto the to be evaluated and record them by techniques [9]. In this manner, the object is digitized as a 3D point cloud. Neither the object nor the 3D sensor is moving, which suggests that separating is driven quickly and effectively.

11.3   Fever Detection Camera

A fever detection camera is used to protect customers and employees from getting the coronavirus. It's focused on the face, so basically the head temperature is measured when customers walk around the store. Thermal imaging cameras can survey people's body temperatures in gatherings in order to find those who have raised temperatures. According to NBC News, more than 11 security companies marketed the technology as a sort of coronavirus detection [10]. Fever is a symptom of COVID-19, the disease caused by the coronavirus. However, there are issues with this technology. According to thermal imaging and virus surveillance experts, thermal imaging is an imprecise method for scanning crowds, and doesn't measure inner-body temperature. These experts also noted that the coronavirus only produces a fever after an individual is infected for days, if there are any symptoms at all. A recent report in Iceland looked at tests taken from a sizable portion of the population and found that 50 percent of all of those who tested positive were asymptomatic.

A thermal imaging camera measures inner-body temperature by scanning people's faces using top-tier sensor technology [14]. The camera can check up to 5 people at the same time for fever. In case an elevated temperature is detected, the system sets off an alarm or even denies access, For example a thermochromic material exhibits a color change when heated, while an electroactive polymer and alarm must generates a mechanical output.

The system is an effective non-contact fully automated solution that provides increased security in areas such as air terminals, health facilities, police stations, schools, businesses, and any large public gathering. The turn-key structure comes pre-configured for fever screening, which makes it ready to run with very little training or planning [11]. The efficient software is intuitive and easy to use so that people can be processed quickly, thereby avoiding bottlenecks and dissatisfied people waiting in lines. The current health crisis introduced by COVID-19 has impelled an increasing number of organizations and businesses to find ways to improve their health security strategies. The proposed system features AI-enabled facial recognition technology and can scan up to 30 people per second and store in excess of 20,000 faces in real-time, identifying them "as known" or "as strangers." The AI scene analytics tool is used to detect scenarios like an individual entering with or without a mask and masks being removed, and assessing the number of people entering a building. The AI Social Distancing tool can recognize if people are maintaining a safe distance from each other by studying real-time video streams from the camera (Figure 11.7). This is all done in real-time with no additional employee required to operate it.

11.3.1   Facial Recognition

Facial recognition is a category of biometric software that maps an individual's facial features mathematically and stores the data as a faceprint. The software uses deep learning algorithms to compare a live capture or digital image to the stored faceprint in order to verify an individual's identity [12]. The software identifies 80 nodal points on a human face. In this context, nodal points are endpoints used to measure variables of a person's face such as the length or width of the nose, the depth of the eye sockets and the shape of the cheekbones. The system works by capturing data for nodal points on a digital image of an individual's face and storing the resulting data as a faceprint [13]. The faceprint is then used as a basis for comparison with data captured from faces in an image or video as shown in Figure 11.8. Despite the fact that the facial recognition system just uses 80 nodal points, it can quickly and precisely identify target individuals when the conditions are favorable. Nonetheless, if the subject's face is partially obscured or in profile rather than facing forward, this type of software is less reliable.

Mobile devices with high-quality cameras have made facial recognition a viable option for authentication and identification. For example, Apple's iPhone X and Xs include Face ID technology that lets users unlock their phones with a faceprint mapped by the phone's camera as shown in Figure 11.9. The phone's software is designed with 3D modeling to restrict being faked by photos or masks, captures and compares more than 30,000 variables. Face ID can be used to authenticate purchases with Apple Pay and in the iTunes Store, App Store and iBooks Store. Apple encrypts and stores faceprint data in the cloud, but authentication occurs directly on the device.

Facial recognition data contains an original facial image and a facial image with augmented features relating to the individual being investigated. Basically, facial recognition helps to verify personal identity by comparing information with a database of known faces to find a match.

11.3.2   Geometric Approach

In the geometric approach for face detection and recognition, the facial action coding system describes all visually discernible facial movement using support vector machines, principal component analysis, linear discriminant analysis, kernel strategies or trace transforms [15]. The geometric component-based frameworks separate and highlight facial landmarks and their geometric relationship. It is also known as the segmentation method.

11.3.3   Holistic Approach

Holistic face recognition utilizes global information from faces to perform face recognition. Various authorities use this technique, in which global information from faces is basically represented by a small number of features derived from the pixel information of face images, in order to find the most suitable match [16]. A couple of strategies tried to use the eyes, a blend of features, and so on. Moreover, some hidden Markov model procedures fall into this category, which are especially known for their application in facial recognition.

11.3.4   Model-Based

Model-based face recognition constructs a model of the human face which is able to capture the facial variations in a pictures as shown in Figure 11.5. A picture can be treated as a high-dimensional vector [17]. This method is incredibly useful to describe a particular feature of an image. The model image is isolated from the planned set as shown in Figure 11.6. Then again, way of thinking and working with collection image to deep face recognition.

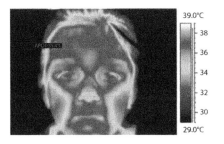 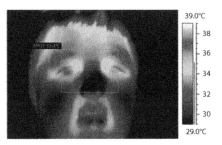

Figure 11.5 Thermal infrared images.

11.3.5   Vascular Network

A facial vascular network is highly characteristic to the individual as shown in Figure 11.12. Facial vein structures provide a unique thermal face signature similar to a fingerprint. In this context, Vascular networks suggest structures of neurons, either normal or phony in nature [18]. Vascular networks can change in accordance with advancing information so the framework creates the best result without hoping to redesign the yield measures. The possibility of Vascular frameworks, which has its establishments in automated thinking, is rapidly getting unmistakable quality in the headway of trading systems.

a) Template Matching
    Template matching techniques are expected to address tests, models, pixels, surfaces, etc. The affirmation work is regularly an association or partition measure.

b) Statistical Approach
    In the statistical approach, the models imparted as features. The affirmation work in a discriminant work. Each image addressed concerning d features. Along these lines, the goal is to choose and apply the beneficial quantifiable strategy for extraction and assessment. There are various quantifiable strategies which are used for facial recognition. These analytical strategies, which are used in two or more social events or working procedures listed below, are listed below.

    – Principal Component Analysis
       One of the most utilized and referred to quantifiable strategies is principal component analysis as shown in Figure 11.10. It is a technique for reducing the dimensionality of large datasets by separating out the principal segment of multidimensional information.

    – Discrete Cosine Transform
       A discrete cosine transform (DCT) expresses a finite sequence of data points in terms of a sum of cosine functions oscillating at different frequencies as shown in Figure 11.11. The DCT depends upon discrete Fourier transform, In this way, dimensional grayscale image with N real numbers to describe the DFT, the same number of numbers you needed to describe the original image.

– Linear Discriminant Analysis
Linear discriminant analysis (LDA) is a method used in statistics, pattern recognition, and machine learning to find a linear combination of features that characterizes or separates two or more classes of objects or events. Not unlike principal component analysis (PCA), LDA attempts to show the distinction between levels. For each level, LDA has a separate projection vector.

– Locality Preserving Projections
In their paper, Xiaofei He and Partha Niyogi [3] discussed locality preserving projections (LPP) as an alternative to principal component analysis (PCA), a linear technique that projects the data to organize and store locations. Model certification estimations generally look for the closest model or neighbors.. Telethermography Devices focus on temperature taking in the return-to-work environment and key challenges and considerations for adapting thermography machines as one of the medical devices.

11.4 Simulation and Analysis

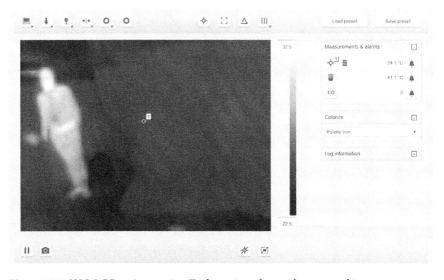

Figure 11.6 YOLO BBox Annotation Tool user interface with annotated image.

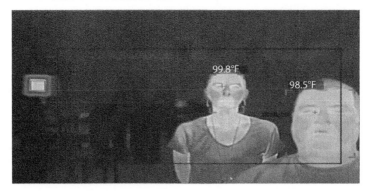

Figure 11.7 Image produced with the IN-DEPTH camera for fever detection.

Figure 11.8 Power heater.

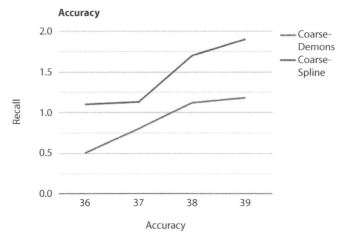

Figure 11.9 Accuracy.

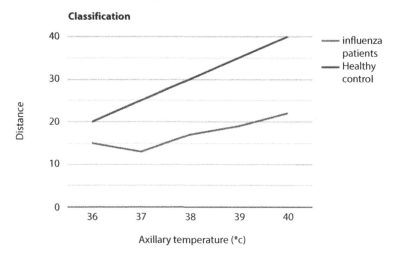

Figure 11.10 Classification.

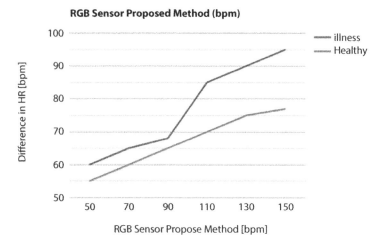

Figure 11.11 RGB sensor proposed method.

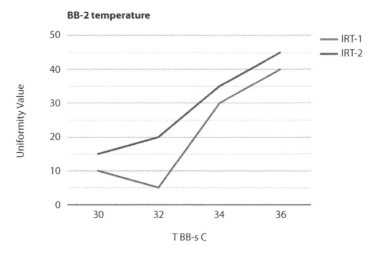

Figure 11.12 BB-2 temperature.

11.5   Conclusion

This chapter presented the basics of a work stream for locating individuals of disease symptoms with a framework that centers around measuring face temperature to guarantee exactness in estimations. Utilizing facial recognition (FR) also limits false-positive readings; for example, an individual conveying a hot beverage. Temperature recognition range can be set with the ideal location separation of up to 3 meters in the framework highlighted by a bi-directional double-channel (infrared light + visible light) camera utilizing a heated sensor and low level interference signals.

References

1. De Jong, J.C., Claas, E.C.J., Osterhaus, A.D.M.E., Webster, R.G., Lim, W.L., A pandemic warning? *Nature*, 389, 6651, 554–554, 1997.
2. Ksiazek, T.G., Erdman, D., Goldsmith, C.S., Zaki, S.R., Peret, T., Emery, S., Rollin, P.E., A novel coronavirus associated with severe acute respiratory syndrome. *N. Engl. J. Med.*, 348, 20, 1953–1966, 2003.
3. Ng, E.Y., Kawb, G.J.L., Chang, W.M., Analysis of IR thermal imager for mass blind fever screening. *Microvasc. Res.*, 68, 2, 104–109, 2004.
4. Lee, C.W., Tsai, Y.S., Wong, T.W., Lau, C.C., A loophole in international quarantine procedures disclosed during the SARS crisis. *Travel Med. Infect. Dis.*, 4, 22–8, 2006.

5. Han, K., Zhu, X., He, F., Liu, L., Zhang, L., Ma, H., Lack of airborne transmission during outbreak of pandemic (H1N1) 2009 among tour group members, China, June 2009. *Emerg. Infect. Dis.*, 15, 1578– 81, 2009. PubMed.

6. Monto, A.S., Gravenstein, S., Elliott, M., Colopy, M., Schweinle, J., Clinical signs and symptoms predicting influenza infection. *Arch. Intern. Med.*, 160, 3243–7, 2000.

7. Surabhi, V., *Automatic Features Identification with Infrared Thermography in Fever Screening*, Doctoral dissertation, Université d'Ottawa/University of Ottawa, 2012.

8. Ring, E.F. and Ammer, K., Standard procedures for infrared imaging in medicine. *Med. Devices Syst.*, 4, 36-1–36-14, Apr 2006.

9. Lahiri, B.B., Bagavathiappan, S., Jayakumar, T., Philip, J., Medical applications of infrared thermography: A review. *Infrared Phys. Technol.*, 55, 4, 221–235, 2012.

10. Rainwater-Lovett, K., Pacheco, J.M., Packer, C., Rodriguez, L.L., Detection of foot-and-mouth disease virus infected cattle using infrared thermography. *Vet. J.*, 180, 3, 317–324, 2009.

11. Huang, L.K. and Wang, M.J.J., Image thresholding by minimizing the measures of fuzziness. *Pattern Recognit.*, 28, 1, 41–51, 1995.

12. Li, C.H. and Lee, C.K., Minimum cross entropy thresholding. *Pattern Recognit.*, 26, 4, 617–625, 1993.

13. Kapur, J.N., Sahoo, P.K., Wong, A.K., A new method for gray-level picture thresholding using the entropy of the histogram, in: *Computer vision, graphics, and image processing*, vol. 29, 3, pp. 273–285, 1985.

14. Otsu, N., Thresholds selection method from grey-level histograms. *IEEE Trans.Syst. Man Cybern.*, 9, 1, 1979, 1979.

15. Yen, J.C., Chang, F.J., Chang, S., A new criterion for automatic multilevel thresholding. *IEEE Trans. Image Process.*, 4, 3, 370–378, 1995.

16. Zack, G.W., Rogers, W.E., Latt, S.A., Automatic measurement of sister chromatid exchange frequency. *J. Histochem. Cytochem.*, 25, 7, 741–753, 1977.

17. Shanbhag, A.G., Utilization of information measure as a means of image thresholding. *CVGIP: Graphical Models Image Proc.*, 56, 5, 414–419, 1994.

18. Mohan, A., Papageorgiou, C., Poggio, T., Example-Based Object Detection in Images by Components. 23, 4, 349–361, 2001.

12

Drones in Smart Cities

Manju Payal[1]*, Pooja Dixit[2] and Vishal Dutt[3]

[1]Academic Hub Ajmer, India
[2]Sophia Girls' College (Autonomous), Ajmer, India
[3]Department of Computer Science, Aryabhatta College, Ajmer, Rajasthan, India

Abstract

The worldview of the internet of things (IoT) is changing physical situations into interactive and smart stages to offer a wide range of creative services upheld by the development of 5G systems. These days, the notoriety of unmanned aerial vehicles (UAVs) is high, and it is normal that, in the coming years, the use of UAVs in everyday life will become much more prominent. These new UAVs utilize novel advances enveloped by the term "internet of things." Today, rambles, or unmanned aircraft systems, are autonomously modified or remotely controlled, either by a remote control or a ground station, and are arranged as organized automated innovations. Tragically, rambles haven't significantly affected rural practices, in any event not up to this point. As of late, there has been a ton of information regarding the matter of automaton applications in horticulture and exactness cultivating. Some noteworthy advances have been created to computerize agribusiness so as to reduce cost and become more beneficial to farmers. The IoT can be used in agribusiness to bolster the design process for small- to large-scale farming. In this chapter, we examine different areas of horticulture and the use of the IoT in these areas. Moreover, recent advancements have repurposed these UAVs for residential applications in different fields. "Smart" rambles is an increasingly modern term, meaning that sensors inside these UAVs feed into a system framework where automatons are associated with different gadgets through internet advances, which empowers correspondence and consequently makes them smart. Farmers can't afford to remain outside this gigantic market.

Keywords: Internet of Things, unmanned aerial vehicles, smart city, information and communication technologies, high-altitude platforms, low-altitude platforms, drones, fifth-generation wireless

*Corresponding author: manjupayal771@gmail.com

Ashutosh Kumar Dubey, Abhishek Kumar, S. Rakesh Kumar, N. Gayathri, Prasenjit Das (eds.) *AI and IoT-Based Intelligent Automation in Robotics*, (205–228) © 2021 Scrivener Publishing LLC

12.1 Introduction

The first drone was introduced by the U.S. Office of Naval Research in a project managed by Elmer Sperry, the founder of Sperry Corporation, a flight navigation control firm. Each since, drones have been implemented for work [1] categorized as dirty, dull, and, dangerous. These types of tasks are also known as the three Ds tasks, and are normally implemented in remote areas [10] sparsely populated by humans. In this way, the impact of drones on the safety and security of individuals was not a huge concern. At present, non-military personnel rambles are becoming increasingly well known among specialists and business visionaries, and with numerous organizations pushing for rambles for conveyance of products and services, the national airspace is expected to be totally redesigned [11]. The Federal Aviation Administration (FAA) requirement of compulsory enrollment of drones is effective in the case of catching violating drones, yet it doesn't provide any preventive arrangements. Moreover, shielding the drones of ordinary citizens from promotion versifies and shielding people and their properties from vindictive automatons is as yet an open issue. Presented below is a brief outline of the various classes and control techniques for drones, followed by the general design of UAV frameworks [10].

12.1.1 Overview of the Literature

There are various types of innovative technologies available for drones [12] that depend on which types of operations are being carried out [2]; however, they are mostly utilized in the military. Nowadays, drones are used in different types of fields like civilian and commercial applications such as crisis management, disaster management, hostile environment, surveillance, search operations, civil security, ad-hoc relay networks, agricultural and remote sensing, wind estimation, traffic monitoring and surveillance, etc. [12]. In addition, one of the most developed areas of drones today is their participation in smart cities. There are some fields available in smart cities like real estate, the market, infrastructure, and communications. The benefits of smart cities apply to everyone, including businesses, citizens, administration, the environment, etc. [3].

The idea of smart cities begins with the innovations required to deliver services more effectively and rapidly to inhabitants. To meet this challenge, drones have a huge capacity for rapidly changing from an advanced plan to the real world, and to assist urban communities by improving areas to live [1]. A drone is also known as an unmanned aerial vehicle (UAV), which is either operated remotely by humans or autonomously fly through programming controlled flight plans. The design of a business ramble mainly consists of the control, information preparing, checking and landing frameworks. The interior framework gives an assortment of capacities extending from routing to information moving to ground transport. Prior to planning an automation for business and ordinary citizen applications, it is essential to make sense of the particulars of certain requirements that must be fulfilled for their proprietors. Park and Dinan thoroughly discussed their structuring of traffic flow optimization in urban areas [4], where the automaton must be progressively solid, with precise route framework, and will most likely be more advanced than other systems. Since urban communities are packed with structures and people, the automatons will be furnished with impact sensors, GPS data (waypoints and routes), and computerized maps.

A smart city is a complicated framework, predominantly composed of information and communication technologies (ICT) targeted towards making the urban communities progressively appealing, increasingly practical, and exceptional spots for development by business enterprises [2]. The significant partners in a smart city include application designers, professional organizations, residents, government and open specialist organizations, inquire about network, and stage engineers. Moreover, the smart city cycle consists of various ICT advancements, improvement stages, upkeep and maintainability systems, community apps, and specialized social and financial KPIs (key performance indicators). Subsequently, IoT frameworks will assume a key job in the arrangement of a huge range heterogeneous foundations [10].

Smart city applications can be categorized based on organize type, adaptability, inclusion, adaptability, heterogeneity, repeatability, and end-client associations [11]. These applications are based on the IoT framework. When all is said and done, these applications can be categorized as individual and home, utilities, versatile, and endeavours. For example, individual and home applications incorporate pervasive e-social insurance services to live independently by means of body area networks (BANs) which help a specialist screen patients remotely [12]. Utilities applications incorporate a decision matrix, smart metering/observing, water monitoring, and video-based reconnaissance. Therefore, versatile applications incorporate intelligent transport systems (ITS) that coordinate traffic control, clog control, and waste management. Furthermore, IoT-based enterprise applications generally comprise a system of things inside a workplace. A few research endeavours have been made to incorporate IoT with smart city conditions. For example, in the far reaching models, conventions and empowering innovations for web-based management of the IoT system in the Padova

Smart City venture. The verification of idea execution with various specialized arrangements intend to screen road lighting, the nature of air and distinguishing proof of most basic issues. A study on the principal IoT components in smart urban communities is presented in [4], which also depicts a contextual investigation on commotion checking. Jeong *et al.* [5] proposed an alternate plan for smart urban communities in which IoT devices were viewed as specialist organizations copying cloud-based services. The proposal offered a more significant level of deliberation to send imaginative universal applications by wiping out the boundaries between physical IoT devices and legitimate (cloud specialist co-ops) universes. A nonexclusive top-down smart city design was proposed in [6] in which specialist co-ops assume the job of focal point data unit that is associated with a lot of IoT-based services. It also offers IoT combined with various ICT advancements for acknowledging smart urban communities [11]. However, since only a few studies exist on IoT and smart urban communities, a combination of these two areas need to be further investigated for thriving IoT-based smart urban areas [10].

The rising number of innovations involving drones are or critical importance to how they are used. Sensors, cameras and GPS receivers are all piece of what's known as "the future of automatons" [9]. IoT services from incredible heights are an additional reality that isn't a long way off; yet there are numerous issues to be settled before the successful utilization of UAVs can be implemented. A lot of these issues involve incorporating security, protection and the board [6].

The uses of UAVs are various, including areas identified as non-military personnel, military, business, and administrative [8]. Models incorporate natural checking (e.g., contamination, plant health, and mechanical mishaps) in the non-military personnel area. In military and legislative areas, we mostly have observation and conveyance applications for the purpose of securing or providing data after a disaster or attack in an area, and to disperse medication or other basic necessities. Business applications center around conveying items and products both in urban and provincial areas [7]. Since UAVs are reliant on sensors, receivers, and programming software, they are considered a feature of the internet of things (IoT), giving a two-path correspondence to applications identified with remote control and observing [6].

The IoT establishes a fast developing frontline condition in which the central idea lies in the organization of an enormous assortment of smart protests so that they can be used and operated comprehensively, either straightforwardly by clients or by extraordinary programming that catches their conduct and targets. The IoT empowers items to become dynamic members of regular exercises, with various promising applications through different correspondence advancements with regards to the "smart city" vision [7]. It was estimated that around 25 billion instantly recognizable objects are predicted to be a piece of this worldwide network by 2020. These projections rely upon considerable implementation of 5G innovations and systems [8].

The IoT objects are becoming increasingly unpredictable, heterogeneous, and exceptionally easy to convey [8]. This change occurs at a cost; the IoT, as a combination of heterogeneous systems, not only has similar security issues to sensor systems, versatile correspondence systems, and the internet, but also brings with it explicit security challenges. As a major aspect of heterogeneous systems, ideas are needed to help propel security ideas such as confirmation, security control, information assurance, classification, digital assault anticipation, and a significant level of approval [9]. These security and protection challenges are not the same as customary internet security issues, since the IoT presents unique challenges in addressing and managing external and internal dangers. In this specific situation, an administrative structure is required for setting and applying rules and approaches in business objects. This system ought to provide guidelines for deciding on techniques that every single business system should provide regarding security and protection such as availability, knowledge activation, and control [12].

12.2   Utilization of UAVs for Wireless Network

12.2.1   Use Cases for WN Using UAVs

The utilization of UAVs as key elements of cutting-edge remote systems comprises one of the most encouraging uses of this innovation. Some of the types of use cases are listed below [10]:

- The first case is the UAV-mounted flying base stations, which involves the total heterogeneous 5G frameworks to upgrade the inclusion and limit of existing remote access technologies [5].
- The second case is the UAV-based drone systems, which permit solid, adaptable, and quick remote associations in open security situations.
- The third case is the UAVs that help earthly systems disperse data and upgrade networks [2].

- The fourth case is the UAVs as flying reception vehicles that can be sent on request to enhance wave interchanges [3], D-arranged multi-input multi-output (MIMO) antenna and gigantic MIMO antenna [1].
- The fifth case gives a reliable IoT uplink connectivity and energy efficiency.
- The sixth case is related to the backhaul of terrestrial networks, which allows reliable high-speed connectivity, agility and cost effectiveness [5].
- The seventh case is related to mobile devices, which use mobile patterns to serve mobile users efficiently.
- The eighth case is related to the users of the wireless infrastructure, which is used for remote sensing, surveillance, package delivery applications, virtual reality cases, etc. [6].
- The ninth case is related to city data, which is used to gather a huge amount of city data in smart city scenarios. It is also used for increasing cellular network coverage.

12.2.2 Classifications and Types of UAVs

The two different ways in which UAVs are classified are by altitude and type as shown in Figure 12.1.

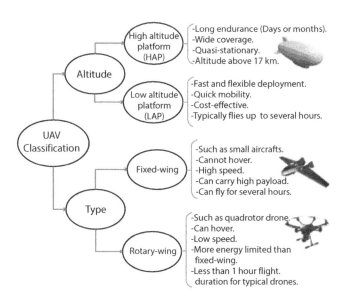

Figure 12.1 Classifications of the UAVs.

1) Altitude: This is the first classification of the UAVs. The altitude is classified into two types – high-altitude platforms (HAPs) and low-altitude platforms (LAPs) [7].

- High-altitude platforms: These quasi-stationary platforms are used in some available applications for wide coverage, long endurance, and altitudes of about 17 km [8].

- Low-altitude platforms: These platforms are available in some available applications for quick mobility, fast and flexible deployment, and are cost-effective and typically file up to several hours.

2) Type: This is the second classification of the UAVs [10]. There are two categories of UAVs – fixed-wing drones and rotary-wing drones.

- Fixed-wing drones: These UAVs are renowned for military and resistance related applications. As shown in Figure 12.2, they simply utilize a wing like a normal airplane to fly. They do not need to exert a lot of energy to stay afloat in the air [11]. Their rigid structure generates lift under the wing due to forward airspeed. Because they use less energy they can fly for a longer time, and are utilized to monitor areas and survey focal points on the ground [11]. They use gas motors rather than electric motors, which increases their flying limit for as long as 16 hours [2]. The disadvantage of these kinds of automatons is that they can't maintain drifting positions, which makes them futile for photography, and they are hard to proper and land. There are various procedures for propelling and handling these kinds of automatons that depend on their size. They can be propelled from a human hand, or a runway might be required if they are too large. They additionally require a higher aptitude level to operate and section point cost [12].

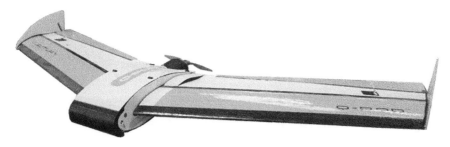

Figure 12.2 An example of a fixed-wing drone.

The DATAhawk and Q200 are two examples of drones consisting of fixed wings that have foreordained airfoil sections (again another variable) which make flight possible by creating lift brought about by the drone's forward velocity. This velocity is as a rule produced by forward push from a propeller being turned by an inside ignition motor or electric engine [1].

There are two types of ailerons in drones: the rudder and elevator [2]. Drones independently rotate around three axes using these ailerons. These axes are opposite to each other. The position of these ailerons is at the drone's center of gravity. The axes are called the lateral axis, vertical axis, and longitudinal axis. The lateral axis is controlled by the elevator; the vertical axis is controlled by the rudder; and the longitudinal axis is controlled by the ailer [5].

- Rotary-wing drones: As shown in Figure 12.3, the wings of these drones have rotors made out of sharp edges that are constantly moving, which produce the wind current essential to move the rudder [10]. In these types of drones, also known as vertical take-off and landing (VTOL) rotorcraft [11] or cancelled VTOL rotorcraft, are ordinarily utilized for operations that need floating flight. They permit a simpler take-off, land heavier payloads, and are more flexible than fixed-wing drones. The most well-known model is the quadrotor helicopter, a multirotor airplane with four rotors that is generally utilized [6].

Figure 12.3 Example of a rotary-wing drone.

Rotary-wing drones consist of 2 or 3 rotor blades that revolve around a fixed mast, which is known as a rotor. These drones come in a wide range of setups, which are listed below [8]:

- A helicopter consisting of one rotor.
- A tricopter consisting of three rotors.
- A quadcopter consisting of four rotors.
- A hexacopter consisting of six rotors.
- A octocopter consisting of eight rotors.

These setups can be further broken down into, for example, a Y6 setup consisting of a tricopter with twin rotors on each arm, one pointing upwards and one pointing downwards, and an X8 consisting of a quadcopter with twin motors on each arm [9].

12.2.3   Deployment of UAVS Using IoT Networks

We consider an area where U resource-constrained IoT devices are sent to regularly monitor and gather data that needs to be processed in a timely manner for proper decision-making. Requests to process the collected data are issued to a set of D UAV-mounted cloudlets, which offer computation offloading services and can serve a maximum of KD IoT devices each. The sets of IoT devices and UAV cloudlets are denoted by U = 1, 2,..., U and D = 1, 2,..., D, respectively [5].

Each IoT device is relied upon to create computational assignments, whereby solicitations of various devices are conveyed to an assigned UAV-mounted cloudlet for handling inside objective idleness limits. Because of the low transmission power, some IoT devices will most likely be unable to come to their particular UAV-mounted cloudlets; along these lines, extra UAVs might be conveyed to serve just as hand-off hubs without being furnished with edge processing capacities. Thusly, in light of the normal interest, a multitude of UAVs are conveyed in 3D space as a completely fit system [6]. Chosen UAVs are furnished with cloudlet assets while others fill in as hand-off hubs to associate IoT devices to their cloudlets. The framework model likewise bolsters situations where a given UAV can fill in as a cloudlet for a lot of IoT devices and as a transfer for different devices. In this instance, we target putting the base number of UAVs in 3D space to deal with all computational outstanding tasks at hand produced by the IoT devices in the system. Each IoT device is related to one of the nearby UAVs indicated as the home UAV that may either hand-off the undertakings to another UAV for calculation or figure the errands locally. The UAV responsible for registering an offloaded task is signified as the cloudlet UAV [10].

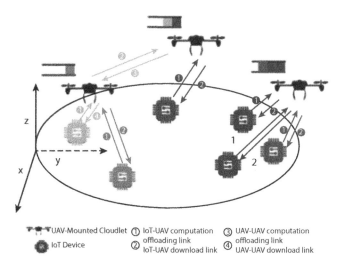

Figure 12.4 Development of UAVs using the IoT.

Figure 12.4 shows a sample network with six IoT devices offloading tasks to three UAV-mounted cloudlets. The device first partners with a nearby UAV to act as its home UAV and uploads its computation workload. After that, the home UAV may compute the tasks locally and convey the results to the respective IoT device upon completion or offload them to another UAV that can deal with the requests. When offloaded to another UAV, the latter computes the task and sends the result back to the home UAV to convey it to the requesting IoT device. For instance, the IoT device in yellow is connected with one UAV; however, the offloaded task is processed by another UAV. The IoT device in blue is, however, served by a nearby UAV that acts as both its home as well as cloudlet UAV [8].

12.2.4   IoT and 5G Sensor Technologies for UAVs

Fifth-generation wireless (5G) technology is relied upon to upgrade mobile broadband, enhance applications that require ultra-reliable low-inertness and extremely high accessibility systems, improve traffic management systems, bolster modern applications, fleet management, logistics, tracking, training, surgery and remote manufacturing [11]. Wireless sensors connected through 5G can be used for smart meters, precision farming, smart agriculture, smart buildings, virtual and augmented reality without range limitations, support of 4K/8K UHD broadcasting, involve enterprises, home and biggest venues offering massive basic machine-type communications (MTC) [2]. The sorts of device interchanges shown in Figure 12.5 can be coordinated with run-of-the-mill human-type communications (HTC) enabled by a 5G designed network [10].

Other 5G use cases that are connected to rambles include computerization and mechanical technology. With the help of 5G systems, automatons have the ability to provide a wide range of applications which provide new advantages to an extensive variety of enterprises [12]. Among the top uses of 5G-empowered automatons are applications identified with development, horticulture, security, law enforcement, fire safety, coast watch, border control, news reporting, utilities, videography, and coordination [2]. Every one of these applications will be attainable since self-governing and view control will be bolstered. So as to empower these use cases, explicit least prerequisites for ethereal vehicles are basic as far as hardware and sensors. The main types of sensor advancements that enable automatons today can be divided into three main classes: (a) flight control, (b) data acquisition, and (c) communication sensors [1].

a) Flight control sensors: These sensors, which evaluate the internal state of accelerometers, are utilized to determine position and direction of the automaton in flight. One

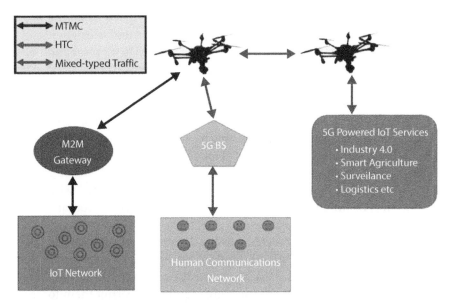

Figure 12.5 Framework of UVAs using 5G.

type of technology senses the micromovement of structures embedded in a small integrated circuit [1]. The thermal sensing technology utilized in accelerometers does not have moving parts, but instead senses changes in the movement of gas molecules passing over a small incorporated circuit [6]. Automatons and UAVs maintain direction and flight ways utilizing inertial measurement units combined with GPS. The inertial measurement units use multi-axis magnetometers (available in one to three tomahawks) [11]. A magnetometer is an instrument that can quantify the Earth's magnetic field. This instrument helps in deciding the direction of a magnetic compass and, thus, of the automaton, which is evaluated in relation to the attractive North. Tilt sensors, along with gyros and accelerometers, provide input to the flight-control system in order to maintain level flight. This is a basic component for UAVs, particularly when the applications require stability (e.g., surveillance, delivery of goods, and so on). Some automatons have engine intake flow and current sensors [5].

These UAVs are controlled with flow sensors to effectively monitor air flow into small gas engines that power some types of drones. These sensors gauge the best possible fuel-to-air ratio at a predetermined engine speed, resulting in reduced emissions and improved power and efficiency. Current sensors are accessible in automatons to monitor and improve power drain and recognize problems in motors or other areas of the framework [6].

b) Data acquisition sensors: Drones are outfitted with a few sensors to collect information required to perform specific errands. Contingent upon the application, the sensor payload contains a suite of instruments used in the advancement of the automatons [5].

For military use cases, UAVs might be furnished with top-of-the-line electro-optical sensors and radar for airborne frameworks [3].

c) Communication systems sensors: These sensors manage and control tasks for UAVs through correspondence frameworks and systems [5]. Because there are different types of automatons, technological advances are required to permit them to speak with one another for security reasons. There are various kinds of correspondences, and most of those utilized in UAVs are recorded. A broad rundown of system conventions and correspondence procedures for nonexclusive IoT devices can be found in reference [12]. In view of the inclusion extend, accessible information rates, and inertness details, it is obvious that 5G innovation would affect automatons' correspondences, enabling a few general applications. In such an applied model, UAVs can shape infrastructure in weaker areas in the IoT and systems engineering, which are deeply interconnected systems for the arrangement for requesting administration; for example, monitoring interactive media gushing [5].

12.3   Introduced Framework

12.3.1   Architecture of UAV IoT

In this method, we concentrate mainly on the security and protection segments upheld by vision-based frameworks [1]. One segment focuses on security, shielding the automaton from aggressors intending to seize it and take control utilizing system and remote channel abuse procedures [12]. A subsequent segment is identified with the security of the payload that fuses propelled encryption and secrecy arrangements. A third PC vision segment is incorporated that offers help and arrangements both for security and protection. This segment presents systems for goal and way confirmation for security, just as conduct examination and scene understanding for protection and wellbeing, individually. Finally, segments for observing and automaton to-ramble correspondence supporting enlistment and directing calculations are a piece of the inserted framework on the versatile IoT gadgets [9].

Non-military UAV systems have three primary components: the unmanned aerial vehicles (UAV), the ground control station (GCS) [11], and the communication link [13]. Additionally, the airplanes consist of an airframe, a propulsion system, a flight controller, and an en-route navigation system, and detect and keep away from framework. All through our review, we just focus on the structure that are applicable to our investigation, and thus consider that the UAV contains a flight controller and a large number of sensors and actuators. There is a high level of engineering in the UAV's framework and its primary components. A concise description of the primary architectures for civilian UAVs is given below [10].

12.3.2   Ground Control Station

Ground control stations allow human administrators to control and also monitor the activities of UAVs. The GCSs change in size depending on the type of activity of the drone. As it were, for recreational smaller than normal and miniaturized scale drone, GCSs are small handheld transmitters utilized by specialists. For strategic and vital automatons, a huge independent office with numerous workstations is utilized as the GCS. A GCS communicates with the automaton by remote control to send orders and constantly gather information, thereby making a virtual cockpit [2].

12.3.3   Data Links

Data links allude to the remote connection of data between the automaton and the GCS. The information that is transmitted depends upon the UAV activity being performed, as shown in Figure 12.6. Automaton missions are arranged and directly transmitted from the GCS to line-of-sight (LOS) missions where control signals can be transmitted through direct radio waves, and beyond line-of-sight (BLOS) missions where the automaton is controlled by means of satellite correspondence or a hand-off airplane which can be the automaton itself [3].

Dependence on a variety of factors will be present by the dependence on common factors; for example, human access, and topographic, spatial, and transient conditions. Below we present some of the current and potential

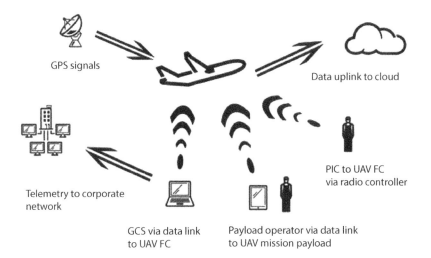

Figure 12.6 Data links.

uses of ordinary citizen rambles, including those that are advantageous and those that are harmful [1].

Figure 12.7 shows some of the types of IoT devices available. These devices are known as heterogeneous IoT devices. They consist of different types of sensors nodes, which are the scalar sensor and multimedia sensor [10]. All sensors have different capabilities. In this figure, the drone is considered the edge server [5]. It performs as a lightweight server and serves one sensor at a particular time. The drone can provide end-to-end connectivity from the sensor to cloud when there is Internet availability or otherwise permit offline accessibility. The data processing is performed at the drone site. The IoT sensor network is used to control the functions. The sensors in this network are considered the nodes which monitor environmental conditions and collect the data; they also collect the actuator devices. Both are used to perform given actions based on the received commands. There are three types of links available as shown in Figure 12.8 [6]:

- Link 1: In this link, sensors are used to collect the data. Then, the collected data is transmitted to the central cloud using

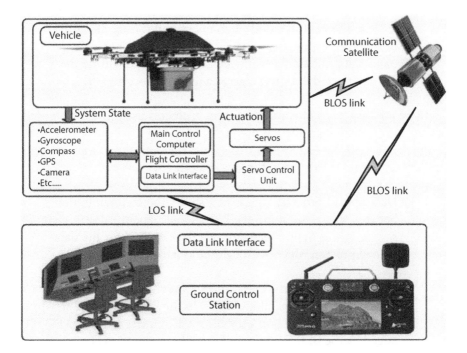

Figure 12.7 Architecture of UAVs.

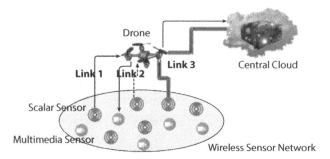

Figure 12.8 Network formed between the wireless sensor network and the drone.

the drone, and when the drone returns to its home location it accesses and processes the retrieved data [1].

- Link 2: In this link, sensors are used to collect data then the data sent to the drone for further processing. Based on the retrieved data, the drone can control the actuator nodes. Since this control is dependent on the recovered data, it is the opposite of Link 1 because no data is transmitted to the central cloud. The drone provides offline data accessibility to the actuator nodes, despite the fact that there is no real-time access to the central cloud [9].

- Link 3: In this link, sensors first collect data and then transfer it to the central cloud in an encrypted format using the drone. The drone only acts as a relay and cannot decrypt data. Data offloading from the drone to cloud can be performed once the drone returns to its home location [8].

There are two types of communication protocols used in the proposed architecture. The first protocol is used to upload data from the sensor node to the drone; and the second protocol is just the opposite of the first, and uploads data from the drone to the sensor node [5].

1) Data upload process: Figure 12.9 shows the communication between the sensor node, the BLE module, and the drone. As shown in this figure, there are two devices used for the data upload process, which are the drone and the BLE module [3].

- First, the drone begins the connection establishment process by sending the connection request to the BLE module [2].
- Second, the connection establishment request is acknowledged by the BLE module, and then the connection is established between the BLE module and the drone [1].

- Third, the BLE module requests data from the sensor node [5].
- Fourth, the sensor node downloads the data in the BLE's local attribute.
- Fifth, the BLE module notifies the drone that it has data to transfer to the drone [2].
- Sixth, the drone sends the attribute read request to the BLE module. If this attribute request is accepted by the BLE module, the drone starts to read the data. It then sends a data acknowledgment to the BLE module, thereby ensuring a reliable link between the drone and BLE module. This process will terminate when the connection between the drone and the BLE module is terminated [10].
- Finally, the BLE module sends a command to the sensor node to save the data until it makes another connection with the drone [1].

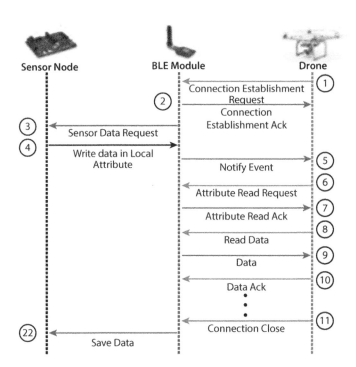

Figure 12.9 Data upload process.

2) Data download process: Figure 12.10 shows the sequence of communication between the sensor node, the BLE module, and the drone during the data download process. There are two devices used in this process, which are the drone and the BLE module [10].

- First, the drone begins the connection establishment process by sending the connection request to the BLE module.
- Second, the connection request to complete the connection establishment process between the BLE module and the drone is acknowledged by the BLE module.
- Third, the drone begins the data download by requesting attribute writing permission from the BLE module of the sensor node [8].
- Fourth, the BLE module acknowledges the drone's request and starts retrieving data from the drone. The BLE module simultaneously sends the command to the sensor node to save those data in flash memory, and the drone receives an acknowledgement that the data was successfully transferred.
- Finally, after the data transfer is successfully completed, the connection between the drone and the BLE module is terminated [9].

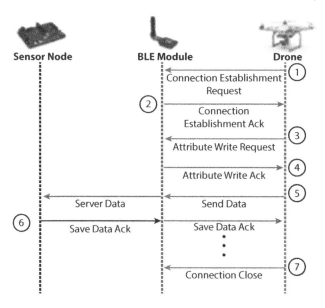

Figure 12.10 Data download process.

12.4   UAV IoT Applications

The implementation of UAV-IoT-enabled frameworks support safe and efficient airspace management with specified rules for drones [1].

The organization of the introduced UAV-IoT structure/design for the protection of automatons enables the creative security applications given below [5].

12.4.1   UAV Traffic Management

Unmanned aerial vehicles (UAVs) sensors have a wide range of roles in various functions. They provide the necessary systems to integrate safely and efficiently into air traffic. For sure, the dramatic development of UAVs over the previous decade and the resulting improvement of business drone's exercises, particularly at low elevation, have started the conversation about automatons' protected activity and secure flight despite expanded air traffic. Unmanned aircraft system traffic management (UTM) is relied upon to oversee drone traffic at low altitudes in airspace, giving a total and exhaustive start to finish administration to collect continuous data on climate, airspace traffic, rambles enrollment, and certifications of automaton administrators between one another (Figure 12.11) [6].

12.4.2   Situation Awareness

The common ground in the situation awareness scenarios that 5G drones [2] will try out is their relevance with the internet of things (IoT), one

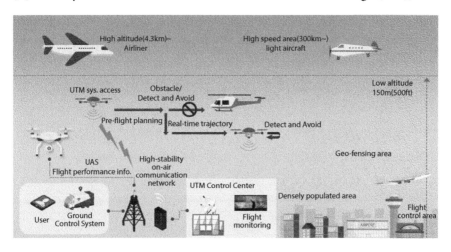

Figure 12.11 UAV traffic management.

of the technological advances behind the 21st century's more disruptive innovations such as smart agriculture and smart city. Outfitting drones with IoT devices allows offering new kinds of services that can only be delivered from the sky. Contingent upon the targeted goals, diverse IoT devices could be considered onboard the drones, including gas sensor, HD camera, humidity/temperature sensor, and so forth [11]. In addition, while UAVs could be sent for a particular strategic activity, such as mail delivery, the on-board IoT devices would provide added value services along with the drones' original tasks. This creates a new ecosystem that bolsters IoT in the sky [10].

In a similar manner, smart agriculture or environmental monitoring situations involve remote inspection and possibly deploying a large number of sensors. The classification of sensor readings by physical site review is a tedious task, whereas if the sensor systems are equipped with networking capabilities for automatic transmission of their readings over a wireless network as shown in Figure 12.12, the radio and core network segments

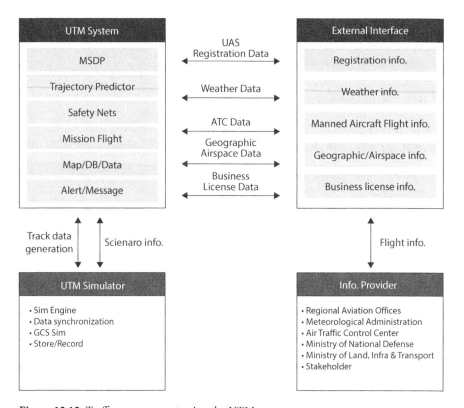

Figure 12.12 Traffic management using the UTM system.

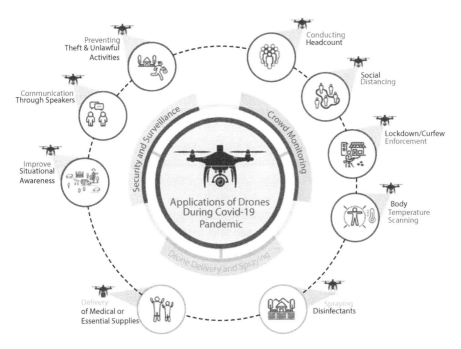

Figure 12.13 Situation awareness.

are subject to significant strain. This is especially true if the sensor density is very large and the network capacity is in short supply [5].

With regards to situation awareness (Figure 12.13), three main scenarios with different network requirements can be identified [12]. The first scenario centers around infrastructure inspection, where the sensing devices are installed onboard the UAV and require the generation and transmission of enormous amounts of information, therefore requiring a high-bandwidth link. The second scenario involves the utilization of UAVs to aid in collecting and transferring data from the sensing devices with communication capabilities deployed on the ground, where the challenge is to deal with the massive amounts of terminal devices. The third scenario centers around location services where utilization of global navigation doesn't apply; for example, indoors and in tunnels [6].

12.4.3   Public Safety/Saving Lives

Natural and man-made disasters destroy environments and put public safety at risk. Included in these are natural disasters such as wildfires, earthquakes, landslides, storms, and tsunamis; and man-made disasters such as chemical, biological, radiological, nuclear or explosive (CBRNE) related events and even terrorist attacks. Under these circumstances, it is difficult and dangerous for relief workers to gain access to regions in order to help. Moreover, catastrophic events can create physical disturbances, which can cause significant damage to urban communities and the vulnerable communications equipment responsible for supporting these areas [2]. Disruptions caused by physical damage to the communications equipment will most likely be unbelievably costly and time-consuming to restore, making it difficult to respond to those impacted by the disaster. Moreover, communication networks will most likely become congested with significant levels of data traffic during disasters as those impacted try to contact loved ones, and hundreds more upload pictures and videos of the damage caused by the disaster, resulting in deterioration of network service, obstruction of new connections, and lost data transmission [5].

Therefore, estimating the damage and providing help in these circumstances must be quick and effective. UAVs can play a vital role here as they are able to assume roles to help relief workers where manned vehicles fall short. To begin with, UAVs can be utilized to take high-resolution images and perform 3D mapping in large-scale disasters such as earthquakes, flooding and rapidly spreading fires to identify hotspot areas that have incurred the most damage and transfer the information in real time to organize relief efforts. The utilization of UAVs provides more cost advantages and faster response times than traditional methods. The utilization of UAVs is less expensive, quicker, and safer than manned aircraft. Also, UAVs can provide high-resolution images and satellites cannot (Figure 12.14) [3].

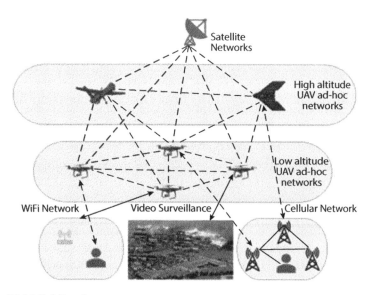

Figure 12.14 Public safety.

UAVs outfitted with thermal cameras can be utilized to quickly locate casualties of disasters no matter the time of day, and especially during nighttime operations. More ground can be covered quickly and efficiently with a swarm of UAVs. Moreover, HD live stream can be transmitted to a bigger monitor to more easily spot subjects in real-time. This permits pilots or command crews to direct rescue teams to the exact location of their subjects, and the aerial view aids in steering those teams around any obstacles or dangers that might be in their way. When a subject has possibly been spotted, zoom cameras can be utilized to assess their well-being to analyze the gravity of the situation and ensure that the rescue teams have the necessary equipment to recover their subject safely [4].

12.5   Conclusion

The concept of smart cities begins with the combination of innovative systems required to deliver services more effectively and rapidly to inhabitants. For this challenge, drones have a great ability to assist in the planning of urban communities to rapidly transform the lives of their inhabitants for the better. An unmanned aerial vehicle (UAV), commonly known as a drone, is either remotely controlled by a human or can fly autonomously using a programming controlled flight plan. The design of a business ramble mainly consists of the control, information preparing, checking and landing frameworks. The interior framework provides a range of abilities extending from route to information move to ground. Prior to planning an automaton for either business or ordinary citizen applications, it is essential to understand the particular needs of the user or proprietor. Park and Dinan thoroughly discussed the structuring of traffic flow optimization in urban areas [4], where the automaton must be progressively solid, with precise route framework, and will most likely be more advanced than other systems. Since urban communities are packed with structures and people, the automatons will be furnished with impact sensors, GPS data (waypoints and routes), and computerized maps.

References

1. Shenoy, J. and Pingle, Y., IoT in agriculture. *International Conference on Computing for Sustainable Global Development*, pp. 1456–1458, 2016.
2. Samir, M., Sharafeddine, S., Assi, C., Nguyen, T., Ghrayeb, A., UAV trajectory planning for data collection from time-constrained IoT devices. *IEEE Trans. Wireless Commun.*, 1–14, 2019.

3. Sun, X. and Ansari, N., EdgeIoT: Mobile edge computing for the Internet of Things. *IEEE Commun. Mag.*, 54, 12, 22–29, 2016.

4. Park, K. and Dinan, E., Traffic control and everything-to-vehicle (v2x) communications, 2018. URL https://ofinno.com/wp-content/uploads/2018/03/Ofinno V2X WP.New.pdf.

5. Jeong, S., Simeone, O., Kang, J., Mobile edge computing via a UAVmounted cloudlet: Optimization of bit allocation and path planning. *IEEE Trans. Veh. Technol.*, 67, 3, 2049–2063, 2018.

6. Mozaffari, M., Saad, W., Bennis, M., Debbah, M., Mobile unmanned aerial vehicles (UAVs) for energy-efficient Internet of Things communications. *IEEE Trans. Wireless Commun.*, 16, 11, 7574–7589, 2017.

7. Yousefpour, A., Ishigaki, G., Gour, R., Jue, J.P., On reducing iot service delay via fog offloading. *IEEE Internet Things J.*, 5, 2, 998–1010, 2018.

8. Zeng, D., Gu, L., Guo, S., Cheng, Z., Yu, S., Joint optimization of task scheduling and image placement in fog computing supported software defined embedded system. *IEEE Trans. Comput.*, 65, 12, 3702–3712, 2016.

9. Yoo, J., Performance Evaluation of Voice Over IP on WiMAX and Wi-Fi Based Networks; Communication Networks 2009. Available online: http://www2.ensc.sfu.ca/~{}ljilja/ENSC427/Spring09/Projects/team1/ensc427-finalreport.pdf (accessed on 5 November 2018).

10. Wu, Q. and Zhang, R., Common throughput maximization in UAV-enabled OFDMA systems with delay consideration. *IEEE Trans. Commun.*, 66, 6614–6627, 2018. [CrossRef].

11. He, X., Yu, W., Xu, H., Lin, J., Yang, X., Lu, C., Fu, X., Towards 3D Deployment of UAV Base Stations in Uneven Terrain. *Proceedings of the 2018 27th International Conference on Computer Communication and Networks (ICCCN)*, Hangzhou, China, pp. 1–9, 30 July–2 August 2018.

12. Alzenad, M., El-Keyi, A., Yanikomeroglu, H., 3D placement of an unmanned aerial vehicle base station for maximum coverage of users with different QoS requirements. *IEEE Wirel. Commun. Lett.*, 7, 38–41, 2018.

13. Muthuramalingam, S., Bharathi, A., Gayathri, N., Sathiyaraj, R., Balamurugan, B., IoT Based Intelligent Transportation System (IoT-ITS) for Global Perspective: A Case Study, in: *Internet of Things and Big Data Analytics for Smart Generation*, pp. 279–300, Springer, Cham, 2019.

13

UAVs in Agriculture

Deepanshu Srivastava, S. Rakesh Kumar* and N. Gayathri

School of Computing Science and Engineering, Galgotias University, Uttar Pradesh, India

Abstract

In this chapter we will discuss the benefits of unmanned aerial vehicles (UAVs). As we all know, there are various advantages and multiple uses of UAVs in the field of science and technology.

Weal ready know that UAV shave beenused in various areas of the armed forces since World War I for surveillance. Now, this technology has also emerged in the fields of farming and agriculture.

The cost of UAVs tends to decrease with an increase in better technology. According to a survey, 85 to 95 percent of growth will occur in agriculture and farming with the help of UAV drones. Surveying fields, forecasting changes in weather, and monitoring rate of photosynthesis can all be successfully achieved with the help of these drones.

It is easy to target problems by surveying an entire farm field with these systems. Continuous monitoring can create a complete record of patterns and growth. Currently there is a high demand for UAVs and the farming and agriculture sectors are also moving towards this new technology to make their operations run more easily and smoothly. Once these tools are implemented in a successful way, they could help the agriculture and farming sector increase their yields.

Keywords: Unmanned aerial vehicles (UAVs), wireless sensor networks (WSNs), multi-sensor systems (MSS), internet of things (IOT)

Corresponding author: s.rakeshkumar@galgotiasuniversity.edu.in

Ashutosh Kumar Dubey, Abhishek Kumar, S. Rakesh Kumar, N. Gayathri, Prasenjit Das (eds.) AI and IoT-Based Intelligent Automation in Robotics, (229–246) © 2021 Scrivener Publishing LLC

13.1   Introduction

Nowadays, unmanned aerial vehicles (UAVs) are more popular in the sector of farming and agriculture. This chapter will discuss the use of drones in smart farming and agriculture to increase sustainability.

RGD-B sensors will be used and we will see the measurement algorithms used in farming and agriculture. Many tests and experiments were conducted, and based on the results it has been observed that this technique would be able to provide good ploughing methods.

This chapter also introduces the new concept of UGVs to address various problems like the traveling salesman problem (TSP) with neighborhoods and aerial measurement with the help of drones due to limited energy.

Precision agriculture has shown growth at a large scale in the field of agriculture and farming practices. This chapter explains how remote sensing, especially satellite remote sensing, can be used in the farm management applications.

Moreover, we will also discuss the use of imaging systems with the help of UAVs which are meant to provide more accurate and detailed data. A combination of robot process automation (RPA) with processing of images at various scales, recognition of different patterns and machine learning (ML) can provide more capabilities to farmers in the field of farming and agriculture. Finally, we will discuss an unmanned aerial system (UAS) platform which also supports agricultural operations [8, 12].

13.2   UAVs in Smart Farming and Take-Off Panel

13.2.1   Overview of Systems

In this era where resources are one of the major concerns due to the population increasing at a greater rate, it is important to use these resources effectively and efficiently, especially in the fields where soil is exploited for crop production.

The growth in the use of UAVs/drones in the field of farming and agriculture benefits farmers by monitoring the presence of light on leaves by viewing the amount of chlorophyll present at that area, as further processing in agriculture sites totally depends on this step.

These UAVs/drones can give a bird's-eye view of the current state of the field, and compared to old satellite technology they can assess all factors, providing more accurate results which were previously only possible in some areas.

These drones have shown an interesting and progressive solution in the field of ploughing and harvesting and allow the overall scanning and surveying of the fields, which makes them very efficient and helpful systems for farmers, which decrease the number of hours they need to work in the field and sometimes provide answers as to how and when their crops are destroyed (see Figure 13.1) [1].

In this chapter we will discuss UAVs with RGD-D sensors which are used for navigation and acquiring data for further processing. The eBee is a fully autonomous and easy-to-use mapping drone, which comes with a RGB-D camera that can take clear images of farming fields and landing segments. One of its advantages in the field is that it costs less compared to other basic solutions.

The global positioning system (GPS) is one of the most important systems for providing information about the location of fields. If factors like positioning and mapping are combined, it would result in much better localization [1, 12].

To monitor soil quality, these drones could be helpful in providing images (see Figures 13.2–13.4), which may not be sufficient and need to be validated at least once for easy surveillance.

The new growth in the field of UAVs in agriculture and farming is greatly reassuring to the framework of society as it can implement better ploughing and harvesting techniques, which result in better crop formation, which could result in a better future. The complete view can be seen in the Figure 13.5.

With the help of these drones, a complete view and report can be generated through RGB-D cameras. Satellite images are also provided, especially

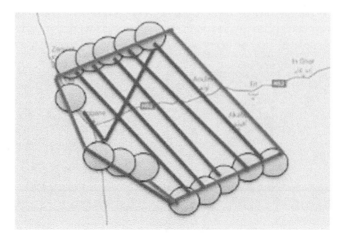

Figure 13.1 Trajectory path for the filed assessment.

Figure 13.2 View of farm field through UAV camera.

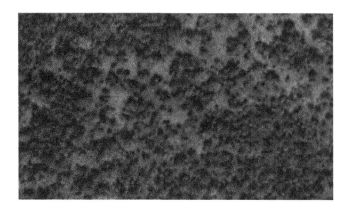

Figure 13.3 View of farm through UAV camera (zoom).

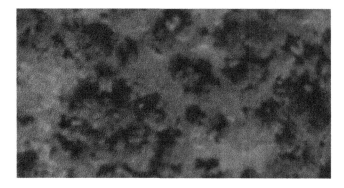

Figure 13.4 View of farm through UAV camera (more zoom).

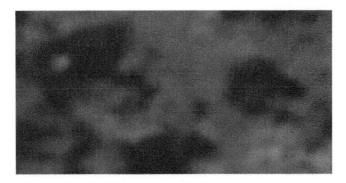

Figure 13.5 View of farm through UAV camera (max zoom).

optical ones, which are quite expensive, so other image solutions exist such as radar images through which one can distinguish between tilled and untilled soil [8]. Due to improvements in technology, we can also detect the type of tillage.

A report can be produced with the help of these drones which analyzes the water level in the plants for better crop growth and can also calculates the hydraulic stress based on its level. Several types of software are available on the market for positioning systems like Parrot Ar.Drone 2.0, which is the software most suitable for the positioning systems [1, 8].

In relation to the environment, drones also plays a vital role in monitoring adverse weather conditions which may harm farmer's crops. To do so, a PID controller is introduced using a sensor with a camera attached to it.

In the acquisition phase, terrain was not properly faced by the camera which resulted in height variations. By using the principal component analysis (PCA) technique it finds its correspondent points in the principal axis with the least variance. In the TOP view of the field, level 3 of ploughing is possible with different height transformations.

After much testing and practice, drones were finally cleared and ready to take-off. According to reports, 50,000 drones were purchased for the testing phase of cropping and farming fields. The Federal Aviation Administration (FAA) has approved the use of drones for agricultural and farming purposes and it expects more drones to be flown in the coming years.

With these drones the specific amount of fertilizers and pesticides applied to crops can be managed. Since these resources are used more efficiently, they cause less harm to the environment. This method can be used in both the agriculture and farming sector, as well as the agricultural chemicals sector.

There are many benefits associated with the use of drones in agriculture and farming, especially in countries that have a variety of crops, plants and species. However, the drones must not be flown above the line of sight, i.e., visual line of sight [2, 12].

13.3   Introduction to UGV Systems and Planning

It is important to plan paths for mobile robot sensors that maximize the utility of data collection, also known as the informative path planning (IPP) problem. In this section we will discuss the new progressive planning solutions that can be used in precision agriculture.

State-of-the-art techniques are used in the agricultural sector to calculate the condition of crops in the field, and with this information increase the number of healthy crops produced. This is known as precision farming.

The growth of healthy crop leads to a healthy environment. Improving the management of fertilizers can reduce the high rate of its use in the world, thereby maintaining the correct nitrogen level.

Data collection is one of the most important functions, i.e., major components, of precision agriculture. It is also a component of unmanned aerial vehicles (UAVs) and unmanned ground vehicles (UGVs) which, when working together, combine the strengths of ground and aerial robots, because even though UGVs can travel long distances, carry large loads, and measure soil data, they cannot obtain aerial imagery.

It would take more and more UGVs to measure soil fertility. For this, we discuss the sampling TSPN problem, which is a non-deterministic problem [3].

Here, we will discuss the concept of orienteering, which is defined as visiting or reaching the control points within a time limit. The result would be better if a UAV is not used alone but instead is used in combination with a UGV for further flight locations and decisions. By using both UAV and UGV together, we can apply several algorithms.

If we include a sampling TSPN problem in which we assume that time is fixed with the UAV and UGV, then real field data can be generated. If we want to visit each node of a crop location, then sensing can be considered as it can provide the trajectory from 0 to total time occupied or used to the path length. The main goal is to get the amount of time spent on the defined location.

So far we have discussed the sampling TSPN and TSPN complete time in measuring the soil field and complete traveling time of field, which is the main difference between sampling TSPN and TSPN and given disk radii.

The general formulations are exponential and polynomial optimal time solution/problem that occurs with these formulas is that they have a fixed number of sample, which can be sorted with the help of UAV battery solution [3].

With the increasing advancements in technology, there has been growth in the use of autonomous underwater vehicles (AUVs) for monitoring surface water, deep water and groundwater systems.

Applying an algorithm to UAVs with UGVs that contains many locations can increase its coverage area and also the amount of battery. In the agriculture and farming field, UAVs and UGVs are widely used for harvesting and many other purposes.

The process of soil measurement is a quite lengthy or slow process. In the TSPN problem, the main target of the problem is to find or get the minimum distance by visiting each and every node at least once. So, the target of the TSPN problem is also to find the minimum path of the covered area.

But, as always, everything has some positive and negative effects; similarly, it may exceed or be at the limit of optimal time, in which case we must find an algorithm in which its complete time is less than its optimal time.

Now we will see how we can analyze the problem of measurement taken by aerial drones through UAVs. The aim of this part is to find the optimal solution which gives maximum profit values.

Now, in this segment, we not only use UAVs/drones but also the combination of UAV+UGV/drones that gives progressive results by going through each node. Both will work simultaneously with the help of each other to give better and better results [3].

To help in precision agriculture, it is also able to control the vision of the UAVs/drones. UAVs/drones have shown the best results in areas such as monitoring wildlife, distance consideration and calculation.

If both techniques combine remote sensing with precision farming, it can give results up to maximum level in areas such as disease and health, which can ensure maximum productivity in the agriculture and farming sectors.

Implementing architecture consist of two parts: Software and Hardware. The hardware structure shows all the physical parts, board systems and other modules such as serial interfaces and all types of relays. The software structure uses the OODA approach for its inside components or frameworks. Its working structure is defined as in Figure 13.6. The detailed description is provided by sensors [4, 11].

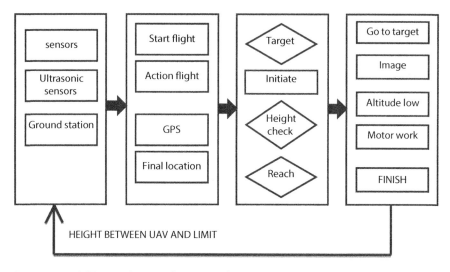

Figure 13.6 OODA working on decision-making process.

13.4   UAV-Hyperspectral for Agriculture

Today, agriculture is one of the most important industries as it is the largest producer of the crops needed to fill the increasing demand for food. With the help of remote sensing, the quality and quantity of all crops are provided, along with detailed information and all variations. The amount of chlorophyll can be estimated by the hyperspectral technique.

After 1970, agricultural applications have been very much supported by the detailed images of satellites, which are used to a very large extent. Recent studies have shown that hyperspectral sensors on UAVs would be very helpful as user-controlled systems; and the paths, i.e., flight paths, provided by this system would be an advantage. Hyperspectral data with the help of lower pixel satellite views can be an answer to high operational costs of UAV high-resolution aerial imaging. Its working structure is defined as in Figure 13.7.

Spectral temporal response surface (STRS) is actually a 4D dataset which is created by temporal and spectral domains. However, everything has some merits and demerits so, it does not give detail for reflectance spectra and uncertainties are not taken into account while observations are weighted. It is also quite difficult to make measurements using sensors.

So, to overcome these disadvantages of STRS, it was further proposed to use the Bayesian theory, which classifies all the uncertainties and with the help of Bayesian interference interpolation these uncertainties are taken into account [5, 9].

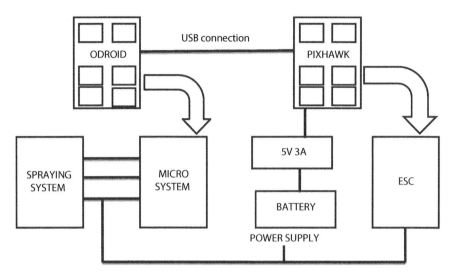

Figure 13.7 System architecture.

Bayesian Theory:

Here, we will consider hyperspectral with multi-spectral sensing image on Bayesian theory.

Let X_{ms} = Spectral response function(SRF) for multispectral
X_{hs}-x = hyperspectral
Now, by the Gaussian theory with marginal is defined as:
$A (X_{ms})$ =P (Xms|ms,sum of all mm)------------------1
$A (X_{hs})$ =P (Xhs|hs,sum of all hh)--------------------2
And,
Prior mean (mean pm) and its distribution (sum of hs) is defined as:
$A (hm|ms)$ =P (X|HM|N,sum of hm|mm).

Bayesian Temporal Interpolation:
STRS is created with the help of multispectral observation. Mathematical representation is given by:

X=By+null;
WhereB=matrix multiplication

Gaussian normal distribution almost reflects the noise. Uncertainty is inversely proportional to sensor precision [5].

On the basis of band by band and temporal and spectral reflectance, STRS is created.

For the efficient and progressive studies, a study was carried out in a potato field in an area in the Netherlands. With its working structure is defined as in Figure 13.8 help of a crop metering device, all spectral measurement of approx. six measurements were taken. For measurement of chlorophyll concentrations, a SPAD-502 meter was used.

High resolution aerial photographs are then converted to reflector with the help of various metadata files. At this experiment level, STRS was constructed and used.

The STRS is created by interpolating the spectral reflectance along the temporal dimension on a band-by-band basis. Probably three STRS were created in which the first one is similar to the second one refers to spectral dimension and temporal dimension, and the third one is temporal inference. Its working structure is defined as in Figure 13.9. Based on these cases and according to the current scenario, as the differences between the spectral characteristics of images is large, the Bayesian calculation or Bayesian imputation is based on that condition [5, 9].

Figure 13.8 UAV-hyper-spectral image.

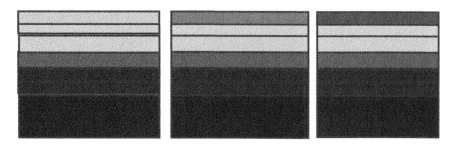

Figure 13.9 Combining UAV-multispectral and UAV-hyperspectral images.

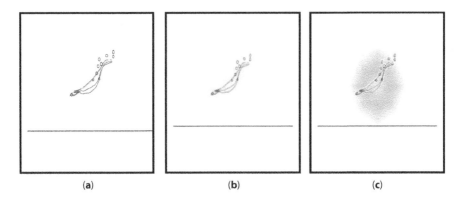

(a)   (b)   (c)

Figure 13.10 Bayesian graphs.

Due to the temporal spline interpolation, spectra changes rapidly. The discrepancies between STRS and the crop scan are completely explained by the field data. Once the canopy is closed, all differences will not be visible. Its working structure is defined as in Figure 13.10. It may improve its performance at a higher level by adding more sensors in temporal and spectral signals provided by the human. The gap between sensor and data requirement can be solved with the help of a useful technique called precision farming.

13.5   UAV-Based Multisensors for Precision Agriculture

With the advancement of technology, UAV systems have shown better results in every sector. These systems have also shown better results in the agricultural sector. The introduction of precision agriculture (PA) has resulted in farming with less human manpower and requiring more high input data.

In this sector, many more techniques have also been tried in order to get a better result but they have some limitations, like satellite remote sensing, which is limited to small-scale agriculture as compared to all the advantages of UAV remote sensing. Here, we will discuss the management in agriculture. Many farming practices, such as applying fertilizers, are based on soil and crop needs [6]. In order to meet these needs, current studies have mainly been dedicated to information technology engineering so as to produce the maximum yield and better farming techniques.

In precision farming, practices that are applied are much better than those in conventional agriculture as it requires spectral and temporal information. As every system has some advantages and disadvantages, some of the disadvantages of satellite remote sensing includeimage resolution and cost [6, 10].

Various research has been conducted targeting the evolving agriculture and farming sector. Recent research has focused on resolving a number of challenges such as in operations, collections, and the cost of products.

One of the areas targeted is providing irrigation management systems for the agriculture sector for delivery of water to crops. Due to less human manpower in farming and agriculture, these targeted changes are necessary and need to be accomplished.

Among the advanced UAV technologies, the cameras installed in drones play a vital role in sensing and displaying the results accurately. Thermal and multi-spectral camera systems with external GPS are components of the main system. A microprocessor, such as Raspberry PI, is a single integrated platform used in the operation of a UAV/drone model.

When several cameras are fitted and installed in the drone model, the cameras must be light-weight, small, and compatible. With minor improvements, these UAV cameras can make the best systems.

Due to some high supplied voltage, acompact flash (CF) memory card present in the camera, resulted in failure. So, in order to overcome this fault, a second power supply was provided with consistent voltage. After the end of several operational tests, some of the operations were limited failures, but so as to overcome these limits, consistent data was produced. After overcoming the failures, multi-targeting image and storage were available, and both its sensors were M-L image coordinated with GPS for the information of that image.

All these functions were introduced and enabled so that the system can work in a broad area of agriculture to easily monitor operations and for easy accessibility and extraction of information [6].

In the first stage, treatment of water is applied to the crops. With the help of conventional irrigation, the irrigation water pattern can be known.

Specific heights are provided to drones as each drone has a some height limit; for example, in the case of multi-spectral imagery it is 44cm and in the case of thermal imagery it is 13cm at the speed of 2.2m/s, with all the GPS trackers being set at their desired locations to get the better output. Its working structure is defined as in Figure 13.11.

These output images were then loaded into professional photo scan systems and were processed with the help of geographical coordinates aided by these initial input images. Its working structure is defined as in Figure 13.12

FLIR systems were used to convert radiometric to kelvin canopy value and provide the information; then, with the help of these information,

Figure 13.11 Image showing the location of a fruit field in a surveyed farm.

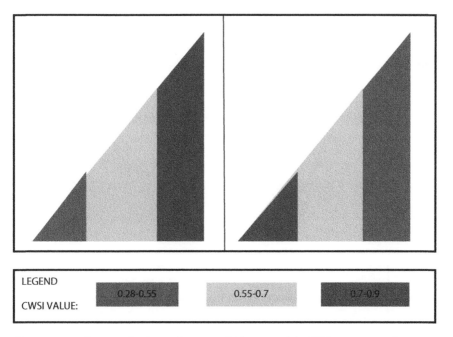

Figure 13.12 These are the thermal images which are used for FLIR systems used to convert radiometric to kelvin canopy value.

the CWSI (crop water stress index) was created, where the canopy values were used (scientists also prefer to use this CWSI information) and these data then processes to GIS systems. Water management, proper schedule of irrigation, problem faced in irrigation path, and maintenance were the most important details derived from the above content [6, 11].

13.6   Automation in Agriculture

Nowadays, robotic process automation (RPA) is a field in which a lot of time is being invested as it is showing impactful and better results. This subject is also being introduced as a course in many universities and colleges. Applications associated with RPA, such as image processing, pattern recognition and machine learning, are used in machine systems to make performing tasks simpler, faster and as cheap as possible.

With the increase in usage of drones, cameras installed in the UAVs can give a complete view from the sky and timely information at a lower cost. Remote sensing drones have shown better performance and results over precision agriculture. In this section we will discuss the problems related to remote sensing with UAVs through sensor-based applications. The thermal images which convert radiometric to kelvin value can be seen in Figure 13.13.

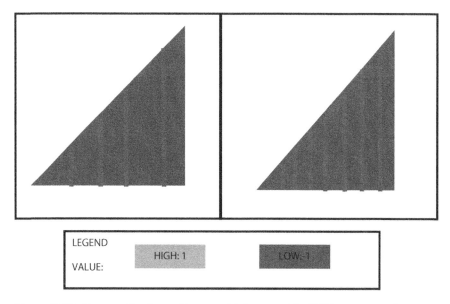

Figure 13.13 These are the thermal images which are used for FLIR systems used to convert radiometric to kelvin canopy value.

Satellites play a major role in the agriculture sector as they can scan the entire area where crops are planted, which is important for farmers. Currently, in many parts of the world it is still not a common practice for farmers to gather and collect all the information taken from satellites and other applications. This is especially true in most of the rural areas where communication connection is not good and people are unaware of smart farming.

Drones have shown that better results in the field of farming and agriculture requires data based on images, as they help in the irrigation process and management of nitrogen and potassium. With the help of these UAV drones, farmers can identify which part of the field needs more improvement and more attention [7].

Drones are used to analyze soil, they also help in surveying fields, irrigation, and in planting seeds at a minimum cost. When cost is at a minimum, everyone, especially farmers, can opt to have UAV drones survey their fields, gather information on areas of every field and much more, which results in better crop yields and food material as well as good quality and effective working.

According to research and advanced studies, the use of UAVs/drones in the sector of agriculture and farming will increase at a higher rate compared to their current use. If it is to become a successful attempt, then it must also work in the field of harvesting and collecting fruits.

Unmanned aircraft systems (UAS) are a component of the aviation system consisting of not only a single UAV drone but also DLS as data link system and GCS as ground control system. They have elevated precision farming to the next level. They are able to capture high pixel pictures from meters of height. UAS systems can be classified into three types: Fixed wings, rotary wings, and flapping wings. There are various categories of aerial sensors, such as Lancaster and Guardian-Z10, which provide high efficiency at a low cost.

Different classes of UAVs are designed based on their capabilities and flight-capacity. GCS is the remote control of these drones. It can also work as a platform for interchange of data. The communications between the GCS and the UAVs take place over wireless data links for each and every level of measurement [7].

In the field of UAVs/drones in agriculture and farming, there are various imaging sensors. In addition to UAS sensors, additional equipment is added such as stabilizing symbols. The Sentera Double 4K sensor exports images in real time. How UAV's work can be seen in the Figure 13.14.

XIMEA is the world's smallest hyperspectral camera sensor. Detection and identification of diseases in sick animals and livestock are possible using this type of sensor. Its working structure is defined as in Figure 13.15

Figure 13.14 UAAVs/drones used for work in the agriculture sector.

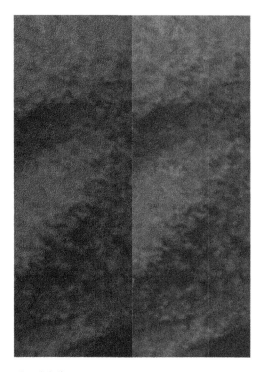

Figure 13.15 Normalized difference vegetation index (NDVI) image and soil image of a crop field.

The correct measurement can be completed by ground sampling distance (GSD). Some of the thermal professional cameras, such as Duo Pro and Vue Pro, are used for UAS. But the prerequisites for the thermal professional cameras are no extra light and optimal weather conditions, so their optimal use would be at night time. Collection of data, analysis, map production, and planning are features that software implements.

Image file formats, such as JPEG or TIFF, determine the quality of the resultant image. Smart farming uses massive amounts of data produced by UAS, such as information about fertilizers, chemicals, soil, etc. In addition to this, IOT systems can be added for biological processes in the agricultural and farming sector.

For remote sensing in precision agriculture, the normalized difference vegetation index (NDVI) is used for assessing crops and measuring chlorophyll and the normalized difference red edge index (NDRE) is suitable for measuring cropslate in the growing season. Because the soil-adjusted vegetation index (SAVI) and the green normalized difference vegetation index (GNDVI) are used for qualitative calculations they are expensive.

Since satellites like WorldView-2 have some limitations, the period from 2000 to 2009 saw a great increase in the use of dronesbecause of their effective results.

Visual sensors in the UAVs/drones indicate which sections of the field need more attention and improvement. The leaf area index (LAI) is used to measure growth and yields. For the classifications of crops, a support vector machine (SVM) is used.

Farmers can apply remote sensing techniques for mapping of soil properties, to detect water level in crop management, and for pest management and nitrogen estimation. Factors that affect the functioning of unmanned aircraft systems, such as noise and heavy winds, can lead to inaccurate results [7, 10, 11].

13.7   Conclusion

In the current UAV market, there is a lot of work being done in the field of visual sensors for UAVs in order to get the desired output. This work will provide a strong foundation for those just starting out in the UAV market. The aim of this chapter was to provide complete information about the various techniques and methodologies used by UAVs/drones to benefit the field of agriculture.

References

1. Tripicchio, P., Satler, M., Dabisias, G., Ruffaldi, E., Avizzano, C.A., Towards smart farming and sustainable agriculture with drones. *2015 International Conference on Intelligent Environments*, pp. 140–143, 2015, July, IEEE.
2. Patel, P., Agriculture drones are finally cleared for takeoff [News]. *IEEE Spectr.*, 53, 11, 13–14, 2016.

3. Tokekar, P., Vander Hook, J., Mulla, D., Isler, V., Sensor planning for a symbiotic UAV and UGV system for precision agriculture. *IEEE Trans. Rob.*, 32, 6, 1498–1511, 2016.

4. Alsalam, B.H.Y., Morton, K., Campbell, D., Gonzalez, F., Autonomous UAV with vision based on-board decision making for remote sensing and precision agriculture. *2017 IEEE Aerospace Conference*, pp. 1–12, 2017, March, IEEE.

5. Gevaert, C.M., Suomalainen, J., Tang, J., Kooistra, L., Generation of spectral-temporal response surfaces by combining multispectral satellite and hyperspectral UAV imagery for precision agriculture applications. *IEEE J. Sel. Top. Appl. Earth Obs. Remote Sens.*, 8, 6, 3140–3146, 2015.

6. Katsigiannis, P., Misopolinos, L., Liakopoulos, V., Alexandridis, T.K., Zalidis, G., An autonomous multi-sensor UAV system for reduced-input precision agriculture applications. *2016 24th Mediterranean Conference on Control and Automation (MED)*, pp. 60–64, 2016, June, IEEE.

7. Kulbacki, M., Segen, J., Knieć, W., Klempous, R., Kluwak, K., Nikodem, J., Serester, A., Survey of drones for agriculture automation from planting to harvest. *2018 IEEE 22nd International Conference on Intelligent Engineering Systems (INES)*, pp. 000353–000358, 2018, June, IEEE.

8. Stehr, N.J., Drones: The newest technology for precision agriculture. *Nat. Sci. Educ.*, 44, 1, 89–91, 2015.

9. Adão, T., Hruška, J., Pádua, L., Bessa, J., Peres, E., Morais, R., Sousa, J.J., Hyperspectral imaging: A review on UAV-based sensors, data processing and applications for agriculture and forestry. *Remote Sens.*, 9, 11, 1110, 2017.

10. Gómez-Candón, D., De Castro, A.I., López-Granados, F., Assessing the accuracy of mosaics from unmanned aerial vehicle (UAV) imagery for precision agriculture purposes in wheat. *Precis. Agric.*, 15, 1, 44–56, 2014.

11. Puri, V., Nayyar, A., Raja, L., Agriculture drones: A modern breakthrough in precision agriculture. *J. Stat. Manage. Syst.*, 20, 4, 507–518, 2017.

12. Veroustraete, F., The rise of the drones in agriculture. *EC Agric.*, 2, 2, 325–327, 2015.

14

Semi-Automated Parking System Using DSDV and RFID

Mayank Agrawal¹, Abhishek Kumar Rawat¹, Archana¹, SandhyaKatiyar¹*
and Sanjay Kumar²

¹Galgotias College of Engineering and Technology, Uttar Pradesh, India
²Galgotias University, Uttar Pradesh, India

Abstract

In this chapter, a new parking system is introduced which uses a pre existing radio-frequency identification (RFID) technology along with destination-sequenced distance-vector (DSDV) routing protocol. RFID and WIFI sensors are used to divide the parking into certain small regions. These regions are governed by different nodes. Each node has a group of assigned areas under it. With the help of these nodes, the nearest vacant parking locations can be identified by the source node. Certain changes have been made in the DSDV protocol for achieving our purpose. This semi-autonomous system has been created for large, hard to manage parking areas.

Keywords: Ad hoc network, autonomous parking services, vehicle locus, radio-frequency identification (RFID) sensors, WIFI sensor, personalized attention network (PANet)

14.1 Introduction

Parking vehicles becomes a major problem when it is done on a large scale due to the increasing demand for parking spaces in urban areas. Due to this growing demand, we need more and more parking spaces. The type of autonomous parking system with robotics is very difficult to set up and needs a completely new infrastructure, which is very expensive and consumes a lot of energy which makes it more difficult to set up in developing

*Corresponding author: san.katiyar@galgotiacollege.edu

Ashutosh Kumar Dubey, Abhishek Kumar, S. Rakesh Kumar, N. Gayathri, Prasenjit Das (eds.) *AI and IoT-Based Intelligent Automation in Robotics,* (247–258) © 2021 Scrivener Publishing LLC nations. Parking can be a daily hassle for some, such as attempting to find a close yet economical space to park for work in an office building. It's also a problem during a particular event, such as thousands gathering around a few blocks or streets during holiday festivals.

The problem lies in the way that these spaces are typically managed, which is proven to be inefficient. Drivers are often left frustrated and spend too much time searching for a spot, due to a lack of immediate awareness of where spaces are open. Predictable, real-time data that allows drivers choose between on-street parking, surface parking lots or garages are not available.

The most crucial aspect of archiving an efficient parking experience is a real-time guidance system to all the parking options and live information updates. This type of live monitoring system is very important in places where there are large events and makes parking autonomous. PANet is a system that provides the nearest optimum parking spot according to your location by using an ad hoc network.

14.2   Ad Hoc Network

The principle of an ad hoc network is multi-hop relaying. In 1994, communication equipment manufacturers developed a low-range, low complexity, low-power network between the different types of devices used for commercial purposes, which later emerged as the ad hoc network.

An ad hoc network is composed of spontaneous devices which connect and communicate with each other individually. It mainly works on the wireless LANs [1]. A wireless ad hoc network does not require a fixed infrastructure, so it is easy to set up and deploy in any type of infrastructure. Wireless ad hoc network is self-organizing; thus, it is easy to adopt the change in the topology. When the cable network is not available in areas like rescue then ad hoc network is the most feasible way to communicate. Routing paths in mobile ad hoc networks can potentially contain multiple hops, with every node in the mobile ad hoc networks acting as a router.

Considering the mobility of the wireless host available in the ad hoc network, each of the nodes are equipped with the capability of the autonomous system without the use of any centralized administration.

14.2.1   Destination-Sequenced Distance Vector (DSDV) Routing Protocol

The distance vector routing protocol illustrated in Figure 14.1 is derived from the Bellman-Ford routing mechanism. It is a table-driven algorithm

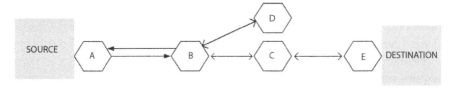

Figure 14.1 Destination-sequenced distance vector routing protocol.

in which each node periodically broadcasts the routing updates. DSDV protocol requires each mobile node in the network to transmit its own routing table to its current neighbors. In all the nodes, each and every node in the table has entries for the destination node in the table and makes the count of the number of hops required for reaching the destination [2]. Every entry has a corresponding sequence number that helps in identifying older entries.

The method which we are using doesn't give a fixed location where you can park but it can tell you the location of the nearest available parking space. It uses DSDV protocols to communicate with each other because there are many moving nodes (mobile device where you can use the map) around the parking. Normally in DSDV, each node maintains one table having information about destination node, next hop, distance, sequence number but, in this system there is a fixed node containing information about destination node, next hop, distance, sequence number, parking available, parking.

14.3   Radio Frequency Identification (RFID)

Radio frequency identification is wireless communication with the use of radiofrequency waves to transfer the data. RFID uniquely identifies your assets that read and capture the information with the tag attached to the object, which provides a unique identifier without coming in contact with them.

There are many types of RFID tags that use radiofrequency waves to set up the communication between the tags and the readers, but there are different methods powering the tags. The tags which use internal battery power are known as active tags [3]. They provide a continuous source of power to power the radio frequency circuit and generate a very low-frequency signal because the client does not need to power the tag.

There is another type of RFID tags which do not need internal power so they are very narrow and have unlimited use for a lifetime [3]. These types of tags are known as passive tags. It is much cheaper to manufacture these tags. According to the regulation transmitter, the passive RFID based system can emit the maximum power allowed by the regulatory board [4].

Nowadays, most of the tags being used are passive tags. Passive tags require very high frequency radio signals from the reader, so their range is very narrow and they have limited memory storage capacity; where active tags transmit signal across a longer range and have high storage and additional information storage capacity.

There are three ways in which RFID tags communicate between the user and the reader: 1) Full duplex (FDX) protocol, in which the information can be sent and received at the same time 2) Half duplex (HDX) protocol, in which it alternates between the links [5] and 3) Sequential (SEQ) protocol, which has predetermined time slots for the transfer.

We are using active RFID tags in this application to setup the communication between the nodes.

14.4   Problem Identification

Now a days advancements in technology has added to the rapidly developing mobility in the country leading to an increase in traffic. How to manage parking spaces to accommodate this increase in traffic is becoming a major issue in urban areas. Therefore, our aim is to find the solution for designing parking garages that are autonomous and affordable by using new technologies and methodologies. The focus of this chapter is to find the empty vehicle locus from the nearby location of the entry location. In this chapter, an attempt is made to setup the contact between the nodes in a Mobile Ad Hoc Network by using the routing algorithm known as the destination-sequenced distance vector (DSDV) routing protocol.

14.5   Survey of the Literature

Daud *et al.* [6] show the performance study of the two routing protocols in distance vector routing protocol and ad hoc on demand vector routing in VANETs. In their study, a new framework is proposed in which a constant Bit Rate bit-rate stream increases and after reaching half, it decreases and the total remains constant.

The comparison is based on the quality of service, such as jitter minimization, of the throughput generated. The study makes the routing algorithm better, which improves the performance in the internet of things environment.

In a research work done by Sallum *et al.* [7] on how routing protocol behaves over the WAVE stack, they show that DSDV is has a better performance in comparison to AODV and OLSR using the NS3 simulation. In this study they observe better performance of the OLSR when the nodes velocity increases.

Corrales and Salichs [8] researched the benefit of RFID in mobile vehicles/robots that can collect information from the board signature and the symbols that humans can recognize from their environment. By doing so, the machine can guess where they are located. RFID works as the wireless sensor between the nodes for transferring the data and help detecting vehicles. In this setup the passive tags are used in the setup of the system because of their high frequency to increase the range and using a large infrastructure.

In study by Longjam and Bagoria [9] the main aim was to do a performance analysis based on packet delivery ratio, throughput, and routing overhead using NS2 to keep the number of nodes constant. When a system setup, a flooding algorithm works in the system which updates the tables at each node. These tables are updated at the time of changes and at regular intervals as performed in DSDV. By using this setup, we are making the very low-cost manageable technology that can be used in any type of topology.

14.6   PANet Architecture

In the PANet architecture shown in Figure 14.2 the chips are the car and the node (A, B, C, D, E) are the fixed nodes that are spread around the parking lot. There are two types of connecting sensors used in the fixed nodes. The first type is RFID sensors which are given to every car at the time of check-in if a car comes near any fixed node it can detect it and then that information can send be sent throughout the whole system.

The second type is wireless sensors, which can communicate with the mobile device of the driver so that the mobile device can know the location of its car. These wireless sensors also help to communicate with one fixed node to another fixed node. These two sensors are used because we want to divide the parking lot into physical areas.

At the user side, which is reprevsented as a chip in the figure, there are also two RFID sensors which are put into their car at the entry point and

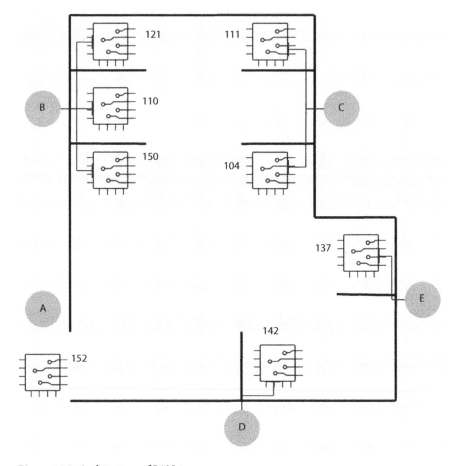

Figure 14.2 Architecture of PANet.

wireless sensors that are present in their mobile device so that they can also communicate with the system.

14.6.1   Approach for Semi-Automated System Using DSDV

Let's suppose node A is our entry point and a car is entering from it and its RFID tag is 152. By using its table node, A determines the closest parking space available. In the table distance of node, D is the smallest, which is having a parking space available. A packet of reserving the place is sent to node D on behalf of RFID tag 152. In node D table at destination D, row sequence number changed to a greater number, parking available is updated to 0 and parking occupied by is updated to 142, RE-152.

This information is sent to throw the whole network. If the car reached the destination and the RFID tag is detected by the RFID sensor 152, the table is again updated and RE-152 changed to 152. Because this car is moved by humans, a human can put the car anywhere without following the instruction. Suppose the car will be parked at node C in the place of node D. RFID sensor of node C can detect the chip 152. But node C does not get any reserve request from 152 it sends a packet in the system for resetting the request coming from 152.

Again, node D table updated row sequence number changed to the greater number, parking available is updated to 1 and parking occupied by is updated to 142. This same thing happens if someone parks a car at in a reserved place. But a new place near that node is searched for that reserved place and a request is sent to that node [17].

14.6.2   Tables for Parking Available/Occupied

Table of node A

Destination	Next hop	Distance	Sequence number	Parking available	Parking occupied by
A	A	0	A-14	0	0
B	B	1	B-11	0	121,110,150
C	B	2	C-15	1	111,104
D	D	1	D-32	1	142
E	E	2	E-03	1	137

Table of node B

Destination	Next hop	Distance	Sequence number	Parking available	Parking occupied by
A	A	1	A-14	0	0
B	B	0	B-11	0	121,110,150
C	C	1	C-15	1	111,104
D	A	2	D-32	1	142
E	C	2	E-03	1	137

Table of node C

Destination	Next hop	Distance	Sequence number	Parking available	Parking occupied by
A	B	2	A-14	0	0
B	B	1	B-11	0	121,110,150
C	C	0	C-15	1	111,104
D	E	2	D-32	1	142
E	E	1	E-03	1	137

Table of node D

Destination	Next hop	Distance	Sequence number	Parking available	Parking occupied by
A	A	1	A-14	0	0
B	A	2	B-11	0	121,110,150
C	E	2	C-15	1	111,104
D	D	0	D-32	1	142
E	E	1	E-03	1	137

Table of node E

Destination	Next hop	Distance	Sequence number	Parking available	Parking occupied by
A	D	2	A-14	0	0
B	C	2	B-11	0	121,110,150
C	C	1	C-15	1	111,104
D	D	1	D-32	1	142
E	E	0	E-03	1	137

14.6.3   Algorithm for Detecting the Empty Slots

In the algorithm, pa, po and re is represent Parking available, Parking occupied by and Reserved tag respectively.

> Step1: Assign available parking spaces to paon source nodes and po with the RFID tags on vehicle which is holding the parking space.
> Step2: The above information should pass to other node while finding the Distance and Next hop to the destination.
> Step3: pd = number of node +1 and pnode=NULL.
> Step4: If pa >0 AND distance to destination node < pd is True then pd = distance to destination node and pnode = destination node.
> Step5: Repeat step4 until All nodes are visited.
> Step6: Signal is sent to the pnode to Decrement the parking available by one and re is appended to the po.
> Step7: If that RFID tag is detected by pnode RFID sensor then reserved RFID tag is UPDATE to RFID tag.
> Step8: Else If that RFID tag is detected on other node then increment parking available by 1 and re tag is removed from that po at pnode.

14.6.4   Pseudo Code

Procedure B_F (List nodes, list connection, node source)
  For each node n in nodes:
  n. predecessor: = null
  if n is Source tn n distance = 0 Else n distance = infinity
  for i from 1 to Size(nodes)-1:
  for each connectionc in connection: u: = c Source and
  n: = c destination
  if u distance +c. weight < n. distance:
  n. distance: =u. distance + c. Weight
  n. distance: = u

Procedure PANet(List nodes, list of distance, list parking available, list parking by occupied, vertex source):

Flag=0 Stod=0
Destination=NULL
For each node n in nodes:
If n. parking available > 0 and flag = = 0: Destination: = n

Stod: = n. distance Flag=1
Else if n. parking available > 0 and flag==1: If n. distance <stod:
Stod: = n. distance Destination: =n
If destination == NULL: Print parking not available
Else: Give the destination.

14.7   Conclusion

This system can replace a preexisting autonomous system, which is both expensive and slow in to execute. The idea is to improvise the parking system which is already present on a sustainable scale. Mapping and real-time tracking can be done using the information presented in this chapter. This system can be further advanced by applying different protocols. Presently, the DSDV protocol is used to transform the source node into a movable node. This protocol can help in implementing this system into commonly used portable devices.

References

1. Babu, G.C., Rao, Pvrd, Srinivas, J., Govardhan, Dr. A., Yesu, Babu, Dr. A., Losad-a location service based on manet for mobile police officers. *Int. J. Eng. Sci. Technol.*, 2, 9, 4838–4843, 2010.
2. Parvathi, P., Comparative analysis of CBRP, AODV, DSDV routing protocols in mobile Ad-hoc networks. *2012 IEEE International Conference on Computing, Communication and Applications*, 9, 6, 1–4, 2007, Article ID 17426.
3. Gutierrez, A., Nicolalde, F.D., Ingle, A., Hochschild, W., Veeramani, R., Hohberger, C., Davis, R., High-frequency RFID tag survivability in harsh environments. *2013 IEEE International Conference on RFID (RFID)*, 2013.
4. Kapucu, K. and Dehollain, C., A passive UHF RFID system with a low-power capacitive sensor interface. *2014 IEEE RFID Technology and Applications Conference (RFID-TA)*, pp. 301–305, 2014.
5. Zhang, Y., Amin, M.G., Kaushik, S., Localization and tracking of passive RFID tags based on direction estimation. *Int. J. Antennas Propag.*, Hindawi Publishing Corporation International Journal of Antennas and Propagation, 9, Article ID 17426, 2007.
6. Daud, S., Gilani, S.M.M., Riaz, M.S., Kabir, A., DSDV and AODV Protocols Performance in Internet of Things Environment. *2019 IEEE 11th International Conference on Communication Software and Networks (ICCSN)*, 6, pp. 466–470, 2020.

7. Sallum, E.E.A., dos Santos, G., Alves, M., Santos, M.M., Performance analysis and comparison of the DSDV, AODV and OLSR routing protocols under VANETs. *2018 16th IEEE International Conference on Intelligent Transportation Systems Telecommunications (ITST)*, pp. 1– 7.
8. Corrales, A. and Salichs, M.A., Use of RFID technology on a mobile robot for topological navigation tasks. *2011 IEEE International Conference on RFID-Technologies and Applications*, pp. 408–414.
9. Longjam, T. and Bagoria, N., Comparative study of destination sequenced distance vector and Ad-hoc on-demand distance vector routing protocol of mobile Ad-hoc network. *Int. J. Sci. Res. Publ.*, 3, 2, 1–7, February, 2013.
10. Kaur, A., Mobility model-based performance analysis of DSDV mobile ad hoc routing protocol. *International Conference on Recent Advances and Innovations in Engineering (ICRAIE- 2014)*, pp. 1–7, 2014.
11. Imran, M. and Qadeer, M.A., Evaluation study of performance comparison of topology-based routing protocol, AODV and DSDV in MANET. *2016 IEEE International Conference on Micro-Electronics and Telecommunication Engineering(ICMETE)*, pp. 207–211.
12. Katiyar, S. and Kumar, S., An Efficient Topology Management Algorithm in MANET. *2018 IEEE International Conference in Advances in Computing, Communication Control and Networking" (ICACCCN-18)*, pp. 267–272, 2018.
13. Communications, I.U. and Information Policy Committee, RFID: The State of Radio Frequency Identification (RFID) Implementation and Policy Implications, *The State of RFID Implementation and Its Policy Implications: An IEEE-USA* White Paper, 2005.
14. Zhi-yuan, Z., He., R., Jie, T., A method for optimizing the position of passive UHF RFID Tags. *2010 IEEE International Conference on RFID- Technology and Applications*, pp. 92–95, October, 2018.
15. Chouhan, T.S. and Deshmukh, R.S., Analysis of DSDV, OLSR and AODV Routing Protocols in VANETS Scenario: Using NS3. *2015 IEEE International Conference on Computational Intelligence and Communication Networks (CICN), IEEE*, pp. 85–89, 2015.
16. Purnomo, M.H., Purnama, I.K.E., Setijadi, E., Performance of the routing protocols AODV, DSDV and OLSR in health monitoring using NS3. *2016 IEEE International Seminar on Intelligent Technology and Its Applications (ISITIA)*, pp. 323–328, 2017.
17. Muthuramalingam, S., Bharathi, A., Gayathri, N., Sathiyaraj, R., Balamurugan, B., IoT Based Intelligent Transportation System (IoT-ITS) for Global Perspective: A Case Study, in: *Internet of Things and Big Data Analytics for Smart Generation*, pp. 279–300, Springer, Cham, 2019.

15

Survey of Various Technologies Involved in Vehicle-to-Vehicle Communication

Lisha Kamala K., Sini Anna Alex* and Anita Kanavalli

Department of Computer Science and Engineering, Ramaiah Institute of Technology, Bangalore, India

Abstract

Prior to the American Civil War (1861–1865), people used to travel from one place to another by walking, ox carts, wagons, etc. Over time, technologies were improved to make the lives of humans easier. To move from one place to another, vehicles were introduced which made it easier to travel long distances in a short amount of time. Even though vehicles have made our lives easier, they are also involved in the traffic accidents which kill thousands of people on roads every day. Road traffic accidents occur due to vehicles colliding, traffic rules not being followed, etc. To overcome these incidents, various techniques are being implemented. So, the main objective of this chapter is to present the various proposed techniques that are involved in vehicle-to-vehicle communication. A brief survey is given of the techniques relating to vehicle-to-vehicle communication; their advantages and disadvantages and how they are used are discussed.

Keywords: Vehicle-to-vehicle communication, VANET, ARM, Zigbee

15.1 Introduction

It is very difficult to imagine our lives without vehicles since they play a very important role in our day-to-day lives. Hence, the traffic on roads has been increasing; and as the number of vehicles increase, the accidents that are occurring have also increased drastically. With this in mind, various

---

Corresponding author: sinialex@msrit.edu

Ashutosh Kumar Dubey, Abhishek Kumar, S. Rakesh Kumar, N. Gayathri, Prasenjit Das (eds.) *AI and IoT-Based Intelligent Automation in Robotics*, (259–270) © 2021 Scrivener Publishing LLC

technologies been introduced for vehicle-to-vehicle communication to prevent collisions between vehicles from occurring. In this chapter, the following techniques involved in vehicle-to-vehicle communication are discussed: ARM and Zigbee-based intelligent vehicle, the use of a VANET-based prototype for V2V communication through WI-FI-based technology, real-time wireless system, IoT approach, and basic message format. The number of accidents on the road can be reduced by considering smart and flexible traffic management systems. When vehicles communicate with each other, a warning can be given regarding an impending collision so that the driver can be alerted, thereby reducing accidents. Nowadays, in most of the expensive cars air bags and air brakes have been introduced for safety reasons. These are designed with sensors and modules which include data processing, making them highly priced options which are unaffordable for many to use.

15.2   Survey of the Literature

Vehicular ad hoc networks (VANETs) play a very significant role in the research conducted for the automotive industry and wireless communication technology. Here, the main feature of VANETs is that mobile nodes are vehicles. These mobile nodes are considered a branch of mobile ad hoc network which helps nearby vehicles communicate. Its own features differ from other networks but the nodes are restricted only to road topology when the vehicles are moving. When the vehicles are moving on the road, details are available based on the information taken from the nearby vehicle and communication takes place [12]. In VANETs the data between the vehicles are data packets which consist of the following parameters: current speed of the vehicle, position of the vehicle, and also how far away the vehicle is [13].

Gupta *et al.* discuss the ad-hoc environment created for three vehicles, focusing on the factors of speed, distance, and position. First the network is formed and the information is transferred through sensors, then the speed of the vehicle is analyzed through GPS. By using sensors, microcontrollers and other communication technologies, communication can take place between vehicles. A signal is then emitted on an LCD device, which alerts the driver to issues regarding speed, position, and distance [5].

The main objective of the study by Meshram *et al.* is to build a VANET application through protocol architecture, control system and also by message structure. A comparative analysis of the proposed system and the existing system was conducted by considering the various factors involved [11].

Feroz *et al.* discuss vehicle-to-vehicle communication through WI-FI. An Arduino controller is used, which basically controls how the system works, and communication between vehicles is carried out using a WI-FI module. The movement of the vehicles is controlled by the controller and a warning system is established to alert the driver [2].

In their study, Vibin *et al.* discuss how the exchange of data between two vehicles is done through two levels: the inter- and intra-vehicular level. The data exchange helps to detect the sudden change that occurs in the movement of vehicles and if any dangerous situations occur an alert will be given to drivers. The data is sent through the BSM format [4].

Chowdhury *et al.* use the IoT approach for vehicle-to-vehicle communication in which numerous data is collected using various sensors and the data that is received is stored in the database using the IoT. If any of the vehicles are moving within the particular range the data that is being stored is shared and this helps to clear the traffic and avoid any dangerous situations that are occurring [3].

Priyanka and Kumar discuss the communication between vehicles using ARM and Zigbee technology. The system is controlled using an ARM controller and communication between vehicles or the information is transferred through Zigbee technology [8].

The main topic of the study by Gowda C.P *et al.* is the establishment of vehicle-to-vehicle communication through its location by taking into consideration latitude and longitude and specifying their relationship. When vehicles are in close proximity an alert message is sent and hence the drivers will be cautioned [7].

The main aim of Nachimuthu *et al.* is to establish good quality service for an intelligent transport system that is helped by Li-Fi technology. Here the data is transmitted wirelessly with the help of Li-Fi–based technology. Li-Fi mainly consists of two types of kits, one is the transmitter and the other is the receiver. The V2V system consists of Li-Fi transmitters placed on a leading vehicle and the Li-Fi receiver placed on a following vehicle, which allows communication to take place between them and an alert will be sent to avoid collision [9]. The review paper by Kavyapriya discusses the various technologies involved in V2V communication for crash avoidance. Li-Fi technology is among the various technologies explained [1].

Limbasiya and Das discuss how vehicle-to-vehicle communication occurs between vehicles and explain how authentication, authority, and security can be achieved [10].

15.3   Brief Description of the Techniques

15.3.1   ARM and Zigbee Technology

The model designed in ARM and Zigbee is the DSRC, which is a default allowing vehicles to communicate in either one or two directional mode. This process is as follows: Ultrasonic, vibration, and temperature sensors are attached to the monitoring ARM controller and show the values via LCD. The sensor values are increased before loading to the controller unit to enhance the output signal. A Zigbee radio frequency (RF) transponder is used for transferring messages between vehicles. The controller is used for making decisions by using configured fuzzy logic based on a shared knowledge. The decision to monitor the vehicle velocity is made (Figure 15.1).

15.3.2   VANET-Based Prototype

To build ad-hoc environment, VANETS may affect the efficiency of the wireless network among vehicles. Inside the automobile are the on-board sensors. These sensors are being used to determine the source, velocity and motion of a vehicle [15].

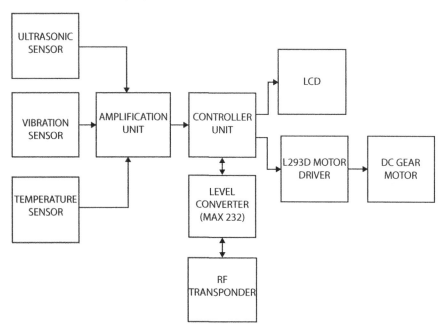

Figure 15.1 Block diagram of ARM and Zigbee for vehicle-to-vehicle communication.

15.3.2.1   Calculating Distance by Considering Parameters

The network model takes into account three automobiles in the wireless vehicle network. Distance is the big problem that nodes need to think about in order to define the neighbors. Ultrasonic sensors for distances are mounted on all four sides of each vehicle [14]. Every vehicle gets its neighboring nodes by its wireless range that is provided to the microcontroller which displays the vehicle "minimum safe distance" on the LCD screen closest to it. Ultrasonic sensor HC-SR04 measures range in the vehicle environment in non-line-of-sight conditions.

15.3.2.2   Calculating Speed by Considering Parameters

An important feature for VANET in pursuing the vehicle is the frequency by which the neighboring vehicles can arrive at it. The IR sensor is considered for calculating the speed of a DC motor, which transfers wheel velocity to the microcontroller and presents it on the comparable motor LCD panel. The entire system's controlling unit or microcontroller is the RF receiver unit that is attached to the L293d; DC motors are configured by a motor driver and DC motor speed is determined using the IR sensor.

15.3.3   Wi-Fi–Based Technology

The Wi-Fi–based model is designed to identify the incoming vehicle and maintain communication with the vehicle through Wi-Fi signals, and transfer data to monitor the speed of the vehicle or redirect the vehicle's course, thereby preventing a collision. The model is implemented by using an Arduino microcontroller. In addition to using an ultrasonic sensor that uses sound waves to detect obstacles, the vehicle is also designed with an alert buzzer that will notify the vehicle's driver of the obstacle.

The device is designed to identify the incoming vehicle and maintain communication with the vehicle through Wi-Fi and transfers data to monitor the speed of the vehicle or to redirect the vehicle's course, thereby preventing collision. The model is been implemented by using Arduino microcontroller. Using an ultrasonic sensor that uses sound waves to detect obstacles, the vehicle was accomplished and an alert buzzer also will be accessed to notify the vehicle driver. Vehicle-to-vehicle connectivity is the real-time wireless transfer of data between motor vehicles. The primary goal of V2V communication is to avoid deaths by permitting vehicles in transit to transmit information to each other about speed and direction. The driver of the car may merely receive an alert if there is a threat of a disaster

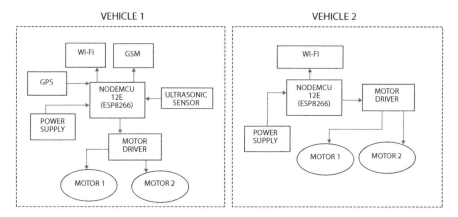

Figure 15.2 V2V communication using Wi-Fi.

or the vehicle itself could take preventive measures to slow itself down by braking. Figure 15.2 shows a schematic diagram of V2V communication using Wi-Fi. This block diagram consists of Node MCU(ESP8266), power supply, ultrasonic sensor, GSM, GPS, and driver motor. The power supply works by transforming AC from a main supply into a steady DC voltage. All units are given a 28-pin ATmega328 controller is being used to monitor the inputs to the external entity by transmission and reception. This also requires modulation of the pulse width (PWM). Ultrasonic sensor is being used to locate nearby obstacles/vehicles consisting of four pins. A GSM modem is a specialized type of modem which accepts a SIM card, and operates over a subscription to a mobile operator, just like a mobile phone. GSM modems can be a fast and efficient way to get started with SMS, as no special subscription to an SMS service provider is required. GSM modems are a cost-effective solution for receiving SMS messages in most regions of the world, since the sender pays for transmitting the message. GPS is a space-based radio-navigation system that records data in all weather conditions wherever there is an unobstructed line of sight to four or more GPS satellites anywhere on or near the Earth.

15.3.4   Li-Fi–Based Technique

The Li-Fi technique offers a V2V communications network that doesn't require a GPS navigation or wireless Wi-Fi or 3G connection. It is recommended to use a sonar programmable interface controller (PIC) which sends a 40 kHz short RF pulse that cannot be heard by the human ear. The microcontroller senses the echo of the signal. Distance is measured from the time it takes for the echo signal to be sent and received. The proposed system needs a transmitter and a receiver at both the back and front sides of a vehicle in each car. To analyze Li-Fi–based technology, the two schemes given below have to be analyzed (Figure 15.3).

- First Scheme
  When vehicle 1 brakes, the vehicle speed sensor detects that the actual speed is significantly lower than the preceding speed. The transmitter situated at the taillights therefore transmits a communication to the second vehicle. The second vehicle collects the message and uses the photodiode at the end. In vehicle 2, an LCD will show a message of (Slow Down).
- Second Scheme
  When vehicle 1 is at the junction T, vehicle 1 emits data on speed to vehicle 2 with LED in the headlights. The photodiode in vehicle 2 receives the details related to speed, so both speeds are contrasted. If vehicle 2 enters the junction as vehicle 1 is traveling at fast speed, the person who is driving is warned to check out other surrounding vehicles. The V2V communication block diagram with Li-Fi technology is shown in Figure 15.4. The source of data, for example

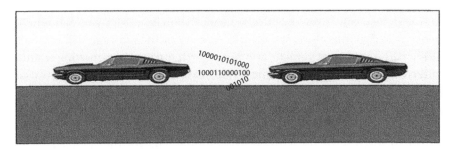

Figure 15.3 V2V communication using Li-Fi in accordance with the First Scheme.

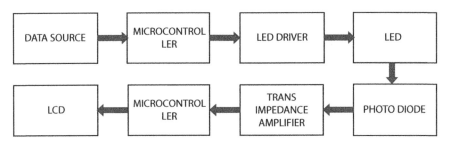

Figure 15.4 Block diagram for V2V communication using Li-Fi in accordance with the Second Scheme.

(Speed Sensor), records the vehicle speed. The sensor speed data are peak-to-peak AC voltages; hence, the microcontroller converts them to DC voltage to read. Next, a microcontroller processes the data (for example to evaluate present and previous speeds). The latest data collected is forwarded to the LED controller. To secure the LED a constant current is maintained by the LED motor. Instead, the LED light transmits the data as a transmitter. The photodiode identifies the emitted light in the form of current in a wireless data transmission by light. A transimpedance amplifier is used to transform the obtained current to voltage. Voltage is eventually handled by the microcontroller, which can be viewed on the LCD screen.

15.3.5   Real-Time Wireless System

The wireless technique requires a solid part made up of various usable subunits, with a receiver and a transmitter inserted in the main part that are needed to transmit and collect data. In case of an emergency, the main unit is the vehicle used to coordinate vehicles to clear the road.

The device will connect with the nearby vehicle and transmit an emergency message; therefore, the vehicle receiver of the message will interact along with the closest vehicle, and henceforth during slow-moving traffic, and connect with both the traffic signals to open up a path through traffic jams. The second subunit is composed of sensors such as sensors for temperature and relative humidity. The wireless sensors include daily cycles of ambient temperature and humidity in real-time. If the temperature recorded reaches the limit, the refrigeration device for the vehicle is triggered. The third subunit is the GPS module which measures the precise velocity, the travel speed and the vehicle position. The GPS is a satellite technique used to monitor the altitude, distance, and position of the vehicle. In this scheme the last subunit is the proximity sensors. The sensors are attached onto the vehicle's back end. In reverse gear such ultrasonic sensors find the difference between barriers and relay data via wireless to the driver's side main unit. The information is displayed on the LCD monitor in real time, i.e., a car speed, the places visited by the vehicle, the temperature and relative humidity of the area, and the distance to the nearest vehicle.

15.4 Various Technologies Involved in V2V Communication

Vehicle-to-vehicle communication requires the use of the various technologies presented in Table 15.1.

15.5 Results and Analysis

Vehicle-to-vehicle technologies were analyzed by considering situations such as collision and delay redundancy that occur in V2V communication and which can be overcome by an alert warning system. These technologies

Table 15.1 Comparison of various technologies involved in V2V communication.

Various technologies for vehicle to vehicle communication	Advantages	Drawbacks
ARM and ZIGBEE based intelligent vehicle for v2v	Reduce road crashes and saves lives	Cost is high, complexity is low, speed of transferring data is slow.
VANET-based prototype	This can be implemented on any kind of vehicles like buses, cars etc.	the cost depends on the hardware and sensors that are used.
WI-FI based technology	A driver can fetch any kind of data like the speed, distance travelled, date, time etc.	Speed is slow when analyzed with LI-FI.
LI-FI based technology	Data density of li-fi is high. It is more efficient in terms of vehicle to vehicle communication [6]	Without the light source internet doesn't work and transferring of data will be difficult.
Real time wireless system	It improves the traffic management system; it is affordable to use	Cost depends on the complexity of the vehicles.

help to improve traffic congestion and traffic safety. In the Li-Fi technique, sending information from one vehicle to the other with LED light is easy. In comparison to Wi-Fi, complications due to traffic congestion are decreased to a very great extent when using Li-Fi. The cost of implementing VANET depends on the kind of hardware components and sensors being considered. As the number of vehicles used in deploying V2V technologies is greater, they will also cost more. The existing technologies described in this chapter have their own advantages and disadvantages.

15.6   Conclusion

Communication between vehicles plays a very important role in providing safety to people. This chapter provided a survey of the literature on various technologies that are involved in vehicle-to-vehicle communication. When considering the advantages and disadvantages of these technologies, extra features can be added for enhancing the system based on the requirements. Hence, vehicle-to-vehicle communication plays a very important role in reducing accidents by making people more aware of situations that occur on the road, thereby saving many lives.

References

1. Kavyapriya, S., Review Paper on Vehicle to Vehicle Communication for Crash Avoidance System. *J. Electrical & Electronic Systems*, 8, 1, 1–4, 2019.
2. Amarsingh Feroz, C., Kavitha, N., Kasthuri, M., Ram Jeya Sudha, R., Vehicle to vehicle communication for collision avoidance. www.nhtsa.gov/technology-innovation/vehicle-vehicle-communication. 5, 7, 544–549, 2019.
3. Chowdhury, D.N., Agarwal, N., Laha, A.B., Mukherjee, A., A vehicle-to-vehicle communication system using iot approach. *2nd International conference on Electronics, Communication and Aerospace Technology (ICECA)*, 2018.
4. Vibin, V., Sivraj, P., Vanitha, Dr.V., Implementation of In-Vehicle and V2V Communication with Basic Safety Message Format. *International Conference on Inventive Research in Computing Applications (ICIRCA)*, 2018.
5. Gupta, N., Rajesh, D., Suryawanshi, Y.A., VANET Based Prototype Vehicles Model for Vehicle to Vehicle Communication. *2017 International conference of Electronics, Communication and Aerospace Technology (ICECA)*, Coimbatore, 207–212, 2017.
6. Kulkarni, S. and Darekar, A., Proposed Framework for V2V Communication using Li-Fi Technology. *2017 International Conference on Circuits, Controls, and Communications (CCUBE)*, Bangalore, 187–190, 2017.

7. Mallikarjuna, G.C.P., Hajare, R., Mala, C.S., Rakshith, K.R., Nadig, A.R., Prtathana, P., Design and implementation of real time wireless system for vehicle safety and vehicle to vehicle communication, *2017 International Conference on Electrical, Electronics, Communication, Computer, and Optimization Techniques (ICEECCOT)*, Mysuru, pp. 354–358, 2017.

8. Priyanka, D.D. and Kumar, T.S., ARM and Zigbee Based Intelligent Vehicle Communication for Collision Avoidance. *International Conference on Advanced Communication Control and Computing Technologies (ICACCCT)*, pp. 230–237, 2016.

9. Nachimuthu, S., Pooranachandran, S., Sharomena Aarthi, B., design and implementation of a vehicle to vehicle communication system using li-fi technology. *Int. Res. J. Eng. Technol. (IRJET)*, 3, 5, 3142–3145, 2016.

10. Limbasiya, T. and Das, D., Secure Message Transmission Algorithm for Vehicle to Vehicle (V2V) Communication. *2016 IEEE Region 10 Conference (TENCON)*, Singapore, 2507–2512, 2016.

11. Meshram, A., *et al.* Design Approach for Vehicle To Vehicle (V2V) Dissemination of Messages in Vehicular Adhoc Network, 4, 7, pp. 65–67, 2014.

12. Liang, W., Li, Z., Bie, R., Vehicular Ad Hoc Network: Architectures, Research Issues, Methodologies Challenges, and Trend. *Hindawi Publishing Corp. Int. J. Distrib. Sens. Netw.*, 2, 6, 1–11, 2015.

13. Doijad, R.G. and Kamble, P.A., Design of Prototype model for Vehicle to Vehicle Secure Formatted Communication. *Int. J. Adv. Res. Comput. Commun. Eng.*, 4, 7, pp. 398–401, 2015.

14. Muthuramalingam, S., Bharathi, A., Gayathri, N., Sathiyaraj, R., Balamurugan, B., IoT Based Intelligent Transportation System (IoT-ITS) for Global Perspective: A Case Study, in: *Internet of Things and Big Data Analytics for Smart Generation*, pp. 279–300, Springer, Cham, 2019.

15. Gayathri, N. and Kumar, S.R., Critical analysis of various routing protocols in VANET. *Int. J. Adv. Res. Comput. Sci. Software Eng.*, 1, 135–141 2015.

16

Smart Wheelchair

Mekala Ajay, Pusapally Srinivas* and Lupthavisha Netam

*Electrical and Electronics Engineering, Department of Electrical Sciences,
Karunya Institute of Technology and Sciences, Coimbatore, India*

Abstract

Thousands of people suffer from disabilities due to health issues or accidents that result in impaired physical mobility. A smart assistive wheelchair can be a boon to people suffering from paralysis below the neck, quadriplegia or congenital gait abnormalities. In our proposed design of a smart wheelchair, the patient will control the chair by simple verbal commands being analyzed by a built-in speech recognition system of Amazon Alexa, a smart home-automation approach. These user's commands are identified for directions. The wheelchair provides a collision-free navigation using sonar sensor. To enable autonomous navigation a MATLAB simulation model is implemented to determine a path planner to the destined location in a local 2D indoor environment. The probabilistic roadmap (PRM) and rapidly-exploring random tree (RRT) algorithms have been used for the same. The integrated patient-monitoring system assists with continuous real-time monitoring of the user's vital body parameters such as heart rate, ECG, patients' physical state and room temperature, and thereby enabling it over an IoT platform for ready reference of the concerned medical authorities, to alert if any parameter goes out of range.

Keywords: Smart wheelchair, health monitoring, IoT, Amazon Alexa, collision-free navigation, path planning algorithms, path planner

16.1 Background

Globally, 250,000–500,000 new cases arise annually on paralysis and spinal cord injuries, and over 80% of the elderly population have mobility

**Corresponding author*: samsrinivas.ss@gmail.com

Ashutosh Kumar Dubey, Abhishek Kumar, S. Rakesh Kumar, N. Gayathri, Prasenjit Das (eds.) AI and IoT-Based Intelligent Automation in Robotics, (271–284) © 2021 Scrivener Publishing LLC

difficulty. Approximately 15% of the world population suffers from a high prevalence of chronic disorders, leading to an increase in disability among a large number of the population. For cases in which it is difficult or impossible to walk, a power wheelchair is a boon. A manual or electric wheelchair works for most of the low and medium level mobility difficulties; however, a certain section of the disabled community remains, who find operating a standard powered wheelchair difficult, such as individuals suffering with impaired vision or affected by spasms or cognitive deficits. Thus, inspired by features from mobile robots, smart assistive wheelchairs capable of storing medical history and providing feasible alternatives for controlling a wheelchair without human intervention can be extremely useful.

To enhance manoeuvrability several alternatives to drive a wheelchair independently are developed such as facial muscle movement based input interface [1], eye-tracking system [2], EMG and hybrid-based HMI [3, 4], head gesture recognition [5, 6], joystick/head-joystick interface [7], hand gesture recognition [8], tongue motion [9], finger movement tracking [10], the conventional touchpad interface [11] and so on. Using an android phone has also been used as an alternative for controlling wheelchairs.

However, implementing these by various sensorial or cognitive disorder patients could be an exhausting task. Wheelchair designs proposing voice control navigation [12] is an attractive approach as it does not require much physical effort to operate. The user can be in a relaxed sitting position and control the wheelchair with clear verbal commands very easily. This can be potentially beneficial for a large section of people using wheelchairs.

Generally, voice control are difficult to implement with utmost accuracy because of various factors such as noise, echo, varied accents, disorganized speech or failure to recognize user's voice by the machine. As shown in Figure 16.1, the proposed wheelchair is enabled with Amazon Alexa through skill development, a smart home-automation approach. Alexa is a virtual assistant AI technology developed by Amazon that is fully capable of voice interactions. Alexa is built on natural language processing (NLP) that is fully capable of identifying speech. It refers to the user's voice recordings with its database to clarify accents and interpret the probable action to be taken; for instance, "to sing a song," "play news" or operate a locally connected device.

Its built-in speech recognition system clears the audio signal by identifying ambience noise, cancelling echo and clearly distinguishing "wake word detection" wherein it turns on only when the word "Alexa" is uttered to avoid false detection and execution of commands.

The fundamental purpose of an assistive wheelchair is to enhance mobility alternatives without much human intervention. Concepts such as path planning and motion planning answer the idea of autonomous navigation.

They cover a range of applications from robotics and virtual prototyping to pharmaceutical drug designing. In our project, we have implemented MATLAB simulation on two different path planning algorithms and derived conclusions. Simulation of a differential drive robot is also implemented as an approach of virtual prototyping of an autonomous wheelchair.

Our proposed model is aimed to assist people with difficult, painful or impossible walking. Manual or electrical wheelchairs perform their work for most of the low and medium level disability cases. A smart wheelchair is designed to provide a certain degree of autonomy when manual control is unfeasible due to the patient's disability. It is specifically aimed at assisting people suffering from paralysis below the neck, quadriplegia or congenital gait abnormalities.

In Figure 16.2 the driver circuit architecture of the proposed wheelchair is shown which makes the model a feasible alternative for the user to control the wheelchair by simple verbal commands on directions. As shown in Figure 16.3, the wheelchair is also enabled with a real-time heath

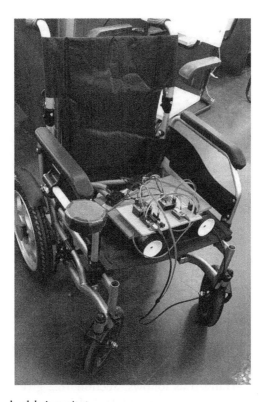

Figure 16.1 The wheelchair project.

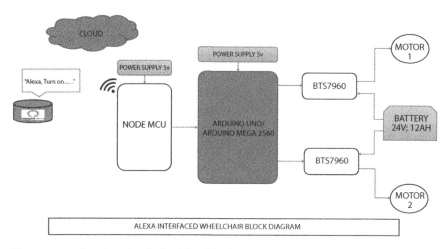

Figure 16.2 Alexa Interfaced wheelchair block diagram.

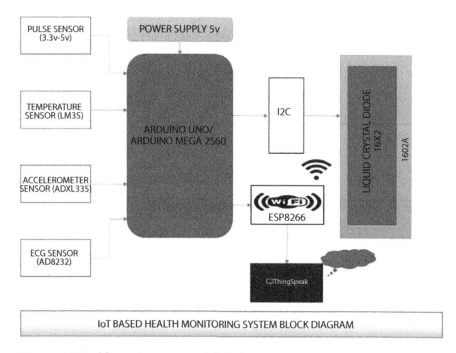

Figure 16.3 Health-monitoring system block diagram.

monitoring system which has been enabled over an IoT platform for constant monitoring of vital parameters.

The chapter is arranged as follows: Section 16.2 gives an overview of the system in detail, Sections 16.3 and 16.4 elaborate on the workings of the system, Section 16.5 focuses on MATLAB simulations on autonomous navigation concepts. Section 16.6 concludes the chapter and Section 16.7 discusses the future work.

16.2 System Overview

The proposed wheelchair, shown in Figure 16.1 has the following major elements:

- Real-time health monitoring using IoT
- Wheelchair's driver circuit and Amazon Alexa interface
- Obstacle detection
- MATLAB simulations on path planning and motion planning

16.3 Health-Monitoring System Using IoT

This section deals with a built-in health-monitoring system which is enabled over an IoT platform for ready access, as shown in Figure 16.3 and Figure 16.4(a). Sensors such as an electrocardiogram (ECG) sensor and pulse sensor have been used to determine body parameters. A room temperature sensor is used to monitor patient's physical environment temperature. These parameters have been sampled to obtain reliable final results. An accelerometer sensor is deployed to determine patient's physical state such as, "sitting" and "trying to get up" body postures on the Y-axis range.

As shown in Figure 16.4(b), all the sampled parameters are enabled over the IoT platform of ThingSpeak via Wi-Fi Module ESP8266. For patient's

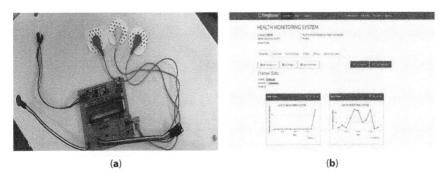

(a)   (b)

Figure 16.4 (a) The health monitoring system circuit; (b) Health parameters obtained on IoT platform.

reference, an LCD interface is also enabled through inter-integrated circuits (I2C) communication protocol.

16.4   Driver Circuit of Wheelchair Interfaced with Amazon Alexa

As shown in Figure 16.2 and 16.5, the components of our wheelchair driver circuit include two BTS7960, Arduino Uno, Alexa virtual assistant, NODE MCU and two DC shunt motors. The DC shunt motors enabled on our wheelchair are powered by a 24Ah battery. Two BTS7960 driver circuit have been used for simultaneous control of the two wheels for directions such as "FORWARD," "REVERSE," "LEFT" and "RIGHT" on user's verbal command.

The driver circuit is programmed on Arduino Uno which is enabled to NODE MCU via serial communication for interfacing with the Amazon Alexa virtual assistant. Sinric mobile application was used in the wheelchair's skill development process with Alexa. The direction control of the two wheels were obtained as shown in Table 16.1.

Figure 16.5 Driver circuit used in wheelchair implementing two BTS7960 driver circuits.

Table 16.1 Motor directions for wheelchair movements.

Direction	Motor 1	Motor 2
Forward	Forward	Forward
Backward	Reverse	Reverse
Right	Forward	Reverse
Left	Reverse	Forward

16.5   MATLAB Simulations

Virtual simulations on MATLAB were implemented to monitor autonomous navigation on a local 2D map. This subsystem on simulations includes the following:

- Obstacle detection
- Optimal path planning based on two path planning algorithms
- Differential drive robot for path following

16.5.1   Obstacle Detection

This subsystem deals with obstacle detection with the help of a sonar sensor. A sonar sensor mounted on a servo motor with an angular range of 180 degree, was programmed through the hardware support package of Arduino on MATLAB to detect obstacles present within the actual distance of 0–12 cm. As shown in Figure 16.6, the same result was obtained on a serial plotter interface for a distance of range 0-50cm. Obstacle's distance detection was done through the formula below:

$$\text{Distance} = (\text{duration} * 0.034) / 2 \qquad (16.1)$$

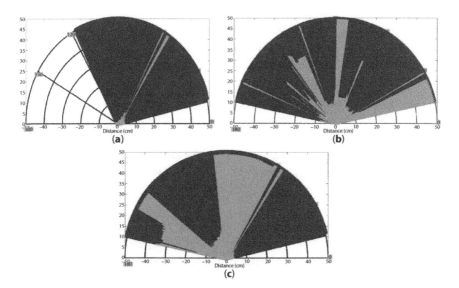

Figure 16.6 (a–c) Serial monitor plotter of the ultrasonic radar system prototype.

In the above formula, duration refers to the time period of echo pin with high input. The number 0.034 is the sound velocity in cm. The product of the two is divided by 2 to give actual distance of the obstacle.

On the serial plotter interface, distance ranges from 0–50 cm. Obstacles detected 50 cm and above are assumed to be equivalent to 50 cm distance. The dark blue area in Figure 16.6 denotes obstacles and light blue area shows the free space.

16.5.2   Implementing Path Planning Algorithms

This subsystem deals with computations and simulation in path planning for an object to move freely among the static obstacles configuration space C0 in a Configuration space (C-space). The complement of C0 with respect to C-space, i.e., C-free, is the free configuration space in the workspace for path planning algorithms. The two primary algorithms implemented are Probabilistic Road Map and Rapidly Exploring Random Tree algorithm for path planning.

a) Implementing Probabilistic Road Map (PRM)
Probabilistic roadmap is a network of simple straight paths that connects collision-free configurations randomly. For problems that involve searching the configuration space of a system for a collision-free path that connects a given start and goal configuration, and also satisfy constraints imposed by complicated obstacles, PRM shows simple and reliable behavior and therefore is widely preferred.

Figure 16.7 shows the basic PRM algorithm. A roadmap graph is initialized where V & E represents vertex and edges. A configuration q is randomly chosen and if object (robot's configuration) is at Q-free; collision detection is implemented here. This process is repeated until N vertices are chosen and for each q, k-closest neighbors are selected. The local planner connects q to q'. Upon successful connection (i.e., collision-free local path) an edge q, q' is added. Figure 16.8 shows the two different ways obtained to reach the goal position when PRM algorithm was implemented on the local 2D map.

b) Implementing Rapidly Exploring Random Tree (RRT)
Figure 16.9 shows the basic RRT algorithm and Figure 16.10 gives the illustration of the algorithm. A simple iteration is performed in which each step attempts to extend the RRT by adding a new vertex which is based on

```
input:
    n:number of nodes to put in the roadmap
    k:number of closest neighbors for each configuration
output:
    A roadmap G = (V,E)

1. V ← ∅
2. E ← ∅
3. while|V|<n do
4.   repeat
5.     q ← a random configuration in Q
6.   untill q is collision free
7.   V ← V ∪(q)
8. end while
9. for all q ∈ V do
10.   Nq ← the k closest neighbors of q chosen from V,according to distance
11.   for all q' ∈ Nq do
12.     if (q,q') ∉ E and Δ(q,q') ≠ NIL then
13.       E ← EU[(q, q')]
14.     end if
15.   end for
16. end for
```

Figure 16.7 The PRM algorithm.

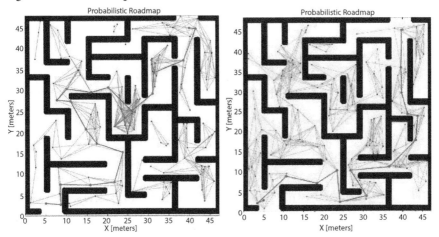

Figure 16.8 (a,b) Results obtained upon implementation of Probabilistic Road Map algorithm.

```
input:
    T =(V,E): an RRT
    q:a configuration towards which the tree T is grown
output:
    connected if q is connected to T otherwise it is a failure

1. repeat
2.    q_new ← extend RRT(T,q)
3. until(q_new=q or q_new=NIL)
4. if q_new=q then
5.    return connected
6. else
7.    return failure
8. end if
```

Figure 16.9 The RRT algorithm.

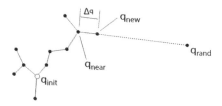

Figure 16.10 RRT Algorithm illustration.

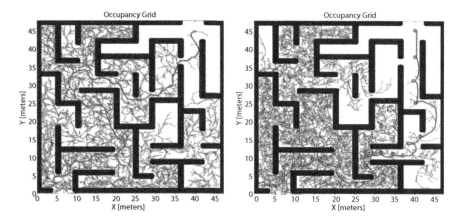

Figure 16.11 (a,b) Results obtained with RRT algorithm.

a randomly-selected configuration. The Δ q function selects the nearest vertex in the already formed RRT to the given sample configuration, q.

In this algorithm each tree is expanded. Considering initialization of two trees of T-initial and T-goal rooted at q-initial and q-goal, a q-rand is generated at uniform distance, and a corresponding q-near is found which is nearest to the node q-rand. Now move step size along the line, i.e., q-near to q-new to further q-rand. If no collision is detected, add q-new to tree. If tree merges, a path is found.

Figure 16.11 shows the results obtained on performing RRT algorithm on the local 2D map. The blue lines in Figure 16.11 show the various branches of the emerging graph to reach the goal point and the red line determines the final path from start to the goal position.

16.5.3   Differential Drive Robot for Path Following

This subsystem deals with simulation of path following through a differential drive robot. A differential wheeled robot is a mobile robot with movement based on two separately driven wheels on either side of the robot body, much similar to our powered wheelchair. Therefore, Kinematics for the same are as follows:

$$\dot{x} = v cos\theta \tag{16.2}$$

$$\dot{y} = v sin\theta \tag{16.3}$$

$$\dot{\theta} = \omega \tag{16.4}$$

Where [x (t), y (t), θ (t)] are the position and orientation of the mobile robot with respect to the mapping frame. These determine the pose of the mobile robot.

A path defined by a set of waypoints was used for the path following of the robot. As shown in Figure 16.12, the waypoints of the path identified by PRM algorithm in Figure 16.8 (a) were used to drive the differential drive robot simulation.

To implement motion planning, a two-wheeled differential drive robot with pure pursuit path following controller was used to drive the robot along the predetermined path. As shown in Figure 16.13 the simulation of a differential drive robot tracing the predetermined path was obtained. The two inputs required by the simulated differential drive robot are linear and angular velocity, which were adjusted according to the powered wheelchair's specification for real-time simulation.

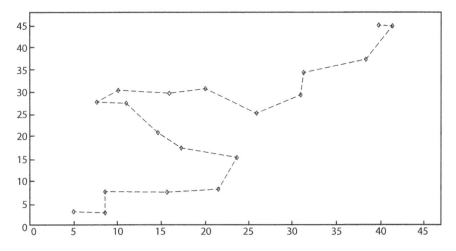

Figure 16.12 Planned trajectory based on waypoints obtained through implementing PRM algorithm.

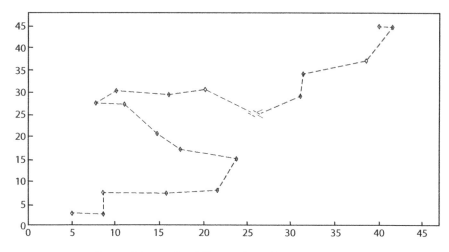

Figure 16.13 Differential drive robot following the path.

16.6   Conclusion

A smart wheelchair was built interfacing Amazon Alexa's built-in speech recognition system to enable directions based on verbal commands. Implementation of the two algorithms, namely, Probabilistic Road Map and Rapidly Exploring Random Tree, on our example map was done on MATLAB software. It is observed that though a PRM algorithm is probabilistically complete and can be easily applied to high-dimensional C-space, it is unlikely to sample nodes on narrow passages and therefore is impractical to implement on surfaces to be constrained. However, a RRT algorithm is useful because of its fast and uniform exploration of the C-space with it's iterative refinement wherein random points in the environment are connected to its closest vertex in the emerging graph. It is then connected to a goal node based on a given threshold.

MATLAB simulations are very convenient, helpful and consistent for implementing different algorithms.

16.7   Future Work

Future work in our project may include implementing the MATLAB simulations in hardware using the hardware support packages to make a fully autonomous wheelchair product. Implementation of LIDAR sensors can be used to perform 360-degree real-time mapping for a distance of 12 m.

Optimal route planning considering barriers such as slope and surface type using a graphical information system can be implemented alongside path planning algorithm. To control wheel motion for proper control of differential robots, a PID controller to control velocities and speed for more accuracy can also be implemented. Moreover, a training wheelchair that behaves well in both a static and moving obstacles environment can be part of the future scope of wheelchair research. This will add autonomous capabilities and help the user drive the wheelchair more efficiently.

Acknowledgment

This project was implemented under the guidance of Electronics Corporation of India Limited (ECIL) under an embedded department. We extend our gratitude to our HoD-EEE, Dr. Immanuel Selvakumar (Karunya Institute of Technology and Sciences), and project guide Dr. R. Meenal for providing technical support.

References

1. Wei, L., Hu, H., Yuan, K., Use of forehead bio-signals for controlling an Intelligent Wheelchair. *2008 IEEE International Conference on Robotics and Biomimetic*, Bangkok, pp. 108–113, 2009.
2. Lin, C.-S., Ho, C.-W., Chen, W.-C., Chiu, C.-C., Yeh, M.-S., Powered wheelchair controlled by eye-tracking system. *Opt. Appl.*, 36, 401–412, 2006.
3. Tsui, C.S.L., Jia, P., Gan, J.Q., Hu, H., Yuan, K., EMG-based hands-free wheelchair control with EOG attention shift detection. *2007 IEEE International Conference on Robotics and biomimetic (ROBIO)*, Sanya, pp. 1266–1271, 2007.
4. Wei, L. and Hu, H., EMG and visual based HMI for hands-free control of an intelligent wheelchair. *2010 8th World Congress on Intelligent Control and Automation*, Jinan, pp. 1027–1032, 2010.
5. Gray, J.O., Jia, P., Hu, H.H., Lu, T., Yuan, K., Head gesture recognition for hands-free control of an intelligent wheelchair. *Ind. Robot Int. J.*, 34, 60–68, 2007.
6. Dey, P., Hasan, M.M., Mostofa, S., Rana, A.I., Smart wheelchair integrating head gesture navigation. *2019 International Conference on Robotics, Electrical and Signal Processing Techniques (ICREST)*, Dhaka, Bangladesh, pp. 329–334, 2019.
7. Rofer, T., Mandel, C., Laue, T., Controlling an automated wheelchair via joystick/head-joystick supported by smart driving assistance. *2009 IEEE*

International Conference on Rehabilitation Robotics, Kyoto, pp. 743–748, 2009.

8. Kundu, A.S., Mazumder, O., Lenka, P.K., Bhaumik, S., Hand gesture recognition based omnidirectional wheelchair control using IMU and EMG sensors. *J. Intell. Rob. Syst.*, 91, 3–4, 529–541, 2018.

9. Huo, X., Wang, J., Ghovanloo, M., Wireless control of powered wheelchairs with tongue motion using tongue drive assistive technology. *2008 30th Annual International Conference of the IEEE Engineering in Medicine and Biology Society*, pp. 4199–4202, 2008, August, IEEE.

10. Wallam, F. and Asif, M., Dynamic finger movement tracking and voice commands based smart wheelchair. *Int. J. Comput. Electr. Eng.*, 3, 4, 497, 2011.

11. Khadilkar, S.U. and Wagdarikar, N., Android phone controlled voice, gesture and touch screen operated smart wheelchair. *2015 International Conference on Pervasive Computing (ICPC)*, pp. 1–4, 2015, January, IEEE.

12. Simpson, R.C. and Levine, S.P., Voice control of a powered wheelchair. *IEEE Trans. Neural Syst. Rehabil. Eng.*, 10, 2, 122–125, 2002.

17

Defaulter List Using Facial Recognition

Kavitha Esther[1]*, Akilindin S.H.[2†], Aswin S.[2‡] and Anand P.[2§]

[1]*Department of Information Technology, Hindustan Institute of Technology and Science, Chennai, India*
[2]*Department of Information Technology, Hindustan Institute of Technology and Science, Chennai, India*

Abstract

In this digital era, where change is the only constant, it is mandatory to evolve and keep up with the fast-paced environment. The key to evolution in the field of technology in the past decade has been artificial intelligence and machine learning. This chapter explores this emerging route to sort out and develop one of the traditional methods of manual recording of identification into automated facial recognition using deep learning. Deep learning is a subset of artificial intelligence that aids in training the system to recognize distinctive patterns, such as faces and objects, in the form of datasets. The inputted data is compared with the prestored data to identify the object. By applying the principals of deep learning, we can identify defaulters (unregistered datasets). That is, it seeks to identify users in the specified facility (in college buses) by accurate identity matching with respect to the prerecorded data that helps to recognize new members/defaulters who are illegally availing college bus services by alerting the listed authorities through email.

The added benefits of the proposed system are it minimizes human error and saves invaluable time. Deep learning minimizes overlapping of similar datasets and helps in accurately determining the student's identity. The suggested system has been developed keeping in mind the affordability and flexibility aspects for ease of use with the combination of powerful face recognition algorithms powered by Python and Raspberry Pi.

*Corresponding author: kavithaesther@hindustanuniv.ac.in
†Corresponding author: Akilindin@gmail.com
‡Corresponding author: Aswins933@gmail.com
§Corresponding author: Iamanandprem@gmail.com

Ashutosh Kumar Dubey, Abhishek Kumar, S. Rakesh Kumar, N. Gayathri, Prasenjit Das (eds.) AI and IoT-Based Intelligent Automation in Robotics, (285–294) © 2021 Scrivener Publishing LLC

Keywords: Deep learning, facial recognition, artificial intelligence, defaulter list, image recognition, object detection

17.1 Introduction

The volume of automation each one of us face in our day-to-day lives is steadily increasing. All industries are striving to develop new technologies with a common goal in mind, which is to make work easier for the end user. One of the key players in the improvement of user experience is artificial intelligence. Its presence has revolutionized interpretation of data and relieved users from information overload by enabling availability of optimal data required. The main reason for its growing demand across multiple platforms and industries is its ability to learn from the inputted data and recognize patterns and process it to predict similar accurate results. With the help of powerful algorithms, the precision of the results is astounding.

The idea is to develop a facial recognition system that identifies the registered students traveling in college buses and signals the authorities when an unregistered student(s) avails the college bus services without prior permission. As part of deep learning, the proposed system can be achieved through object detection algorithm (Figure 17.1).

The initial step of the process is to identify key focal points that are needed to differentiate each object (features of a student's face) and recording it for accurate identification. This will aid in distinguishing the

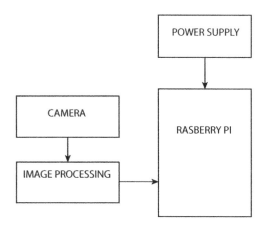

Figure 17.1 Block diagram depicting the data flow [5].

registered students from the unregistered students (defaulters/intruders) through frame-by-frame analysis from the obtained video feed. After successfully storing students' identification, a histogram showcasing the relation between recognized IDs (students) and video playing period is generated. Additionally, to emphasize the difference between recognized IDs (students) and the live number of students in the bus are visualized through flames through this program.

17.2 System Analysis

17.2.1 Problem Description

With a major part of technology moving towards automation, the focus is on leveraging deep learning to convert the old-fashioned method of manual identification of defaulters to automated facial recognition that spots and alerts the listed authorities about the unregistered students (defaulters) that are availing the college bus facilities without authorization using object detection algorithm.

17.2.2 Existing System

The existing system of identifying defaulters that are using college buses without prior registration has been through weekly manual identification of defaulters by the staff in charge. This traditional method of tracking lacks consistency and accuracy. This also includes loopholes that are taken advantage of by students without prior registration and acknowledgement.

A few examples of the limitations of the existing system are i) College bus drivers permitting unregistered students to avail college transportation services. This leads to overcrowding of buses and can affect the safety of the passengers traveling. ii) It also limits seat availability, which distresses pass holders who cannot get a seat [6].

This dishonest usage of university transportation results in a consecutive increase of the number of illegal transporters. This system needs to be eliminated for the safety and comfort of travelers.

17.2.3 Proposed System

There are three major stages in the proposed system (Figure 17.2). The first stage is the image capturing and processing in which the face of each

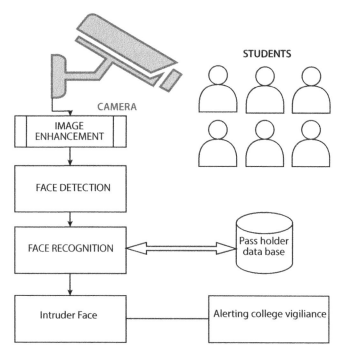

Figure 17.2 Architecture of the proposed system [3].

student that has been authorized to travel in college buses is stored in the database for recognition. This step is crucial as it assists in identifying the registered students from the defaulters and it is an absolute necessity for the database to be updated regularly for accurate reading. Also, it is obligatory for the registered face to be clearly captured for more precise reading [4].

The second stage of the proposed system is image detection. The real-time image captured while entering the bus is compared with the stored IDs to verify whether the student traveling is registered or not. The placement of the camera at optimal location is vital to capture the complete features of the student's face and for better accuracy. If the recognized student does not match the list of stored student database, it captures and stores the face of the presumed defaulter [8].

The third stage of the proposed system is email alerts. The stored faces of the defaulters that are in the vehicle are emailed to the listed authorities through simple mail transfer protocol (SMTP) to the college management [3].

17.3   Implementation

17.3.1   Image Pre-Processing

The objective of pre-processing is to process the obtained image and improve the quality of the image through inflation to remove unintentional suppressions and distortions that lead to imprecise identification. This is achieved through different methods of geometric transformations such as scaling, translation and rotation, which positively impacts on the quality of the image extracted and produces precise results during image analysis.

17.3.2   Polygon Shape Family Pre-Processing

After processing the image, it is crucial to filter out all the essential features of the image, which is done using polygon shape pipelines as it supports in achieving accurate results in image enhancement. It also assists with fine tuning the processed image in accordance with thresholds and segmentation to extract precise features of the image. This technique identifies all features of the person accurately and delivers better results.

17.3.3   Image Segmentation

The extracted image is partitioned by the process of image segmentation, i.e., it attaches a label to each of the identified pixels. The obtained image is partitioned into multiple segments (pixel sets) called superpixels. By assigning labels to the obtained image, the analysis of the data becomes easier and helps detect the specified boundaries to differentiate between dissimilar images.

Every pixel in the selected region is attributed to a specific characteristic such as color, texture or intensity. Pixels that share common characteristics are grouped under the same label for easier identification. The advantage of using image segmentation to label pixels is that it finds patterns that helps in matching the identity by its texture and boundary shape [9].

17.3.4   Threshold

In this technique, the gray scale image is converted to a binary image based on the threshold value. It is crucial to select the correct threshold value (or values for multiple levels) for higher precision and coverage. It produces a histogram that is generated from the set of pixels that have been previously segmented. Similarly, the clusters in the image are identified by the peaks and valleys in the histogram (Figure 17.3) [2].

These clusters are continuously refined to smaller clusters by repeated process until no clusters are formed. Even while applying the same technique to multiple frames the single-pass efficiency can be maintained. This technique has the ability to differentiate between active objects and a static environment that helps to identify the objects in video tracking [1].

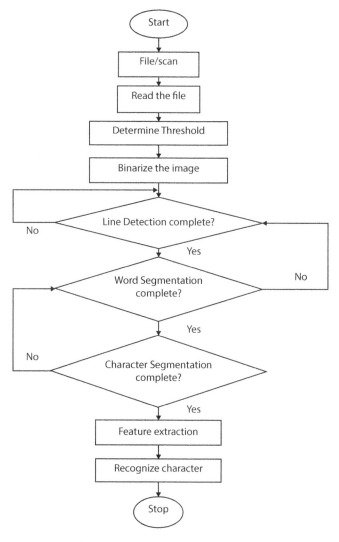

Figure 17.3 Flow chart of the proposed system [6].

17.3.5 Edge Detection

The detection of regions and boundaries are critical for image processing, any misinterpretation will greatly impact the results and lead to inaccuracy. The key to edge detection lies in adjusting the intensity of the image to identify the region boundaries. One of the limitations of the edge detection is that the image must be in closed region boundaries for object detection. Using edge detection technique applied to the spatial-taxon region can identify the disconnected edges that are part of an illusory contour.

17.3.6 Region Growing Technique

The real-time image captured under different lighting can cause variations in the image recorded. Therefore it is essential to train the algorithm to identify similar pixels and group them together using the region growing technique. This technique assumes that the neighboring pixels bounded in the same region have similar values.

When the similarity condition is satisfied, that particular pixel is assigned to the same cluster that its neighboring pixel belongs to. This assists in identifying the key focal points of the student's features in the submitted image.

17.3.7 Background Subtraction

Background subtraction technique assists in detecting the live objects in movement from the static background detected through the video feed. The recorded video has two components: the required object and the background image.

This technique helps to extract the identified object from its background for further processing and cancels out the noises that are captured along with the image technique.

17.3.8 Morphological Operations

Morphology helps to compare the inputted recorded image with the stored image from the database to identify whether the identity of student who has entered the college bus matches with the identity stored in the database.

The value of each pixel in the inputted image is compared to the value of pixel of the stored image. If the number of pixels matched has a high probability, then the system recognizes the student as a registered student. If the pixel matching has a low probability or minimum, then the system recognizes the student as a defaulter [3].

17.3.9   Object Detection

Object detection detects semantic objects of a specified class such as identification of recorded students' appearances from digital images and videos. Two features of object detection are face detection and face recognition. Each object class is classified based on its unique set of features. These unique features (such as eyes, nose, mouth) aid in object recognition [6].

17.4   Inputs and Outputs

The clear images and details of each registered student are prestored in the database for future identification and processing. As the student enters the college bus, the system records the facial features of the student and compares the inputted data with the stored data for analysis.

Case I: If the segmented pixels match the details of the student stored in the database, the system stores the recorded details for training to produce accurate results.
Case II: If the segmented pixels fail to match the details of the student stored in the database, the system stores the recorded image in the database and alerts the listed authorities through email using the SMTP.

17.5   Conclusion

The traditional method of identifying defaulters traveling in college buses through means of manual recognition lacks accuracy and reliability. Therefore, in an effort to replace the traditional system through automated

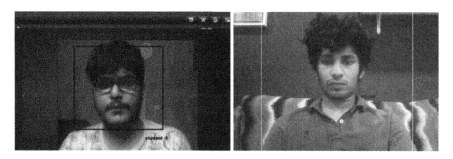

Figure 17.4 Identifying whether the inputted data is a student or an intruder [8].

facial recognition, the proposed system has two important features, which are image detection and image recognition (Figure 17.4).

Polygon shaped image pre-processing helps to identify the features of the student's face accurately. The recorded face is separated from the background through a series of techniques that helps to precisely identify the key features. Through morphological operations, the inputted data is compared with stored data to identify defaulters. If the recorded data does not match the stored data, the recorded image is stored in the database and emailed to the listed authorities, alerting them of the defaulters.

References

1. Bhatia, R., Biometrics and Face Recognition Techniques. *Int. J. Adv. Res. Comput. Sci. Softw. Eng.*, 3, 5, 93–99, 2013.
2. Syed Navaz, A.S., Sri, T.D., Mazumder, P., Professor, A., Face Recognition Using Principal Component Analysis and Neural Networks. *Int. J. Comput. Networking, Wirel. Mob. Commun.*, 3, 1, 2250–1568, 2013.
3. Dhavalsinh, A.M.K. and Solanki, V., A Survey on Face Recognition Techniques. *J. Image Process. Pattern Recognit. Prog.*, 4, 6, 11–16, 2013.
4. Yusuf, M., Ginardi, R.V.H., A.S.A., Rancang Bangun Aplikasi Absensi Perkuliahan Mahasiswa dengan Pengenalan Wajah. *J. Tek. ITS*, 5, 2, 766–770, 2016.
5. Ruiz-del-Solar, J. and Navarrete, P., Eigenspace-based face recognition: a comparative study of different approaches. *IEEE Trans. Syst. Man, Cybern. Part C.*, 35, 3, 2005.
6. Turk, M.A. and Pentland, A.P., Face recognition using eigenfaces. *Proceedings. 1991 IEEE Computer Society Conference on Computer Vision and Pattern Recognition*, pp. 586–591, 1991.
7. Coding, J., Untan, S.K., Muliawan, M.R., Irawan, B., Brianorman, Y., Komputer, J.S., Metode Eigenface Pada Sistem Absensi. *J. Coding, Sist. Komput. Untan*, 03, 1, 41–50, 2015.
8. Murthy, G.R.S. and Jadon, R.S., A review of vision based hand gesture recognition. *Int. J. Adv. Sci. Tech. Res.*, 3, August 2002, 760–768, 2014.
9. Vengatesan, K., Kumar, A., Karuppuchamy, V., Shaktivel, R., Singhal, A., Face Recognition of Identical Twins Based On Support Vector Machine Classifier. *2019 Third International conference on I-SMAC (IoT in Social, Mobile, Analytics and Cloud) (I-SMAC)*, Palladam, India, pp. 577–580, 2019.

18

Visitor/Intruder Monitoring System Using Machine Learning

G. Jenifa*, S. Indu, C. Jeevitha and V. Kiruthika

KPR Institute of Engineering and Technology, Coimbatore, Tamil Nadu, India

Abstract

Home security systems play a predominant role in the modern era. The purpose of the security systems is to protect the members of the family from intruders. The main idea behind these systems is to provide security for residential areas. In today's world, securing our home plays a major role in society. Surveillance from homes to huge industries, plays a significant role in making us feel secure. There are many machine learning algorithms for home security systems but the Haar-cascade classifier algorithm gives a better result when compared with other machine learning algorithms. This system implements face recognition and face detection using Haar-cascade classifier algorithm; OpenCV libraries are used for training and testing of the face detection process. In the future, face recognition will be used everywhere in the world. It is creating magic in every field with its advanced technology. A visitor/intruder monitoring system using machine learning is used to monitor the person and find out whether the person is known or unknown based on the captured picture. Here, local binary pattern histogram (LBPH) face recognizer is used. After capturing the image, it is compared with the available dataset, then the respective name and picture is sent to the specified email to alert the owner.

Keywords: Local binary pattern histogram (LBPH), OpenCV, face recognizer, email

*Corresponding author: gjenifa@gmail.com

Ashutosh Kumar Dubey, Abhishek Kumar, S. Rakesh Kumar, N. Gayathri, Prasenjit Das (eds.) *AI and IoT-Based Intelligent Automation in Robotics*, (295–304) © 2021 Scrivener Publishing LLC

18.1   Introduction

Modern digital home security systems are very efficient in tracking intruders. In today's world, everyone prefers to work outside the home, but at the same time they want to be sure their homes are secure. Therefore, detection and recognition of objects through image processing are very important elements of automatic systems for home security [1]. Studies have shown that simply by having a security system, your home is much less likely to be targeted by intruders. There are many systems that exist in the machine learning projects for home security systems. Each one differs and is unique in its technology. These systems are more like door security systems, but not exactly. Each system has its own advantage. One of the advantages of the system is to reduce cost and time.

The main objective of this chapter is to secure the home from any intruders to avoid theft. With the help of the monitoring system the owner can easily identify the person who visits their home even when they are not at home. A machine learning algorithm is employed with Raspberry Pi and a web camera [5]; and a Haar-cascade classifier algorithm is used for recognition and detection of the human face. Machine learning algorithms are the most accurate way of identifying the image and producing an accurate result. This system allows homeowners to monitor visitors or intruders who are in front of their home and are able to see their faces through email, which helps the owners identify visitors/intruders easily within a short amount of time. To make advancements in this system one can use deep learning algorithms. Since it is a home security system, machine learning algorithms are capable of getting a better result within a short span of time.

18.2   Machine Learning

Machine learning is undeniably one of the most influential and powerful technologies in today's world. Machine learning is the scientific study of algorithms and statistical models that computer systems use to perform a specific task without using explicit instructions. Machine learning algorithms build a mathematical model based on sample data, known as training data, in order to make predictions or decisions without being explicitly programmed to perform the task. Machine learning focuses on making these predictions using a computer. The future in the areas of machine learning is unpredictable; therefore, these algorithms can exceed human expectations in the near future. There are three types of machine learning: supervised learning, unsupervised learning, and reinforcement learning.

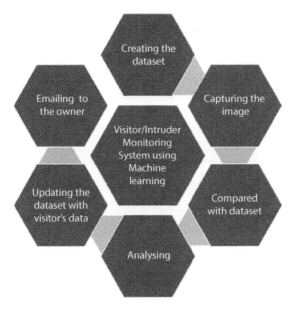

Figure 18.1 Process of visitor/intruder monitoring system.

18.2.1   Machine Learning in Home Security

Machine learning (ML) in the field of home security is enabling home automation and reducing human interaction. This will make the home more secure. There are numerous ML applications in the home security system such as collecting data of family members, relatives, and frequent visitors. This data can be used to automate the process with maximum accuracy and to improve the quality of the outcome. Machine learning concepts play a major role in today's home security system [15]. The simple concept behind the home security system is monitoring the entry point into the home with a web camera. With the help of minimum human interaction, accurate and reliable results can be reached and the number of crimes happening in our homes can be reduced. This system will provide a more detailed account of any activities than any human security guard. Processes that are included in the Visitor/Intruder Monitoring System is shown in the Figure 18.1.

18.3   System Design

The details of the proposed visitor/intruder monitoring system using machine learning are presented here. The main aim is to design and

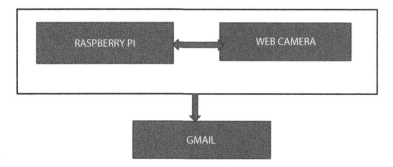

Figure 18.2 Block diagram of visitor/intruder monitoring system.

develop a monitoring system using machine learning to protect homes from intruders and view those who visit the home [3]. With the help of this system the owner can monitor his/her house even when they are away. A block diagram of the system is shown in Figure 18.2.

18.4   Haar-Cascade Classifier Algorithm

Haar-cascade is a machine learning object algorithm used to identify objects in an image or video [2]. It is a machine learning-based approach where a cascade function is trained from a lot of positive and negative images [8]. OpenCV allows one to create their own classifier that is used to detect other objects by training the created classifier [13]. It is then used to detect objects in other images. This system mainly has three processes:

1. Creating the dataset.
2. Training the model.
3. Recognizing the face.

18.4.1   Creating the Dataset

Here, frontal face recognition is used to identify the human face. The image of a single person's face is captured [6]. A single person's face is captured a number of times from the front and at side angles. A frequent visitor to the home can be added in the dataset. The captured image is converted to grey scale and the size of the image is converted to a small picture and stored in the dataset [14].

18.4.2   Training the Model

The dataset is trained randomly after adding a new person's face in the dataset.

18.4.3   Recognizing the Face

After training the model, the captured image is compared with the dataset. After comparing, if the image is in the dataset, then the name of the person is sent to the owner's email [10]. If the person is not in the dataset, then the person's image is sent to the owner's email. From the email, he/she will be able to identify the person who is visiting their home. With the help of this system, one can reduce time and cost.

18.5   Components

The hardware requirements for this system includes:

1. Raspberry Pi
2. Web camera

18.5.1   Raspberry Pi

The main component of the project is Raspberry Pi, which is a low-cost, credit-card-sized computer that plugs into a computer monitor or TV developed by The Raspberry Pi Foundation. In the Raspberry Pi computer, an SD card inserted into the slot on the board acts as the hard drive. It is powered by USB and the video output can be hooked up to a traditional TV set, a more modern monitor, or even a TV using the HDMI port [11]. The model used here is the Raspberry Pi 3 B+ shown in Figure 18.3. Raspbian OS is installed in the memory card. In this model the Raspberry Pi is connected to the web camera through port 0 of Raspberry Pi.

Figure 18.3 Raspberry Pi.

Figure 18.4 Zebronics Crystal Plus web camera.

18.5.2   Web Camera

A web camera plays an important role in face detection and face recognition. It is a video camera that feeds or streams an image or video in real time to or through a computer to a computer network such as the internet. In Raspberry Pi, the standard USB web camera is used to take pictures and video. The web camera used here is Zebronics Crystal Plus (Figure 18.4). The reason for choosing this web camera is that even when the surrounding is dark, we can turn on the light in the web camera to makes the face even more clear. Using the Haar-cascade algorithm, when the motion is detected, the webcam will capture a high-resolution picture.

18.6   Experimental Results

Using Haar-cascade algorithm, the dataset for housemates is created by capturing 'n' number of images of each person, the model is trained and the faces are detected and recognized. If the webcam captured face is matched with the dataset face, then an email is sent to the owner of the house indicating the name and their image [7]. If the captured picture is not in the dataset, then the email is sent to the owner as describing unknown with their image.

Pseudocode of face recognition:

- Importing necessary libraries.
- Creating a function for known person detected; if person is known, then an email is sent to the specified email ID as subject "their name" has arrived and the captured image is added.
- Or else send an email to specified person as "Unknown intruder detection" and add the captured image.

When the motion is detected, the image is captured and compared with the dataset and the image is matched with the dataset, then their name will be mentioned in the email along with their image or if the image is not matched with the dataset, then the intruder image is sent along with notification as unknown intruder detected [9]. We can also add our frequently visiting relatives to our dataset by adding their image to the dataset, so that the owner need not be worried about the known visitors. OpenCV works better in grey scale than color images [12]. The image will be resized as the face will be in the middle of the image or else it will be cropped and failed to recognize the person.

The owner can monitor the house with the help of the email image. It updates the motion in the front of the house and informs through email. The reason for choosing email is that nowadays everyone has their own email ID with a protected password, where only they can access the email [4].

The person in the picture is someone in the household; when this person arrives in front of the house, the camera captures the image and compares it with the dataset [16]. Figure 18.5 shows the sequence of messages sent to the owner when motion detected. After the comparison, the result is found as the image matched with the dataset created, and along with the image, their name is sent to the owner through email, as shown in Figure 18.6.

Figure 18.5 Mail sent to the given email ID.

Figure 18.6 Final outcome with image and name (Known person).

Figure 18.7 Final outcome with image as mentioned "unknown person" (Unknown intruder).

Figure 18.8 After adding a frequent visitor to the dataset, the result is "Indu has arrived."

When the captured image is not matched with the already created dataset, then the intruder's image is sent to the owner as Unknown intruder detected, as shown in Figure 18.7.

When the captured image is of a frequent visitor to the house, an email is sent to the owner along with the visitor's name, as shown in Figure 18.8.

18.7   Conclusion

The Machine-Learning-enabled visitor/intruder monitoring system helps to monitor the home using the Haar-cascade classifier algorithm. Upon implementing these technologies, this system can create an alert to the owner when a person visits their house. This system reduces the need for human intervention and makes everything easier for the owner. It is also cost-efficient and convenient to use. Even if the owner is away from home, they can monitor their house using this system. This system has maximum predictive accuracy, i.e., 95% accuracy.

Acknowledgment

The authors would like to express special thanks to Assistant Professor Ms. G. Jenifa for the guidance and support provided during our UG project.

This project was only possible with her motivation and patience, which helped in doing the research for our project and applying some new technologies throughout the project. We are grateful to all the faculty members of the Computer Science Department for their valuable suggestions regarding our project. We would especially like to thank our professor, Dr. K. Vishnu Kumar, the head of the Computer Science Department, for his continuous encouragement.

References

1. Priya samyuktha, M., Siva bharathi, K., Sivagami, A., Haar Cascade Algorithm for the visually Impaired to Detect and Recognize Objects. *Int. J. Eng. Res. Technol. (IJERT)*, 5, 04, 256–261, April-2016.
2. Cuimei, L., Zhiliang, Q., Nan, J., Jianhua, W., Human face detection algorithm via haar cascade classifier combined with three additional. *13th IEEE International Conference on Electronic Measurement & Instruments (ICEMI)*, ICEMI.2017.8265863, pp. 483–487, 2017.
3. Repalle, S.A. and Kolluru, V.R., Intrusion Detection System using AI and Machine Learning Algorithm. *Int. Res. J. Eng. Technol. (IRJET)*, 04, 12, 1709–1715, Dec-2017.
4. Faughnan, S.Y., Smart Surveillance as an Edge Network Service from Haar-cascade. *4th IEEE International Conference on Collaboration and Internet Computing*, pp. 256–265, Oct 2018.
5. Babanne, V., Mahajan, N.S., Sharma, R.L., Gargate, P.P., Machine Learning based Smart Surveillance System, *3rd International Conference*, ISMAC47947. 2019, pp. 84–86, 2019.
6. Sharifara, A., Mohd Rahim, M.S., Anisi, Y., A general review of human face detection including a study of Haar feature-based cascade classifier in face detection. *International Symposium on Biometrics and Security Technologies*, pp. 73–78, 2014.
7. Khan, M., Chakraborty, S., Astya, R., Face Detection and Recognition using OpenCV, *International Conference on Computing, Communication, and Intelligent Systems*, ICCCIS 48478. 2019, pp. 116–119, 2019.
8. Prathaban, T., Thean, W., Sazali, M.I.S.M., A Vision based home security system using OpenCV on Raspberry Pi. *AIP Conference Proceedings*, vol. 2173, 1, 2019.
9. Manjunatha, R. and Nagaraja, Dr. R., Home Security System and Door Accss Control Based on Face Recognition. *Int. Res. J. Eng. Technol. (IRJET)*, 04, 03, 437–442, 2017.
10. Senthamizh Selvi, R., Sivakumar, Sandhya, Siva sowmiya, S., Face Recognition using Haar-Cascade Classifier for Criminal Identification. *Int. J. Recent Technol. Eng.*, 7, 6S5, 1871–1876, 2019.

11. Shah, A.A., Zaidi, Z.A., Chowdry, B.S., Real time face detection/monitoring using Raspberry Pi and MATLAB. *10th IEEE International Conference on Application of Information and Communication Technologies*, pp. 1–4, 2016.

12. Umme, A. and Virendra, P., Face recognition using modified deep learning neural network. *8th International Conference on Computing Communication and Networking Technologies*, pp. 1–5, 2017.

13. Vaidya, B., Patel, A., Panchal, A., Mehta, R., Smart home automation with a unique door monitoring system for old age people using python, OpenCV, Raspberry Pi. *International Conference on Intelligent Computing and Control System*, pp. 82–86, 2017.

14. Shendkar, B., Kasurde, A., Patil, N., Lotket, M., Home Automation using Face Profiling. *Int. Res. J. Eng. Technol. (IRJET)*, 04, 04, 696–699, 2017.

15. Filali, H., Riffi, J., Mahraz, A.M., Tairi, H., Multiple Face detection based on machine learning. *International Conference on Intelligent Systems and Computer Vision (ISCV)*, pp. 1–8, 2018.

16. Faisal, F., Hossain, S.A., Smart Security System using Face Recognition on Raspberry Pi, *13th international Conference on software, knowledge, Information Management and applications*, pp.1–8, 2019.

19

Comparison of Machine Learning Algorithms for Air Pollution Monitoring System

Tushar Sethi* and R. C. Thakur

Department of Instrumentation and Control Engineering (ICE), Netaji Subhas University of Technology (NSIT), Dwarka, New Delhi, India

Abstract

Today, air pollution is one of the topics that needs to be addressed with new, bold and effective techniques in order to control pollution levels. Recently, there has been a rapid rise in the amount of dangerous pollutants released into the air such as sulfur dioxide, nitrogen dioxide, particulate matter 2.5 ($PM_{2.5}$) and particulate matter 10 (PM_{10}), ammonia and ozone. The increase in pollutants has mainly been due to human activities. In this chapter, data has been captured and collected by the Open Government Data (OGD) Platform India, which has been released under the National Data Sharing and Accessibility Policy (NDSAP) and various extensive open sources. The main purpose of this data is to compare the different machine learning algorithms and check their accuracy for the pollution detection systems. The algorithms used are multiple linear regression (MLR), random forest regression (RFR), decision tree regression (DTR), support vector regression (SVR) and extreme gradient boosting (XGBoost).

Keywords: Air pollution, machine learning, Python, random forest, decision tree regression

19.1 Introduction

Air pollution is one of the most pressing issues around the world, which has led to a lot of research being done today in order to reduce pollutants

---
Corresponding author: tushar2071996@gmail.com

Ashutosh Kumar Dubey, Abhishek Kumar, S. Rakesh Kumar, N. Gayathri, Prasenjit Das (eds.) AI and IoT-Based Intelligent Automation in Robotics, (305–322) © 2021 Scrivener Publishing LLC

or identify the best practices and methods to hold down pollutant levels. The most dangerous and deadly pollutants present in the air are particulate matter 2.5 ($PM_{2.5}$), carbon monoxide, sulfur dioxide and nitrogen dioxide. So, in order to stop pollutant levels from increasing, we first need to know at what levels they are present in the air; and, more importantly, we need to know in advance what will be the levels of these pollutants in the future. Here, machine learning comes into the picture. By using machine learning and different algorithms we can predict what the levels of air pollutants will be in the near future. But the main question remains; how to decide which algorithms to use for the pollution monitoring systems, and hence the comparison of these algorithms is required to check their accuracy.

Machine learning is the technique used to predict future values using the provided past values. It is one of the most used scientific methods of analytical models and algorithms that processors use to accomplish a specific task without the use of unambiguous directives rather than relying on patterns and inference instead. Machine learning or computer studying itself is a form of artificial intelligence (AI) that enables the system to gain knowledge without being completely educated. This special ability to process and tackle any new piece of information by itself using the algorithm is done by utilizing the power of Python and its libraries.

The process of training and predicting involves the use of specialized algorithms [3]. We need to train the model using the dataset that we have created or captured and make the modifications using data wrangling; and then the trained algorithm uses this training knowledge to make predictions for the future values. Machine learning algorithms predicting the future can be roughly classified into three categories, which are supervised learning, unsupervised learning, and reinforced learning. Supervised learning allows us to showcase a specific class of problem that uses a model to show specific mapping between input examples and the target variable and it uses labels. In unsupervised learning there isn't any use of labels. In reinforced learning there is not a particular fixed action to take, rather it depends on what action yields the maximum reward. It works on the greedy approach.

The proposed system will check for the accuracy of different algorithms used to predict data for future values of pollution and discover the best algorithms for the same.

19.2   System Design

There are mainly two phases in which the task will be executed.

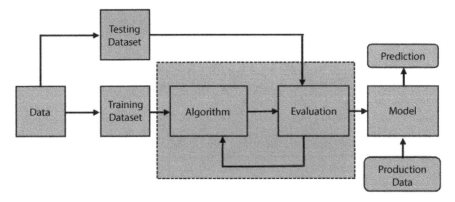

Figure 19.1 Work flow.

a) Training Phase
The model is trained with the data in the dataset on all the algorithms. Training and testing of data is mainly divided into 80:20 ratio. Machine learning algorithms, such as multiple linear regression (MLR), random forest regression (RFR), decision tree regression (DTR), support vector regression (SVR) and XGBoost (XGB), are used to train datasets [8]. After the testing is completed, the final accuracy depends on parameters such as Precision, Detection Rate and Overall Accuracy for the purpose of air pollution detection.

b) Testing Phase
The model is then tested to predict the desired values and corresponding errors and then finding the precise algorithm providing the least error and highest accuracy. Four of the algorithms are trained and tested and the one which performs the best will be chosen for the further prediction part. The flow of working is shown in Figure 19.1.

The use of industrial grade sensors to monitor industrial processes in real time and later achieving their interconnection is called the Industrial Internet of Things.

19.3   Model Description and Architecture

Modeling and implementation will be done in several steps, which will include the data processing along with training and testing and visualization [7].

Steps that will be followed are as follows and can be seen in Figure 19.2.

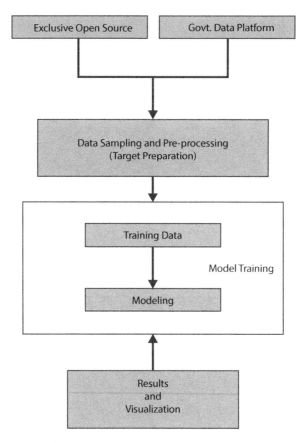

Figure 19.2 System architecture.

- Predominant parameter identification
- Collection of data
- Data crunching and pre-processing
- Training and testing the model
- Comparing algorithms for best accuracy results
- Evaluation
- Visualization

19.4   Dataset

a) Data Collection
Data has been collected mainly from the Open Government Data (OGD) Platform India and various exclusive open sources for training the model

using different algorithms, eventually utilizing the pattern to find out the maximum accuracy and lowest error among the different algorithms [2].

b) Sampling and Pre-processing

Most of the raw data captured is messy and needs to be taken care of. This part involves cleaning the raw data by deleting all the null values and inconsistent data. Data wrangling is done to check for the cleanliness in the data set and then trimming the rest of the data, making is easier for evaluation and training [9]. The different parameters therefore have been normalized to standard values in order to find the predominant parameter among them and therefore are considered for further testing and training evaluation. The data frame of training and testing data can be seen in Figure 19.3 [11].

The attributes considered in the dataset are as follows:

- State
- City
- Date
- Time
- $PM_{2.5}$
- PM_{10}
- NO_2
- NH_3

state	city	station	date	time	PM2.5	PM10	NO2	NH3	SO2	CO	OZONE	AQI
Andhra_Pr	Amaravati	Secretaria	03-01-2020	10:00:00	68	64	17	4	28	31	40	68
Andhra_Pr	Rajamahe	Anand Kal	03-01-2020	10:00:00	67	70	23	2	13	49	77	77
Andhra_Pr	Tirupati	Tirumala, 1	03-01-2020	10:00:00	32	64	26	5	6	19	16	32
Andhra_Pr	Visakhapa	GVM Corp	03-01-2020	10:00:00	93	93	31	3	9	57	61	93
Andhra_Pr	Amaravati	Secretaria	05-01-2020	06:00:00	60	55	20	5	18	29	53	60
Andhra_Pr	Rajamahe	Anand Kal	05-01-2020	06:00:00	48	52	25	3	12	43	67	67
Andhra_Pr	Tirupati	Tirumala, 1	05-01-2020	06:00:00	36	41	31	5	5	33	14	41
Andhra_Pr	Visakhapa	GVM Corp	05-01-2020	06:00:00	27	43	23	3	11	44	61	61
Andhra_Pr	Amaravati	Secretaria	06-01-2020	03:00:00	54	54	15	5	21	30	51	54
Andhra_Pr	Rajamahe	Anand Kal	06-01-2020	03:00:00	48	53	24	3	13	39	69	69
Andhra_Pr	Tirupati	Tirumala, 1	06-01-2020	03:00:00	24	35	29	5	6	16	16	35
Andhra_Pr	Visakhapa	GVM Corp	06-01-2020	03:00:00	53	63	24	3	12	48	59	63
Andhra_Pr	Amaravati	Secretaria	06-01-2020	06:00:00	59	57	15	5	20	30	63	63
Andhra_Pr	Rajamahe	Anand Kal	06-01-2020	06:00:00	55	58	24	3	14	43	82	82
Andhra_Pr	Tirupati	Tirumala, 1	06-01-2020	06:00:00	22	34	26	4	6	17	15	34
Andhra_Pr	Visakhapa	GVM Corp	06-01-2020	06:00:00	65	72	25	3	12	50	70	72
Andhra_Pr	Amaravati	Secretaria	06-01-2020	11:00:00	66	61	15	5	23	36	57	66
Andhra_Pr	Rajamahe	Anand Kal	06-01-2020	11:00:00	74	70	22	3	13	48	82	82
Andhra_Pr	Tirupati	Tirumala, 1	06-01-2020	11:00:00	20	30	23	4	5	16	14	30
Andhra_Pr	Visakhapa	GVM Corp	06-01-2020	11:00:00	83	86	27	3	12	55	77	86
Andhra_Pr	Amaravati	Secretaria	07-01-2020	12:00:00	69	63	15	5	24	37	54	69
Andhra_Pr	Rajamahe	Anand Kal	07-01-2020	12:00:00	78	72	22	3	14	48	80	80
Andhra_Pr	Tirupati	Tirumala, 1	07-01-2020	12:00:00	19	30	22	4	5	16	14	30
Andhra_Pr	Visakhapa	GVM Corp	07-01-2020	12:00:00	85	88	28	3	12	55	76	88
Andhra_Pr	Amaravati	Secretaria	07-01-2020	02:00:00	131	94	15	5	26	34	60	131
Andhra_Pr	Rajamahe	Anand Kal	07-01-2020	02:00:00	109	90	21	3	17	42	86	109

Figure 19.3 Sample data frame.

- SO$_2$
- CO
- Ozone
- AQI

19.5 Models

a) Multiple Linear Regression

Multiple linear regression (MLR) is a predictive analysis technique which uses multiple independent explanatory parameters to foresee the output-dependent parameter [3, 13]. A linear relationship is established between the independent variables and the dependent variable as a result of MLR.

The MLR equation is:

$$y_i = \beta_0 + \beta_1 x_{i1} + \beta_1 x_{i1} + \ldots + \beta_p x_{ip} + \epsilon$$

Where, for observations:

y_i = Dependent variable which corresponds to Predominant Parameter

x_i = Explanatory variables which correspond to other parameters such as PM$_{10}$, Ozone, NO$_2$, NH$_3$, SO$_2$ and PM$_{2.5}$

β_0 = y-intercept (constant term)

β_p = Regression Coefficient Corresponding

ϵ = The observation error (also known as the residuals)

The MLR model is established based on the following conventions [10]:

- There is a linear alliance between the independent explanatory variable and the dependent response variable.
- The independent explanatory variables are not fully correlated to each other as it would affect the final predictions.
- Residuals should be normally distributed.

b) Decision Tree Regression

This decision tree regression (DTR) model is used to predict a target variable by learning from the training set. It learns decision rules which can be used for prediction. The name of the model is enough to visualize the type of model it infers [4]. DTR is a tree-like model which learns from a different series of questions. It is an attractive model if we care about the interpretability and is a lot easier as it requires less data cleaning.

Though there are many more methods and algorithms that can also do the same work, a decision tree is preferred because of its graphical or hierarchical structure [12]. This structure is not only able to present the deep level of information and insight more effectively, but the time complexity is also reduced to a certain extent [14]. When a decision tree is fitted on a training dataset, one of most significant parts is to choose the top few nodes of the tree based on which the tree is parted and which is done productively in decision tree regression.

c) Random Forest Regression
Random forest regression (RFR) can be understood as an advanced tree algorithm which operates by constructing multiple decision trees while training the model and getting the mean prediction of the individual trees [5]. The fundamental idea behind RFR is to merge multiple decision trees rather than relying on the individual decision tree in determining the final output. The tree structure of Random Forest Regression Technique can be visualized in Figure 19.4. It mainly uses a bagging ensemble method that is used to train individual models parallelly.

d) Support Vector Regression
The support vector regression (SVR) algorithm is one of the most powerful algorithms as it allows us to control how much error can be tolerated by the model. It also allows us to choose how resilient we are against errors, both

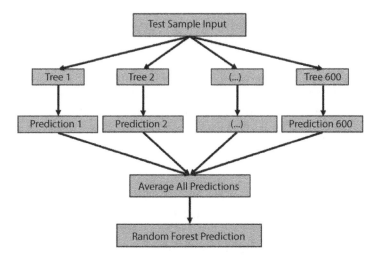

Figure 19.4 System architecture.

through a tolerable error brim and through modifying our tolerance of crossing the satisfactory error frequency [6]. SVR uses small sets of training points in the decision function, making it more memory efficient. To perform SVR we need to maintain some of the following basic steps [15]:

- Collection of a training set.
- Choosing a kernel and its parameters and also any regularization required.
- Formation of a correlation matrix.
- Training the model approximately to get contraction coefficients.
- Use of these coefficients to create and estimator.

e) Extreme Gradient Boosting

Extreme gradient boosting (XGBoost) algorithm is one of the most optimized distributed gradient boosting libraries designed specifically for distributed environments. It is a highly flexible, efficient and portable boosting library and has the ability to solve data science and machine learning problems accurately and perform them in a fast way, limiting the time complexity to its minimal. This algorithm is a perfect example of an engineering goal pushed to its limits for computational resources for boosted tree algorithms. This algorithm has several useful features such as:

- Scattered implementation with preprogrammed handling of missing variables.
- Continuous training of the model enabling further boosting of the optimization of the model.

This algorithm uses an approach of ensembling where new models are created to reduce the rate of errors made by the existing model. The addition of other or the new models is sequential till the time the error falls below the desired value, and as the name suggests, it uses gradient descent algorithm to minimize the error value while there is addition of new models in the existing model.

19.6   Line of Best Fit for the Dataset

A best fit line, commonly known as the trend line, is the line which passes through most of the points. It represents the least squared error and is based on the least squared method. It provides the overall best approximation of

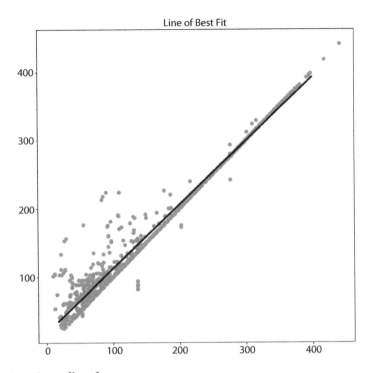

Figure 19.5 Line of best fit.

the provided dataset. The method of using the trend line is that we need to use the two variables, which in our case are the independent variables and the dependent variable. In Figure 19.5, the dataset is represented by the scatter plot in blue and the regression line or the trend line is represented in black.

19.7   Feature Importance

Feature importance is one of the major parts while working with the machine learning models, as we need to be clear about all independent features which will have a positive and high impact on the dependent feature. By referring to the graph in Figure 19.6 we can easily see that one of the features which has a huge positive impact on the dependent feature is $PM_{2.5}$ and therefore we now have a clear understanding of the dataset and all of the features which are quite important.

Some of the useful features of feature importance which help a model to be precise and give accurate results are summarized below.

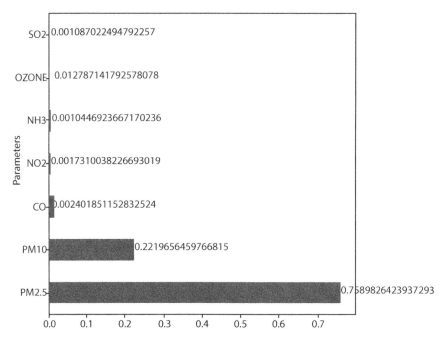

Figure 19.6 Feature importance.

- Curse of dimensionality, popularly known as overfitting: In order to make a generalized model we have to find the importance features which have a significant impact on the model accuracy.
- Occam's razor is another advantage of feature selection as we want our model to be quite explainable and simple.

	PM2.5	PM10	NO2	NH3	SO2	CO	OZONE	AQI
PM2.5	1.000000	0.847821	0.452296	0.514462	0.127736	0.349025	–0.131209	0.985440
PM10	0.847821	1.000000	0.507776	0.501298	0.099759	0.330761	–0.158430	0.872710
NO2	0.452296	0.507776	1.000000	0.391747	0.027716	0.149404	–0.113338	0.463397
NH3	0.514462	0.501298	0.391747	1.000000	0.043533	0.209216	–0.228292	0.519951
SO2	0.127736	0.099759	0.027716	0.043533	1.000000	0.087520	0.023599	0.125297
CO	0.349025	0.330761	0.149404	0.209216	0.087520	1.000000	–0.144244	0.375208
OZONE	–0.131209	–0.158430	–0.113338	–0.228292	0.023599	–0.144244	1.000000	–0.137347
AQI	0.985440	0.872710	0.463397	0.519951	0.125297	0.375208	–0.137347	1.000000

Figure 19.7 Pearson's correlation coefficient.

- High quality of data, when given as input to the model, will provide high quality of output, resulting in greater accuracy.

And to better visualize the graph we can also use Pearson's correlation coefficient table shown in Figure 19.7 in order to understand it in a much more mathematical manner. It is a filter-based method where we look at the absolute values of the Pearson's correlation between the target value and the numerical features in the data.

19.8   Comparisons

In order to closely observe the accuracy of the models, comparison analysis is done and graphs are plotted where the actual value is represented by the blue line and the predicted value is represented by the orange line. The graphs in Figures 19.8 to 19.12 denote the number of entries on the x-axis while the y-axis denotes the presence of predominant parameter of pollutants.

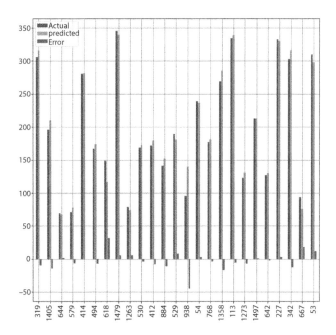

Figure 19.8 Results of Multiple Linear Regression comparing the true values and the predicted values along with their respective errors.

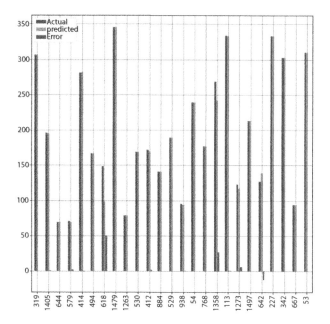

Figure 19.9 Results of Decision Tree Regression comparing the true values and the predicted values along with their respective errors.

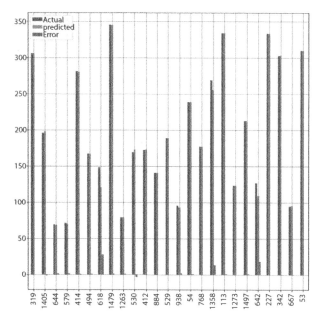

Figure 19.10 Results of Random Forest Regression comparing the true values and the predicted values along with their respective errors.

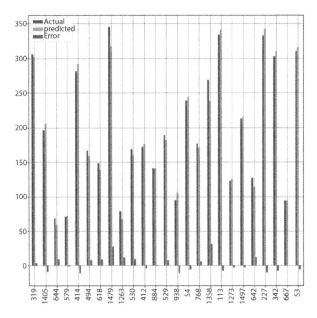

Figure 19.11 Results of Support Vector Regression comparing the true values and the predicted values along with their respective errors.

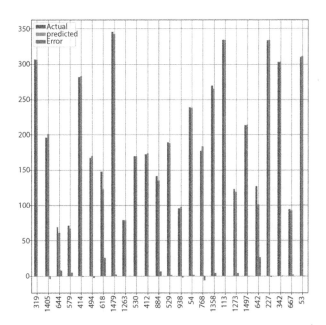

Figure 19.12 Results of Extreme Gradient Boost comparing the true values and the predicted values along with their respective errors.

19.9   Results

Table 19.1 shows the obtained errors for different models from the trained model for tested dataset.

a) Plots
- Scatter Plot Matrix
The scatter plot matrix is used to visualize relationships between different dependent and independent variables. Figure 19.13 shows the relationship between the dominant pollutants and their significant linear correlations.

- Heat Maps
Figure 19.14 shows a heat map which is a pictorial representation of information that uses a method of color-coding to visualize different values [1]. These maps provide the insight that is not readily visible at first glance or any of the different plots. It is extremely necessary and useful to visualize a general and pictorial perspective of numerical values.

Table 19.2 shows the root mean square error predicted by various machine learning models along with their respective accuracy.

- Performance Analysis
Figure 19.15 shows the performance graph showing the respective accuracies between different models.

19.10   Conclusion

This research began with a collection of data for training and testing the models. Furthermore, the training dataset was applied to different models for calculating errors and accuracies. Upon comparing the testing dataset with the prediction for different machine learning models for air pollution monitoring we were able to come to the conclusion that the random forest regression model has the least number of errors and an accuracy of approximately 97% under supervised learning. There is a scope of advancement ahead which could include real-life data collection using an IoT prototype and sensors under more circumstantial situations such as wind velocity, atmospheric pressure above sea level, movement of vehicles, construction work, rains, etc. The collected data can be bundled with all these parameters, which could provide more accurate and place-oriented output.

Table 9.1 Error obtained in each model.

Machine learning models	Errors			
	R^2	RMSE	MAE	RMSLE
Multiple Linear Regression (MLR)	0.9965	5.4969	3.4799	0.0517
Decision Tree Regression (DTR)	0.9955	6.2370	2.3546	0.0563
Random Forest Regression (RFR)	0.9983	3.8577	1.7016	0.0423
Support Vector Regression (SVR)	0.9165	27.0026	19.0723	0.1686
Extreme Gradient Boosting (XBG)	0.9950	6.5498	3.8303	0.0511

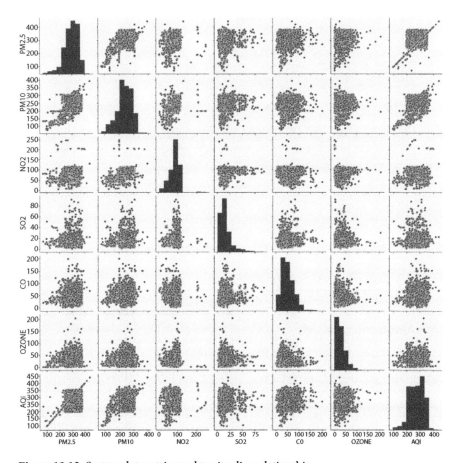

Figure 19.13 Scatter plot matrix used to visualize relationships.

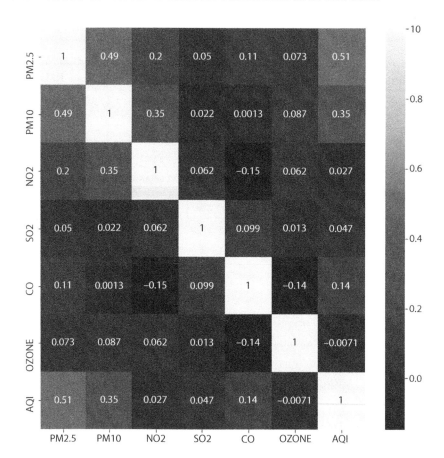

Figure 19.14 Heat map.

Table 9.2 Trained model performance.

	Parameters	
Machine learning models	**Error**	**Accuracy**
Multiple Linear Regression (MLR)	5.4969	94.5031
Decision Tree Regression (DTR)	6.2370	93.763
Random Forest Regression (RFR)	3.8577	96.1423
Support Vector Regression (SVR)	27.0026	72.9974
Extreme Gradient Boosting (XBG)	6.5498	93.4502

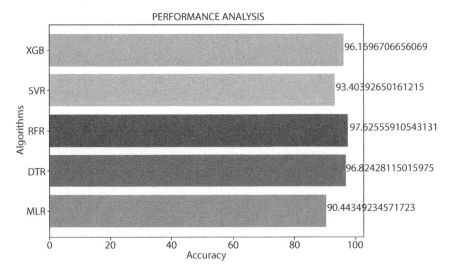

Figure 19.15 Performance analysis.

References

1. Mahesh Babu, K. and Beulah, J., Air Quality Prediction based on Supervised Machine Learning Methods. *Int. J. Innovative Technol. Exploring Eng.*, 8, 94, 206–212, 2019.
2. Esther Pushpam, V., Kavitha, N., Karthik, A., IoT Enabled Machine Learning for Vehicular Air Pollution Monitoring. *2019 International Conference on Computer Communication and Informatics (ICCCI)*, 2019.
3. Deshmukh, A. C R, C., Gandhi, N. D K, P., Astu, V., Detection and Prediction of Air Pollution using Machine Learning Models. *Int. J. Eng. Trends Technol.*, 59, 4, 204–207, 2018.
4. Bhalgat, P., Pitale, S., Bhoite, S., Air Quality Prediction using Machine Learning Algorithms. *Int. J. Comput. Appl. Technol. Res.*, 8, 9, 367–370, 2019.
5. Rubal, and Kumar, D., Evolving Differential evolution method with random forest for prediction of Air Pollution. *Procedia Comput. Sci.*, 132, 824–833, 2018.
6. Amado, T. and Dela Cruz, J., Development of Machine Learning-based Predictive Models for Air Quality Monitoring and Characterization. *TENCON 2018 - 2018 IEEE Region 10 Conference*, 2018.
7. Vineeta, A.B., Asha, S.M., Pranay, M., Machine Learning based Prediction System for Detecting Air Pollution. *IJERT*, 8, 9, 155–159, September 2019.
8. Srivastava, C., Singh, S., Singh, A., Estimation of Air Pollution in Delhi Using Machine Learning Techniques. *2018 International Conference on Computing, Power and Communication Technologies (GUCON)*, 2018.

9. Pant, A., Workflow of a Machine Learning Project, in: *Medium*, 2019, [Online]. Available: https://towardsdatascience.com/workflow-of-a-machine-learning-project-ec1dba419b94.

10. Kenton, W., How Multiple Linear Regression Works, in: *Investopedia*, 2020, [Online]. Available: https://www.investopedia.com/terms/m/mlr.asp.

11. Gargava, D., Real Time Air Quality Index From Various Locations. [online] Open Government Data (OGD) Platform India, 2020. Available at: https://data.gov.in/resources/real-time-air-quality-index-various-location.

12. Li, L., Classification and Regression Analysis with Decision Trees, in: *Medium*, 2019, [Online]. Available: https://towardsdatascience.com/https-medium-com-lorrli-classification-and-regression-analysis-with-decision-trees-c43cdbc58054.

13. Li, L.N., Gong, X.P., Dai, L.C., Zhan, X.H., The Regression Models of PM2. 5 and Other Air pollutants in Wuhan. *Adv. Mat. Res.*, 864, 1356–1359, 2014. Trans Tech Publications Ltd.

14. Das, A. and Desarkar, A., Decision Tree-Based Analytics for Reducing Air Pollution. *J. Inf. Knowl. Manage.*, 17, 02, 1850015, 2018.

15. www.aionlinecourse.com, 2018. [Online]. Available: https://www.aionlinecourse.com/tutorial/machine-learning/support-vector-regression.

20

A Novel Approach Towards Audio Watermarking Using FFT and CORDIC-Based QR Decomposition

Ankit Kumar[1*], Astha Singh[1†], Shiv Prakash[1‡] and Vrijendra Singh[2§]

1Centre for Advanced Studies, Dr. A.P.J Abdul Kalam Technical University, Lucknow, Uttar Pradesh, India
2Indian Institute of Information Technology (IIIT), Allahabad, Uttar Pradesh, India

Abstract

Digital media containing images, audio, video, etc., is accessed very frequently today. With the huge access to digital data, their security threat becomes one of the major concerns. Data ownership can be stolen by an imposter. Cases of data piracy and data ownership have been observed and explored by many previous techniques and studies. However, imposters are still looking for a crack intended to destroy the media's security feature and access it without a license. The study in this chapter explores the methodology to secure digital audio signal by introducing the concept of watermarking, in which, rather than using obsolete watermarking design, one of the novel hybrid decomposition techniques using fast Fourier transform (FFT) and CORDIC-based QR decomposition are used together to factorize audio signal and hide a watermark image in it. The watermark image is enrolled in the encryption technique using cyclic coding and Arnold's cat map to ensure dual-layer encryption. The challenging task is to maintain the quality of watermarked audio in terms of its imperceptibility. The other challenge explored in this study is carrying out the extrication of the obscured bits back from the watermarked audio file which is reconstructed into the watermark image that must be recognized enough to describe ownership. A watermark image of size

*Corresponding author: 7667ankit@gmail.com
†Corresponding author: astha0532@gmail.com
‡Corresponding author: shivprakash@cas.res.in
§Corresponding author: Vrij@iiita.ac.in

Ashutosh Kumar Dubey, Abhishek Kumar, S. Rakesh Kumar, N. Gayathri, Prasenjit Das (eds.) AI and IoT-Based Intelligent Automation in Robotics, (323–338) © 2021 Scrivener Publishing LLC

16×16 pixels is taken and is inculcated in the digital audio of 44.1 kHz sampling rate. The watermarked audio file is also appointed against various signal processing attacks and the hidden watermark is re-extracted in the respective conditions. Another challenge of this study is to stabilize the quality and avoid distortion from the extracted watermark bits enough to justify the ownership information.

Keywords: Audio watermarking, FFT transformation, CORDIC-based QR decomposition, encryption, normalized cross-correlation (NCC), peak signal-to-noise ratio (PSNR)

20.1   Introduction and Related Work

Digital media is accessed very frequently in the distributed environment, bringing with it security concerns. Digital rights management is one of the buzz terms which seek the attention of every researcher. The security of the digital rights of a user over his/her media file preserves his/her intellectual property and credit for his/her contribution. Nowadays, cyber imposters are spread across the globe and looking to break the security parameters to enable the unauthorized access and sale of genuine media. These types of unauthorized actions are very commonly practiced by using malware scripts, appointed by an imposter, which is intended to destroy the ownership stamp that acts as a security agent. Previously explored technologies to introduce the security measures of digital media in order to preserve its ownership have recommended the concept of watermarking theory. In a watermarking theory, watermark bits, signature, image or any other user's uniquely representative data is implanted in the audio signal in a way that does not destroy the balance among robustness, payload and the imperceptibility. This study deals with the security of audio digital media in which the most challenging concern is to preserve its ownership and secure its transaction in the distributed environment. The traditional approach to preserve the user's rights over the audio media is practiced through its watermarking, but audio signals are very sensitive against noise and any modification in the audio files may leave noticeable distortion to the human ear as proved by existing work. Another major challenge of audio watermarking is the flawless extraction of the watermark bits from the host audio data through which ownership can be satisfied.

Previously published techniques of watermarking are lacking somewhere to establish a robust security design for audio media. Such a technique coined by Akhaee *et al.* [1] practiced the implementation of data embedding in audio media using transformation in point-to-point graph (PPG) domain. This method lacks the ability to preserve the good quality of imperceptibility of host and extracted subject. Another previous approach on digital audio watermarking with the use of SVD and Fourier transform was discussed by Ozer *et al.* [2]. This security design fails to rescue the watermark bits upon the implication of attacks-related signal processing on watermarked audio. Audio watermarking based on a QIM and DWT scheme was also discussed earlier by Bhat *et al.* [3] which was unable to preserve good PSNR value for resulting watermarked signal; however, on the positive side, it facilitates robustness of watermark data under several attacks. Another practiced technique was coined by Hu *et al.* [4] is based on echo hiding design; but later it was found that the increasing payload is not tolerated by the host audio signal and results in distortion. Another method using SVD and dither modulation for hiding watermark bits in the host audio signal was also discussed by Hu *et al.* [5]. Signal processing attacks are found to be effective in the discussed technique and ultimately seem unsuitable to preserve the watermark bits. Overall, the previously presented watermarking designs have some constraints left and they fail to somehow resolve the audio media's ownership issues. The most common unacknowledged challenge in the aforementioned literature review is the flawless extraction of watermark data, which is subjected to resolve ownership issues.

The major contribution of the proposed work is to build a novel watermarking design using the decomposition of the host audio signal at the hybrid level. In the proposed design, the factorization of the host audio is executed in order to attain an appropriate region in a signal matrix which can be utilized to inculcate a watermark data. The combination of the fast Fourier transform (FFT) and CORDIC-based QR decomposition technique, which is a new combination, is implemented in this study. The standard host audio file is primarily enrolled in the FFT transformation in which host audio is decomposed into frequency coefficients energy subbands. The appropriate frequency coefficients are further appointed into the QR decomposition technique in which two fixed-sized orthogonal matrices are disintegrated from the host audio signal. The resulting Q-matrix and R-matrix are the orthogonal matrix and the upper triangular matrix respectively. In this work, the diagonal elements of the resulting R-matrix that contain eigenvalues are found to be very stable, which are taken for the embedding operation. The watermark bits are implanted at the least bits of such eigenvalues using specific randomly generated keys. The watermark data is chosen as an image which has undergone encryption technique, before the embedding process, in which the watermark image is encrypted using cyclic code and further by Arnold's cat map. This dual encryption practice is helpful to secure the watermark image even after its extraction from the audio signal. After the embedding, the quality of watermarked audio is checked in terms of peak signal-to-noise ratio (PSNR). The quality of withdrawal watermark bits is also checked with and without the influence of the various common types of attacks and the entire result is found to satisfy the standard acceptance rate. This chapter is divided into the following illustrated sections: Section 20.2 demonstrates the problem and presents the proposed methodology; Section 20.3 is reserved for the algorithm design; Section 20.4 contains the experiment results; and Section 20.5 gives concluding remarks about the work.

20.2   Proposed Methodology

In the proposed methodology, the endorsed watermarking technique is investigated over the standard data set of audio files of 44.1 kHz sampling rate containing standard types such as blues, classic and pop. Each audio signal has a different variation of frequency and amplitude according to its music information. A watermark image of size 16×16 is selected for embedding. The encryption of watermark is done using generation polynomial in which redundant bits are added with watermark bits and generate cyclic code which is linear and invariant to the shifting. The encrypted watermark bits are again scrambled using Arnold's cat map [6] using a key which determines the number of iterations for the random arrangement of the bits. The final encrypted image is embedded in the host audio using uncorrelated pseudo-random sequence [10] that contains 1s and 0s of a specific length which is used as a key for inculcation. As discussed earlier, the host audio first undergoes FFT decomposition and then the CORDIC QR which generates the final upper triangular R-matrix. The elements of the R-matrix are generated through the decomposition of stable frequency coefficients of the host signal. The binary values of the diagonal elements [11] of the R-matrix are considered to be most stable and used as the embedding region in the proposed methodology as these stable bits can tolerate the chances of distortion of an audio signal. The sample of host audio of type blues and the watermark image is presented in Figure 20.1.

The flow chart of the complete procedure is shown in Figure 20.2. For embedding purposes, the host audio is reshaped first in a 2-dimensional vector of size 512×512. This vector is further decomposed and participates in the watermarking process as shown in Figure 20.2.

As disclosed in Figure 20.2, the bits of watermark are inculcated into the least bits of the diagonal elements of matrix R using the PN

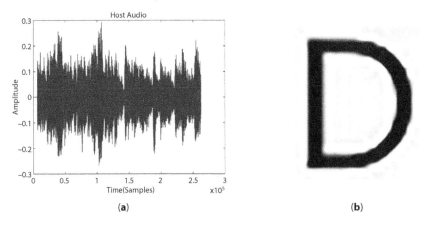

Figure 20.1 (a) Host audio (Blues); (b) watermark image.

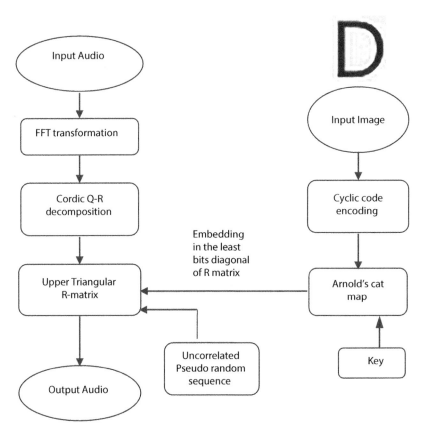

Figure 20.2 Flow chart of the complete process of watermark embedding.

(pseudo-random) sequence as a key. The same process is applied for the extraction of the watermark image whose algorithm is described in the Section 20.3.

20.2.1   Fast Fourier Transform

Fast Fourier Transform (FFT) is used to represent a signal in the frequency domain. It basically generates the non-collapsing frequency bands of a signal in which each frequency band represents pixel values based on data information carried by pixels. In other words, the magnitude of the whole data of the signal is segmented into coefficient bands of fixed size based on frequency information. FFT is much similar as DCT (Discrete Fourier transform) but its computation time is 3 times better than DCT. In the presented technique, the audio signal is reshaped into a 2D matrix and it's FFT [7] coefficients are decomposed into fixed-size non-overlapping frequency energy bands. The low- and high-frequency subbands are not utilized in the embedding process since they contain essential information which may not tolerate any manipulation. The information in the high-frequency coefficient band may easily be lost due to compression; hence it is not a good idea to hide a watermark in such a frequency coefficient. The general equation of the FFT is given below:

$$F[a] = \sum_{p=0}^{n-1} F[p] e^{-j2\pi ap/n}$$

(20.1)

$$e^{-j2\pi ap/n} = -j\sin\left(\frac{2\pi ap}{n}\right) + \cos(2\pi ap/n)$$

Here, F[a] is the representation of input matrix 'a' in frequency domain. It is similar to DFT [8] but its computation time is $O(N log_2 N)$, which is faster than DFT. The frequency coefficients of a signal matrix represent the intensity of its pixel values. The frequency bands are in the form of real and imaginary components which contain the information of the signal. The energy of each frequency band is computed by the following equation:

$$E = \sum_I f(I)^2$$

(20.2)

Here, E is the energy magnitude of an energy band and $f(I)^2$ is the square of the function of its intensity value. In the proposed technique, middle energy frequency coefficients are enrolled in CORDIC-based QR decomposition to find stable elements which can participate in the embedding procedure.

20.2.2 CORDIC-Based QR Decomposition

The decomposition method, i.e., CORDIC-based QR, is practiced, which is nothing but the coordinate rotation digital computer (CORDIC) method that contains shift and addition operation. The CORDIC algorithm performs rotation and vectoring mode operation to calculate vector rotation and rotation angle in order to perform QR decomposition of a matrix. The component of vectoring mode forced the lower triangular element of a matrix 0 and the rotation mode rotates the vector by an angle between $-\pi/2$ and $+\pi/2$. Hence, QR decomposition [13] is executed using vectoring mode followed by a series of rotation modes which come under "Givens transformation." QR decomposition of a matrix is implemented using Givens transformation, which forces the alignment of the first vector with the X-axis and then the rest of the vector is rotated with the same angle. After this transformation, the entry of the lower part of triangular matrix gets nullified and the residual upper part of triangular matrix is generated. The audio signal is reshaped into 2D square matrix A and its QR decomposition is evaluated:

$$CORDIC(A) = QR \qquad (20.3)$$

Here, an orthogonal matrix is Q and the other matrix is R, which is the upper triangular matrix. The general equation of the CORDIC algorithm in rotation mode is:

$$X_{k+1} = x_k - y_K P_k 2^{-k} \qquad (20.4)$$

$$Y_{k+1} = y_k + x_K P_k 2^{-k}$$

$$Z_{k+1} = z_k - P_k \tan^{-1}(2^{-k})$$

Here, P_k describes the angle of rotation that possesses value ± 1. Z is an angle accumulator that possesses value 0 or +1. The CORDIC algorithm generates the following result after performing a finite number of iterations on word length m:

$$X_m = A_m(X_0 \cos Z_0 - Y_0 \sin Z_0) \qquad (20.5)$$

$$Y_m = A_m (Y_0 \cos Z_0 + X_0 \sin Z_0)$$

$$Z_m = 0$$

$$A_m = \prod_{k=0}^{m} \sqrt{1 + 2^{-2k}}$$

Here, A_m is the computational gain. The general equation of the CORDIC algorithm in vectoring mode is:

$$X_m = A_m \sqrt{X_0^2 + Y_0^2} \qquad (20.6)$$

$$Y_m = 0$$

$$Z_m = Z_0 + tan^{-1} (Y_0/X_0)$$

$$A_m = \prod_{k=0}^{m} \sqrt{1 + 2^{-2k}}$$

From the CORDIC algorithm, the Givens transformation is applied to the square matrix A using an orthogonal matrix G, also called the rotator, which generates the required R upper triangular matrix.

$$G = \begin{bmatrix} \cos\phi & \sin\phi \\ -\sin\phi & \cos\phi \end{bmatrix} \qquad (20.7)$$

Here, ϕ is a rotation angle which is chosen appropriately.

$$\begin{bmatrix} \cos\phi & \sin\phi \\ -\sin\phi & \cos\phi \end{bmatrix} \times \begin{bmatrix} A_{m-1, k} \\ A_{m,k} \end{bmatrix} = \begin{bmatrix} R_{11} \ R_{12} \ ... \ R_{1k} \\ 0 \ R_{21} \ ... \ R_{2k} \end{bmatrix}$$

$$\uparrow \qquad\qquad\qquad \uparrow \qquad\qquad\qquad \uparrow$$

Rotator matrix (G)   Input host matrix A of size n×n   Upper triangular matrix R

Here, $m \in \{2,3,...n\}$ and $k \in \{1,2,3....n\}$. Rotation angle ϕ is calculated as:

$$\phi_{m,n} = tan^{-1}(R_{m,n}/R_{m-1,n})$$
(20.8)

The rotator matrix initiates zeroing the bottom element of the R matrix and leaves the upper triangular matrix, which is further utilized for the embedding process.

20.2.3   Concept of Cyclic Codes

Cyclic code encryption [12] is used to add some redundant bits with data bits in order to generate the codeword. In the proposed technique, bits of the watermark image are encrypted using (7, 4) cyclic code in which every 4-bit long message is added with 3 redundant bits using generation polynomial and produce a 7-bit codeword that is linear and invariant of shifting.

20.2.4   Concept of Arnold's Cat Map

The encrypted watermark resulting from the cyclic coding is again transformed by using the Arnold's cat map transformation using some specific times of scrambling iteration which ensures the dual security of the watermark image. The general equation of Arnold's cat map transformation [6] for an image is given below:

$$\Gamma \begin{bmatrix} X \\ Y \end{bmatrix} = \begin{bmatrix} X+Y \\ X+2Y \end{bmatrix} mod\ n$$
(20.9)

The X and Y are the directions in which a part of an image is sheared and its position jumbled. The flow chart of extraction process is shown in Figure 20.3

Figure 20.3 shows the process of watermark extraction in which the same path is followed, as used during the embedding, to extract the hidden watermark bits. These bits are reconstructed into image finally.

20.3   Algorithm Design

A. Algorithm of Watermark Embedding

The audio file of sampling rate 44.1Khz is reshaped into 2-dimensional space of size 512×512 and its matrix values is generated, which is undertaken in the decomposition procedure.

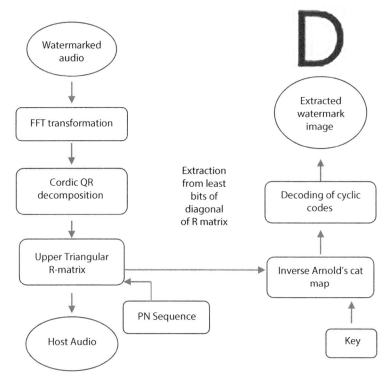

Figure 20.3 Process of watermark extraction.

Step 1: Audio signal is transformed from the special domain to frequency domain using FFT transformations which splits the host matrix into energy bands based on its frequency, and middle frequency bands are selected for the next level of decomposition.

$$FFT(A)=[LH]$$

Here, input host matrix is transformed into middle frequency coefficient matrix (LH), which is the part that contains both low and high values of pixels of data.

Step 2: The selected mid-bands are supplied to CORDIC-QR decomposition.

$$CORDIC(A)=QR$$

Step 3: Watermark image of size 16×16 is selected and supplied for encryption. First, cyclic code encoding has been performed.

The cyclic coding of 7×4 is applied in which 4 is the watermark bits and 7 is the codeword or encoded bits, which contain 3 extra redundant bits that are added using generation polynomial.

$$C(x) = W(x).G(x)$$

$$G(x) = x^3 + x + 1$$

Here, $C(x)$ is the codeword or encoded bits, $W(x)$ is the watermark bits and $G(x)$ is the generation polynomial.

Step 4: Arnold's cat map is applied to the $C(x)$ codeword using key=7, which iterates the scrambling 7 times and generates the encrypted codeword.

Step 5: The least bits of diagonals of R matrix are used as embedding region and the encrypted watermark bits are implanted into it using two pseudo-random sequences (PN1 and PN2) as a key.

$$If \; A(k)=0$$

$$R_n=R_n+PN1$$

$$If \; A(k)=1$$

$$R_n=R_n+PN2$$

$$end$$

Here, $A(K)$ is the scrambled codeword generated after Step 5. The R_n is the least bit of diagonal element of n-th position in S matrix. The PN1 and PN2 are the pseudo-random sequence.

Step 6: The embedded watermarked audio is reconstructed after applying inverse process of CORDIC-QR decomposition and the inverse function of FFT, which is finally reshaped to generate the watermarked audio.

B. Algorithm of Watermark Extrication

Step 1: The input watermarked signal is reshaped into 2D space and decomposed into frequency sub-band in which middle frequency band is selected.

$$FFT(A)=[LH]$$

Step 2: The middle energy band of watermarked audio is decomposed using QR decomposition in which R matrix is extracted.

Step 3: The encrypted bits of watermark are extracted from the least bits of the diagonal elements of R matrix.

If correlation (R_n and PN1) > correlation (R_n and PN2)

Then A(k)=0

If correlation (R_n and PN2) >= correlation (R_n and PN2)

Then A(K)=1

Step 4: The encoded watermark bits A(K) is supplied to inverse of Arnold's cat map using key value 7.

Step 5: The descrambled watermark bits are then supplied to inverse of cyclic code of size 7×4, in which the 3 redundant bits are removed from the 7-bit long codeword, leaving a data bit that is 4-bit long. In this way, the entire data bits are recovered and reconstructed to an image.

20.4   Experiment Results

The experiment is carried out on 3 types of audio files named Blues, Classical and Pop. All the audio files have different music frequencies and amplitudes and they are reshaped in 512×512 size matrix for the embedding process. Figure 20.4 shows the GUI representation of watermarking an audio file of type 'Blues' in which the blue color signal is the host audio and green color signal is the watermarked audio. GUI also shows the quality of watermarked audio after embedding in which the PSNR of watermarked audio is 37.7dB. The watermark image is re-extracted from the host signal using the extraction algorithm and the watermark quality is depicted by the GUI in terms of the PSNR [9] which is 66.02dB and the value of its normalized cross-correlation and the bit error rate (BER) is 0.89 and 0.10 respectively, which are found to be satisfying.

Figure 20.5 shows the watermark image before and after the extraction process. And so the quality of the extracted watermark image is determined, which is shown to be 66.02dB PSNR.

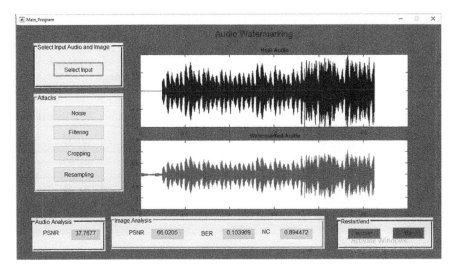

Figure 20.4   Process of audio watermarking in MATLAB.

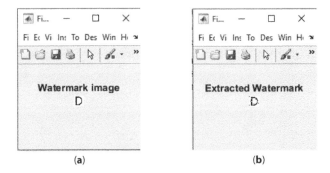

Figure 20.5   (a) Watermark image before embedding; (b) watermark image after the extraction.

The PSNR values of the watermarked audio of all the types are also shown in Table 20.1. The average value of PSNR watermarked audio is 36.75dB, which satisfies the acceptance rate and is now easily distributed in a shared network without letting imposters know about the hidden data.

The robustness of the scheme is tested by conducting several attacks on different audio files containing the watermark image (Figure 20.6). The attacks [12] named as noise, filtering, cropping, and resampling are first tested on an audio file of type 'Blues' and the watermark images in the respective attacks are extracted. The samples of the extracted watermark images are shown in Figure 20.6, which are collected from the attacked (Noise, Filtering, Resampling) watermarked audio of type 'Blues.'

Table 20.1 Evaluation of audio signals and the respective extricated watermark image.

Quality analysis of audio		Quality analysis of extracted watermark image		
Type of audio	PSNR of watermarked audio (dB)	BER	NC	PSNR (dB)
Blues	37.76	0.02	0.88	66.02
Classic	35.74	0.01	0.90	61.74
Pop	36.15	0.03	0.94	54.08

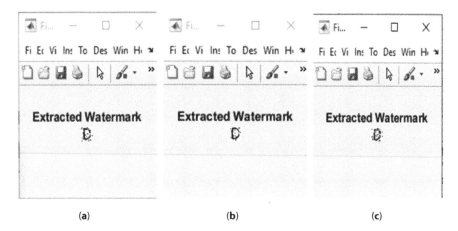

(a)   (b)   (c)

Figure 20.6 Sample of watermark image extracted from the attacked—(a) noise, (b) filtering, (c) resampling—watermarked audio.

The average PSNR value of all the extracted watermark images in Figure 20.6 is 56.207dB. Now, the experiment is extended for other types of audio files containing watermark images which are exposed to 4 types of attacks (Noise, Filtering, Cropping, and Resampling), and the watermark images are extracted from the respective audio files [13] and their quality is analysed using the value of PSNR, BER, and NC. Table 20.2 shows the results of the quality assessment of extracted watermark images for different audio types under several different attacks. The respective values are found to satisfy the acceptance rate required to prove ownership. Table 20.2 comprises with the results of the quality measurement of extracted watermark images under different attacks.

Table 20.2 Quality analysis of extracted watermark images under various attacks.

Audio files with respective attacks		Quality analysis of extracted watermark images		
Audio type	Attacks	BER	NC	PSNR (dB)
Blues	Noise attack	0.34	0.86	60.026
	Audio Filtering	0.10	0.84	49.211
	Crop attack	0.44	0.96	59.385
	Resampling the rate	0.11	0.85	43.484
Classic	Noise attack	0.03	0.88	58.823
	Audio Filtering	0.01	0.81	48.414
	Crop attack	0.03	0.92	60.519
	Resampling the rate	0.12	0.82	51.568
Pop	Noise attack	0.25	0.91	50.020
	Audio Filtering	0.03	0.84	47.709
	Crop attack	0.03	0.95	52.779
	Resampling the rate	0.12	0.80	51.457

20.5   Conclusion

The combination of FFT and CORDIC-based QR decomposition is successfully implemented on audio files of sampling rate 44.1 kHz. The watermark payload of size 16×16 is implanted into the elements of the diagonal part of the matrix R of host audio. The extraction of the watermark image also follows the same steps as followed in embedding. The average PSNR of watermarked audio is 36.75dB. The values of NC, PSNR, and BER are also estimated for the extracted watermark subject with and without the implication of signal processing attacks. The respective results are found to be good and ensure the significance of the proposed technique in order to increase the security of digital audio while minimizing ownership disputes.

References

1. Akhaee, M.A., Saberian, M.J., Feizi, S., Marvasti, F., Method based obscuring data in audio signal using correlated quantization followed by histogram-based detector. *IEEE Trans. Multimedia*, 11, 5, 834–842, 2009.

2. Ozer, H., Sankur, B., Memon, N., An audio watermarking structure using SVD disintegration technique, Proc. Seventh ACM workshop on multimedia and data privacy, MMSEC-2005. *EURASIP J. Adv. Signal Process*, 2005, 658950, 51–56, 2005.

3. Bhat, V.K., Sengupta, I., Das, A., A robust method uses singular value decomposition for an adaptive audio watermarking system in wavelet domain. *Digital Signal Process.*, 20, 6, 1547–1558, 2010.

4. Hu, P., Peng, D., Yi, Z., Xiang, Y., Robust time-spread echo watermarking using characteristics of host signals. *Electron. Lett.*, IEEE, 52, 1, 5–6, 2016.

5. Hu, H.T., Hsu, L.Y., Chou, H.H., Perceptual-based DWPT-DCT framework for selective blind audio watermarking. *Signal Process.*, 105, 316–627, 2014. https://doi.org/10.1016/j.sigpro.2014.05.003.

6. Sharma, B. and Dave, M., Robust Hybrid Image and Audio Watermarking Using Cyclic Codes and Arnold Transform. *International Conference on Communication and Electronics Systems-2019*, Coimbatore, India, pp. 309–315, 2019.

7. Dhar, P.K. and Echizen, I., Robust FFT Based Watermarking Scheme for Copyright Protection of Digital Audio Data. *2011 7th International Conference on Intelligent Information Hiding and Multimedia Signal Processing*, Dalian, 2011, 181–184, 2011.

8. Karajeh, H. *et al.*, proposed a watermarking system relied on dual decomposition using DWT and Schur technique, published in Spinger Science, in: *Multimedia Tools and Applications*, vol. 78, pp. 18395–18418, 2019.

9. Subir, and Joshi, A.M., DWT-DCT based blind audio watermarking using Arnold scrambling and Cyclic codes. *International Conference on Signal Processing and Integrated Networks (SPIN-2019)*, Noida, pp. 79–84, 2016.

10. Chen, K., Yan, F., Iliyasu, A.M. *et al.*, Watermarking system using Dual Quantum Audio procedure relied on Quantum Discrete Cosine Transform. *Int J Theor. Phys.*, 58, 502–521, 2019. https://doi.org/10.1007/s10773-018-3950-9.

11. Dwivedi, A., Kumar, A., Dutta, M.K., Burget, R., Myska, V., An Efficient and Robust Zero-Bit Watermarking Technique for Biometric Image Protection. *International Conference on Signal Processing (TSP)-2019*, Budapest, Hungary, pp. 236–240, 2019.

12. Vivekananda Bhat, K., Das, A.K., Lee, J., A Mean Quantization Watermarking Scheme for Audio Signals Using Singular-Value Decomposition. *IEEE Access*, 7, 157480–157488, 2019.

13. Gupta, A., Kaur, A., Dutta, M.K., Schimmel, J., Perceptually Transparent & Robust Audio Watermarking Algorithm Using Multi Resolution Decomposition & Cordic QR Decomposition. *International Conference on Signal Processing (TSP)-2019*, Budapest, Hungary, pp. 313–317, 2019.

21

Performance of DC-Biased Optical Orthogonal Frequency Division Multiplexing in Visible Light Communication

S. Ponmalar* and Shiny J.J.

*Department of Electronics and Communication Engineering,
Thiagarajar College of Engineering, Madurai, India*

Abstract

An orthogonal frequency division multiplexing (OFDM) scheme is used to achieve high data rate and good performance under various channel conditions. The negative peaks in the OFDM signal are clipped based on the DC bias applied to the system which proportionally increases the peak-to-average power ratio (PAPR). The PAPR can be optimized by modulating the signal using a direct-current optical orthogonal frequency division multiplexing (DCO-OFDM) scheme. In the proposed model, the negative peak of the transmitting signal is accurately clipped off, thereby improving the performance of the modulating scheme. The optical characteristics of the LED and the photodiode are demonstrated in the transmitter and receiver respectively. The results of the system show that the DCO-OFDM enhances the visible light communication in various channels with the increasing number of users.

Keywords: Visible light communication, clipper, DCO-OFDM, Hermitian symmetry, quadrature amplitude modulation, orthogonal frequency division multiplexing

Corresponding author: sponmalar1976@gmail.com

Ashutosh Kumar Dubey, Abhishek Kumar, S. Rakesh Kumar, N. Gayathri, Prasenjit Das (eds.) AI and IoT-Based Intelligent Automation in Robotics, (339–354) © 2021 Scrivener Publishing LLC

21.1   Introduction

Visible light communication (VLC) is a data communications variant which uses visible light between 400 and 800 THz (780–375 nm). VLC is one of the advances used in optical wireless communications technologies [14, 23]. It works in a similar way as optical fiber; however, the mechanism of transmission is free space. The innovation of light-emitting diode (LED) has enabled incredible progress to be made in light communication [12]. LEDs are regularly utilized for transmitting information; however, the transmitter and consequently the receiver must be in view of each other. VLC utilizes LED because of the fact that the transmitter sends information by rapidly flickering light, which might be unnoticeable to the human eye [11]. The detector receives the flickering light faster and decodes the transmitted information. One advantage of VLC is that it is frequently implemented since it's affordable, smaller, low power and prevents radio obstruction. Applications include vehicle-to-vehicle information transmission utilizing headlights, position identification, AI-enabled vehicle frameworks, image sensor communication, web access and sound video transmission [8–10]. VLC will have an extraordinary impact in future areas of communication and is easily executed for a lot of uses.

Orthogonal frequency division multiplexing (OFDM) is a type of digital transmission and a method of encoding digital data on multiple carrier frequencies to reduce interference and crosstalk [1, 3]. As opposed to transmitting a high-rate stream of data with a single subcarrier, OFDM utilizes a large number of closely spaced orthogonal subcarriers that are transmitted in parallel. Each subcarrier is balanced with a conventional digital modulation scheme at low symbol rate. Moreover, the combination of many different subcarriers enables data rates practically like those in conventional single-carrier modulation schemes within equivalent bandwidth [6, 25].

The OFDM scheme varies from traditional frequency division multiplexing in the following ways:

1. Multiple carriers convey the information stream,
2. The subcarriers are orthogonal to each other, and
3. A guard interval is added to each symbol to diminish the channel delay spread and inter-symbol interference.

Optical wireless communication is an energy-efficient and cost-effective response for rapid and secure remote connections. Orthogonal frequency division multiplexing (OFDM) is a key procedure for 4G remote communications, which is also broadly used in numerous applications. Since

OFDM systems possess properties, such as high spectral efficiency, and reduce intersymbol interference (ISI), these days optical OFDM has garnered a lot of attention, both in academia and industry. As of late, there are numerous mainstream optical OFDM strategies like [7, 15–17] Flip-OFDM, asymmetrically clipped optical OFDM (ACO-OFDM), DC-biased optical OFDM (DCO-OFDM), and unipolar OFDM (U-OFDM). OFDM is presently considered as a modulation method for optical framework. In conventional OFDM, the signals are transmitted in bipolar and complex structure. In any case, such signals aren't reasonable for transmission in IM/DD optical remote framework [20–22]. In this way, Hermitian evenness is applied to the signal. This modifies the bipolar and sophisticated signals into applicable/valid signal.

In wireless optical signals, an intensity modulation is practiced by LEDs and direct detection using a sophisticated photodiode. In DC biased OFDM, a DC bias is added to the signal [2] Because of the enormous peak-to-average power proportion of OFDM, even with an outsized bias some negative peaks of the signal will be cut. To maintain a strategic distance from the negative signals, DCO-OFDM adds a DC bias to the valid bipolar OFDM signals. Since the DC-biased signals can't totally get obviate negative-valued data, the signals under zero must be cut.

21.2   System Model

21.2.1   Transmitter Block

The transmitter block of DCO-OFDM is shown in Figure 21.1. Input bit steam is mapped according to modulation scheme, e.g., quadrature

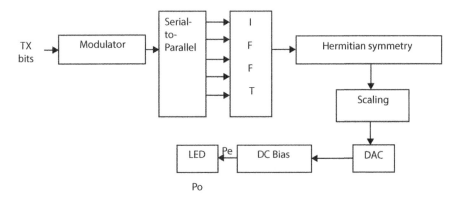

Figure 21.1 Transmitter block of DCO-OFDM.

amplitude modulation (QAM). The serial-to-parallel converter is used to convert the serial signals into parallel signals [5].

The inverse fast Fourier transform is used to convert the frequency domain signals into the time domain signals. The Hermitian symmetry is used to obtain the real valued signal, which means it clipped off the negative signal [26]. In scaling, the signal is multiplied with a constant value. After the digital signal is scaled, it is passed through a digital-to-analog converter to obtain the analog signal [18]. Finally, a DC bias is added with the resulting signal to drive the light-emitting diode and transmit the signal over the channel.

21.2.2   Receiver Block

The receiver block of DCO-OFDM is shown in Figure 21.2. The signal obtained by the channel is collected by the photo detector. An amplifier is used to mitigate the effect of path loss. An ADC converter is used to obtain the digital signals and transmit them to the parallel-to-serial converter to convert the parallel signal into serial signal [24]. After parallel-to-serial conversion, fast Fourier transform is performed to obtain the frequency domain signals. The demodulator is used to recover the original signal.

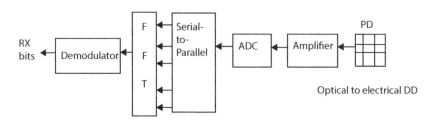

Figure 21.2 Receiver block of DCO-OFDM.

21.3   Proposed Method

To expel the negative peaks, a proper DC bias is applied to the unipolar signal. A cyclic prefix is added to the signal. As OFDM signals have extremely high PAPR, an outsized DC bias is required [28]. In any case, it makes the framework useless for optical power. So, a moderate DC bias is applied. A perfect optical modulator is utilized accordingly, and the intensity of output optical signal is legitimate relative to the information current. The subsequent signal is transmitted over an additive white Gaussian noise (AWGN) channel [27, 30]. On the recipient side, the received signal is first changed over from an optical signal to an electrical signal utilizing a photodiode. Presently, the attached cyclic prefix and the signal are changed over from sequential to parallel. The signal at that point goes through the fast Fourier transform block. At that point it is demodulated and changed over from corresponding to sequential information.

21.3.1   Simulation Parameters for OptSim

The specifications of DCO-OFDM with different parameters in OptSim are shown in Table 21.1.

Table 21.1 Simulation parameters of DCO-OFDM.

Parameters	Value	Units	Range
Bit rate	10	Gb/s	[0,∞]
Number of subcarrier	8		[1,32]
Cyclic prefix	0.25	Fraction baud	[0,4]
QAM bit number	4		
Samples per bit	13		[]
Baud rate	2.5	Gbaud/s	[0,52]
Reference frequency	193.4	THz	[0,∞]
Reference wavelength	1550	Nm	[0,∞]
Quantum efficiency	0.7		[0,1]
Responsivity	0.8751	A/W	[0,∞]
Maximum value before clipping	0	a.u	
Minimum value before clipping	-1.8	a.u	

21.3.2   Block Diagram of DCO-OFDM in OptSim

The block diagram of DCO-OFDM is simulated using OptSim is shown in Figure 21.3. Input bit steam is mapped consistent with modulation scheme Quadrature AM (QAM), which consists of both in-phase and quadrature signal [4, 19]. The serial-to-parallel converter is employed to convert the serial signals into parallel signals. The inverse fast Fourier transform is

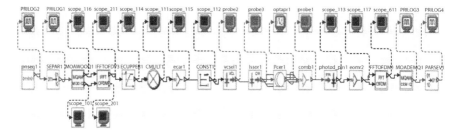

Figure 21.3 Block diagram of DCO-OFDM.

employed to convert the frequency domain signals into the time domain signals. It consists of both in-phase and quadrature component [13]. The Hermitian symmetry (electrical clipper) is employed to get the real-value signal, which suggests it clipped off the negative signal [26]. In scaling (multiplier), the signal is multiplied with a systematic value. After the digital signal is scaled, it's a trained digital-to-analog converter for getting the analog signal. Eventually, a DC bias is added with the resulting signal to drive the light-emitting diode and transmit the signal through optical fiber [30]. Electrical and logical scopes are employed to view the information signals.

The signal obtained by the channel (fiber) is collected by the photodetector. An amplifier is employed to mitigate the effect of path loss. An ADC converter is employed to get the digital signals and given to parallel-to-serial converter to convert the parallel signal into serial signal [24]. After parallel-to-serial conversion, fast Fourier transform is performed to get the frequency domain signals, which have both in-phase and quadrature signals. The demodulator employed to recover the original signal is QAM demodulator. It contains both the in-phase and quadrature phase signal. Electrical scope and logical scope are employed to view the data signals.

21.4   Results and Discussion

Figure 21.4 shows the input data signal for DCO-OFDM method.

The input signal is given to the serial-to-parallel converter, which converts the serial signals into parallel signals as shown in Figure 21.5.

The parallel signal is mapped according to the quadrature amplitude modulation (QAM) scheme. It consists of both in-phase and quadrature signals [4]. Figure 21.6 shows the in-phase modulated signal.

The modulated signal is given to the inverse fast Fourier transform block, which converts the frequency domain signals into the time domain

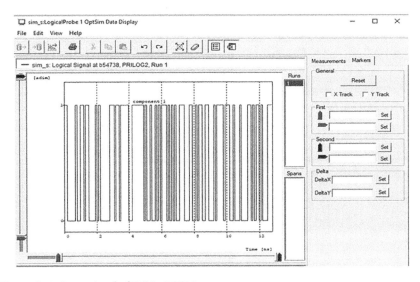

Figure 21.4 Input signal of DCO-OFDM.

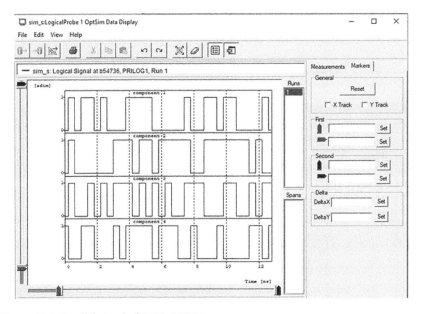

Figure 21.5 Parallel signal of DCO-OFDM.

signals [19]. Figure 21.7 shows the time domain in-phase inverse FFT (IFFT) signal.

The Hermitian symmetry is employed to obtain the real-value signal, which means it clipped off the negative signal [26]. The signal coming from

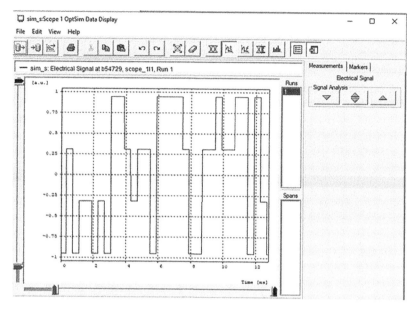

Figure 21.6 Modulated signal of DCO-OFDM.

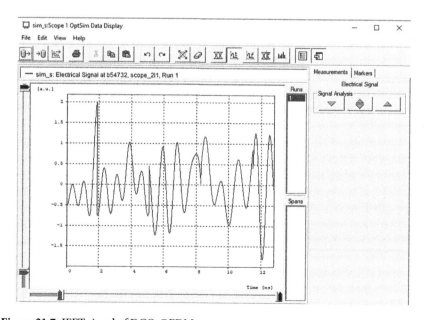

Figure 21.7 IFFT signal of DCO-OFDM.

the QAM modulator has both positive and negative signals. The electrical clipper clipped off the negative signal comes from the modulator and allows only positive signals. The positive clipped signal is shown in Figure 21.8.

The clipped signal is given to the multiplier. In scaling, the signal is multiplied with a constant value. Figure 21.9 shows the scaling signal multiplied by a constant factor of 2.

After the digital signal is scaled it is passed through a digital-to-analog converter to obtain the analog signal [29]. Finally, a DC bias is added with the resulting signal to drive the light-emitting diode and transmit the signal through a channel. Figure 21.10 shows the DC bias signal.

Figure 21.11 shows the optical spectrum for a vertical cavity surface-emitting laser (VCSEL) with 3.42044 mW or -9.6592 dBm power in the range of [193.362; 193.466] THz.

Figure 21.12 shows the optical spectrum for a CW Lorentzian laser with 0.999967 mW or -0.000144433 dBm power in the range of [193.362; 193.466] THz.

Figure 21.13 shows the optical spectrum for fiber with 0.639124 mW or -1.94415 dBm power in the range of [193.362; 193.466] THz.

Figure 21.14 shows the optical combiner spectrum with 7.82915 mW or 8.93715 dBm power in the range of [193.362; 193.466] THz.

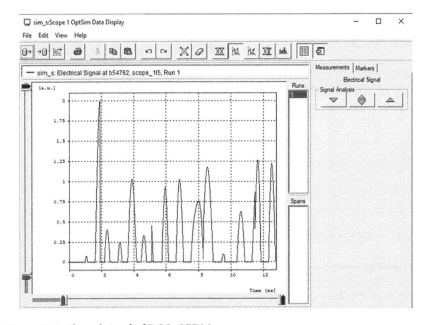

Figure 21.8 Clipped signal of DCO-OFDM.

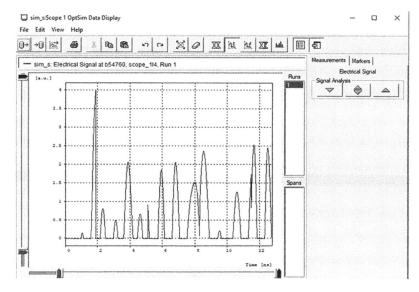

Figure 21.9 Scaled signal of DCO-OFDM.

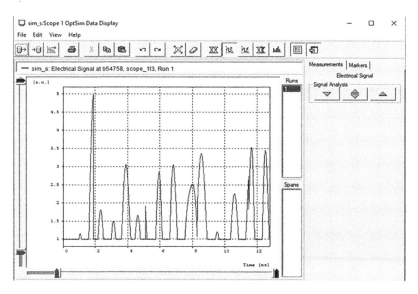

Figure 21.10 DC-biased signal of DCO-OFDM.

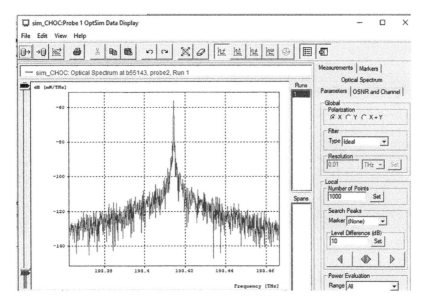

Figure 21.11 VCSEL optical spectrum of DCO-OFDM.

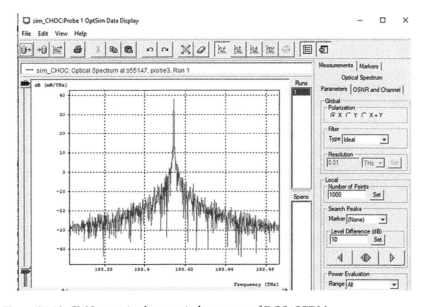

Figure 21.12 CW Lorentzian laser optical spectrum of DCO-OFDM.

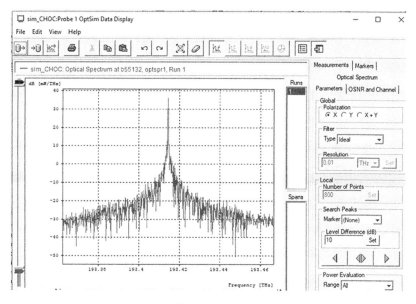

Figure 21.13 Fiber optical spectrum of DCO-OFDM.

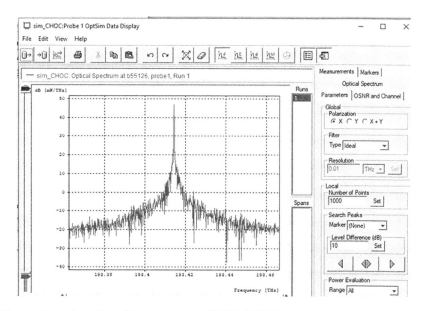

Figure 21.14 Optical combiner spectrum of DCO-OFDM.

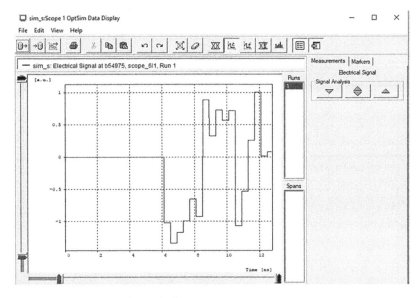

Figure 21.15 Demodulated signal of DCO-OFDM.

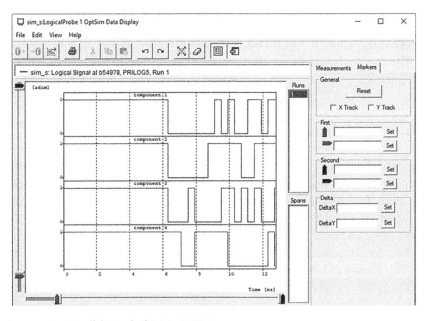

Figure 21.16 Parallel signal of DCO-OFDM.

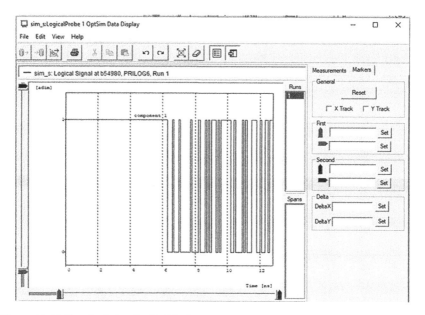

Figure 21.17   Received signal of DCO-OFDM.

Figure 21.15 shows the demodulated signal of DCO-OFDM after passing through the channel.

After the negative signal is clipped off between 0 to 6 values, the obtained received signal of DCO-OFDM is shown in Figure 21.16.

The received signal after clipping the remaining negative part is shown in Figure 21.17.

21.5   Conclusion

The optical wireless communication technique has been in incredible demand over the past few years. To cope with the latest technological advancements, the study in this chapter proposes a completely unique modulation technique of DCO-OFDM. To remove the negative peaks, an appropriate DC bias is applied to the signal. It has been implemented using different modulation techniques under various channels. Based on the simulations on RSoft's OptSim, it has been concluded that the input with combined positive and negative signals contains the required information in the positive half, which was extracted by a clipper that clipped off the unwanted signal. The specified information is obtained at the output with nothing lost. It has also been evaluated because the power is inconsistent; the right power allocation isn't found to be accurate. So as to eliminate this drawback (i.e., imperfect power allocation), proper power allocation algorithms are often developed. For future technological purposes, DCO-OFDM will continue to be used and further improvements will be implemented.

References

1. Armstrong, J., OFDM for optical communications. *J. Lightwave Technol.*, 27, 3, 189–204, Feb. 1, 2009.
2. Ling, X., Wang, J., Liang, X., Ding, Z., Zhao, C., Offset and power optimization for DCO-OFDM in visible light communication systems. *IEEE Trans. Signal Process.*, 64, 2, 349–363, Jan. 2016.
3. Proakis, J.G. and Salehi, M., 4th Ed., McGraw-Hill, New York, NY, USA, 2001.
4. Lee, S.C.J., Randel, S., Breyer, F., Koonen, A.M.J., PAM-DMT for intensity-modulated and direct-detection optical communication systems. *EEE Photon. Technol. Lett.*, 21, 23, 1749–1751, Dec. 1, 2009.
5. Dissanayake, S.D., Panta, K., Armstrong, J., A novel technique to simultaneously transmit ACO-OFDM and DCO-OFDM in IM/DD systems, in: *Proc. IEEE GLOBECOM Workshops*, pp. 782–786, Dec. 2011.
6. Armstrong, J. and Lowery, A.J., Power efficient optical OFDM. *Electron. Lett.*, 42, 6, 370–372, Mar. 2006.
7. Dissanayake, S.D. and Armstrong, J., Comparison of ACO-OFDM, DCOOFDM and ADO-OFDM in IM/DD systems. *J. Lightwave Technol.*, 31, 7, 1063–1072, Apr. 1, 2013.
8. Sun, Y., Yang, F., Cheng, L., An overview of OFDM-based visible light communication systems from the perspective of energy efficiency versus spectral efficiency. *IEEE Access*, 6, 60824–60833, 2018.
9. Bykhovsky, D. and Arnon, S., Multiple access resource allocation in visible light communication systems. *J. Lightwave Technol.*, 32, 8, 1594–1600, Apr. 15, 2014.
10. Li, J.J. and Richardson, T., Visible light communication: Opportunities, challenges and the path to market. *IEEE Commun. Mag.*, 51, 12, 26–32, Dec. 2013.
11. Deng, X., Mardanikorani, S., Wu, Y., Arulandu, K., Chen, B., Khalid, A.M., Linnartz, J.-P. M. G., Mitigating LED nonlinearity to enhance visible light communications. *IEEE Trans. Commun.*, 66, 11, 5593–5607, Nov. 2018.
12. Deng, X., Wu, Y., Khalid, A.M., Long, X., Linnartz, J.-P. M. G., LED power consumption in joint illumination and communication system. *Opt. Express*, 25, 16, 18990–19003, Aug. 2017.
13. Deng, X., Arulandu, K., Wu, Y., Mardanikorani, S., Zhou, G., Linnartz, J.-P. M. G., Modeling and analysis of transmitter performance in visible light communications. *IEEE Trans. Veh. Technol.*, 68, 3, 2316–2331, Mar. 2019.

14. Mardanikorani, S., Deng, X., Linnartz, J.-P.M. G., Efficiency of power loading strategies for visible light communication, in: *Proc. IEEE Globecom Communication. Workshops*, vol. 7, 2019 983, pp. 1–6, Dec. 2018.

15. Dissanayake, S.D., Comparison of ACO-OFDM, DCO-OFDM and ADO-OFDM in IM/DD systems. *J. Lightwave Technol.*, 31, 7, 1063–1072, April 1, 2013.

16. Islim, M.S., A generalized solution to the Spectral Efficiency Loss in Unipolar Optical OFDMbased systems. *IEEE International Conference*, pp. 5126–5131, June, 2015.

17. Baxley, R.J., Achievable Data Rate Analysis of Clipped FLIP-OFDM in Optical Wireless Communication. *J. Wireless Commun. Networking*, pp. 1203–1207, Dec 2012.

18. Barrami, F., Low Complexity direct detection optical OFDM systems for high data rate communications, Thesis, 55–82, April 2015.

19. Mathur, G., Performance Analysis of MIMO OFDM System for Different Modulation Schemes under Various Fading Channels. *Int. J. Adv. Res. Comput. Commun. Eng.*, 2, 5, 2098–2103, May 2013.

20. Fernando, N., Flip-OFDM for Unipolar Communication Systems. *IEEE Trans. Commun.*, 60, 12, 3726–3733, Dec 14, 2011.

21. Islam, R., Analysis of DCO-OFDM and Flip-OFDM for IM/DD Optical-Wireless System. *8th international Conference on Electrical and Computer Engineering (IEEE)*, Dhaka, Bangladesh, pp. 32–35, Dec 14.

22. Saju, S.C., Comparison of ACO-OFDM and DCO-OFDM in IM/DD systems. *IJERT*, 4, 04, 2278–2281, April 2015.

23. Zhang, Y.Y., Yu, H.Y., Zhang, J.K., Zhu, Y.J., Signal-cooperative multilayer-modulated VLC systems for automotive applications. *IEEE Photonics J.*, 8, 1, 1–9, 2016.

24. Liu, X., Gong, C., Li, S., Xu, Z., Signal characterization and receiver design for visible light communication under weak illuminance. *IEEE Commun. Lett.*, vol. 20, 7, 1349–1352, 2016.

25. Li, Y., Majid, S., Robert, H., Haas, H., Optical OFDM with single-photon avalanche diode. *IEEE Photonics Technol. Lett.*, 27, 9, 943–946, 2015.

26. He, C. and Armstrong, J., Clipping noise mitigation in optical OFDM systems. *IEEE Commun. Lett.*, 99, 1–1, 2016.

27. Aly, B., Performance analysis of adaptive channel estimation for U-OFDM indoor visible light communication. *Radio Science Conference*, pp. 217–222, 2016, IEEE.

28. Zhou, J. and Qiao, Y., Low-PAPR asymmetrically clipped optical OFDM for intensity-modulation/direct-detection systems. *IEEE Photonics J.*, 7, 3, 1–8, 2015.

29. Alaka, S.P., Narasimhan, T.L., Chockalingam, A., Coded Index Modulation for Non-DC-Biased OFDM in Multiple LED Visible Light Communication. *Vehicular Technology Conference*, pp. 1–5, 2016, IEEE.

30. Long, S., Khalighi, M.A., Wolf, M., Bourennane, S., Investigating channel frequency selectivity in indoor visible-light communication systems. *IET Optoelectron.*, 10, 3, 80–88, 2016.

22

Microcontroller-Based Variable Rate Syringe Pump for Microfluidic Application

G. B. Tejashree[1], S. Swarnalatha[1], S. Pavithra[1‡],
M. C. Jobin Christ[2†] and N. Ashwin Kumar[3*]

[1]Department of Biomedical Engineering, Rajalakshmi Engineering College,
Chennai, India
[2]Department of Biomedical Engineering, Rajalakshmi Engineering College,
Chennai, India
[3]Department of Biomedical Engineering, SRM Institute of Science and Technology,
Kattankulathur, India

Abstract

Microfluidics is the science of controlling fluid flow, usually at smaller volume ranges of micro- or nanoliters, used in biomedical research. The syringe pumps currently on the market are essential at this point in time but expensive. In this work, a cost-effective prototype of a syringe pump with variable flow rates is designed and developed with an achievable volume of 1 mL per minute. Mechanical design of the developed syringe pump consists of a lead screw controlled by stepper motor using an Arduino-based microcontroller. The prototype is adaptable and programmable with high accuracy and adjustable flow rate in a simple mechanical system. Thus, our project provides a flexible platform for controlling one or more syringe pumps simultaneously with different flow rates. It is a compact, inexpensive, easy to operate, programmable and easily reconfigurable device.

Keywords: Syringe pump, Arduino, microfluidics

[*]Corresponding author: ashwinkn@srmist.edu.in
[†]Corresponding author: jobinchrist.mc@rajalakshmi.edu.in

Ashutosh Kumar Dubey, Abhishek Kumar, S. Rakesh Kumar, N. Gayathri, Prasenjit Das (eds.) AI and IoT-Based Intelligent Automation in Robotics, (355–370) © 2021 Scrivener Publishing LLC

22.1   Introduction

Microfluidics is widely used in bioengineering and biomedical research as well as fields like chemistry and nanotechnology [1]. In recent times, microfluidic systems have become one of the more prolific tools for researchers in the chemical and biological sciences [3]. Microfluidics has become attractive for bioengineering and biomedical research, especially due to requirements of small volumes of reagents and samples in research devices [2]. Microfluidic chips fabricated using poly dimethyl-siloxane (PDMS) and glass help in sensing, imaging and quantification of biochemical compounds in applications, such as immunoassays, separation of proteins, DNA and cell sorting and cell manipulation [19] of living cells, allowing researchers to reveal cell functions and processes [4]. Also, they provide a platform for many analytical chemistry techniques such as electrophoresis and chromatography [7, 19]. However, microfluidic systems are not limited to biological research alone, as they have also been used in the field of nanotechnology [7] to produce high-quality nanomaterials.

Infusion pumps are used to deliver fluids in large or small amounts of drugs over a period of time in a hospital environment [19]. A similar medical device also used in the hospital environment is called as infusion pump [3]. In biomedical research, the injection of fluids with a microfluidics device at a micro or nano volume of samples is controlled using syringe pumps [17]. Both of these systems work by a similar mechanism wherein the precision of syringe pumps is greater compared to infusion pumps. Other advantages of the syringe pump is its settling time and stability, and the ability to easily adapt and operate at the picoliter scale. Commercially available syringe pumps consist of one syringe operating at single flow rate.

One of the best tools for fluid injection in microfluidic systems is a syringe pump. High-precision and pulseless syringe pumps have been developed for microfluidic applications. To reach this level of performance, the manufacturing companies upgraded syringe pumps by adding motors with hundreds of thousands of steps, automatic motor gears to adjust the speed depending on the flow rate, and fine mechanical contact between the moving mechanical pieces. These syringe pumps are generally expensive when it comes to microfluidic applications [8] (see Figure 22.1) and are capable of providing only a single flow rate at a time.

The main idea behind this project is to design a low-cost syringe pump which delivers different flow rates with different viscosities of different liquids. In this study we explain the design and implementation of a low-cost syringe pump that uses Arduino microcontroller to control a NEMA-14

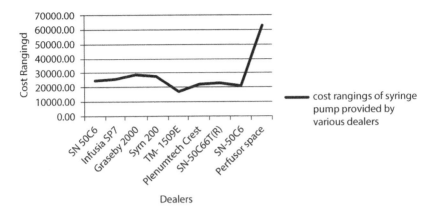

Figure 22.1 Cost range of syringe pumps provided by various dealers.

stepper motor, which in turn actuates the plunger and thus flow into micro-fluidic chips.

22.2 Related Work

A study conducted of varying designs and methods for fabrication of controlled syringe pumps used for microfluidics applications describes the design and function of an open-source syringe pump [1]. The pump is actuated by a stepper motor, which is controlled by Arduino with UI and a desktop application for remote control. This study serves as a reference for the pump's functional analysis.

In another study, a design for a microcontroller-based syringe pumps was proposed for multiple uses according to their location, which describes the need to control specific parameters based on its use. This new approach was proposed to implement more than one application of a syringe pump in a single hardware setup [14]. The control for this system was given with the help of a microcontroller, and a webpage was also developed for the same to help the user record, retrieve and access information about the operating conditions [15]. This study influenced the design for hardware as well as the design for user interface.

The design for a microcontroller-based syringe pump involved variable and low delivery rates for the administration of small volumes [3]. Syringe pumps are highly useful in delivering an exact quantity of a substance at specific periods of time as required [7]. A cost-effective working prototype for a syringe pump providing variable and low delivery rates and for administration of small volumes has been designed. Thus, this study serves as a reference for fabrication of syringe pump that is capable of delivering volumes as small as 0.1 milliliters with extraordinary accuracy with respect to both flow rate and volume [20].

A study on the open source Poseidon syringe pump system was also conducted and the results analyzed. The Poseidon syringe pump is an open source alternative to existing commercial systems [9]. The Poseidon system is used to illustrate design principles that can facilitate the adoption and development of open-source bio instruments. The Poseidon system is designed using a 3D printer, which makes the system costly [10]. This design mainly influenced the principles of functionality, robustness, simplicity, modularity, benchmarking, and documentation.

22.3 Methodology

The design and hardware components used for developing the syringe pump [4] are explained in this section; also elaborated are the principles and procedures that are followed throughout the design and development of the hardware. This pump design aims to be simple yet efficient. The complete methodology for development of the syringe pump is in Figure 22.2 [2]. The development of the syringe pump began with the brainstorming [4–6] in order to identify the most efficient and cost-effective design.

The prototype was first involved in designing of the hardware and purchase of relevant materials for the project. Secondly, the code was developed similar to the existing open source codes to run the stepper motor. Once the hardware was developed, the code was modified according to the desired result of the hardware [18]. The synchronization between design of hardware and software plays a major role in developing such systems with better accuracy.

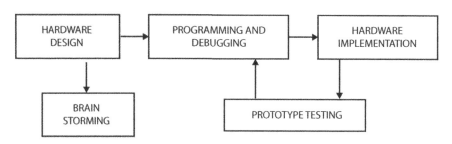

Figure 22.2 Flowchart showing the steps involved in developing the syringe pump.

22.3.1   Hardware Design

The materials used in the fabrication of the mechanical assembly of the syringe pump are shown in Figure 22.3a. Nylon blocks are used for fabrication of the syringe holder that holds the syringe and movable parts that pushes the plunger of the syringe. The exceptional dimensional stability is one of the main reasons for choosing nylon material. Figure 22.3b (i) shows the Allen grip screws of different sizes; and the different-sized bolts used in the device to avoid the movement of the system are shown in Figure 22.3b (ii).

A stainless-steel rod of 8 mm of 2 mm pitch (see Figure 22.3b (iii)) was used for connecting the motor's coupler and fixed block along with movable block in between which a screw for the 8 mm screw rod is placed. This pitch was used as it has an excellent ability to convert rotational motion into linear motion, which is shown to be accurate in the flow rate of the syringe pump. The base on which the entire hardware is assembled is an aluminum metal frame box, as shown in Figure 22.3b (iv). The dimensions of materials are given in Table 22.1.

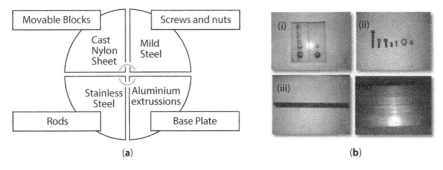

(a)   (b)

Figure 22.3 (a) Material used and components made are provided for mechanical assembly of the syringe pump. (b) (i) Movable blocks, (ii) screws, (iii) stainless-steel rod, and (iv) aluminum block.

Table 22.1 Dimensions of materials used in the fabrication of the mechanical assembly of the syringe pump.

Material	Dimensions
Aluminum	31 cm*40 mm*40 mm
Syringe Holder	80 mm*38 mm*20 mm
Movable Part	100 mm*48 mm*20 mm
Disposable plastic syringe	1ml, 3 ml

22.3.2   Hardware Interface with Software

Hardware implementation was performed using an Arduino Uno micro-controller board as a control interface to operate the bipolar stepper motor, wherein the stepper motor is coupled to a linear threaded rod with a coupler. An Arduino Uno controller board has 14 input/output digital pins, 6 analog pins, 16 MHz crystal oscillator [8], universal serial bus, power input and a reset button. For the input connections, eight digital input pins were connected to a 4×4 keypad interface [8] and three digital pins were connected to an A4988 driver.

A simple circuit to drive the stepper motor in both directions is built on the breadboard connected to the Arduino microcontroller [4]. The microcontroller was activated by a 5V logical supply and the A4988 stepper motor driver was powered from an output pin of the Arduino board. The input voltage (V_{in}) and ground pin (GND) of the microcontroller are connected to the driver driving voltage (V_{dd}) and GND pins of the driver. The step and direction pins of the driver are connected to corresponding digital pins of the microcontroller as indicated in the stepper motor program of Arduino IDE. The sleep and reset pins are usually shorted. The motor voltage V_{MOT} and GND are connected to power supply ranging from 8V to 35V in a series connection with decoupling capacitor of 100 µF [5] for safeguarding the driver from voltage spikes. The motor has four color-coded wires with bare lead termination. Out of two coils, one coil is coded with black-green and the other coil coded with red and blue color-coded wires respectively. The color-coded wires are connected to 1A, 1B and 2A, 2B pins of the A4988 driver. This constitutes the electrical circuit of our syringe pump [11].

As shown in Figure 22.4, when the external voltage is given to the circuit, the stepper motor shaft starts to rotate. This direction of rotation of

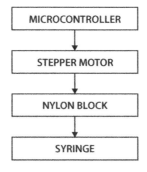

Figure 22.4 Block diagram of hardware implementation.

motor causes rotation of the linear threaded rod with help of the coupler connected between them [12]. The rotation of the screw rod rotates the screw with the movable block fixed on either side of the non-threaded rod to move further. The syringe loaded with solution moves linearly at the same direction of the screw fixed with the threaded rod. This later pushes the plunger of the syringe, thus leading to discharge of the fluid from the syringe [8]. The materials used on the device have been selected with due attention to high performance at low cost.

22.3.3   Programming and Debugging

The programming, as shown in Figure 22.5, involves the selection of stepper motor using keypad interface, once the stepper motor is selected (either stepper motor 1, 2 or both), then the serial monitor displays the message to select the type of the syringe, whether 1 ml or 3 ml, then the amount to

```
Input    : Steps per revolution , delay
Output : Rotation of stepper motor , fluid discharge.
Initialization of keypad , stepper motor , On=4 , Fiv =5 ,O =6, W=7;
 1:   if key pressed = 0
          return 0;
 2:   else
 3:       Switch (key pressed)
 4:           Case 1:
 5:               for x= 0 to 51
 6:                   for j = 4 or 5 do (syringe volume)
 7:                       for k = 6 or 7 (fluid used)
 8:                           enable stepper motor 1;
 9:                           increment x value;
                         break;
10:           Case 2:
11:               for y= 0 to 51
12:                   for j = 4 or 5 do (syringe volume)
13:                       for k = 6 or 7 (fluid used)
14:                           enable stepper motor 1;
15:                           increment y value;
                         break;
16:           Case 3:
17:               for x= 0 to 51 and y = 0 to 51
18:                   for j = 4 or 5 do (syringe volume)
19:                       for k = 6 or 7 ( fluid used)
20:                           enable stepper motor 1 & 2;
21:                           increment x & y value;
                         break;
22:       End switch;
23:   End if;
```

Figure 22.5 Algorithm for fluid discharge from syringe.

be discharged is entered, and the program goes into the respective loop of the values entered.

22.4   Result

The final prototype shown in Figure 22.6 has fixed parts, such as the syringe holder and the motor mounting block shown in Figure 22.7a-b that are fabricated separately.

Different syringe volumes were used in the experiments. This is carried out to measure the performance of the developed syringe pump system. For fixed motor speed, only the volume of the syringe is changed and the corresponding time taken is noted. The same procedure was repeated three times to detect the amount of ejected volume along with respective times and deviations for each case. The data observed were noted and the data plot shown in Figure 22.8 was created.

As can be seen from Figure 22.8, the volume discharged in 60 seconds, as noted in Table 22.2.

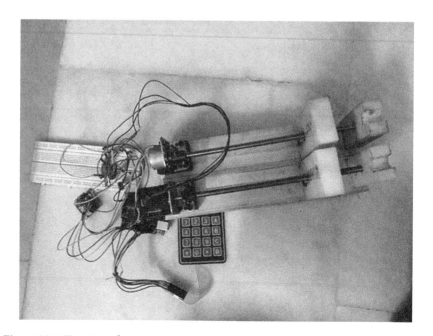

Figure 22.6 Top view of prototype.

(a)   (b)

Figure 22.7 (a) Syringe holder and (b) Stepper motor.

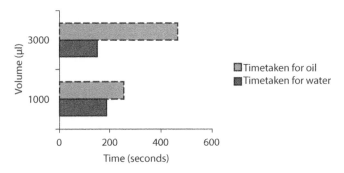

Volume Vs Maximum Time-taken

Figure 22.8 Comparison plot indicating maximum time taken by oil and water to completely discharge the volume of 1000 ml and 3000 ml from a syringe attached to the syringe holder of the prototype.

The deviation in time for complete discharge of oil and water is shown in Figure 22.9 and noted in Table 22.3.

22.5   Inference

The hardware is actuated by application of a software program and after observations are noted and corresponding data are plotted on graphs.

Table 22.2 Volume of the syringe discharged in 60 seconds.

Volume (μl)	η (cP)	Fluid used	Syringe inner diameter (mm)	Total discharge time (sec)	Volume discharged in 60 seconds (μl)
1000	1	Water	4.78	187	375
3000	55	Water	8.66	254	1100
1000	1	Oil	4.78	151	300
3000	55	Oil	8.66	465	500

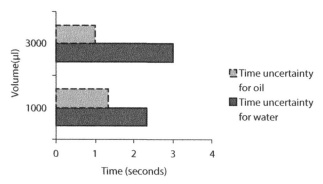

Figure 22.9 Comparison plot indicating maximum deviation in time taken by oil and water to completely discharge the volume of 1000 μl and 3000 μl from a syringe attached to the syringe holder of the prototype.

Table 22.3 Maximum deviation in time taken for discharge of oil and water.

Volume (μl)	Fluid used	Syringe inner diameter (mm)	Deviation
1000	Water	4.78	±2.33
3000	Water	8.66	±3
1000	Oil	4.78	±1.33
3000	Oil	8.66	±1

These observations are done to observe the flow rate of liquids having different viscosities, time, and syringe diameter with error percentage. In this work, we have used 2 types of syringes (purchased from BD Company) with total volume of 1 mL and 3 mL diameter; the inner diameter of the 1 mL syringe was 4.78 mm and that of the 3 mL syringe was 8.66 mm respectively. Also, the developed prototype was further characterized by loading with varied viscosities such as distilled water and oil (coconut oil).

22.5.1   Viscosity (η)

Viscosity is the internal resistance of liquid in the presence of sheer stress. It plays an important role in the time it takes to discharge the entire volume of liquid. The reciprocal of the viscosity is called the fluidity [16]. The viscosities of the liquid used were 1 cP and 55 cP for water and oil respectively. The reason for using two liquids is to find the difference in flow rate and time taken for liquid to discharge.

22.5.2   Time Taken

Time taken is the maximum time it takes for liquid to discharge completely from the syringe. The maximum and minimum time taken for oil and water was noted. As shown in Figure 22.10, the time taken to discharge 1 ml of water (η=1 cP) and oil (η=55 cP) was 187 seconds and 254 seconds respectively. The same process was repeated using 3 ml, and it took a

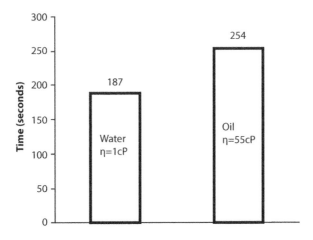

Figure 22.10 Graph indicating the difference in time taken for complete discharge of 1000 µl due to the difference in viscosity of the two fluids used in the syringe (water and oil).

maximum time of 151 seconds and 465 seconds for water (η=1 cP) and oil (η=55 cP) respectively.

22.5.3   Syringe Diameter

According to Poiseuille's equation, the volume flow rate is directly proportional to the diameter of the syringes [13]. The diameter of the syringe used also plays an important role in time taken for discharge of the liquid, as shown in Figure 22.11. The inner diameter of the syringe being used also influences flow rate of liquid. The inner diameter of 1 mL syringe was 4.78 mm and that of 3 mL syringe was 8.66 mm. The following parameters are inferred from the observation obtained by testing the hardware developed.

22.5.4   Deviation

Deviation denotes the significant value by which the measurement differs from a fixed value such as the mean. The error in flow rate of the proposed syringe pump ranges from ±0.33% (dotted circle) to ±3.0% (solid-lined circle) (Figures 22.12 and 22.13), which is comparable to most commercial-grade syringe pumps in which flow rate error ranges from ±2% to ±5% [11].

22.6   Conclusion and Future Works

The design and implementation of a high-performance, cost-efficient syringe pump device has been fabricated and parameters were evaluated.

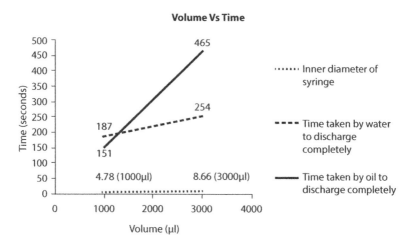

Figure 22.11 Volume vs Time plot with respect to inner diameter of syringe.

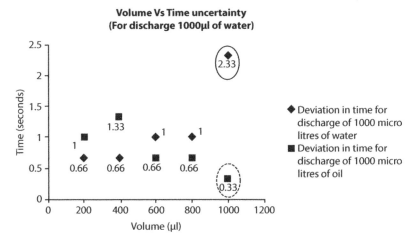

Figure 22.12 Volume (1000 μl) vs Time uncertainty (seconds).

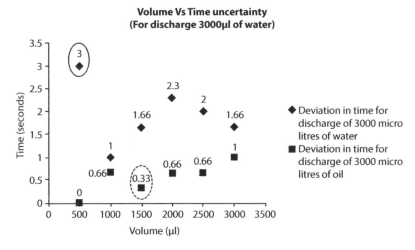

Figure 22.13 Volume (3000 μl) vs Time uncertainty (seconds).

The applicability of this technical solution is perceived to be major application in the field of microfluidics and biomedical engineering research. This adaptable and programmable syringe pump provides high accuracy and adjustable flow rate in a simple mechanical manner. The overall work is compared with different syringes, and viscosity and time of delivery were measured. The obtained flow rate errors of the proposed syringe pump range from ±0.33% to ?3%, which is comparable to most commercial-grade syringe pumps in a larger volume with the percentage ranges from ±2% to ±5%. After fabrication of the syringe pump, it was tested and it was concluded that it is capable of delivering volumes as small as 0.2 ml to as large as 3ml at flow rate of 6.25 μL/s. The accuracy and precision of the prototype was studied with respect to both flow rate and volume. From an economical point of view, the costs are relatively lower in comparison with similar, classical solutions currently being practiced. Presently, the hardware developed is capable of providing two variable flow rates simultaneously and this system of parallel functioning for more than two variable flow rates can be achieved by replacing the Arduino Uno microcontrollers with an Arduino Mega microcontroller, which has more ports, greater speed, larger memory bounds, and thus provides a better processing speed, which prevents the delay in signal. The entire prototype costs approximately ₹2000 or approximately 27 US$. Other future works involve the development of user interface and achievement of flow rates in the nanoliter range.

References

1. Assuncao, R., Barbosa, P., Ruge, R., Guimaraes, P.S., Alves, J., Silva, I., Marques, M.A., *Developing the control system of a syringe infusion pump*, research gate publications, Porto, Portugal, 2014.

2. Periyasamy, A., Kumar, R.J., Karuppiah, T., Microfluidic Syringe Pump using Arduino. *Int. J. Adv. Res. Electr. Electron. Instrum. Eng.*, 8, 4, 2019.

3. Sung, C., Kamath, R.R., Cui, Y., Ouyang, C., Carstens, E., Design of a Novel Mechanical Syringe Pump for Neonatal Care in Low-Resource Settings. *IEEE Global Humanitarian Technology Conference*, 2011.

4. Maillefer, D. and Gamper, S., High Performance Silicon Micropump for Disposable Drug Delivery System, in: *Institute of Microsystems*, IEEE, 2001.

5. Quattromani, E., Hassler, M., Rogers, N., Fitzgerald, J., Buchanan, P., Smart Pump App for Infusion Pump Training, in: *Clinical Simulation in Nursing*, vol. 17, pp. 28–37, April 2018.

6. ElKheshen, H., Deni, I., Baalbaky, A., Dib, M., Hamawy, L., Ali, M.A., Semi-Automated Self-Monitored Syringe Infusion Pump. *International Conference On Computer And Applications (Icca)*, 2018.

7. Lei, I.N., Wen, S., Wu, Z., Xu, Q., Design and Testing of a Micro-Syringe Pump Driven by Piezoelectric Actuator. *International Conference on Advanced Robotics and Mechatronics (ICARM)*, 2016.

8. Tee, K.S., Saripan, M.S., Yap, H.Y., Soon, C.F., Development Of A Mechatronic Syringe Pump To Control Fluid Flow In A Microfluidic Device Based On Polyimide Film. *IOP conference series: materials science and engineering.*, 2017.

9. Junwu, K., Zhigang, Y., Taijiang, P., Guangming, C., Boda, W., Design nd test of a high-performance piezoelectric micropump for drug delivery. *Sens. Actuators, A*, 121, 156–161, 2005.

10. Amarante, L.M., Newport, J., Mitchell, M., Wilson, J., Laubach, M., An Open Source Syringe Pump Controller for Fluid Delivery of Multiple Volumes. *eNeuro*, 6, 5, ENEURO.0240-19.2019. 2019.

11. Jarfarzadeh, M. and Farokhi, F., Design and construction of an automatic syringe injection pump. *Pac. Sci. Rev. A: Nat. Sci. Eng.*, 18, 2, 132–137, July 2016.

12. *International Conference on Advancements of Medicine and Health Care through Technology;* 12th - 15th October 2016, Cluj-Napoca, Romania, Springer Nature, 2017.

13. Goyal, M., Saurav, K., Tiwari, G., Rege, A., Saxena, A., IV (Intravenous) Tube Flow Control Device with IOT. *2020 IEEE International Students' Conference on Electrical, Electronics and Computer Science (SCEECS)*, 2020.

14. Khan, M.A., Mazhar, O., Tehami, S., Designing of Microcontroller based Syringe Pump with Variable and Low Delivery Rates for the Administration of Small Volumes. *2015 IEEE 21ˢᵗ International Symposium for Design and Technology in Electronic Packaging (SIITME)*, 2015.

15. Nisar, A., Afulzpurkar, N., Mahaisavariya, B., Tuantranont, A., MEMS-based micropumps in drug delivery and biomedical applications. *Sens. Actuators, B*, 130, 917–942, 2008.

16. Rodriguez, S.M., Galindo, A.S., Llamazares, C.M.F., Herce, J.L., Lopez, I.G., Alvarez, A.C., Saez, M.S., Developing a drug library for smart pumps in a pediatric intensive care unit. *Artif. Intell. Med.*, 4, 54155–161, 2012.

17. Islam, R., Rusho, R.Z., Sheikh Md, Rabiul Islam Design and Implementation of Low Cost Smart Syringe Pump for Telemedicine and Healthcare. *International Conference on Robotics, Electrical Signal Processing Techniques (ICREST)*, 2019.

18. Tebrean, B., Crisan, S., Muresan, C., Crisan, T.E., Low Cost Command and Control System for Automated Infusion Devices, in: *Electrical Engineering and Measurements Department*, Technical University of Cluj-Napoca, Romania, 2017.

19. Soenksen, L.R., Kassis, T., Noh, M., Griffith, L.G., Trmper, D.L., Closed-loop feedback control for microfluidic systems through automated capacitive fluid height sensing, https://pubmed.ncbi.nlm.nih.gov/29437172/, 2017.

20. Badamasai, Y.A., The Working Principle of an Arduino, 978-1-4799-3/14/2014 *IEEE*, https://ieeexplore.ieee.org/abstract/document/6997578, 2014.

23

Analysis of Emotion in Speech Signal Processing and Rejection of Noise Using HMM

S. Balasubramanian

M.Tech Embedded System Technology (ECE), SRM Institute of Technology, Ramapuram, Chennai, Tamil Nadu, India

Abstract

Noise has always been a particular issue for accurate emotion recognition in speech. Therefore, this chapter will first focus on the distraction of noise in speech. Our study proposes an acoustic function known as Mel-frequency cepstral coefficients (MFCCs) for better robustness. The MFCC extraction process combines short-term evaluation with long-term evaluation. Secondly, a spectral subband focal point of mass criterion with higher robustness to improve noise is proposed with an MFCC extraction algorithm in conjunction with a hidden Markov model (HMM) set of rules. Our experiments on speech recognition emotion has various tiers of signal-to-noise ratio (SNR) and reveal that this proposed approach works well for noise robustness and live performance, which accounts for the increased popularity of emotion speech recognition. Experiments related to audio statistics assess the efficiency of our proposed technique. The outcomes will show that response reputation associated with audio statistics will enhance and increase robustness and the better overall performance by evaluating distinctive sorts of emotion information.

Keywords: Strong noise, speech, emotion recognition, MFCC, HMM, SNR

Email: balasundar717@gmail.com

Ashutosh Kumar Dubey, Abhishek Kumar, S. Rakesh Kumar, N. Gayathri, Prasenjit Das (eds.) AI and IoT-Based Intelligent Automation in Robotics, (371–384) © 2021 Scrivener Publishing LLC

23.1   Introduction

The majority of tests on voice emotion popularity are controlled to track emotional collection. Even so, to minimize noise effect, acquiring voice facts in real-life frameworks typically is not the same as in lab conditions. The voice features amassed as sensible set continually go along with heritage noise. The surround noise crashes actual audio traits and typical criterion of speech signals, making it effortless to create one type of voice indicator and having a horrific impact on extracted audio functions, thereby influencing the authenticity of the result of voice emotion reputation.

Thus, up to now, few tests conducted in emotion speech reputation have considered speech indicators under ambient noise conditions. Focusing the trouble of noise, most of the contemporary research effort is directed towards pre-treating signal noise. For example, Schuller *et al.* [1] studied the influence of additive noise of different signal-to-noise levels on the performance of speech emotion recognition. In Chinese academy of acoustics Wuhan University of Technology, Professor Yan and his team [2] proposed a new method for emotion popularity under ambient noise conditions. Moreover, it's a far better path for robust speech emotion extraction from environmental traits. Iliev and Scordilis [3] studied about valid and noise robustness of the acoustic flow signal in voice emotion recognition. It was shown that the glimpse airflow feature shows better noise robustness through experiments on voice emotion recognition with White Gaussian Noise. In the past decade, Weninger *et al.* [4] applied non-negative matrix factorization (NMF) in automatic speech recognition for enhanced robustness by introducing and evaluating different kinds of NMF-based features for emotion recognition. Thus, to obstruct noise in speech emotion, methods have been sought by some scientists which bypass this issue and conquer the robustness by multimodal popularity. Poria *et al.* [5] pondered using features from multimodal content and suggested a process for identification of emotions in a multimodal stream.

Yan *et al.* [6] proposed a sparse kernel reduced-rank regression (SKRRR) fusion method for bio-modal emotion identification based on diverse audio information. Zhang *et al.* [7] utilized an approach based on a multimodal deep convolution neural network (DCNN) for bio-modal emotion identification based speech emotion depending on numerous audio facts. Somandepalli *et al.* [8] established a brand new multimodal approach to recognize emotions in real time. For recognition of human emotions for improved human-robot interaction, Boccanfuso *et al.* [9] applied infrared (IR) thermography to monitor facial expressions, and applied artificial intelligence (AI) strategies for characterizing thermal records based on emotional condition. Mitra *et al.* [10] widely used the MFCC technique to investigate the impact of reverberation and noise on depression prediction because the features of this technique are designed for noise robustness and damped oscillator cepstral coefficients [12].

Gong and Poellabauer [11] assessed an approach which can directly access original audio records rather than utilizing a manual method of engineering.

Even though there has been recent progress in techniques notable for improving the overall performance of speech emotion recognition systems under natural noise conditions, the reputation of speech emotion recognition under original conditions has not been realized for a wide range of applications. The main purpose of speech recognition is to look inside the noise situation to split acoustic functions that can adequately recognize emotions by speech statistics and display awesome noise robustness [19].

A wavelet-based method is used for analyzing time-localized events in noisy time series. In view of the fact that numerous wavelet bases have numerous capacities for time-recurrence confinement, we can pick out reasonable wavelet bases with fantastic editability as per numerous signs [15]. We do biomodal emotion recognition based on audiovisual informations by making a decision extent fusion, which improves quality and takes advantages of different kinds of information [17].

One audio feature used for better robustness is MFCC. Our MFCC extraction process combines short-term evaluation with long-term evaluation. Secondly, a spectral subband focal point of mass criterion with higher robustness to improve noise is proposed with an MFCC extraction algorithm in conjunction with a hidden Markov model (HMM) set of rules [18]. Our experiments on speech recognition emotion has various tiers of signal-to-noise ratio (SNR) and reveal that this proposed approach works well for noise robustness and live performance, which accounts for the increased popularity of emotion speech recognition. Experiments associated with audio information are shown to evaluate the efficiency in techniques such as the one proposed by us [13].

23.2   Existing Method

In the current method, exposure to noise over a long period of time is predicted using the subdivided bands of the maximum benefit wave packet and contemporary subband range is mixed with wavelet-packet cepstral coefficient for collecting unique audio characteristics with appropriate noise efficiency. In this framework, in order to extract strong voice emotion characteristics, a set of policies have been created exclusively on frame assessment using the long-term weighted wavelet packet supplied [13]. To produce emotional speech data using at various SNR levels, a long-term frame analysis weighted wavelet packet cepstral coefficient (LW-WPCC) feature is used for analysis and validation. Its overall performance via experiments is based totally on audio recordings of various SNR tiers. The disadvantages of this feature are:

- LW-WPCC function illustrations advanced noise reduction, but accuracy of reputation is low compared with proposed acoustic models.
- Emotion reputation based on audio visible information shows higher overall performance, but not higher than speech emotion recognition.
- Overall performance is not as high as speech emotion recognition [14].

23.3   Proposed Method

Speech is a vocal technique used in conversation by humans to express thoughts and feelings by articulate sounds. Knowing the mood of an individual immediately during communication is simply identification; however, the detection of mood in an oblique verbal exchange is intelligence. For this, intelligent machines require a few limitations which include amplitude, pulse, frequency, harmonics, pitch, shape and Mel-frequency cepstrum. The raw aural voice is first transformed to signal form, the characteristic extraction is made from the signal by using Mel-frequency cepstral coefficients for higher robustness [20]. Then the extracted feature is implemented through which characteristic choices are trained by means of hidden Markov model (HMM) and k-nearest neighbor (KNN) classifiers and fertile output on the first-rate emotion is received. The advantages of this proposed method are:

- It removes transient noise effectively from the features.
- The accuracy of recognition and its performances was high compared with existing acoustic models.
- The reason for developing this method is to assist humans in saving time.

23.3.1   Proposed Module Description

Components of the proposed module are outlined in Figure 23.1 and briefly described below.

a) Pre-processing
The pre-processing approach may also be used to improve the information in an image, setting it up for the following level of statistical thinking and cognitive devices. So, in order to achieve better introductory costs, it is much more important to have a successful pre-processing stage; in this way, utilizing the pre-processing technique effectively makes the framework of the proposed approach basically stronger through appropriate image enhancement, noise removal, image thresholding, and skew correction/detection technique [16].

b) Feature Extraction
In artificial intelligence (AI), structure prominence besides in picture pre-processing and the extraction technique starts from a basic arrangement of evaluated records and builds derived values meant to be non-repetitive and enlightening, encouraging the subsequent mastering and

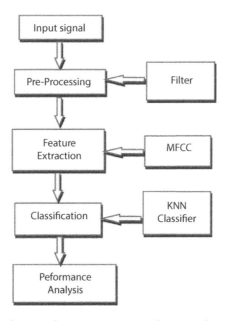

Figure 23.1 Outline of proposed emotion extraction from speech.

principle steps, and from time to time prompting higher human understanding. Feature extraction is associated with dimensionality reduction.

At the point when the information for a calculation is probably too significant to be treated and is suspected of being redundant (for instance, a comparable estimation in the two feet or meters, or the monotony of images exhibited as pixels), that factor may be thoroughly converted directly into a reduced representation of features, also known as a feature vector. Determining which parts of a function are important is called function selection. The selected features are required to contain input information so that the ideal project can be implemented by utilizing this preferred reduced representation to complete the initial record.

Feature extraction consists of lessening the quantity of sources required to depict good-sized fact sets while examining complex facts; one of the severe problems stems from the quantity of variables covered. Analysis with infinite variables usually requires a large amount of memory and power for calculation moreover, it may make a counting sort over fit to preparing appraisals and sum up inadequately to new models. Characteristic extraction requires a standard time period for techniques to build blends of the factors to get around such problems, even depicting records with sufficient exactness. Many AI professionals has been given exact feature extraction methods in every development versions.

23.3.2   MFCC

Mel-frequency cepstral coefficients (MFCCs) are coefficients that collectively make-up an MFC. They are derived from a type of cepstral representation of the audio clip—a nonlinear "spectrum-of-a-spectrum." The difference between the MFC and the cepstrum is that in MFC, the frequency bands are equally spaced on the Mel scale, which approximates the human auditory system's response more closely than the linearly spaced frequency bands directly used in ordinary cepstrum. This frequency warping allows for better sound representation such as in audio compression.

Extraction of the best parametric representation of acoustic signals is important for producing better recognition performance. The efficiency of this stage is critical for the next phase because it impacts the way it behaves. MFCC is based on human hearing perceptions which cannot perceive frequencies over 1 kHz. Likewise, MFCC is based on the known variation of the human ear's critical bandwidth frequency [8–10]. MFCC has a filter which is spaced linearly at low frequencies below 1000 Hz and logarithmic spacing above 1000 Hz. A dynamic field can be obtained on a Mel frequency scale to get essential phonetic features in speech.

It has been determined that MFCC consists of seven computational processes. Every process has its own capacity and clinical methodologies, which are shown in Figure 23.2 and are briefly discussed below.

a) Pre-Emphasis

Here, a study is discussed which is based on passing a signal through a filter that emphasizes higher frequencies. This method will increase signal strength at higher frequencies.

$$Y[n] = X[n]\ 0.90\ X\ [n-1] \tag{23.1}$$

Consider that a = 0.90, which makes up 90% of any one sample which is presumed to come from a previous sample.

b) Framing

Speech samples obtained from an analog-to-digital converter (ADC) are segmented into a small frame with a length within the range of 20 to 40 msec. the voice signal is divided into frames of 'N' samples. Adjacent frames are separated by m (m < n). Common values used are m = 100 and n = 256.

c) Hamming Windowing

A hamming window is used as a window shape which considers the following block in the feature extraction processing chain and integrates all the frequency lines nearby.

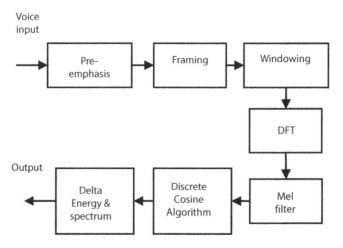

Figure 23.2 MFCC process.

The features of the hamming window are given as:
If the window is defined as W(n), $0 \le n \le$ N-1

Where,
   N = Number of samples in every frame
   Y(n) = Output signal
   X(n) = Input signal
   W(n) = Hamming window
   In which case the result of the windowing signal is given below:

$$Y(n) = X(n) * W(n) \tag{23.2}$$

$$w(n) = 0.54 - 0.46 \ cos\left[\frac{2\pi n}{N-1}\right] 0 \le n \le N-1 \tag{23.3}$$

d) Fast Fourier Transform
Fourier transform is used to convert each frame of N samples from time domain to frequency domain. Fourier transform converts the glottal pulse U[n] and the vocal tract impulse response H[n] in the time domain. This statement supports the following equation:

$$Y(w) = FFT[h(t) * X(t)] = H(w) * X(w) \tag{23.4}$$

The Fourier transform of X (t), H (t) and Y (t) are X (w), H (w) and Y (w) respectively.

e) Mel Filter Bank Processing
The FFT spectrum has a frequency range which is very wide and voice signals do not follow the linear scale. The bank of filters shown in Figure 23.3 perform according to Mel scale.
   In the figure a set of triangular filters are shown which can be applied to compute a weighted sum of filter spectral components so that the output of the engineering process approximates a Mel scale. The magnitude frequency response of every filter is triangular in shape and equal to unity at the center frequency and decrease linearly to zero at the center frequency of two adjacent filters [19]. Subsequently, each of the filter outputs is the sum of their filtered spectral components. Next, the following equation is applied to calculate Mel for the given frequency f in Hz:

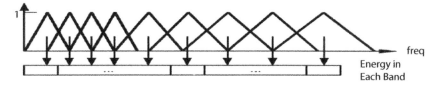

Figure 23.3 Mel scale bank of filters.

$$F(Mel) = [2595 * \log10[1 + f]700] \tag{23.5}$$

f) Discrete Cosine Transform
Discrete cosine transform (DCT) is an alternative way to convert the log Mel spectrum into various time domains. The results of this conversion is known as Mel frequency cepstrum coefficient. The set of coefficients is referred to as acoustic vectors. In this way, every input utterance is transformed into a succession of acoustic vectors.

g) Change in Energy and Spectrum
The voice signal and the frames change; for example, the slope of the formant at its transitions. That is why there may be a need to add features related to the change in cepstral features over time. Thirteen delta or velocity features (12 cepstral features plus energy), and 39 double delta or acceleration features are added. The energy in a frame for a signal X in a window from time sample t1 to time sample t2 is represented in the following equation:

$$Energy = \Sigma X^2[t] \tag{23.6}$$

All of the 13 delta features represent the change between frames in the equation, which is known as the cepstral or energy feature, while each of the 39 double delta features represent the change between frames in the corresponding delta features.

$$d(t) = \frac{c(t+1) - c(t-1)}{2} \tag{23.7}$$

23.3.3   Hidden Markov Models

Hidden Markov models (HMM) are generative models, which is a verification method using undetectable (i.e., hidden) systems.

Hidden Markov models are a specific kind of Bayesian network. The HMM algorithm was created by Leonard E. Baum and Lloyd R. Welch. HMM is firmly identified before taking a shot at the ideal nonlinear filtering issue by Ruslan L. Stratonovich, who was the first to portray the forward-in reverse system [20].

In simpler Markov models (same as Markov chain), the state is clearly recognizable to the user, and subsequently the state change probabilities are the fundamental parameters, while in the hidden Markov model, the state isn't straightforwardly noticeable, anyway the result (as data or "token" in the going with), dependent on the state, is self-evident. Each state has a probability assignment over the possible yield tokens. Thusly, the game plan of tokens delivered by a HMM gives some information about the gathering of states, this is in any case called design hypothesis, a subject of sentence structure acceptance.

The modified HMM refer to the state arrangement via which the model passes, not to the parameters of the model, the version continues to be refer to as a hidden markov version regardless of whether or not these parameters are known precisely [12].

HMM are specially known for their utilization in reinforcement learning and temporary pattern recognition, like hand writing, speech, gesture recognition, part of speech tagging, genetic information and partial discharges.

A hidden Markov version can be regarded as speculation of a blend model where hidden values (or factors idle), which controls the blend components to be selected for each idea, are linked through the Markov method is not independent of one another. Until the end, hidden Markov mode has been added up to pairwise Markov models and triplet Markov models that allows the technique of an increasing number of complex information structures and the displaying of non-stationary information.

a) Viterbi Algorithm

The Viterbi algorithm is a dynamic programming algorithm for finding the most likely sequence of hidden states, called the Viterbi path, that results in a sequence of observed events, especially in the context of Markov information sources and hidden Markov models (HMM).

The algorithm has found application in conventional software in decoding the convolutional codes utilized in both CDMA and GSM satellite, digital cellular, deep-space communications, dial-up modems, and 802.11 wireless LANs. Moreover, it's currently utilized in speech recognition, keyword spotting, speech synthesis, computational linguistics, and bioinformatics. For example, in speech to text (speech recognition), the acoustic signal is treated as an observed sequence of events, and a string of text is considered the "hidden cause" of the acoustic signal. The Viterbi algorithm finds the most probable string of text given the acoustic signal [13].

b) Baum-Welch Algorithm
The Baum–Welch algorithm is a marvellous example of the EM algorithm used to unknown parameters of a hidden Markov model (HMM). It uses a back and forth algorithm to compute the statistics for the expectation step.

A hidden Markov model depicts the joint likelihood of an assortment of "hidden" and observed discrete random variables. It depends on the supposition that the i-th hidden variable given the $(i-1)$-th hidden variable is independent of previous hidden variables, and the current observation variables depend only upon the current hidden state.

The Baum–Welch algorithm utilizes the well-known EM algorithm to locate the maximum likelihood estimate of the parameters of a hidden Markov model given a set of observed feature vectors [19].

c) Forward Algorithm
The forward algorithm, in context of a hidden Markov model (HMM), is utilized to calculate a "belief state"—the chance of a state at a certain time, given the history of evidence. The process is otherwise known as filtering. The forward algorithm is closely related to, but different from, the Viterbi calculation.

The forward and backward algorithms must be placed within the context of probability as they appear to simply be names given to a set of standard mathematical procedures within a few fields. For example, neither the forward nor Viterbi algorithm app0ears in the *Cambridge Encyclopedia of Mathematics*. The main observation to take away from these algorithms is how to organize Bayesian updates and and inference to be efficient in the context of directed graphs of variables.

For an HMM, such as the one in Figure 23.4, this possibility is shown as $P(x_t y_{1:t})$. Here, $x(t)$ is the hidden state which is shortened as x_t and $y_{(1:t)}$ are the comments 1 to t.

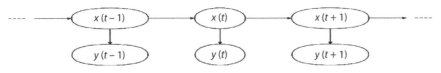

Figure 23.4 Algorithm for an HMM.

d) Time-Inhomogeneous Hidden Bernoulli Model

The time-inhomogeneous hidden Bernoulli model (TI-HBM) is an alternative to the hidden Markov model (HMM) for automatic speech recognition. Instead of HMM, the state transition process in TI-HBM is not a Markov-dependent process, but a generalized Bernoulli (independent) process. This difference leads to the elimination of dynamic programming at state-level in the TI-HBM decoding process. In this way, the computational complexity of IT-HBM to evaluate probability and state estimation is $O(NL)$, instead of $O(N^2L)$, in the case of HMM, where N and L are number of states and observation sequence length respectively. TI-HBM can model acoustic-unit duration, such as phone/word duration, by using a built-in parameter called survival probability. The TI-HBM is less difficult and quicker than HMM in a phoneme recognition task, but its performance is comparable to HMM [18].

e) Filtering

The errand in filtering is to compute, given the model's parameters and an association of perceptions, the conveyance over hidden situations of the ultimate dormant variable closer to the end of the succession; for example, *figure* $P(x(t) \mid y(1),...,y(t))$. This errand is typically utilized when the grouping of latent factors is thought of as the basic expresses that a procedure travels through at a succession of purposes of time, with comparing perceptions at each point in time. At that point, it is normal to get some information about the condition of the procedure toward the end.

f) Smoothing

That is like filtering but receives a few records about the dispersion of an inactive variable, some locations in an arrangement, for example, to compute $P(x(k) \mid y(1),...,y(t))$ for some $\kappa < t$. From the perspective depicted over, this can be thought of as the probability distribution over hidden states for a point in time k previously, comparative with time t.

23.4   Conclusion

This chapter focused on emotional speech recognition under background noise conditions. The issue of noise in speech was highlighted and an acoustic function was proposed; with Mel-frequency cepstral coefficients (MFCC) being used to improve robustness. The MFCC feature extraction is combined with short-term and long-term frame evaluations. In addition, a parameter of subband spectral-mass center has the appropriate strength for the additive noise and provides a MFCC with a set of rules along with a hidden Markov model (HMM) algorithm. Moreover, speech tests on emotion recognition of different ranges of SNR showed more robustness to noise. Tests dependent on sound informational indexes were used to survey the viability of the proposed approach.

References

1. Schuller, B., Seppi, D., Batliner, A., Maier, A., Steidl, S., Towards more reality in the recognition of emotional speech. *Proc. IEEE Int. Conf., Acoust., Speech Signal Process.*, pp. 941–944, Apr. 2007.

2. Cai, S., Jin, X., Gao, S., Pan, J., Yan, Y., Subband energy regular perception linear prediction coefficients for noise robust speech recognition. *J. Acoust.*, 37, 6, 667672, 2012.

3. Iliev, A.I. and Scordilis, M.S., Spoken emotion recognition using glottal symmetry. *EURASIP J. Adv. Signal Process.*, Hindawi Publishing Corporation EURASIP, 2011, Article ID 624575, 11, 2, Jan. 2011.

4. Weninger, F., Schuller, B., Batliner, A., Steidl, S., Seppi, D., Recognition of nonproton typical emotions in reverberated and noisy speech by nonnegative matrix factorization. *EURASIP J. Adv. Signal Process.*, 2011, Hindawi Publishing Corporation EURASIP J. Adv. Signal Processing Volume 2011, Article ID 838790, pp. 3,4,5,6 https://doi.org/10.1155/2011/838790 838790, Dec. 2011.

5. Poria, S., Cambria, E., Howard, N., Huang, G.-B., Hussain, A., Fusing audio, visual and textual clues for sentiment analysis from multi modal content. *Neurocomputing*, 174, 5059, Jan. 2016.

6. Yan, J., Zheng, W., Xu, Q., Lu, G., Li, H., Wang, B., Sparse kernel reduced-rank regression for bimodal emotion recognition from facial expression and speech. *IEEE Trans. Multimedia*, 18, 7, 13191329, Jul. 2016.

7. Zhang, S., Zhang, S., Huang, T., Gao, W., Multimodal deep convolutional neural network for audio-visual emotion recognition. *Proc. ACM Int. Conf. Multimedia Retr.*, 281–284, 2016.

8. Somandepalli, K., Gupta, R., Nasir, M., Booth, B.M., Lee, S., Narayanan, S.S., Online affect tracking with multimodal kalman filters, in Proceedings of the 6th International Workshop on Audio/Visual Emotion Challenge, ser. AVEC '16. New York, NY, USA: ACM, pp. 59–66, 2016

9. Boccanfuso, L., Wang, Q., Leite, I., Li, B., Torres, C., Chen, L., Salomons, N., Foster, C., Barney, E., Ahn, Y.A., Scassellati, B., Shic, F., A thermal motion classier for improved human-robot interaction. *Proc. 25ᵗʰ IEEE Int. Symp. Robot Hum. Interact. Commun. (RO-MAN)*, New York, NY, USA, p. 718723, Aug. 2016.

10. Mitra, V., Tsiartas, A., Shriberg, E., Noise and reverberation effects on depression detection from speech. *Proc. IEEE Int. Conf. Acoust., Speech Signal Process. (ICASSP)*, Shanghai, China, p. 57955799, Mar. 2016.

11. Gong, Y. and Poellabauer, C., Continuous assessment of children's emotional states using acoustic analysis. *Proc. IEEE Int. Conf. Health care Inform. (ICHI)*, Park City, UT, USA, p. 171178, Aug. 2017.

12. Huang, Y., Ao, W., Zhang, G., Novel sub-band spectral centroid weighted wavelet packet features with importance-weighted support vector machines for robust speech emotion recognition. *Wireless Pers. Commun.*, 95, 3, 2223–2238, 2017, https://doi.org/10.1007/s11277-017-4052-3.

13. Huang, Y., Ao, W., Zhang, G., Li, Y., Extraction of adaptive wavelet packet lter bank-based acoustic feature for speech emotion recognition. *IET Signal Process.*, 9, 4, 341–348, Jun. 2015.

14. Coifman, R.R., Meyer, Y., Wickerhauser, M.V., Wavelet analysis and signal processing, in *Wavelets and their applications*, M.B. Ruskai *et al.* (Eds.), Jones and Bartlett, USA, pp. 153–178, 1992

15. Mallat, S., *A Wavelet Tour of Signal Processing*, 3rd ed., p. 263395, Academic, Press, Burlington, VT, USA, 2009.

16. Yue, L., Research on speech emotion recognition based on optimal wavelet packet decomposition, M.S. thesis, Southeast Univ., Nanjing, China, *Optimal wavelet packet decomposition for rectal pressure signal feature extraction 2012 IEEE Fifth International Conference on Advanced Computational Intelligence (ICACI)*, 18-20 Oct. 2012 INSPEC Accession Number: 13327116, 19, 2013, 2014.

17. Herman sky, H. and Morgan, N., RASTA processing of speech. *IEEE Trans. Speech Audio Process.*, 2, 4, 578–589, Oct. 1994.

18. Kim, C. and Stern, R.M., Power function-based power distribution normalization algorithm for robust speech recognition. *Proc. IEEE Work-shop Autom. Speech Recognit. Understand*, p. 188193, Nov./Dec. 2009.

19. Nagasubramanian, G., Sankayya, M., Al-Turjman, F., Tsaramirsis, G., Parkinson Data Analysis and Prediction System Using Multi-Variant Stacked Auto Encoder. *IEEE Access*, 8, 127004–127013, 2020, https://doi.org/10.1109/ACCESS.2020.3007140.

20. Huang, Y., Xiao, J., Tian, K., Research on Robustness of Emotion Recognition under Environmental Noise Conditions speech. *Proc. IEEE Int. J.*, 7, 142009–142021, 2019.

Securing Cloud Data by Using Blend Cryptography with AWS Services

Vanchhana Srivastava*, Rohit Kumar Pathak and Arun Kumar

Department of Computer Science and Engineering, Centre for Advanced Studies, Dr. A.P.J. Abdul Kalam Technical University, Lucknow, Uttar Pradesh, India

Abstract

Large amounts of data are stored by users on cloud storage for further use. There are various security measures which need to be addressed when the data is stored on the cloud, like confidentiality, integrity and availability of data (also known as the CIA triad). Generally, the data which is stored on cloud by the cloud service provider is in the original form, and users use their own encryption algorithm for securing their data. In this work, we use Amazon Web Services (AWS) for storing our data by encrypting it with the existing algorithm. Here, the data is always stored in AWS storage, i.e., dynamo DB (database), in the encrypted form with the help of our algorithm, and when others need that data, then a request is sent to the owner regarding access to data and after verification the access is approved.

Keywords: Quantum cryptography, AWS, DynamoDB, elliptic curve digital signature algorithm (ECDSA)

24.1 Introduction

When something is stored on a cloud that means it is stored on internet servers instead of your computers. It is like having an extra hard drive, one which you can access anytime and anywhere, which is connected to the internet. In the cloud, there are several servers which manage their databases and applications [1]. By using cloud-based applications called web apps, we can access our data from anywhere via our internet browser.

Corresponding author: iamvanchhana@gmail.com

Ashutosh Kumar Dubey, Abhishek Kumar, S. Rakesh Kumar, N. Gayathri, Prasenjit Das (eds.) AI and IoT-Based Intelligent Automation in Robotics, (385–398) © 2021 Scrivener Publishing LLC

By using web apps, like google docs, we can create several projects and access them from any computer, and to do that we only need a device that is connected to the internet. Storing, processing or accessing the data or applications from the cloud servers is known as cloud computing [2]. Just like in the diagram in Figure 24.1 showing an overview of the cloud, many servers are present and each of them manage their applications and databases [3].

For the cloud computing, security becomes a major concern as most of the attacks and threats occur on cloud data [24]. There are several types of threats that need to be addressed since, as we know, in today's world there is extensive use of the internet due to the proliferation of social networks, mobile devices, social interaction, web use, business, financial transactions, etc. [4], from where data is being generated in very large amounts and getting transferred.

With the generation of so much sensitive data, the attacks on the network are also increasing [21]. Nowadays, there is a great need for security of data on cloud so as to protect it from being stolen, altered, being sent by unauthorized users, being lost, getting into the wrong hands, being misused or leaked [5]. The several threats which cloud computing faces regarding its storage, applications or virtual desktops are shown in Figure 24.2.

The incentive for doing this work is that the data which gets stored in the cloud generally suffers from data loss/leakage or several other problems like misuse of data, data theft, etc. [6]. The objective is to find a better solution for these discussed problems by encrypting the data with an existing algorithm and then storing it on an AWS database, thereby preventing data from being accessed or altered by an unauthorized person [7].

The introductory part of this chapter contains a brief discussion of the following topics: AWS [8], quantum cryptography and elliptic curve digital

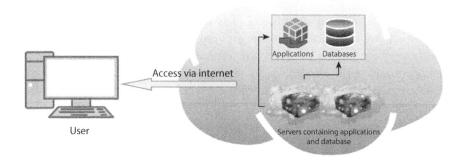

Figure 24.1 Overview of the cloud.

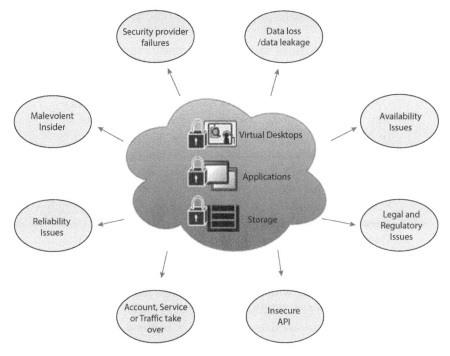

Figure 24.2 Threats in cloud computing.

signature algorithm (ECDSA). The other parts of this chapter cover the following topics: Section 24.2 discusses the background of the existing algorithms BB84 and ECDSA [9]. Section 24.3 is about the methodology, Section 24.4 shows the results, and lastly Section 24.5 consists of the conclusion and future work.

24.1.1   AWS

Amazon Web Services (AWS), as the name suggests, is an Amazon product and one of the first cloud service providers, which is the most popular and best service provider on the market [20]. It is a secure cloud service platform that offers computing power, storage, content delivery and functionality to scale up businesses [10]. Some of its features are:

- On-demand provisioning
- Scalability in minutes
- Pay-as-you-consume
- Efficiency of experts
- Measurability

There are several domains in AWS service, some of them are:

- Compute: Provides computation power and also Elastic Compute Cloud.
- Security and Compliance: Identity and access management (IAM) systems provide access to authorized persons [11].
- Key Protection: Protects keys, i.e., public and private keys, from others.
- Storage: Amazon S3 or Amazon Simple Storage Service has authentication mechanisms to protect the buckets and objects type files which are stored in a bucket folder; Amazon S3 Glacier consists of archival type storage where data which does not need to be retrieved frequently is stored [12].
- Database Services: Relational database services (RDS) such as Arora work like SQL database and works 5 time faster; based on the principle of Dynamo, Amazon DynamoDB is a NoSQL database which provides its users scalability and fast performance [13]. With this service users can create tables and store as much data as they want in them and can also retrieve it. It provides users with data backup so that their data remains secure, i.e., on-demand backup and restore. It has many benefits such as no servers to manage, performance at scale, enterprise ready, etc.

24.1.2   Quantum Cryptography

The BB84 protocol is the quantum key distribution (QKD) used in quantum computing or cryptography. The thing that makes quantum cryptography different from classical cryptography is that it doesn't work on mathematics, it works on quantum mechanics [14]. Quantum cryptography is continuously moving forward, which makes it useful for providing protection to the keys from attackers. It makes use of the rules and regulations of quantum mechanics to make it a new vernacular of secret writing. One quantum cryptographic primitive could be the assigning of keys using quantum. By making the use of the quantum properties, such as illumination, optical fibers, beams, and transmission of radio or optical signals in free space, we can achieve the quantum keys. It works on 'q' bits rather than traditional bits [15]. Figure 24.3 gives an overview of quantum cryptography where there are two channels, i.e., public and quantum channel; in the quantum channel the polarizers are being transferred in the form of photons for carrying out communication [16].

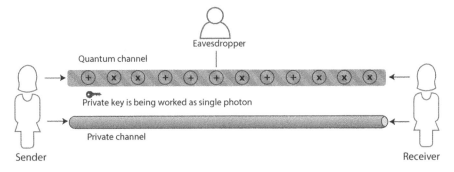

Figure 24.3 Overview of quantum cryptography.

24.1.3   ECDSA

The elliptic curve digital signature algorithm (ECDSA) is the combination of elliptic curve and the digital signature algorithm, where elliptic curve provides the same level of security instead of having a small key size [17]. There are some advantages of elliptic curve, which are that it is faster, provides low power consumption, low memory usage and low CPU utilization, and the digital signature [25] in it is used for maintaining the authentication of the user identity and integrity of the message. It provides a high level of security during the exchange of message or information. There is a need to provide safeguards against unknown access or alteration, especially to secure media for e-governance and e-commerce.

24.2   Background

In the existing method, first the quantum keys are generated with the help of BB84 (Bennett and Brassard 84) through the quantum channel. In this method, the sender passes the randomly guessed polarized state through the quantum channel [18].

Then, at the receiver side the same process happens and after that the receiver sends its guessed states to sender and then after matching receiver's state, sender sends back the mismatched state to the receiver, and hence the matched state becomes the key for both parties. Figure 24.4 shows the key generation using BB84 in quantum cryptography [19]. After generating the keys from the above method, the other part is generating the elliptic curve keys.

In this method, first the private keys are generated and then with the help of "generator," public keys are generated [18]. With the help of public

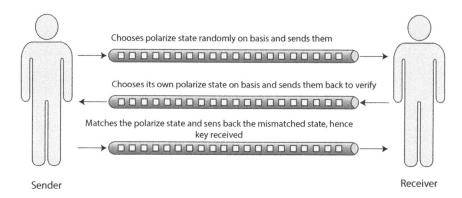

Figure 24.4 Quantum key generation using BB84.

keys, private keys and quantum keys, secret keys are generated on both sides [22] as shown in Figure 24.5.

After getting the keys, the message needs to be encrypted with the keys. In this method, first the message is encoded with the points on the elliptic curve. Then, with the help of randomly selected positive integer the message is encrypted with the private key, and for decryption, the receiver's

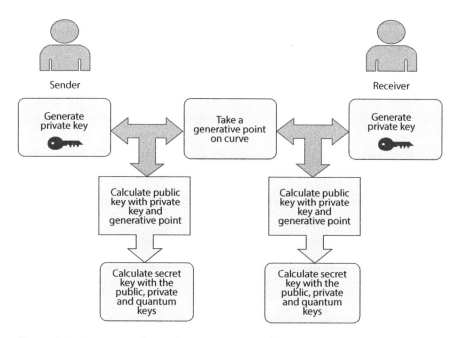

Figure 24.5 Generation of secret keys in existing method.

secret key is used. Now, after encrypting the message, authentication is provided by taking any two prime numbers on the basis of some parameters and then calculating the third with the help of the previous two prime numbers [18]. Hence, these three prime numbers will become the domain parameters, then the private and public keys are calculated with the help of domain parameters.

As illustrated in Figure 24.6, the signature is generated by choosing a random number on the basis of some parameters and then there is generation of the hash value of the message and then the hash value of message and the signature, both of which are sent to the receiver. Then the verification process is done on the receiver side; for that an original copy of the domain parameters are obtained and then the hash value of the message is again generated so as to match with the sender's message hash value. Then, the signature is verified and if the value of both, i.e., signature and hash value of message, is the same it gets accepted, otherwise the presence of a third user is indicated [23].

DynamoDB provides security to all the data stored in the indexes, streams and backups. DynamoDB uses AWS Key Management Service (AWS KMS) to provide an additional layer of security to protect data from all types of unauthorized access through encryption. DynamoDB provides additional storage for the data to protect it from any type of loss and to provide backups. It also plays a major role in providing secure services from AWS to end-user.

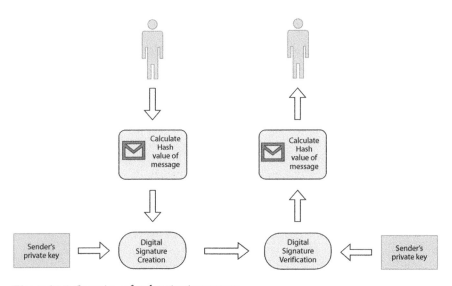

Figure 24.6 Overview of authentication process.

24.3   Proposed Technique

In the section, an overview of how the proposed method works is presented. In this work, we use AWS as cloud storage. Here, the sender first encrypts the message using BB84 with ECDSA and then stores it on an AWS server for serving receivers.

Figure 24.7 shows how communication is first established between the sender and the AWS DynamoDB as well as how storing is done from raw message to the encrypted message overcloud server, i.e., DynamoDB. Figure 24.8 shows how secret keys are created at the initial level of communication between a sender and first receiver and that the key is stored for further distribution to other receivers. Initially, the receiver will request a secret key then the sender will verify the authenticity of the receiver; after authentication the sender will provide the key to the receiver. In this process, all secret key generation and key sharing was done using ECDSA with BB84.

After receiving the secret key, the receiver will request that the data be sent to the AWS server that he/she wants to access. After getting the

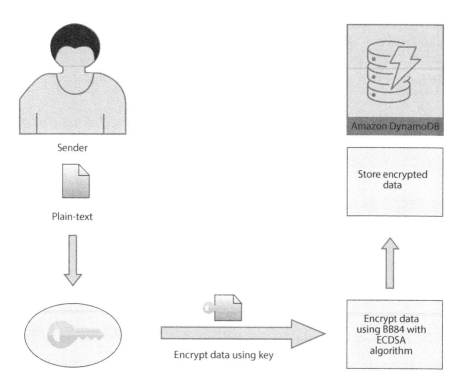

Figure 24.7 Storing the message after encryption in DynamoDB.

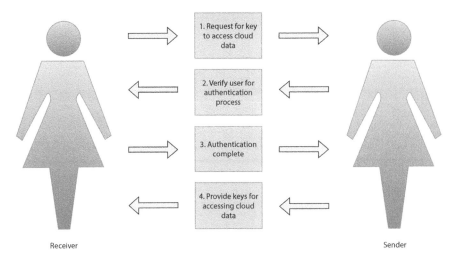

Figure 24.8 Sending the secret key after authentication.

data, the receiver will decrypt the message using the same secret key that is received from the sender. In Figure 24.9, we can see how the receiver will put in a request to the AWS server and how he/she received the data after decryption.

24.3.1   How the System Works

1. The sender will encrypt the message using ECDSA with BB84.
2. After encryption, the sender will store that message on the AWS dynamo DB.
3. When the receiver wants to access that data stored on the AWS server then he/she will request the secret key from sender using BB84.
4. The sender will generate that secret key after the authentication of the receiver and store it for further distribution.
5. After receiving the secret key from the receiver, the sender will request for the data from the AWS DynamoDB.
6. When the receiver receives the data from the server then he decrypts the data using that secret key.
7. In the future, when any new user requests data, then after authentication, the sender will share the same secret key that he/she has stored after generating it the first time.

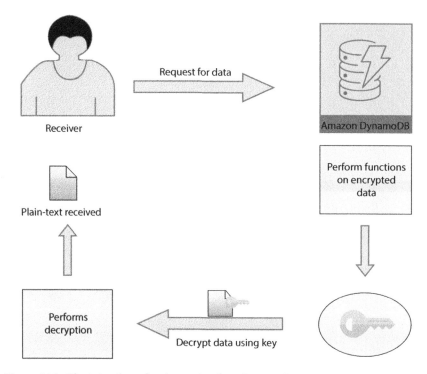

Figure 24.9 Obtaining data after decryption from DynamoDB.

24.4   Results

In this section, we will discuss the output that we obtained after the implementation of the existing technique.

In Figure 24.10 we have taken data to encrypt using ECDSA with BB84 and based on that we generated two points after encryption. That two points are the encrypted data which is going to be stored on Amazon Web Services.

Figure 24.11 shows an overview of the DynamoDB on Amazon Web Services in which we have created a table with the name "cloudsec."

Here, Figure 24.12 shows that the encrypted data is stored in table cloudsec. In this table, those two encrypted data points are stored as point 1 and point 2.

Figure 24.13 shows the obtained result after decryption at the receiver end. Here, first the signature verification process is done and after that the decryption process is done and at last we can see that the original message and decrypted message are the same.

```
Enter the message need to be incripted8975897462357988715752553
Encrypted message 4644 5131
```

Figure 24.10 Output after the message encryption.

Figure 24.11 Overview of creation of the table on DynamoDB.

Figure 24.12 Encrypted message stored on DynamoDB.

```
sinature has been varified
decrypted message is 8975897462357988715752553
```

Figure 24.13 Output of the message after decryption.

24.5   Conclusion

With the help of existing encryption technique, i.e., blend of BB84 and ECDSA, a new dimension in the storage of cloud can be realized. This technique not only provides data secrecy but also gives the surety of non-repudiation of the data. The algorithm applied to the AWS public cloud is very uncomplicated and methodical. This algorithm can also be used for encrypting data in various fields like business and healthcare. Various other encryption techniques can also be used on the cloud to protect data from being misused.

References

1. Kumar, P.R., Raj, P.H., Jelciana, P., Science Direct Procedia Computer Science Exploring Data Security Issues and Solutions in Cloud Computing. *Procedia Comput. Sci.*, 125, 2009, 691–697, 2018.
2. Fu, J., Liu, Y., Chao, H., Member, S., Bhargava, B.K., Secure Data Storage and Searching for Industrial IoT by Integrating Fog Computing and Cloud Computing, IEEE Transactions on Industrial Informatics, 14, 1–10, 2018.
3. Basu, S., Cloud Computing Security Challenges Solutions-A Survey, Annual Computing and Communication Workshop and Conference (CCWC), 8, 347–356, 2018.
4. Subramanian, N. and Jeyaraj, A., Recent security challenges in cloud computing. *Comput. Electr. Eng.*, 71, July 2017, 28–42, 2018.
5. Cook, A. *et al.*, Internet of Cloud: Security and Privacy Issues. 39, pp. 71–301, 2018.
6. Hourani, H., Cloud Computing: Legal and Security Issues. *2018 8th Int. ci. Inf. Technol.*, pp. 13–16, 2018.
7. Cook, B., *Formal Reasoning About the Security*, vol. 2, Springer International Publishing, USA, 2018.
8. Swedha, K. and Dubey, T., Analysis of Web Authentication methods using Amazon Web Services. *2018 9th Int. Conf. Comput. Commun. Netw. Technol.*, pp. 1–6, 2018.
9. Kittur, A.S. and Pais, A.R., A new batch verification scheme for ECDSA A~ signatures. Indian Academy of Sciences, 0123456789, https://doi.org/10.1007/s12046-019-1142-9, 2019.
10. Gayatri, P., Venunath, M., Subhashini, V., Umar, S., Securities and threats of Cloud Computing and Solutions. *2018 2nd Int. Conf. Inven. Syst. Control, no. Icisc*, pp. 1162–1166, 2018.
11. Kumar, R. and Goyal, R., On cloud security requirements, threats, vulnerabilities and countermeasures: A survey. *Comput. Sci. Rev.*, 33, 1–48, 2019.

12. Madhuri, T. and Sowjanya, P., Microsoft Azure v/s Amazon AWS Cloud Services: A Comparative Study, International Journal of Innovative Research in Science, Engineering and Technology, 5, 3904–3908, 2016.

13. Rasheed, Y., Qutqut, M.H., Almasalha, F., Overview of the Current Status of NoSQL Database Overview of the Current Status of NoSQL Database, *IJCSNS*, 19, 47–53, April, 2019.

14. Charles, Quantum Cryptography: Public Key Distribution and Coin Tossing, *Theoretical Computer Science*, 560, pp. 7–11, 2014.

15. Tang, Y. *et al.*, Measurement-Device-Independent Quantum Key Distribution over Untrustful Metropolitan Network. *Physical Review X*, 011024, 1–8, 2016.

16. Shenoy-hejamadi, A., Pathak, A., Radhakrishna, S., Quantum Cryptography: Key Distribution and Beyond. *QUANTA*, 6, 1, 1–47, 2018.

17. Van Rijswijk-deij, R., Jonker, M., Sperotto, A., On the Adoption of the Elliptic Curve Digital Signature Algorithm (ECDSA) in DNSSEC, International Conference on Network and Service Management (CNSM) 12, 258–262, 2016.

18. Srivastava, V. and Pathak, R.K., Using a blend of Brassard and Benett 84 Elliptic Curve Digital Signature for secure cloud data communication. *Accept. Int. Conf. Electron. Sustain. Commun. Syst. (ICESCS 2020) International Conf. Electron. Sustain. Commun. Syst. (ICESCS 2020)*, 2020.

19. Nurhadi, I., Quantum Key Distribution (QKD) Protocols: A Survey. *2018 4th Int. Conf. Wirel. Telemat.*, pp. 1–5, 2018.

20. Kotas, C., Naughton, T., Aws, A., A Comparison of Amazon Web Services and Microsoft Azure Cloud Platforms for High Performance Computing, *IEEE International Conference on Consumer Electronics (ICCE)*, 36, pp. 1–4, 2018.

21. Nagasubramanian, G., Sakthivel, R.K., Patan, R., Gandomi, A.H., Sankayya, M., Balusamy, B., Securing e-health records using keyless signature infra-structure blockchain technology in the cloud. *Neural Comput. Appl.*, 32, 3, 1–9, 2018.

22. Kumar, S.R., Gayathri, N., Balusamy, B., Enhancing network lifetime through power-aware routing in MANET. *Int. J. Internet Technol. Secured Trans.*, 9, 1-2, 96–111, 2019.

23. Sakthivel, R.K., Nagasubramanian, G., Al-Turjman, F., Sankayya, M., Core-level cybersecurity assurance using cloud-based adaptive machine learning techniques for manufacturing industry. *Trans. Emerging Telecommun. Technol.*, 9, 14, e3947, 2020.

24. Chandran, R., Kumar, S.R., Gayathri, N., Designing a Locating Scams for Mobile Transaction with the Aid of Operational Activity Analysis in Cloud. *Wireless Pers. Commun.*, 1, 1–14, 2020.

25. Sharma, S.K., Modanval, R.K., Gayathri, N., Kumar, S.R., Ramesh, C., Impact of Application of Big Data on Cryptocurrency, in: *Cryptocurrencies and Blockchain Technology Applications*, 4, 181–195, 2020.

Index

Printed and bound by CPI Group (UK) Ltd, Croydon, CR0 4YY

27/10/2024